Communications
in Computer and Information Science   1012

Commenced Publication in 2007
Founding and Former Series Editors:
Phoebe Chen, Alfredo Cuzzocrea, Xiaoyong Du, Orhun Kara, Ting Liu,
Krishna M. Sivalingam, Dominik Ślęzak, and Xiaokang Yang

More information about this series at http://www.springer.com/series/7899

Luca Longo · M. Chiara Leva (Eds.)

Human Mental Workload

Models and Applications

Second International Symposium, H-WORKLOAD 2018
Amsterdam, The Netherlands, September 20–21, 2018
Revised Selected Papers

 Springer

Editors
Luca Longo ⓘ
Dublin Institute of Technology
Dublin, Ireland

M. Chiara Leva
Dublin Institute of Technology
Dublin, Ireland

ISSN 1865-0929   ISSN 1865-0937 (electronic)
Communications in Computer and Information Science
ISBN 978-3-030-14272-8   ISBN 978-3-030-14273-5 (eBook)
https://doi.org/10.1007/978-3-030-14273-5

Library of Congress Control Number: 2019932782

This Springer imprint is published by the registered company Springer Nature Switzerland AG
The registered company address is: Gewerbestrasse 11, 6330 Cham, Switzerland

Preface

This book endeavors to stimulate and encourage discussion on mental workload, its measures, dimensions, models, applications and consequences. It is a topic that demands a multidisciplinary approach, spanning across human factors, computer science, psychology, neuroscience, statistics, and cognitive sciences. This book presents recent developments in the context of theoretical models of mental workload and practical applications.

The book and its central theme arose in the context of the Second International Symposium on Mental Workload, Models and Applications (H-WORKLOAD 2018), sponsored by the Netherlands Aerospace Centre (NLR) and supported by the Irish Ergonomics Society. It contains a revision of the best papers presented at the symposium and selected through a strict peer-review process. From the content of these research contributions, it is clear that mental workload is a very complex construct, thought to be multidimensional and multifaceted, with no clear and accepted definition. This is confirmed by the different modeling approaches that consider different factors and employ distinct strategies for their aggregation. Despite this uncertainty in modeling mental workload, it is clear that this construct is key for predicting human performance.

The nature and efforts required by the modern workplace is shifting toward more complex cognitive demands, as Professor Catherine Burns pointed out, and predicting the influence of new interactive technologies on human work is a critical capability for the practitioners of the future. The capacity to assess human mental workload is a key element in designing and implementing processes capable of monitoring interactions between automated systems and the humans destined to use them. Similarly, mental workload assessment is key for designing instructions and learning tools aligned to the limitations of the human mind. Unfortunately, mental workload measurement is not trivial. Some of the articles published in this book applied psychological subjective self-reporting measures, others made use of physiological or primary task measures, and some a combination of these. We believe the adoption of a multidimensional approach is fundamental to further understand the complex construct of mental workload and to fully grasp its nature. A number of research articles in this book have started focusing on the development of novel models of mental workload employing data-driven techniques, borrowed from machine learning as subfield of artificial intelligence, whose explanatory capacity over the topic is still to be explored. This last area is a field where traditional human factor approaches and novel data-driven modeling approaches can cross paths and perhaps trace a new fundamental research direction that should be further explored and promoted.

We wish to thank all the people who helped in the Organizing Committee for the Second International Symposium on Mental Workload, Models and Applications (H-WORKLOAD 2018). In particular the local chairs, Rolf Zon, Wendy Duivestein, Tanja Bos, and many more of the members of the Scientific Committee. We want to also thank the main sponsors of the event, the Netherlands Aerospace Centre and the Irish Ergonomics Society, without which neither the conference nor the book would have been realized. A special thanks goes to the Dublin Institute of Technology as well as all the reviewers of the Program Committee who provided constructive feedback. A special thanks goes to the researchers and practitioners who submitted their work and committed to attending the event and turning it into an opportunity to meet and share our experiences in this fascinating topic.

January 2019   Luca Longo
                                                            M. Chiara Leva

Organization

Organizing Committee

General Chairs, Editors, and Program Chairs

Luca Longo   Dublin Institute of Technology, Ireland
M. Chiara Leva   Dublin Institute of Technology, Ireland

Local Chairs

Rolz Zon   Netherlands Aerospace Centre, The Netherlands
Tanja Bos   Netherlands Aerospace Centre, The Netherlands

Program Committee

Aghajani Haleh   Baylor Scott & White Research Institute, USA
Balfe Nora   Trinity College Dublin, Ireland
Barge Roland   Rolls-Royce, UK
Bellini Emanuele   LOGOS Ricerca & Innovazione, Florence, Italy
Bos Tanja   Netherlands Aerospace Centre, The Netherlands
Brookhuis Karel   Rijks Universiteit Groningen, The Netherlands
Byrne Aidan   ABMU Health Board, UK
Cahill Joan   Trinity College Dublin, Ireland
Cain Brad   C3 Human Factors, Canada
Castor Martin   GEISTT, Sweden
Cerrato Loredana   EITDigital, Sweden
Charles Rebecca   Cranfield University, UK
Costa Antonio Pedro   Aveiro University, Portugal
Edwards Tamsyn   NASA Ames/San Jose State University, USA
Genga Glauco   Institute of Aerospace Medicine, Italy
Galicic Matjaz   Arcadis, UK
Golightly David   HFRG, University of Nottingham, UK
Greiner Birgit   University College Cork, Ireland
Hines Andrew   University College Dublin, Ireland
Kane Bridget   Karlstad University, Sweden
Kenvyn Fiona   Metro Trains Melbourne, Australia
Konstandinidou Myrto   NCSR Demokritos, Greece
Maij Anneloes   Netherlands Aerospace Centre, The Netherlands
Massaiu Salvatore   IFE, Norway
Mijovic Pavle   mBrainTrain, Serbia
Mills Ann   Railway Safety Standards Board, UK
O'Sullivan Leonard   University Limerick, Ireland

Contents

About the Editors

Dr. Luca Longo is currently Assistant Professor at the Dublin Institute of Technology, Technological University Dublin, where he is a member of the Applied Intelligence Research Centre and ADAPT, the Global Center of Excellence for Digital Content and Media Innovation. His core theoretical research interests are in artificial intelligence, specifically in automated reasoning and machine learning. He also performs applied research in mental workload modeling. He is author of 45+ peer-reviewed articles appeared in conference proceedings, book chapters, and journals in various theoretical and applied computer science fields. Luca was awarded the National Teaching Hero in 2016, by the National Forum for the Enhancement of Teaching and Learning in Higher Education.

Dr. Maria Chiara Leva is Lecturer at the Dublin Institute of Technology in the College of Environmental Health. She is also a visiting research fellow in the Centre for Innovative Human Systems at Trinity College Dublin. Her area of expertise is human factors and safety management systems. Chiara holds a PhD in human factors conferred by the Polytechnic of Milan, Department of Industrial Engineering. Her PhD focused on human and organizational factors in safety-critical system in the transport sector. She is the co-chair of the Human Factors and Human Reliability Committee for the European Safety and Reliability Association and has been working in ergonomics and risk assessment as a consultant since 2008. She has more than 56 publications on human factors, operational risk assessment, and safety management in science and engineering journals.

Models

Understanding, Supporting, and Redesigning Cognitive Work

Catherine M. Burns[✉]

Systems Design Engineering, University of Waterloo, Waterloo, Canada
catherine.burns@uwaterloo.ca

Abstract. Cognitive work analysis (CWA) is a framework that has been used in many settings to describe various aspects of work. This paper outlines how CWA can be used to understand work and mental workload. The work domain, control task, and strategies analysis can be useful to understand the nature of work, work allocation and mental workload. Finally, the prediction of work patterns is discussed. Predicting the influence of new technologies on human work is a critical capability for the human factors practitioners of the future.

Keywords: Cognitive Work Analysis · Mental workload · Task analysis · Function allocation

1 Introduction

As Wickens [23] introduced at H-WORKLOAD last year, studies of mental workload began in the 1960's and have accelerated through the decades. Mental workload is certainly not a mature science, and I expect that it will always be an exciting area of study. Exciting new methods of being able to compute and predict mental workload are emerging [12–15, 18]. While it is true that studies of mental workload measurement techniques such as the NASA-TLX have reached maturity, there is a significant new challenge on the horizon. That challenge is the prediction of the impact on humans of new technologies. New forms of automation and artificial intelligence have the potential to impact human work at a cognitive level we have not seen before (e.g. [5, 6, 11, 20]). Being able to predict the impact of these new technologies, so that benefits and risks can be anticipated, will be an important contribution to society for those who practice human factors and ergonomics.

Our last significant technological revolution was the arrival of the internet, and it dramatically changed the nature of human work and communication around the world. In 1982, a New York Times article made reasonable predictions that the emergence of the internet would improve communications, allow individuals to create their own content, and blur lines between home and work by allowing more work at home. Other implications such as advanced globalization, economic shifts and the development of social and political hacking through things like fake news were not predicted. Had we been able to predict some of these effects, safeguards and more effective responses could have been developed. There are some differences though in these two technological revolutions. The internet largely was about connectivity, and improved connectivity was perhaps not in the domain of human factors professionals. However, the reallocation of human decision

© Springer Nature Switzerland AG 2019
L. Longo and M. C. Leva (Eds.): H-WORKLOAD 2018, CCIS 1012, pp. 3–12, 2019.
https://doi.org/10.1007/978-3-030-14273-5_1

making to automation and artificial intelligence, and the resultant supervisory control problems land squarely within the expertise of our community. I am not arguing that human factors practitioners become futurists, but we do have an important role to play in the careful prediction of how new technologies will influence how people work and live.

Suppose a client asks you whether bringing in a new artificial intelligence system will allow her physicians to make better decisions. The core question of whether decision making will better with the new tool can be answered (relatively) easily. The tool can be analyzed and its accuracy compared to expected human performance. If funding allows, we can run a study to compare the performance of physicians using the tool, against the performance of those physicians who are not using the tool. These are all good questions, and solid approaches exist for answering these questions. More challenging questions though are:

- Will I still need as many physicians?
- Should I still pay the physicians the same amount?
- How will this tool influence their mental workload?
- Will I be expecting my physicians to analyze more cases per day?
- Does the tool take away their decision-making latitude, making them mechanical tool users where before they had rich and empowered positions?
- Is the tool telling them enough of how it made its decisions that they can justify their case to a concerned family member, or defend themselves in a negligence case?

These are the challenging questions of how people work with technology today. I firmly believe that we have an important role in being a part of that conversation. Our field has the tools and methods that can begin to identify these kinds of issues. Our approaches are systematic and scientific and can move us away from the realm of speculation. In this paper, I will discuss how one of our tools, Cognitive Work Analysis (CWA), can be used for mental workload analysis. From this abstraction, I believe that most of our work analysis approaches can be used to answer mental workload prediction questions. Although I am using CWA as my base for discussion, there are many methods within our human factors toolbox that can be used to model and understand mental workload (e.g. [13, 23]). I want to encourage us to think of the decision latitude we give our users through design, how we can make decision making more effective, and how we can predict the adaptation of work.

Cognitive Work Analysis (CWA) is well known as a framework for analyzing work [16, 17, 22]. CWA takes a multi-faceted view of human work, looking at work through five different lenses: domain constraints (work domain analysis), tasks and information processing (control task analysis), strategies, social, organizational constraints, and worker competencies. Many times, CWA is used in environments that are, by their very nature, complex and CWA is a useful method for unpacking that complexity and identifying the areas where users need more support for their work. In particular, the first three phases of CWA, work domain analysis, control task analysis, and strategy analysis reveal important aspects of human work and how to design healthy and effective work.

CWA is inherently focused on the analysis of work, and yet, CWA is not used explicitly for mental workload analysis by most CWA practitioners. In many ways, this is something of a lost opportunity. CWA can help to investigate work and to understand when work is complex, when the mental workload is high, or when work could be supported with technology. In this paper, I will step through the first three phases of CWA, identifying the mental workload implications implied by the models.

2 Work Domain Analysis: Building Decision Latitude

Work domain analysis (WDA) is known for its functional description of the work environment. In many ways, WDA is the differentiating analysis of CWA, providing a different view of the work environment than most other analyses provide. The WDA uses the abstraction hierarchy [17, 22] as its most common model, which looks at the world the person must operate in, the purposes of that system and how that system operates. The abstraction hierarchy is grounded on the assumption that an operator will be working towards a successfully functioning work system, and responding within the constraints of that system to achieve the required purposes. For a human factors practitioner, conducting a WDA brings the practitioner into the world of the operator, helps to show areas of complexity for that operator, makes the goals of the operator and their action possibilities apparent to the analyst. A WDA does not specify actions, or user interface technologies, or even ideal approaches. A WDA is not a human-centered analysis; it is an objective analytical re-engineering of the work environment to bring a greater understanding of the needs of workers in that environment. The human-centered, work-centered or human factors oriented advantages of WDA come from how the analysis is used, not from the analysis itself.

The abstraction hierarchy has implications for understanding mental workload. First, expert workers understand the components and constraints of their environment with more clarity than novice workers [2]. At first, this additional knowledge, of being aware of all the various purposes, components, processes and action possibilities, might seem like higher mental workload. However, with expertise being aware of purposes and action possibilities makes that worker a better decision maker. The awareness that various solutions are possible creates decision latitude for that worker through competency (Fig. 1). Work with higher levels of decision latitude is known to create more empowering and healthier work [8]. The work may still be stressful, and the mental workload may still be high, but the nature of that mental workload is more rewarding.

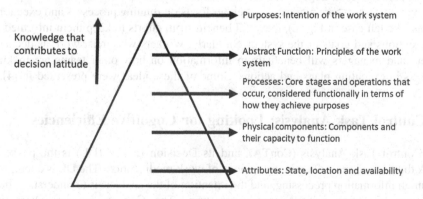

Fig. 1. Understanding functional relationships and purposes leads to more decision latitude for decision makers.

The corollary of this implication is that when we design better displays for workers, showing them more of the intention of the work system, and their capabilities to react to situations, we change the nature of their work. We know from research that we create workers capable of better diagnoses and better able to mitigate situations. We can develop workers with a greater sense of competency and empowerment to take successful action in their work environments. Figure 2 illustrates different intention and action distributions, described along the structure of the abstraction hierarchy.

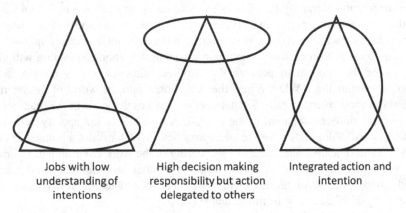

| Jobs with low understanding of intentions | High decision making responsibility but action delegated to others | Integrated action and intention |

Fig. 2. Different role allocations with different mixes of intention understanding and capability for action.

Often the complexity of work requires the distribution of work through functional stratification. In several projects, we have developed role allocation maps along the abstraction hierarchy, and patterns like those in Fig. 2 have been noticed. Examples include Ashoori [1] which looked at roles across a team in a labor and delivery unit of a hospital and Hajdukiewicz [7] who looked at role division during surgery.

Not every role can have integration between the intentions and actions of the work system, particularly in larger work contexts where the distribution of work is required. However, in cases where workers must either focus on running processes and executing actions (the left case in Fig. 2), they will benefit from efforts to keep them informed of the intentions and goals of the system. Similarly, workers who must work as decision makers and managers will benefit from information on how other teams are making progress in executing plans and actions. Some of these ideas were presented in [4].

3   Control Task Analysis: Looking for Cognitive Efficiencies

The Control Task Analysis (ConTA), and its Decision Ladder (DL) is the phase of CWA that is used most often in discussions of work modification. The DL is a template of human information processing, and the intention of the analysis is to understand how tasks are triggering various processing steps. The ConTA presents alternative behaviors, with knowledge-based behavior and cognitively costly analytical decision-making at its top, and more efficient and less effortful heuristic and rule-based processing at the bottom of the DL (Fig. 3). The analysis intends to understand when cognitively effortful work is occurring and whether there is an opportunity to replace that work with approaches that are less effortful. The ConTA also models expertise and acknowledges that less experienced workers may spend more time in the more effortful processing. Experienced workers facing new situations will also revert to these processes at times when their experience cannot provide the heuristics for more efficient decision making.

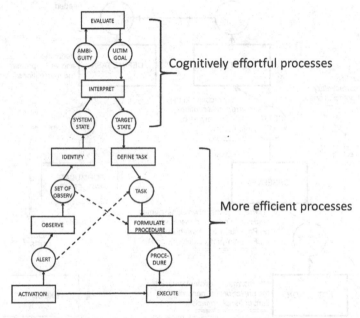

Fig. 3. The decision ladder can identify cognitively effortful processes.

A second application of the DL can be to identify technologies that are adding unnecessary mental workload. The DL can show where information is missing, and work processes become less efficient. We developed The DL below (Fig. 4) by observing pharmacists as they processed prescriptions and checked for medication issues [9]. The DL helped to identify that information such as allergy information or interactions was often not shared with the pharmacist. Because this information was missing, the pharmacist would need to go through an extra problem-solving process to identify these issues, possibly communicating with the patient or their physician. Including this information with the prescription or the medication record would have allowed these pharmacists to work more efficiently. A small change in information could have generated a significant improvement in mental workload.

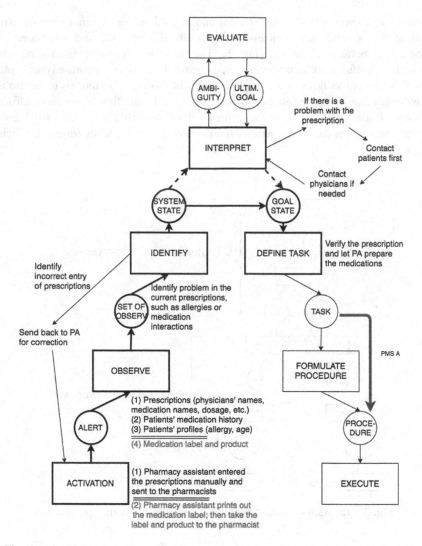

Fig. 4. Identifying technology that increases mental workload in the decision ladder.

4   Strategies Analysis: Understanding How Work Adapts

The Strategies Analysis (SA) looks at the different ways people can solve the same problem. Unlike the ConTA, the focus is not on information processing or decision-making. In this case, understanding the variety of pathways and what triggers put people on those paths is important. Most often, the triggers for different strategic paths are either particular contexts, the experience of the user, or different mental workload levels (Fig. 5). We know well that under high mental workload users will take different approaches, either shedding tasks or building workarounds. The SA can in this way be used to investigate high mental workload situations and to ask users how they adapt to these situations.

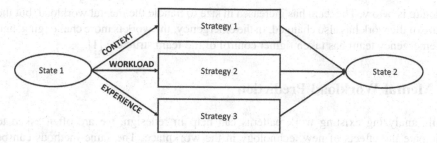

Fig. 5. Context, mental workload, and experience determine the strategies that are chosen.

Some of the adaptation strategies we have seen in other work has been adjusting mental workload patterns or reducing communication. In some cases, team structures have shifted to handle higher mental workload conditions. In the figure below (Fig. 6) we show strategic shifts in team composition to handle the additional mental workload of an emergency delivery. The normal delivery team structure is at the top; the emergency team

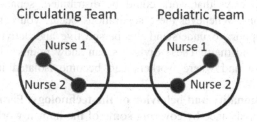

Strategy 1: Team configuration under normal conditions.

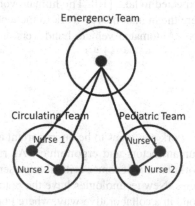

Strategy 2: Team configuration under high mental workload and critical conditions, centralized control.

Fig. 6. Different strategies for different mental workload situations, normal (*on top*) or emergency (*lower figure*) [1].

structure is below. The team has increased in size to handle the mental workload, but the nature of the work has also changed. In the emergency, the work is more challenging, and the emergency team has taken tighter control of the team structure [1].

5 Mental Workload Prediction

While analyzing existing work patterns can help in redesign, we are often asked to anticipate the effects of new technology in the workplace. The same methods can be used prospectively to predict where new technologies may add or reduce work, require new function allocations, or require additional information support. There are several specific ways to predict work.

- **Comparison of similar environments.** Models of similar work environments can be compared, and the differences in one work environment used to understand the other environment. Examples of these comparisons are [3, 21]. To make these comparisons, the two environments must share some functional similarity.
- **Analysis of the "cut points" in models.** Whenever work must be distributed over people, over function, or over process, "cut points" in work occur. Figure 2, for example, showed two ways that work could be distributed: separating decision making from operations. Whenever these separations occur, you can predict that workers will need support to understand the perspective and activities from the other work zones around them. These divisions can show points where situation awareness can be lost and where workers can become isolated in their work processes.
- **Analysis of the functionality and behavior of the technology.** Particularly when technologies provide assistance by covering some of the human work, it becomes critical to understand how that technology will interact. The decision ladder can be used to develop detailed and sensitive function allocation models, that show what roles the technology is expected to take [10]. The human work should be studied at the transition points, where the human moves work to the technology or takes work over from the technology. (Automated vehicle handovers are a classic example of this problem).

6 Conclusion

The understanding of human work continues to be an important and exciting field, even years after the origins of human factors and ergonomics. As rich and complex technologies are added to the workplace, it becomes critical to understand how people will interact with these technologies. New technologies have the potential to replace human work, but this needs to be done in a collaborative way, where humans and technologies are partners. This partnership means providing the communication to support smooth work transitions and continuing to position humans in roles where they have decision latitude as well as good situation awareness of actions that are occurring under their supervision.

Mental workload will remain a critical issue for the future, in particular, as humans move to more supervisory roles. The mental workload of working with technologies such as automation, artificial intelligence, and more complex systems, is still only loosely understood. More research is needed that explores the mental workload of working with these new technologies. Further, there is a need for a more finely understood concept of mental workload. There is great promise emerging in the development of new mental workload measurement techniques, from physiological measurements and neuroergonomic viewpoints to machine learning models. This conference, and the papers included in this issue, contribute invaluably to these new directions.

References

1. Ashoori, M., Burns, C.M., Momtahan, K., d'Entremont, B.: Using team cognitive work analysis to reveal healthcare team interactions in a labor and delivery unit. Ergonomics **57**, 973–986 (2014). https://doi.org/10.1080/00140139.2014.909949
2. Burns, C.M.: CWA: models of expertise. In: Ward, P., Schraagen, J.M., Gore, J., Roth, E. (eds.) Oxford Handbook of Expertise: Research and Application. Oxford University Press (in press). https://doi.org/10.1093/oxfordhb/9780188795772.001.0001
3. Burns, C.M., Bisantz, A.M., Roth, E.M.: Lessons from a comparison of work models: representational choices and their implications. Hum. Fact. **46**, 711–727 (2004). https://doi.org/10.1518/hfes.46.4.711.56810
4. Burns, C.M., Torenvliet, G., Scott, S., Chalmers, B.: Work domain analysis for establishing collaborative work requirements. In: Proceedings of the 53rd Annual Meeting of the Human Factors and Ergonomics Society, pp. 314–318. HFES, Santa Monica (2009). https://doi.org/10.1177/154193120905300432
5. Cahill, J., et al.: Adaptive automation and the third pilot: managing teamwork and workload in an airline cockpit. In: Longo, L., Leva, M.C. (eds.) H-WORKLOAD 2017. CCIS, vol. 726, pp. 161–173. Springer, Cham (2017). https://doi.org/10.1007/978-3-319-61061-0_10
6. Edwards, T., Martin, L., Bienert, N., Mercer, J.: The relationship between workload and performance in air traffic control: exploring the influence of levels of automation and variation in task demand. In: Longo, L., Leva, M.C. (eds.) H-WORKLOAD 2017. CCIS, vol. 726, pp. 120–139. Springer, Cham (2017). https://doi.org/10.1007/978-3-319-61061-0_8
7. Hajdukiewicz, J.R., Vicente, K.J., Doyle, D.J., Milgram, P., Burns, C.M.: Modeling a medical environment: an ontology for integrated medical informatics design. Int. J. Med. Inform. **62**, 79–99 (2001). https://doi.org/10.1016/S1386-5056(01)00128-9
8. Karasek, R.A.: Job demands, job decision latitude, and mental: strain: implications for job redesign. Admin. Sci. Quart. **24**, 285–308 (1979). https://doi.org/10.2307/2392498
9. Keresteglioclu, D., Burns, C.M., Grindrod, K.: Building bridges between physicians and pharmacists: an interprofessional approach to electronic health record requirements. In: HFES 2016 International Symposium on Human Factors and Ergonomics: Shaping the Future, pp. 9–14. HFES (2016). https://doi.org/10.1177/2327857916051000
10. Li, Y., Wang, X., Burns, C.M.: Modeling automation with cognitive work analysis to support human-automation coordination. J. Cogn. Eng. Decis. Mak. **11**, 299–322 (2017). https://doi.org/10.1177/1555343417709669

11. Li, Y., Wang, X., Burns, C.M.: Improved monitoring performance of financial trading algorithms using a graphical display. Proc. Hum. Factors Ergon. Soc. Annu. Meet. **62**(1), 187–191 (2018). https://doi.org/10.1177/1541931218621045
12. Longo, L.: Designing medical interactive systems via assessment of human mental workload. In 2015 IEEE 28th International Symposium on Computer-Based Medical Systems (CBMS), pp. 364–365. IEEE, June 2015
13. Longo, L., Leva, M.C.: Human Mental Workload: Models and Applications, vol. 726. Springer, Cham (2017). https://doi.org/10.1007/978-3-319-61061-0
14. Mijović, P., Milovanović, M., Ković, V., Gligorijević, I., Mijović, B., Mačužić, I.: Neuroergonomics method for measuring the influence of mental workload modulation on cognitive state of manual assembly worker. In: Longo, L., Leva, M.C. (eds.) H-WORKLOAD 2017. CCIS, vol. 726, pp. 213–224. Springer, Cham (2017). https://doi. org/10.1007/978-3-319-61061-0_14
15. Moustafa, K., Luz, S., Longo, L.: Assessment of mental workload: a comparison of machine learning methods and subjective assessment techniques. In: Longo, L., Leva, M.C. (eds.) H-WORKLOAD 2017. CCIS, vol. 726, pp. 30–50. Springer, Cham (2017). https://doi.org/ 10.1007/978-3-319-61061-0_3
16. Naikar, N., Moylen, A., Pearce, B.: Analysing activity in complex systems with cognitive work analysis: concepts, guidelines and case study for control task analysis. Theor. Issues Ergon. Sci. **7**, 371–394 (2006). https://doi.org/10.1080/14639220500098821
17. Rasmussen, J.: The role of hierarchical knowledge representation in decision making and system management. IEEE Trans. Syst. Man Cybern. **15**, 234–243 (1985). https://doi.org/10. 1109/tsmc.1985.6313353
18. Rizzo, L., Longo, L.: Representing and inferring mental workload via defeasible reasoning: a comparison with the NASA task load index and the workload profile. In: AI^3@AI*IA, 1st Workshop on Advances in Argumentation in Artificial Intelligence co-located with XVI International Conference of the Italian Association for Artificial Intelligence (AI*IA 2017), Bari, Italy, 16–17 November 2017 (2017)
19. Rizzo, L., Dondio, P., Delany, S.J., Longo, L.: Modeling mental workload via rule-based expert system: a comparison with NASA-TLX and workload profile. In: Iliadis, L., Maglogiannis, I. (eds.) AIAI 2016. IAICT, vol. 475, pp. 215–229. Springer, Cham (2016). https://doi.org/10.1007/978-3-319-44944-9_19
20. Smith, K.T.: Observations and issues in the application of cognitive workload modelling for decision making in complex time-critical environments. In: Longo, L., Leva, M.C. (eds.) H-WORKLOAD 2017. CCIS, vol. 726, pp. 77–89. Springer, Cham (2017). https://doi.org/10. 1007/978-3-319-61061-0_5
21. St. Maurice, J., Burns, C.M.: Using comparative cognitive work analysis to identify design priorities in complex socio-technical systems. In: 2015 International Symposium on Human Factors and Ergonomics in Health Care: Improving the Outcomes, vol. 4, no. 1, pp. 118–123 (2015). https://doi.org/10.1177/2327857915041019
22. Vicente, K.J.: Cognitive Work Analysis: Toward Safe, Productive, and Health Computer-Based Work. LEA, Mahwah (1999)
23. Wickens, C.D.: Mental workload: assessment, prediction and consequences. In: Longo, L., Leva, M.C. (eds.) H-WORKLOAD 2017. CCIS, vol. 726, pp. 18–29. Springer, Cham (2017). https://doi.org/10.1007/978-3-319-61061-0_2

Assessing Workload in Human-Machine Teams from Psychophysiological Data with Sparse Ground Truth

David Dearing[(⊠)], Aaron Novstrup, and Terrance Goan

Stottler Henke Associates, Inc.,
1107 NE 45th Street, Suite 310, Seattle, WA 98105, USA
{ddearing, anovstrup, goan}@stottlerhenke.com

Abstract. Data-driven approaches to human workload assessment generally attempt to induce models from a collection of available data and a corresponding ground truth comprising self-reported measures of actual workload. However, it is often not feasible to elicit self-assessed workload ratings with great frequency. As part of an ongoing effort to improve the effectiveness of human-machine teams through real-time human workload monitoring, we explore the utility of transfer learning in situations where there is sparse subject-specific ground truth from which to develop accurate predictive models of workload. Our approach induces a workload model from the psychophysiological data collected from subjects operating a remotely piloted aircraft simulation program. Psychophysiological measures were collected from wearable sensors, and workload was self-assessed using the NASA Task Load Index. Our results provide evidence that models learned from psychophysiological data collected from other subjects outperform models trained on a limited amount of data for a given subject.

Keywords: Workload assessment · Transfer learning ·
Human-machine teams · Psychophysiological sensors ·
Human-automation interaction · Machine learning

1 Introduction

Effective human workload assessment techniques have long been sought after by researchers in hopes of preventing fatigue, stress, and other negative influences on performance [1–3]. One particular application of such techniques is to diagnose performance successes and failures in human-machine teams to help identify effective training and design interventions. A wide range of research suggests that problems in such teams are greatly exacerbated by the harmful effects that high cognitive demands can have on human operator performance [4–12]. Many approaches have been proposed for assessing human workload, ranging from theory-driven models to data-driven computational models [13]. In the case of computational models, machine learning can be used to train a model directly from measurable factors—producing a model by finding patterns and relationships between an individual's measurable factors and a corresponding performance measure.

© Springer Nature Switzerland AG 2019
L. Longo and M. C. Leva (Eds.): H-WORKLOAD 2018, CCIS 1012, pp. 13–22, 2019.
https://doi.org/10.1007/978-3-030-14273-5_2

In this paper, we report on our initial efforts to induce such a data-driven workload model in situations where there is only a sparse amount of data for a given human operator. Our research focuses on improving the effectiveness of human-machine teams through real-time human workload monitoring captured by wearable sensors. More specifically, we describe our progress in the context of an ongoing effort to develop an extensible modeling framework and software system for real-time human state assessment in human-machine teaming environments.

The remainder of this paper is organized as follows. Section 2 describes related work in human workload assessment and the challenges of machine learning with sparse data. Section 3 describes the design of a comparative study to evaluate the utility of the transfer learning technique with psychophysiological data for human workload monitoring. Section 4 presents the experimental results. Finally, Sect. 5 presents the conclusions and future work.

2   Related Work

Traditional approaches to producing an index of workload have typically been theory-driven, following a top-down approach that begins with a hypothesis based on existing knowledge and then moves towards the measurement and quantification of the factors believed to influence workload [14–16]. Recently, however, there has been an increased focus on data-driven approaches [13, 17–19]. Unlike theory-driven approaches, these data-driven approaches can induce a workload model bottom-up from data acquired through subjective self-report measures and other measurable factors. In particular, there has been a rise in the use of psychophysiological data to generate these data-driven models, in part because such measures can be captured unobtrusively with wearable sensors and, thus, fully integrated into real-world work environments [20–23]. However, these data-driven approaches still rely on self-assessed workload ratings to serve as the labeled ground truth for training a machine learning classifier. Because these self-reports often require the full cognitive attention of the user, it is often infeasible to elicit these self-assessed ratings with great frequency (i.e., while performing attention-demanding tasks like driving or flying). In such situations, where there is sparse subject-specific ground truth data from which to develop accurate predictive models of workload, a more effective alternative might be to utilize models produced from the labeled data collected from *other* subjects. This technique, called *transfer learning*, has been used in other applications where it is expensive or impossible to collect the needed training data and rebuild the models [24]. Although the psychophysiological data from other subjects may not be completely consistent with a new subject's profile, it may still contain useful information, as people may exhibit similar responses to the same task [25].

3   Design and Methodology

This section describes the design of a comparative study to evaluate different approaches to inducing a workload model from psychophysiological data. In particular, we are interested in the value of transfer learning in situations where there is sparse ground truth for a given human operator (i.e., labeled psychophysiological data) from which to develop accurate predictive models of workload. This would be the case when, for example, a new operator joins a human-machine team and no physiological measures or self-assessed workload ratings have yet to be collected. Our research centers on examining the following hypotheses:

Hypothesis 1: Given a sparse amount of psychophysiological data for a particular human operator, a workload model induced from that sparse data and the data collected from all *other* human operators will outperform a workload model trained using the data for that operator alone.

Hypothesis 2: Given a sufficient volume of psychophysiological data for a particular human operator, an operator-specific workload model will outperform a model trained using data from the all *other* human operators.

3.1 Dataset

We utilized an existing dataset consisting of psychophysiological measures collected as part of a formal study conducted by the Air Force Research Laboratory (AFRL) Human Universal Measurement and Assessment Network (HUMAN) Laboratory. In this study, a total of 13 participants were instrumented with wearable sensors to collect physiological data consisting of respiration measures, electrocardiography (ECG) measures, and electroencephalography (EEG) measures (see Table 1 and [26] for details). Each participant was monitored while operating a remotely piloted aircraft simulation program and workload was self-assessed using the NASA Task Load Index (NASA-TLX) [27].

Table 1. Summary table of dataset features.

Independent Features		
Respiration Features	**ECG Features**	**EEG Features**
Amplitude	Heart Rate	Electrodes: F7, F8, T3, T4, Fz, O2
Cycle Time	Filtered Heart Rate	Frequencies: Alpha, Beta, Delta,
Inspiration Time	Heart Rate Variability	Gamma1, Gamma2,
Duty Cycle	Interbeat Interval	Gamma3
	Heart Rate Trend	Measures: Power, Saccade

Dependent Feature						
NASA-TLX	Sessions	Trials	Min	Max	High Workload	Low Workload
Composite Score	104	205	2.2	94.4	105 Trials	100 Trials

Over the course of ten days, each participant experienced two training sessions and eight data collection sessions. Each session included two seven-minute trials of a target tracking task that played out along distinct scripted timelines during which the participant manually tracked either one or two targets (among other independent variables to vary the task demand). This resulted in a total of 104 data collection sessions with 205 individual trials (data was either missing or erroneous for three of the trials). When each trial of the tracking task ended, participants were asked to fill out a new NASA-TLX questionnaire. The NASA-TLX scale, which is built upon six factors and their individual weights, has been widely used by human factors researchers over the last four decades. Each 7-min trial of an operator's session is labeled with a single, static NASA-TLX composite measure of perceived workload. The physiological measures were collected constantly throughout each trial.

3.2   Workload Model Training

As part of an ongoing effort to improve the effectiveness of human-machine teams through real-time human workload monitoring, Stottler Henke is developing an extensible modeling framework and software system for real-time human state assessment in human-machine teaming environments. The system, called *Illuminate*, employs machine learning techniques to induce a workload model from psychophysiological data and can—in real-time—update its internal model as new labeled data is made available. This enables us to evaluate *adaptive* models that incrementally incorporate operator-specific data (e.g., after each session; see Fig. 1), thereby addressing complications typically associated with the analysis of biometric data, including: the non-stationarity of psychophysiological data [28] and the initial sparsity (or lack) of operator-specific data. Workload models are trained to predict either high or low workload for an operator, based on the self-reported composite NASA-TLX measure that corresponds with the physiological measures for each trial.

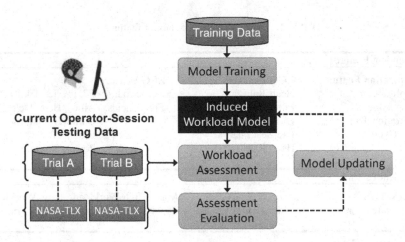

Fig. 1. Diagram of the general experimental workflow for training, evaluating, and updating the workload model for each individual operator session (consisting of two trials).

Data Preparation. Prior to model training, we first normalize the measures on a per-operator basis and designate each trial as either a high or low workload based on the normalized composite NASA-TLX measure (low workload being less than the 50th percentile). Psychophysiological measures are aligned by their individual timestamps and down-sampled to a frequency of 2 Hz with a five-second rolling average, so as to synchronize the measurements collected by the various sensors.

Model Training and Evaluation. Our system uses machine learning classification techniques to induce a workload model for each individual operator and uses that model to assess an operator's workload at a given moment in time. For these experiments, we utilize the Weka implementation of a multinomial logistic regression model with a ridge estimator [29, 30]. For the purposes of our comparative evaluation, we trained models for each operator using three configurations (see Fig. 2):

- *Transfer learning model*: We use a leave-one-out approach in which one operator at a time is taken to be the "current" operator and the data for all of the *other* operators provides the basis for training a transfer learning model.
- *Session-specific model*: For each "current" operator, a session-specific model is trained using the data for all of that operator's *previous* sessions. That is, when evaluating data for the nth session, the corresponding model has been trained on all data for the current operator's first $n - 1$ sessions.
- *Combination model*: As with the session-specific model, the combination model for each "current" operator is updated between each session so that it has been trained on data for all *previous* sessions. It uses model stacking to combine the session-specific model with that operator's corresponding transfer learning model by including the output of the transfer learning model as an additional input when training the session-specific model.

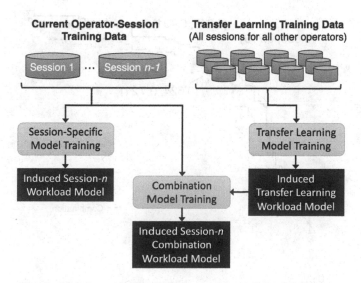

Fig. 2. Diagram outlining the three model training configurations.

These configurations are meant to simulate a human-machine team scenario in which the system initially has a sparse amount of human operator-specific data from which to develop predictive models of workload (i.e., for a new human operator). As the operator completes additional sessions and provides workload feedback (e.g., NASA-TLX measure of perceived workload), the system updates its internal model for subsequent workload assessment. Note that each model is evaluated only on data for sessions 2 – 8—there is no session-specific model for the first session.

4   Results and Discussion

Here we describe the results of our comparative evaluation of the three configurations for model training and evaluation that are described in Sect. 3.2. Because the underlying models are binomial logistic regression models with probabilistic output (as opposed to binary output), when evaluating the models on a given trial we average the workload assessment scores over all instances for that trial. To measure the performance of each model, we calculate the sensitivity and specificity metrics. Sensitivity provides an estimate of how good the model is at predicting a high level of workload, whereas specificity estimates how good the model is at predicting a low level of workload. We plot these measures on a Receiver Operating Characteristic (ROC) curve, a graphical representation wherein the points of the curve are obtained by moving the classification threshold from favoring a correct assessment of low workload to favoring a correct assessment of high workload. Each chart also indicates the point with the "optimal" threshold, maximizing Youden's J statistic [31].

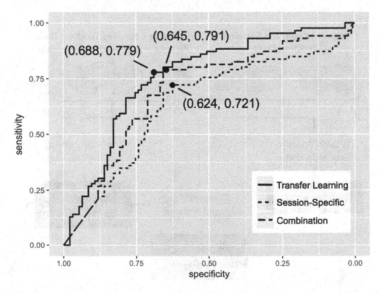

Fig. 3. ROC curve comparing each model configurations, averaged across all 13 operators.

For each of the three evaluation configurations, the chart in Fig. 3 shows the ROC curve averaged across all operators and sessions. Figure 3 shows that the transfer learning model outperforms not only the session-specific model, but also the combination model. These difference between the transfer learning model and the session-specific model is statistically significant (p-value of 0.006), as is the difference between the combination and session-specific models (p-value of 0.005). This provides evidence toward confirming our first hypothesis that psychophysiological data collected from other operators can be used to train a predictive workload model. However, the fact that the transfer learning model outperformed the combination model that utilizes psychophysiological data for the current subject with the results of the transfer learning model was unexpected but not significant (p-value of 0.129).

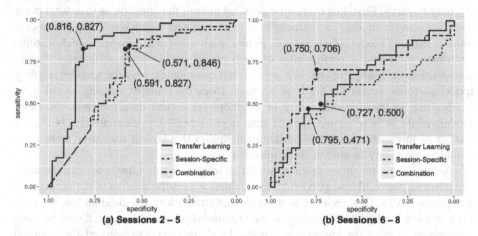

Fig. 4. ROC curves comparing each of the three model configurations, averaged across all 13 operators for (a) the first four sessions and (b) the final three sessions.

To better understand how the session-specific and combinations models performed over time (e.g., with additional training data from later sessions), we partitioned the evaluation data to compare the results of the first four sessions (sessions 2–5) with the results of the final three sessions (sessions 6–8), which resulted in partitions with roughly balanced class labels. As the ROC curves in Fig. 4 illustrate, the combination model actually outperforms the transfer learning model for sessions 6–8 (i.e., when there are four or more sessions of labeled training data available for each operator). Comparing the optimal points on each curve, we can see that the transfer learning model's performance drops during the later sessions (from a J of 0.643 to 0.266), whereas the performance of the combination model improves in the later sessions (from a J of 0.418 to 0.456).

5 Conclusion and Future Work

In this paper, we have described a comparative evaluation to test our hypothesis that transfer learning is useful in situations where there is insufficient subject-specific data to develop accurate predictive models of human workload. Our results provide evidence that models learned from psychophysiological data collected from other subjects outperform models trained on a limited amount of data for a given subject (*Hypothesis 1*). More specifically, with little or no data, a transfer learning model trained on all other-subject data performed best. Once a sparse amount of subject-specific data was available, a combination model induced from the output of the transfer learning model and the subject-specific psychophysiological measures generally outperformed the transfer learning model alone.

There remain several items to be answered by future work as well as by our own ongoing research. First, this evaluation does not answer the question as to at what point a session-specific model (i.e., induced only from a subject's own data) outperforms the transfer learning model (*Hypothesis 2*). Future work is needed to inspect which features contribute most to the performance of each model and how those features change across the three configurations. We are also left questioning why the transfer learning model performs worse for the later sessions. Does the transfer learning model have trouble due to the non-stationarity of psychophysiological data (whereas the other models adapt as new subject-specific data is collected)? Or, alternatively, is this an artifact of this particular dataset? Additional studies that collect data over more trials would be necessary to answer these questions.

Another topic for future research would be to vary the dividing line between what constitutes a high and low workload. Our evaluation uses the median of the normalized composite NASA-TLX measure as a simple and straightforward dividing line between high and low workload. Depending on the task and application domain, it may be more appropriate to raise (or lower) that threshold. Alternatively, to account for potential learning effects across sessions, a per-subject adaptive threshold may yield better results. The results of our comparative evaluation highlight the threshold for each model that produces the best balance of sensitivity and specificity. However, depending on the target application, it may be more appropriate to favor specificity or sensitivity so as to more accurately predict a high or low workload, respectively.

Lastly, a more accurate model might be produced by first identifying a relevant subset of other subjects within the transfer learning data. In particular, if individual differences are high (as is often the case with psychophysiological data), a more accurate model might be induced based only on data collected from people who appear to have similar physiological responses. This is something we plan to explore in our ongoing work to improve the effectiveness of human-machine teams through real-time human workload monitoring.

Acknowledgments. This material is based upon work supported by the United States Air Force under Contract No. FA8650-15-C-6669. Any opinions, findings and conclusions or recommendations expressed in this material are those of the author(s) and do not necessarily reflect the views of the United States Air Force.

References

1. Hancock, P.A.: Whither workload? Mapping a path for its future development. In: Longo, L., Leva, M.C. (eds.) H-WORKLOAD 2017. CCIS, vol. 726, pp. 3–17. Springer, Cham (2017). https://doi.org/10.1007/978-3-319-61061-0_1
2. Longo, L.: Mental workload in medicine: foundations, applications, open problems, challenges and future perspectives. In: 2016 IEEE 29th International Symposium on Computer-Based Medical Systems (CBMS), pp. 106–111 (2016). https://doi.org/10.1109/cbms.2016.36
3. Wickens, C.D.: Mental workload: assessment, prediction and consequences. In: Longo, L., Leva, M.C. (eds.) H-WORKLOAD 2017. CCIS, vol. 726, pp. 18–29. Springer, Cham (2017). https://doi.org/10.1007/978-3-319-61061-0_2
4. Balfe, N., Crowley, K., Smith, B., Longo, L.: Estimation of train driver workload: extracting taskload measures from on-train-data-recorders. In: Longo, L., Leva, M.C. (eds.) H-WORKLOAD 2017. CCIS, vol. 726, pp. 106–119. Springer, Cham (2017). https://doi.org/10.1007/978-3-319-61061-0_7
5. Chen, J.Y., Haas, E.C., Barnes, M.J.: Human performance issues and user interface design for teleoperated robots. IEEE Trans. Syst. Man Cybern. Part C (Appl. Rev.) 37(6), 1231–1245 (2007). https://doi.org/10.1109/tsmcc.2007.905819
6. Edwards, T., Martin, L., Bienert, N., Mercer, J.: The relationship between workload and performance in air traffic control: exploring the influence of levels of automation and variation in task demand. In: Longo, L., Leva, M.C. (eds.) H-WORKLOAD 2017. CCIS, vol. 726, pp. 120–139. Springer, Cham (2017). https://doi.org/10.1007/978-3-319-61061-0_8
7. Fan, J., Smith, A.P.: The impact of workload and fatigue on performance. In: Longo, L., Leva, M.C. (eds.) H-WORKLOAD 2017. CCIS, vol. 726, pp. 90–105. Springer, Cham (2017). https://doi.org/10.1007/978-3-319-61061-0_6
8. Hancock, P.A., Williams, G., Manning, C.M.: Influence of task demand characteristics on workload and performance. Int. J. Aviat. Psychol. 5(1), 63–86 (1995). https://doi.org/10.1207/s15327108ijap0501_5
9. Longo, L.: Experienced mental workload, perception of usability, their interaction and impact on task performance. PLoS ONE 13(8), e0199661 (2018). https://doi.org/10.1371/journal.pone.0199661
10. Orasanu, J.M.: Shared problem models and flight crew performance. In: Johnston, N., McDonald, N., Fuller, R. (eds.) Aviation Psychology in Practice. Ashgate Publishing Group, Aldershot (1994). https://doi.org/10.4324/9781351218825
11. Smith, A.P., Smith, H.N.: Workload, fatigue and performance in the rail industry. In: Longo, L., Leva, M.C. (eds.) H-WORKLOAD 2017. CCIS, vol. 726, pp. 251–263. Springer, Cham (2017). https://doi.org/10.1007/978-3-319-61061-0_17
12. Tong, S., Helman, S., Balfe, N., Fowler, C., Delmonte, E., Hutchins, R.: Workload differences between on-road and off-road manoeuvres for motorcyclists. In: Longo, L., Leva, M.C. (eds.) H-WORKLOAD 2017. CCIS, vol. 726, pp. 239–250. Springer, Cham (2017). https://doi.org/10.1007/978-3-319-61061-0_16
13. Moustafa, K., Luz, S., Longo, L.: Assessment of mental workload: a comparison of machine learning methods and subjective assessment techniques. In: Longo, L., Leva, M.C. (eds.) H-WORKLOAD 2017. CCIS, vol. 726, pp. 30–50. Springer, Cham (2017). https://doi.org/10.1007/978-3-319-61061-0_3
14. Kantowitz, B.H.: Mental workload. In: Hancock, P.A. (ed.) Advances in Psychology, vol. 47, pp. 81–121. North-Holland (1987). https://doi.org/10.1016/s0166-4115(08)62307-9

15. Longo, L., Barrett, S.: A computational analysis of cognitive effort. In: Nguyen, N.T., Le, M. T., Świątek, J. (eds.) ACIIDS 2010. LNCS (LNAI), vol. 5991, pp. 65–74. Springer, Heidelberg (2010). https://doi.org/10.1007/978-3-642-12101-2_8

16. Moray, N. (ed.): Mental Workload: Its Theory and Measurement, vol. 8. Springer, New York (2013). https://doi.org/10.1007/978-1-4757-0884-4

17. Appriou, A., Cichocki, A., Lotte, F.: Towards robust neuroadaptive HCI: exploring modern machine learning methods to estimate mental workload from EEG signals. In: Extended Abstracts of the 2018 CHI Conference on Human Factors in Computing Systems, p. LBW615. ACM (2018). https://doi.org/10.1145/3170427.3188617

18. Wilson, G.F., Russell, C.A.: Real-time assessment of mental workload using psychophysiological measures and artificial neural networks. Hum. Factors 45(4), 635–644 (2003). https://doi.org/10.1518/hfes.45.4.635.27088

19. Zhang, J., Yin, Z., Wang, R.: Recognition of mental workload levels under complex human–machine collaboration by using physiological features and adaptive support vector machines. IEEE Trans. Hum.-Mach. Syst. 45(2), 200–214 (2015). https://doi.org/10.1109/thms.2014.2366914

20. Prinzel III, L.J., Parasuraman, R., Freeman, F.G., Scerbo, M.W., Mikulka, P.J., Pope, A.T.: Three experiments examining the use of electroencephalogram, event-related potentials, and heart-rate variability for real-time human-centered adaptive automation design. Report TP-2003-212442, NASA, Langley Research Center, Hampton (2003)

21. Roscoe, A.H.: Assessing pilot workload. Why measure heart rate, HRV and respiration? Biol. Psychol. 34(2–3), 259–287 (1992). https://doi.org/10.1016/0301-0511(92)90018-p

22. Veltman, J.A., Gaillard, A.W.K.: Physiological workload reactions to increasing levels of task difficulty. Ergonomics 41(5), 656–669 (1998). https://doi.org/10.1080/001401398186829

23. Verwey, W.B., Veltman, H.A.: Detecting short periods of elevated workload: a comparison of nine workload assessment techniques. J. Exp. Psychol.: Appl. 2(3), 270 (1996). https://doi.org/10.1037/1076-898X.2.3.270

24. Pan, S.J., Yang, Q.: A survey on transfer learning. IEEE Trans. Knowl. Data Eng. 22(10), 1345–1359 (2010). https://doi.org/10.1109/tkde.2009.191

25. Wu, D., Lance, B.J., Parsons, T.D.: Collaborative filtering for brain-computer interaction using transfer learning and active class selection. PLoS ONE 8(2), e56624 (2013). https://doi.org/10.1371/journal.pone.0056624

26. Hoepf, M., Middendorf, M., Epling, S., Galster, S.: Physiological indicators of workload in a remotely piloted aircraft simulation. In: 18th International Symposium on Aviation Psychology, pp. 428–433. Curran, Dayton (2015)

27. Hart, S.G., Staveland, L.E.: Development of NASA-TLX (task load index): results of empirical and theoretical research. In: Advances in Psychology, vol. 52, pp. 139–183. North-Holland (1988). https://doi.org/10.1016/s0166-4115(08)62386-9

28. Christensen, J.C., Estepp, J.R., Wilson, G.F., Russell, C.A.: The effects of day-to-day variability of physiological data on operator functional state classification. NeuroImage 59(1), 57–63 (2012). https://doi.org/10.1016/j.neuroimage.2011.07.091

29. Le Cessie, S., Van Houwelingen, J.C.: Ridge estimators in logistic regression. Appl. Stat. 41(1), 191–201 (1992). https://doi.org/10.2307/2347628

30. Witten, I.H., Frank, E., Hall, M.A., Pal, C.J.: Data Mining: Practical Machine Learning Tools and Techniques. Morgan Kaufmann, Burlington (2011). https://doi.org/10.1016/c2009-0-19715-5

31. Youden, W.J.: Index for rating diagnostic tests. Cancer, 3(1), 32–35 (1950). https://doi.org/10.1002/1097-0142(1950)3:1<32::aid-cncr2820030106>3.0.co;2-3

The Evolution of Cognitive Load Theory and the Measurement of Its Intrinsic, Extraneous and Germane Loads: A Review

Giuliano Orru and Luca Longo[✉]

School of Computing, College of Health and Sciences,
Dublin Institute of Technology, Dublin, Ireland
Luca.Longo@dit.ie

Abstract. Cognitive Load Theory has been conceived for supporting instructional design through the use of the construct of cognitive load. This is believed to be built upon three types of load: intrinsic, extraneous and germane. Although Cognitive Load Theory and its assumptions are clear and well-known, its three types of load have been going through a continuous investigation and re-definition. Additionally, it is still not clear whether these are independent and can be added to each other towards an overall measure of load. The purpose of this research is to inform the reader about the theoretical evolution of Cognitive Load Theory as well as the measurement techniques and measures emerged for its cognitive load types. It also synthesises the main critiques of scholars and the scientific value of the theory from a rationalist and structuralist perspective.

Keywords: Cognitive Load Theory, Cognitive load types ·
Intrinsic load, Extraneous load, Germane load · Measures ·
Instructional design · Efficiency

1 Introduction

The construct of Cognitive Load (CL) is strictly related to the construct of Mental Workload (MWL). The former has evolved within Educational Psychology [1], while the latter within Ergonomics and Human Factors [2]. Despite their independent evolution within different disciplines, both are based upon the same core assumption: the limitations of the human mental architecture and the cognitive capacities of the human brain and its working memory [3, 4]. In a nutshell, as professor Wickens suggested [5], mental workload is equivalent to the amount of mental resources simultaneously elicited by a human during the execution of a task. In order to achieve an optimal performance, the working memory limits should not be reached [3, 4]. If this occurs, the mental resources are no longer adequate to optimally execute the underlying task. Within Ergonomics, the construct of Mental Workload has evolved both theoretically and practically. A plethora of ad-hoc definitions exist as well as several domain-dependent measurement techniques, measures and applications [1]. While abundance of research exists, the science of Mental Workload is still in its infancy because any of the proposed measures can generalise the construct itself. Similarly, within Educational

L. Longo and M. C. Leva (Eds.): H-WORKLOAD 2018, CCIS 1012, pp. 23–48, 2019.
https://doi.org/10.1007/978-3-030-14273-5_3

Psychology, despite Cognitive Load Theory (CLT) is one of the most invoked learning theory for supporting instructional design [6], research on how to develop highly generalisable measures of Cognitive Load is limited. Also, it is unclear how its three types of load – intrinsic, extraneous and germane – can be measured and how they interact with each other. The aim of this paper is to provide readers with the theoretical elements underpinning the construct of Cognitive Load. This is done from an evolutionary perspective of the measurement techniques and measures emerged from the three types of load, accompanied with a critical discussion of their scientific value.

The remainder of the paper is structured as follows. Section 2 presents the key theoretical elements and assumptions of Cognitive Load Theory, as appeared in the literature. Section 3 focuses on a review of the measurement techniques and measures emerged for its intrinsic, extraneous and germane loads. Section 4 builds on this review by emphasising the open debate on the scientific value of CLT. Section 5 highlights new perspectives and research on CLT and the reconceptualization of its cognitive load types, as recently emerged in the literature. Section 6 summarises this study with final remarks suggesting novel research directions.

2 Cognitive Load Theory

Cognitive Load Theory (CLT) is a cognitivist learning theory aimed at supporting instructors in the development of novel instructional designs aligned with the limitations of the human cognitive architecture. In a nutshell, this architecture is the human cognitive system aimed at storing information, retrieving and processing it for reasoning and decision making [7]. CLT is based upon the assumption of *active processing* that views the learner as actively engaged in the construction of knowledge [8]. In other words, learners are actively engaged in a process of attention to relevant material and its organisation into coherent structures that are integrated with prior knowledge [9]. Another premise of CLT is the *dual-channel* assumption by which processing of information occurs in two distinct channels: an auditory and a verbal channel. The former processes auditory sensory input and verbal information while the latter processes visual sensory inputs and pictorial representations [10]. An essential component of this architecture is its memory that can store information for short and long term. According to another premise, *the limited capacity* assumption of CLT, the former memory, also referred to working memory, is conscious and limited, while the latter is unconscious and unlimited [2]. Baddeley [3] and Paivio [4], following Miller proposal [7], support the view that when working memory has to deal with new information, it can hold just seven chunks at a time. However, if these chunks are related and if they have to be processed, human beings are capable to handle just two or three at the same time [11]. Expanding the capacity of working memory coincides with learning [2]. Learning take places by transferring pieces of information from working memory to long term memory [3, 4]. According to Schema Theory, this transfer of information allows the construction of knowledge, in long term memory, in the form of schema [12]. To construct a schema means to relate different chunks of information from a lower level to a higher level of complexity and to hold them as a single unit that can be understood as a single chunk of information [12]. In turn, schema can be retrieved to solve a problem, a task, or more generally to answer a question in educational contexts. Schema construction is believed to reduce the load in working memory [2]. The expansion of long term memory can be achieved by a reduction of the load of working memory. Leaving sufficient cognitive resources in working memory to process new information is one of the core objectives of educational instructional design. In fact, if the amount of information that has to be held in working memory lies within its limits, the learning phase is facilitated. Contrarily, if the amount of information overcomes these limits, an overload situation occurs and the learning phase is hampered (Fig. 1).

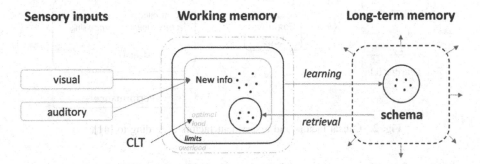

Fig. 1. A representation of the mental architecture and the role of Cognitive Load Theory (CLT) in connection to working memory and schema construction

A core construct within CLT is Cognitive Load (CL), believed to be multidimensional. Intuitively it can be defined as the mental cost imposed by an underlying cognitive task on the human cognitive system [13]. It is possible to distinguish two types of factors that can interact with cognitive load: causal and assessment factors (Fig. 2). The formers affect cognitive load while the latter are affected by cognitive load. The causal factors include:

- features of the task (T) such as structure, novelty and pressure;
- the features of the environment (E) such as noise and temperature where a task (T) is executed and their interaction (ExT);
- the characteristic of a learner (L) such as capabilities, cognitive style and prior knowledge;
- the interaction between environment and learner characteristics (ExL);
- the interaction between task, environment, learner's characteristics Ex(TxL).

The assessment factors can be conceptualised with three dimensions: mental load, mental effort and mental performance. Mental load is imposed by the task (T) and/or by demands from the environment. It is a task-centred dimension, independent of the subject, and it is considered constant. Mental effort is a human-centred dimension that reflects the amount of controlled processing (capacity or resources allocated for task demands) in which the individual is engaged with [13]. It is affected by the task-environment interaction (ExT), the subject characteristics interaction with the environment (ExL) and the interaction of the learner with the task in the environment (Ex(TxL)). Similarly, the level of mental performance is affected by the factors that affect mental effort [4]. Other factors might affect cognitive load [14, 15] and research in the field has not produced a comprehensive list yet [16].

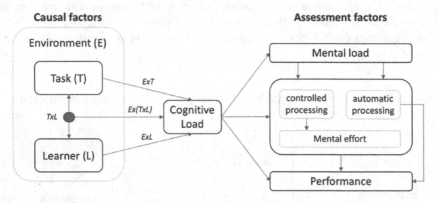

Fig. 2. Causal factors and assessment factors according to [41].

Starting from the research of Halford et al. [17] on the difficulty in processing information with multiple elements at the same time during problem solving, Sweller defined the degree of complexity of these elements as 'element interactivity' [18]. Starting from this definition, two types of cognitive load has emerged: the *intrinsic* and the *extraneous* loads. Intrinsic load refers to the numbers of elements that must be processed simultaneously in working memory (element interactivity) for schema construction. 'This type of load cannot be modified by instructional interventions because it is intrinsic to the material being dealt with. Instead, extraneous cognitive load is the unnecessary cognitive load and can be altered by instructional interventions' [2]. Sweller stated that the basic goal of Cognitive Load Theory is the reduction of extraneous load: this is a type of ineffective load that depends on the instructional techniques provided by the instructional format to complete a task [2]. This view is supported by Paas and colleagues that refers to extraneous load as the cognitive effect of instructional designs that hamper the construction of schema in working memory [19]. Beside, intrinsic and extraneous, Sweller defined another type of load: the *germane* load [2]. This is the extra effort required for learning (schema construction). It is possible to use this effort when intrinsic and extraneous loads leave sufficient working memory resources. This extra effort increases cognitive load, but it is connected to learning, thus, it facilitates schema construction. Germane load is the effective cognitive load and it is the result of those beneficial cognitive processes such as abstractions and elaboration that are promoted by 'good' instructional designs [20]. Reducing extraneous load and improving germane load by developing schema construction and automation should be the main goal of the discipline of instructional design. The three types of load emerged within Cognitive Load Theory, and their role, can be summarised in Fig. 3.

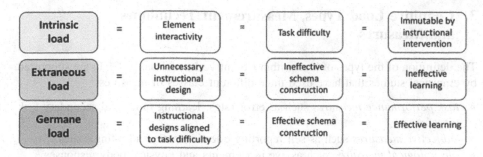

Fig. 3. Definitions and role of the cognitive load types of Cognitive Load Theory.

Sweller and colleagues, with their attempt to define cognitive load within the discipline of Educational Psychology and for instructional design, believed that the three types of load are additive. This meant that the total cognitive load experienced by a learner in working memory while executing a task, is the sum of the three types of load, these being independent sources of load [2] (Fig. 4).

Fig. 4. Additive definition of overall cognitive load.

Figure 5 depicts the relationship between the three types of cognitive load, as proposed in [21]. In condition A (overload), cognitive load exceeds the limits of the working memory of the learner due to an increment in the extraneous load. In turn errors are more frequent, longer task execution times occur, sometimes even leading to the inability to perform an underlying task. In condition B there is spare working memory capacity and the learners can perform optimally on an underlying task. With spare capacity, CLT proposes to increase the germane load in order to activate learning tasks, as in condition C.

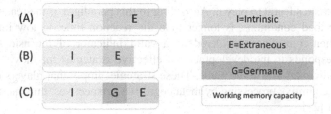

Fig. 5. Relationship between the three types of cognitive load

3 Cognitive Load Types, Measurement Techniques and Measures

The definition of the types of load within Cognitive Load Theory (CLT) are supported by empirical studies that have used three different classes of measures:

- *task performance measures* such as error rates, learning times and secondary task measures;
- *subjective measures* such as self-reporting questionnaires and rating scales;
- *physiological measures* such as eye movements and physical body responses.

Within Educational Psychology, the focus has always been on the first two classes: task performance and subjective measures. The reason is intuitive since physiological measurement techniques require special equipment to gather data, trainer operators to use this equipment and they are intrusive, most of the time not suitable for empirical experiments in typical classrooms. Additionally, evidence suggests they did not prove sufficient sensitivity to differentiate the three cognitive load types [13] envisioned in CLT. As a consequence, the next sections mainly focus on research studies that employed task performance and subjective measures.

Miwa et al. [21] developed a task-performance based method for cognitive load measurement built upon the *mental chronometry paradigm* [22], in line with the tri-archic view of load [2]. The mental chronometry assumes that reaction time can reveal the quantity of intrinsic, extraneous and germane loads coming from the corresponding cognitive processes. The hypothesis behind their experiment is that if, in the 8×8 Reversi game (Fig. 4), the three types of cognitive load are manipulated by changing the presentation of the information to the players, it is possible to measure them by observing their reaction time of players between movements of discs on the board. To manipulate the intrinsic load, on one hand, an advisor computer agent provides some hints to participants on the possible subsequent move (low intrinsic load condition, Fig. 6 left). On the other hand, in another condition, no hints are provided (high intrinsic load condition, Fig. 6 right). In addition to this, in order to manipulate extraneous load, the white and black discs are changed with two different letters from the Japanese alphabet. Since these 2 letters are perceptually similar, they are expected to lead to higher perception and understanding exerted by participants. Eventually, the germane load is manipulated by altering the instructions presented to participants. In order to exert more germane load, each participant is requested to report, after the game, the heuristics learnt to play it. According to this paradigm, if the reaction time, in high intrinsic load conditions, is longer than the reaction time, in low intrinsic load conditions, then it can be considered as a valid indicator of intrinsic load. Here, learning corresponds to the development of effective strategies for moving discs that can lead a participant to win the game. These strategies imply that players control and regulate their cognitive processing by meta cognitive perspectives, thus increasing their germane load [21].

Low Intrinsic Load,
with agent hints

High Intrinsic Load, with no hints
and Japanese characters

Fig. 6. Low and high extraneous load conditions in the 8 × 8 Reversi game [35].

The research attempt by Miwa and colleagues [21] is indeed useful to investigate the discrimination between the three types of load and to provide guidelines on how to design experiments that contribute to the definition of cognitive load. Their preliminary findings suggest the three types of load are separable. However, it was executed in a highly controlled environment and not in more natural settings such as in a typical classroom, thus limiting the generalisability of their findings.

3.1 Subjective Measures of Cognitive Load

Gerjets et al. [23] proposed two experiments on the use of hypermedia environments for learning on the topic of probability theory. In the first experiment, the validity of multimedia principles [10] in hypermedia environments has been tested. In the second experiment, an analysis of the ability of learners to impact their performance according to their prior experience was performed. A subjective 9-point Likert scale is employed to measure the three types of load during learning (Table 1).

Table 1. Subjective rating scale to measure cognitive load types from [23]. Each item has to be rated on a 9 point Likert scale (1 = extremely easy, 9 = extremely difficult)

Type of load	Scale
Intrinsic load	How easy or difficult do you consider probability theory at this moment?
Extraneous load	• How easy or difficult is it for you to work with the learning environments? • How easy or difficult is it for you to distinguish important and unimportant information in the learning environments? • How easy or difficult is it for you to collect all the information that you need in the learning environment?
Germane load	Indicate the amount of effort you exerted to follow the last example

Depending on the prior knowledge of learners, high intrinsic and extraneous loads should lead to poor learning outcomes while high germane load should lead to good learning outcomes. Unfortunately, in this study no evidence of this connection has been found. Consequently, authors claim that subjective rating scales are valid if learners are able to distinguish the types of cognitive load. In other words, in order to be sensitive to the differences in loads, learners should be aware of the cognitive process connected to the experienced load. To achieve this, training learners on Cognitive Load Theory can facilitate their understanding of the three types of load. However, this is not an easy condition to achieve. In fact, for instance, the level of difficulty (intrinsic load) could be due to the poor instructional design that increase the extraneous load, or due to the natural complexity of an underlying learning task. A novice learner could find this distinction really hard to understand and could not be able to comprehend if the own difficulty in learning can be attributed to the instructional design (extraneous load) or the complexity of the task (intrinsic load).

Corbalan et al. [24] hypothesises that, in order to prevent cognitive overload, it is possible to adapt task difficulty and the support of each newly selected learning task to the previous knowledge and experience of a learner and his/her perceived task load [24]. This can be done by employing some external agent, the learner him/herself, or both. The hypothesis was tested by employing two subjective rating scales, one for task load and one for germane load (as per Table 2). This hypothesis was tested by performing an empirical 2×2 factorial design experiment with health sciences students. The design variables where the factors adaptation (absence or presence of the agent) and the control over task selection (program control or shared control program/learner).

Table 2. Measurements of task and germane load on a 7-point scale from [24] (1 = extremely low, 7 = extremely high)

Type of load	Scale
Task load	Rate your effort to perform the task
Germane load	Evaluate the effort invested in gaining understanding of the relationship dealt with in the simulator task

Findings suggest that, on one hand, the presence of adaptation delivered more efficient learning and task involvement. On the other hand, shared control produced a higher task involvement when compared to program task selection. Learning here refers to good learning outcomes and lower effort exerted in the underlying learning tasks. Task involvement refers to good learning outcomes and higher effort exerted in the learning task. Both the cases prevented cognitive overload [24].

Ayres hypothesised that, by maintaining the extraneous and the germane loads constant, students can identify changes in the 'element interactivity' within problems by means of subjective measures, and thus successfully quantify the intrinsic cognitive load [25]. In his study, extraneous and germane loads are maintained constant by not providing any instructional hint. Learners had to solve a set of four brackets-expansion problems without any explicit instructions (source of extraneous load) and without any didactic feedback (source of germane load). The bracket-expansion problems required a series of four operations in which the level of difficulty increased. Under this instructional condition, any change in the overall cognitive load is due to change in the element interactivity (source of intrinsic load). Intrinsic load is measured by a subjective measure, as depicted in Table 3. After each operation, learners had to rate its difficulty. The hypothesis is that higher intrinsic load should correspond to more errors.

Table 3. Subjective rating scale of intrinsic load on a 7-point scale from [1] (1 = extremely easy, 7 = extremely difficult)

Type of load	Scale
Intrinsic load	How easy or difficult you found each calculation?

The authors tested their hypothesis with two experiments. In the first, students had low prior mathematical knowledge while in the second, participants had a wider range of mathematical skills. In the first experiment, students could recognise task difficulty since subjective intrinsic load was highly correlated with the errors committed by themselves. In the second experiment, although students did not commit many mistakes, they still could detect differences in task difficulty. These findings support the high sensitivity and reliability of the employed self-reporting measure. Additionally, the takeaway of this study is that, by keeping constant two sources of load out of three, it is possible to get a measure of the remaining dependent load. Transitively, it turns out that, by keeping constant the extraneous and the intrinsic loads, any change in cognitive load, irrespective of the measurement technique employed, corresponds to variations in the dependent variable, the germane load.

Gerjets et al. [26] investigated how to enhance learning through a comparison of two instructional designs on the same topic: how to calculate the probability of a complex event. The first design condition included worked out examples, while the latter included modular worked examples. To measure the experienced cognitive load of learners in each condition, a modified version of the NASA-Task Load Index was (Table 4) [27]. Readers are referred to [27] for the original version.

Table 4. Modified version of the NASA-TLX from [26] where each scale ranged from 0 to 100 (low level to high level)

Type of load	Scale
Task demands (intrinsic load)	How much mental and physical activity did you require to accomplish the learning task? (Thinking, deciding, calculating, remembering, looking, searching)
Effort (extraneous load)	How hard did you have to work to understand the contents of the learning environment?
Navigational demand	How much effort did you invest to navigate the learning environment?
Understanding	How successful did you feel in understanding the contents?
Stress	How much stress did you experience during learning?

Within Cognitive Load Theory, Sweller [2] stated that task demand is caused by the degree of element interactivity of the task (intrinsic load), while the effort is exerted to achieve an effective understanding of the instructional material. The navigational demands are related to those activities not strictly directed to learning. In this line, Gerjets and colleagues stated that the scale for task demands is aimed at quantifying the intrinsic load of the instructional material, the effort scale at quantifying the germane load and the scale for navigational demands is aimed at quantifying the extraneous load [26]. The hypothesis of the experiment is that the modular presentation of worked examples can increase the germane load more than their molar – as a whole – presentation. Unfortunately, findings did not provide evidence about any increment of the germane load. As a possible interpretation, the authors suggested that the instructional explanations provided during the task to increase the germane load, and the self-explanation derived using worked out examples, created a redundant information and the illusion of understanding hampered the learning instead of improving it. However, in a prior experiment, Gerjets et al. [26] have successful demonstrated that, in an example based learning, the modular presentation of worked examples can actually reduce the intrinsic load and improves the germane load more than the molar presentation of the same problem. The modular presentation provides a part-whole sequencing of the solution procedures whereas the molar presentation provides the solutions of the procedures as a whole. The segmentation of the presentation of the worked example led to a decrease in the degree of interactivity as well as in the number of simultaneous items. In turn, this led to a decrease in the intrinsic load. According to the authors, these findings are more relevant to novice learners, whereas the same instructional design could be redundant for more expert learners because the degree of their expertise increases. Consequently, in the case of expert learners, the molar presentation of solution procedures is a more appropriate instructional design. The modified version of the NASA-TLX, employed in this study, has been applied also in [28]. Here, authors focused on the effects of different kinds of computer-based graphic representations in connection to the acquisition of problem-solving skills in the context of probability theory. Despite different experiments, [26, 29] and [28] did not provide evidence on the reliability and validity of the subjective rating scale employed. Therefore, it can be only hypothesised that this scale is sensitive to the three types of load conceived within CLT.

Galy et al. [30] tested the additivity between the intrinsic, the extraneous and the germane loads by manipulating three factors believed to have an effect on each of them. In detail, this study assumed that task difficulty is an indicator of intrinsic load, time pressure of extraneous load and the level of alertness of germane load. The effect on the experienced overall cognitive load is connected to the manipulation of the extraneous and intrinsic loads which are respectively estimated by the self-reporting of notions of tension (time pressure) and mental effort (task difficulty). The level of alertness is measured by the French paper-and-pencil version of the Thayers's Activation-Deactivation Checklist [31]. Questions are listed in Table 5. For each word in the deactivation list, each student had to tick one from the "not at all", "don't know", "little" and "much" labels. These labels are respectively mapped to weights (1, 2, 3 and 4). The responses were counted up to have a measure of four factors: general activation (GA), deactivation sleep (DS), high activation (HA), and general deactivation (GD). The GA/DS ratio yielded an alertness index.

Table 5. Self report scales of cognitive loads types from [30]. Intrinsic and extraneous load are in the scale 0 to 10 (low time pressure/mental effort to high effort/considerable effort)

Type of load	Scale
Intrinsic load	Rate the mental effort (task difficulty) you experienced during the task
Extraneous load	Rate the tension (time pressure) you experienced during the task
Germane load	Select one of the following responses ("not at all", "don't know", "little" and "much") for each of 20 listed adjectives: active, energetic, vigorous, full of, lively, still, quiet, placid, calm, at rest, tense, intense, clutched up, fearful, jittery, wide-awake, wakeful, sleepy, drowsy, tired

The experimental task consisted of a memory recalling activity with 2 digit numbers (low difficulty) or 3 digit numbers (high difficulty) in four conditions: low difficulty and low time pressure, low difficulty and high time pressure, high difficulty and low time pressure, high difficulty and high time pressure. The difference in cognitive load due to variations in task difficulty and time pressure with respect to the different levels of alertness can be taken as an indicator of differences in the contribution of germane load. In low difficulty and low time pressure conditions, germane load is believed to be substantially inexistent, but in high difficulty and high time pressure conditions, it is assumed that the learner has to employ specific strategies to execute the memory task and thus generating germane load. Authors believed that germane load, as a function of alertness, corresponds to the subject's capability to select strategies to be employed while performing the learning task. However, the implementation of these strategies is determined by the amount of free cognitive resources determined by task difficulty and time pressure [30]. Consequently, the authors claimed that alertness is a germane load factor depending on the quantity of working memory resources left by the intrinsic and extraneous load experienced.

Leppink et al. [32] developed a new instrument for the measurement of intrinsic, extraneous and germane loads. The authors consider the critique of Kalyunga et al. [33] about the expertise reversal effect and its consequences on the learning and on the different types of load. According to this, the same instructional feature may be associated with germane load for a learner and with extraneous load for another learner, depending on the level of expertise and on the level of prior knowledge. To develop a more sensitive instrument to detect changes in cognitive load types, they proposed a multi-item questionnaire (Table 6). Authors conducted experiments in four lectures of statistics, asking to rate difficult or complex formulas, concepts and definitions using the scales in Table 6. In a number of studies, Leppink and colleagues verified 7 hypotheses regarding the reliability of the new instrument compared with other instruments, used in the past, to measure intrinsic load [25], extraneous load [34], germane load [35] and for overall cognitive load [36]. They also tested five hypotheses connected to the expected relationship between prior knowledge and intrinsic load, and between prior knowledge and learning outcomes. Through an exploratory analysis, it has emerged that the reliability of the rating scale was positive, the extraneous load and the germane load elements were negatively correlated and the elements that were supposed to measure intrinsic load were not correlated to germane load.

Table 6. Multi-subjective rating scales of cognitive load types from [32] in the scale 0 to 10 (0 = not at all, 10 = completely).

Type of load	Scale
Intrinsic load	• The topic/topics covered in the activity was/were very complex • The activity covered formulas that I perceive as very complex • The activity covered concepts and definitions that I perceived as very complex
Extraneous load	• The instruction and/or explanation during the activity were very unclear • The instruction and/or explanation were, in terms of learning, very ineffective • The instruction and/or explanations were full of unclear language
Germane load	• The activity really enhanced my understanding of the topic(s) covered • The activity really enhanced my knowledge and understanding of statistics • The activity really enhanced my understanding of the formulas covered • The activity really enhanced my understanding of concepts, definitions

Eventually, the elements that were expected to measure intrinsic load had moderate correlation with extraneous load. The validity of the scales was verified by comparing the subjective ratings with the learning outcomes assessed by a performance test. As hypothesised, a high prior knowledge corresponded to a low intrinsic load. Extraneous cognitive load was higher when a problem was solved by an unfamiliar format and germane load was higher when a problem was solved by a familiar format. There is partial evidence that higher germane load, as measured by multiple subjective scales, lead to higher results on post-task test performance.

Leppink and colleagues [37] criticised their own previous study [32] mentioning the uncertainty of their multiple subjective rating scales to represent the three different types of cognitive load. The main reasons of their critique are three: (1) the correlation between germane load and the learning outcomes, in the task performance, was lower than expected and not statistically relevant (2) the previous experiments were all focused on a single topic, namely statistic (3) the manipulations applied in [32] did not lead to the expected differences in the measurement of the three different cognitive load types [37]. In summary, their psychometric instrument might have measured only the level of expectation instead of the actual invested effort devoted in the complexity of the activity (intrinsic load), its ineffective explanations (extraneous) and its understanding (germane). To evaluate a more direct relation between the three types of load and the learning outcomes, a randomized experiment was performed, with bachelor students who received a description of the Bayes theorem. To measure the three different types of load, the authors changed the order of the rating scales and added three items to it (as per Table 7). These items were supposed to contribute to the evaluation of the internal consistency of the theoretical assumption that the three types of load are separated, additive and independent. Findings suggest that two items improved the internal consistency of the mental effort for intrinsic and extraneous loads but not for germane load, suggesting its re-definition [6].

Table 7. Informed subjective rating questionnaire proposed in [39] available to learners while rating different learning scenarios on a 7-point Likert scale (1 = very low, 7 = very high)

Type of load	Scale
Intrinsic load	I invested a very high mental effort in the complexity of this activity
Extraneous load	I invested a very high mental effort in unclear and ineffective explanations and instructions in this activity
Germane load	I invested a very high mental effort during this activity in enhancing my knowledge and understanding

Zukic and colleagues [38] focused on the assessment of the validity of the instrument developed in [37] as well as its internal consistency and its capability to correlate with learning outcomes. In their study, the correlations between intrinsic and extraneous load and between extraneous and germane load were statistically significant. A low degree of experienced intrinsic load and a high degree of reported germane load could explain the improvement of the learning outcomes. Additionally, a regression analysis verified that the items associated to the germane load could actually explain the perceived learning. Eventually, a confirmatory factor analysis supported the development of a three-dimensional model that includes the three types of load. The main take away of this study is that germane load can be measured as an independent source of load.

Klepsch et al. proposed an alternative way to measure the three load types reliably and validly [39]. The novelty of their approach is the use of two forms of ratings: informed and naïve. According to this, they conducted an experiment with two different group of learners. The first, the informed rating group, was trained on how to differentiate the three types of load through a theoretical explanation of CLT and its assumptions. The second, the naïve rating group, did not receive the training on CLT.

Learners were asked to rate 24 learning scenarios grouped in 5 different domains (language learning, biology, mathematics, technology and didactics). To detect changes

Table 8. Informed subjective rating questionnaire proposed in [39] available to learners while rating different learning scenarios on a 7-point Likert scale (1 = very low, 7 = very high)

Type of load	Scale
Intrinsic load	During this task, Intrinsic Load was...
Extraneous load	During this task, Extraneous Load was...
Germane load	During this task, Germane Load was...

in the cognitive load experienced by the two groups of learners, only one type of cognitive load was manipulated at a time. The learners in group one received the questionnaire in Table 8, while those in group two received the questionnaire in Table 9 Both the groups received also an additional question on perceived overall cognitive load adapted from [36]. The participants in the informed ratings group correctly discriminated intrinsic, extraneous and germane loads in line with the expectations. However, participants, in the Naïve ratings group, correctly discriminated only the intrinsic and the extraneous loads but they were not able to differentiate germane load.

Table 9. First version of the Naïve rating scales questionnaire proposed in [39] 7-point Likert scale (1 = completely wrong, 7 = absolutely right)

Type of load	Scale
Intrinsic load	• For this task, many things needed to be kept in mind simultaneously • This task was very complex
Germane load	• For this task, I had to highly engage myself • For this task, I had to think intensively what things meant
Extraneous load	• During this task, it was exhausting to find the important information • The design of this task was very inconvenient for learning • During this task, it was difficult to recognize and link the crucial information

A reliability analysis of the scales was executed, by task, using the Cronbach alpha measure based on the formula presented in [40]. This allowed to compute the mean of several given alpha values based on sampling distribution. The validity of the measure was analysed by comparing the ratings of learners with the expectations for each type of load for each task. A very low reliability was detected for all the tasks, in the informed ratings group, this being an indicator of the capability of learners to differentiate the types of load separately. However, in the naïve ratings groups, reliability was high, suggesting how the three types of load were not clearly separable. In particular, germane load was the dimension that was not discriminable across the two groups. Starting from this unsatisfying finding, the authors developed a new scale for germane load (Table 10).

Table 10. Second version of the Naïve rating questionnaire proposed in [39] with a new scale for the germane load on a 7-point Likert scale (1 = completely wrong, 7 = absolutely right)

Load type	Scale
Germane load	• I made an effort, not only to understand several details, but to understand the overall context • My point while dealing with the task was to understand everything correctly • The learning task consisted of elements supporting my comprehension of the task

Subsequently, they evaluated the overall new questionnaire with a larger sample. A new experiment was conducted with a group of students who received 8 tasks, one at a time, designed to induce more or less germane load. Here, in contrast to the first study, and in line with the idea of doing experiments in more realistic learning environments, each learning task was designed to induce changes in the three types of load. For intrinsic load, the degree of interactivity of the tasks was manipulated. For extraneous load, different learning formats were considered, some employing text and pictures together, some individually and some with additional non-relevant information. Eventually, germane load was manipulated by creating tasks aimed at eliciting different degrees of deeper learning processes. A reliability and validity analysis, conducted as in the first experiment, confirmed that it is possible to measure the three types of load separately, in line with the triarchic theory of load [2].

3.2 Task Performance and Self-reported Measures

Deleeuw and Mayer tested the separability of the three types of load in a multimedia lesson on the topic of electric motors [41]. Two experiments were executed: one with a pre-question on the content of the lesson aimed at motivating learners to focus on deeper cognitive processing, and one without. Authors manipulated extraneous load providing redundant instructional designs to learners. Similarly, they manipulated intrinsic load through changes on the complexity of the sentences that explained the lesson. Eventually, they examined the differences in the germane load by comparing students with high scores on a test of problem solving transfer, against students with lower scores. The authors evaluated the sensitivity of the response time to a secondary task during learning for measuring the extraneous load, the effort ratings during learning for measuring the intrinsic load, and the self-reported difficulty rating, after learning, for measuring the germane load (as per Table 11). In details, the secondary task consisted of a visual monitoring task where learners had to recognise a periodic change of colour and to press the space bar each time this colour change took place.

Table 11. Subjective rating scales and secondary task reaction time proposed by [41] on a 9-point Likert Scale (1 = extremely low, 9 = extremely high for intrinsic load and 1 = extremely easy, 9 = extremely difficult for germane load)

Types of load	Scale/measure
Intrinsic load	Your level of mental effort on this part of the lesson
Germane load	How difficult this lesson was
+	
Extraneous load	Measured by the response time to a secondary task
	At each of eight points in an animated narration, the background colour slowly changes (pink to black)
	Learner is required to press the spacebar of the computer as soon as the color changes

The findings of the experiment supported the triarchic theory of cognitive load [2]. Students who received redundant information needed longer reaction time than students who did not receive redundant instructional design. The explanation about the electric motor has been provided by learners using different sentences with different levels of complexity. The scale for intrinsic load reflected higher effort for high complexity sentences and lower effort for low complexity sentences. Students who reported a lower and a higher transfer reflected their difficulty by the rating scale provided: low transfer reflected high difficulty, high transfer reflected low difficulty. Thus, the authors showed that these different measures of load (reaction time, effort and difficulty) are sensitive to different types of load (extraneous, intrinsic, germane) [41]. The three different variables analysed (redundancy and complexity of statement, high or slow capacity of transfer to solve a problem) are strongly correlated with the three different types of load, thus providing evidence for their good sensitivity. Eventually, authors recommended a replication of their research study in other contexts and with different students because the measurement of the three cognitive load types might be often intrusive, creating an artificial learning situation. In addition, the study did not account for the prior knowledge of learners, (most of them had a low prior knowledge) as an important variable that could influence the overall perception of load.

Cerniak et al. [34] hypothesised how the split attention effect, proposed by Sweller [2], could be mediated not only by a reduction of extraneous cognitive load but also by an increase of germane load (germane load explanation) [42]. An experiment, conducted in a learning context on physiological processes of a nephron, was aimed at testing the above the research hypothesis. Authors employed the reaction time on a secondary as a task performance measure, in order to detect variations in the overall cognitive load between learners who received an integrated format of instructional designs and learners who received a split source format. The former learners were expected to experience less overall load because the integrated format was believed to decrease their extraneous load. The latter learners were expected to experience more overall load due to the split attention effect believed to increase their extraneous load, as suggested in [43]. In the experiment, learners had to press the space bar of the keyboard of a computer every time a stimulus appeared on the screen (for example the change of a colour). The longer time required to react to this secondary task, the higher cognitive load exerted on the primary task. Eventually, subjective ratings were applied to measure the three types of load, as per Table 12.

Table 12. Subjective rating scales for the cognitive load types proposed by [34] on a 6-point Likert Scale (1 = not at all, 6 = extremely)

Type of load	Scale
Intrinsic load	How much difficult was the learning content for you?
Extraneous load	How difficult was it for you to learn with the material?
Germane load	How much did you concentrate during learning?

Findings showed that there is no difference in the overall cognitive load between learners who received the split source format and those who received the integrated source format. As a consequence, the former learners increased their extraneous load and decreased their germane load, whereas the latter learners decreased their extraneous load and increased their germane load. This confirms that the extraneous and germane loads partially mediate the split attention effect. However, authors brought forward a critique whereby there could be a possible confusion between the two different questions designed for intrinsic and extraneous loads. Learners could have the impression to answer the same question. In fact, in a new learning context, learners might not be able to identify the source of difficulty that means the content or the instructional material delivered. The authors spotted a high correlation between the extraneous and the germane loads through an analysis of the learning outcomes. However, they did not state that these measures of loads were aimed at tackling different working memory resources. As a consequence, the relation between learning processes and working memory capacity was not demonstrated.

4   Synthesis and Observations on the Scientific Value of Cognitive Load Theory

According to the literature review conducted in the previous sections, it appears evident that the three types of load envisioned in Cognitive Load Theory – intrinsic, extraneous and germane – have been mainly measured by means of subjective rating scales. This has more a practical explanation because self-reporting scales are easier to use and they do not influence the primary task when compared to secondary task measures. They can be administered post-learning tasks and they are aimed at representing a perceptual subjective experience of a learner for an entire learning session. This is in contrast to secondary task measures which, even if more sensitive to variations of cognitive load, they are more intrusive since they alter the natural execution of a learning task. A number of researchers brought forward critiques on Cognitive Load Theory in relation to its theoretical clarity [44, 45] and its methodological approach [46]. According to these critiques, the assumptions of CLT appear circular because its three types of load are believed not to be empirically measurable. Empirical research is based on observed and recorded data and it derives knowledge from actual experience rather than from a theory, a belief or a logic coming from first principles 'a priori'. This is the case of subjective rating scales aimed at measuring the cognitive load types. Regardless of the way these scales relate to the evaluation of the different cognitive load types, all of them underlie the phenomenon they are pretending to measure in their premises or suppositions, namely the definitions of intrinsic, extraneous and germane loads (Fig. 7, left). In other words, the premises of CLT – its cognitive load types – are believed to be confirmed by the data coming from their measurements circularly, without empirical evidence.

In addition, the fact that human cognitive processes, related to the same instructional design, can be regarded as germane load in one case and as extraneous load in another case, it means that CLT can account for nearly every situation [45]. This critique also refers to the 'Expertise Reversal Effect' [47]. In fact, on one hand, some instructional design, such as written explanations followed by a graphic element to enhance its understanding, can be useful for a novice learner, by reducing the extraneous load and increasing the germane load. On the other hand, the same graphical aid can be useless for an expert learner because it can reduce germane load and increase extraneous load. In fact, for an expert, it can be redundant to read instructional designs just registered and automatized in own memory, hampering understanding and learning. Depending on the degree of expertise, the same instructional design can lead to germane or extraneous load, emphasising the circularity of CLT (Fig. 7, right). The theoretical differences regarding the types of load are based on the subjective experienced load of learners, implying that they are able to differentiate them by their own. This issue, as discussed above, depends on the way the questions are formulated, and on the familiarity of learners on the different cognitive load types, and their prior knowledge. All these variables are not easy to monitor and control, they can create confusion on the source of the supposed experienced load. Under a strict scientific view, the evaluation of this supposed load does not come from the experience of the learners, rather from the principles of the theory is based upon.

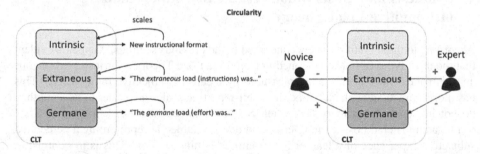

Fig. 7. The circularity of the load types of Cognitive Load Theory (left) and the 'expertise reversal effect' by which different cognitive processes can be regarded differently (right)

To analyse the scientific value of CLT, two different methodological approaches have been followed: the rationalism of Karl Popper [48, 49] and the structuralist approach of the theories of Joseph Sneed [50]. Under the former approach, it is not possible to consider CLT scientific because its basic principles, namely the three different types of load, cannot be tested by means of any experimental method, consequently they are not falsifiable [46] (Fig. 8, left). To be scientific, the measures should be sensitive to the different types of load. From a strict rationalist point of view, a measure is scientific if it does not presuppose the assumptions that it shall measure in its rationale [46]. However, as previously discussed, most of the subjective rating scales, conceived for the cognitive load types, contain the variables they pretend to measure. This implies that the logic of the questions influences the logic of the answers. In turn, the measures of the loads can be obtained 'a priori', by setting the questions to validate the theory they are pretending to verify, and not through any authentic experience of cognitive load. CLT should provide empirical evidence about the cognitive load types. Unfortunately, this has not convincingly emerged in the literature of

Educational Psychology, Instructional Design and Cognitive Load Theory, justifying the scepticism regarding the possibility to measure the three different types of load.

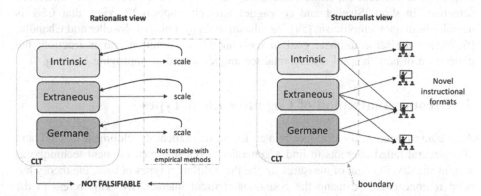

Fig. 8. The rationalist view of Cognitive Load Theory (left) and the structuralist view (right)

The second methodological approach to analyse CLT is based upon structuralism [50–53]. Under its logic, the scientific value of the theoretical principles of CLT does not depend on their empirical validity. Rather it depends upon their effectiveness to form the ground of the structure of a theory that consents to derive specific predictions on how detailed instructional manipulations can affect learning outcomes [46]. The structuralist analysis considers the fundamental assumptions of CLT as theoretical axioms. The empirical content of these axioms is valid in the context of the theory if they contribute to expand the theory itself (Fig. 8, right). Regardless whether it is possible to validate some research predictions or not, these predictions can still expand the theory. In fact, CLT has been extensively adopted for the design of several new instructional formats, expanding its boundaries [46]. As discussed in the previous sections, several research experiments have been performed in different learning contexts. In each of this, the intrinsic, extraneous and germane loads have been manipulated, individually or in pair by employing the traditional experimental/control group design. In turn, the cognitive load of learners and their learning outcomes where analysed [6]. If this analysis showed that learning has been actually facilitated, and statistical power held, then it means that a new instructional design was conceived as it actually promoted one or more types of load. Similarly, starting from the study of the 'Goal free effects' compared to the traditional ways to solve a problem (means analysis), Sweller and his colleagues have produced various novel findings and approaches to inform instructional design. Yet, Plass et al. [54] provided a complete list of CLT effects such as the 'Worked completion effect' [55], the 'Split attention effect' [56] the 'Redundancy effect' [57], the 'Modality effect' [58], the 'Expertise reversal effect' [47] and the 'Collective working memory effect' [11]. As a consequence, according to a structuralist point of view, Sweller stated that CLT has been developed and evolved as a consequence of these contributions and experiments [6]. They defend the fact that the three types of load were not elaborated a priori, rather they have been developed according to experimental findings that are falsifiable in their nature. In fact, it is still possible to replicate the experiments and obtain opposite findings. However, what cannot be considered falsifiable is only the definition of the three types of load employed in different experiments because the measures adopted are not considered scientific. In short, Sweller and colleagues strongly support the view that CLT is actually built upon empiricism [59]. As educational psychologist, Sweller and Chandler [60] share the same ultimate goal in the context of cognition and instruction: the generation of new, helpful instructional techniques aimed at improving learning.

5   Reconceptualization of Cognitive Load Types

As a consequence of the critiques related to the theoretical development of CLT and after several failed attempts to find a generally applicable measurement technique as well as the development of measures for the three different types of load, the theory has been re-conceptualised using the notion of element interactivity. This refers to the numbers of elements that must be processed simultaneously in working memory for schema construction and their interactions [18]. In this update of CLT, the element interactivity now defines the mechanisms not only of intrinsic load, but also of extraneous load [6]. In detail, the extraneous load is related to the degree of interactivity of the elements of the instructional material used for teaching activities, and instructional designs should be aligned to this. These designs should not focus on enhancing the number of items to be processed by learners, otherwise the resulting load could be considered extraneous. In other words, when instructional designs do not add instructions that increase the number of elements that must be processed within working memory, then the germane load of learners can be triggered. In this case, existing instructions can facilitate the use of working memory allocated for the intrinsic load. Additionally, germane load is no longer an independent source of load, it is a function of those working memory resources related to the intrinsic load of the task. In turn, intrinsic load depends on the characteristic of the task, extraneous load on the characteristic of the instructional material, on the characteristic of the instructional design and on the prior knowledge of learners. Eventually, germane load depends on the characteristics of a learner which equates to the resources of working memory allocated to deal with the intrinsic load [6] (Fig. 9).

The main theoretical contradiction before the reconceptualization of CLT was the additivity and the compensability of germane and extraneous loads. Here, the critical point is that, if extraneous load decreases, while keeping intrinsic load constant, then germane load should increase too. However, the measures for the three cognitive loads appeared in the last 30 years, confirm that this compensation does not have empirical evidence: the total cognitive load does not remain constant but changes [6]. After the reconceptualization (Fig. 9), germane load is related to that part of working memory that deals with the degree of element interactivity of the task. It can be promoted by creating instructional design aligned to it but it also depends on the intrinsic load, and as a consequence, it is not clearly measurable [6]. In fact, germane load now forms a balanced whole with extraneous load without creating logical and empirical contradictions. If intrinsic load remains constant but extraneous load changes, the overall

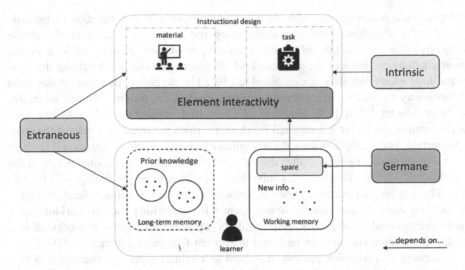

Fig. 9. Redefinition of the cognitive load types and their roles.

cognitive load changes too because more or less working memory resources are devoted to deal with the degree of element interactivity. At a given level of knowledge and expertise, intrinsic load cannot be altered without changing the content of the material presented to learners altogether. Extraneous load, instead, can be altered by changing the instructional procedures. Yet, germane load coincides to those working memory resources allocated to deal with the degree of element interactivity inherent to an underlining learning task. Although germane load has now a fundamental role to deal with intrinsic load, the additivity of CLT still holds in the two remaining theoretical assumptions: the intrinsic and the extraneous load. According to this reconceptualisation, most of the critiques related to the circularity of CLT do not longer stand according to Sweller. Additionally, Sweller and colleagues, as in [59], consider the unidimensional subjective rating scale of mental effort proposed by Paas et al. [13] a valid measure of overall cognitive load. In fact, if intrinsic load is kept constant, it is feasible to measure the extraneous load by only altering the instructional designs between an experimental and a control group. It is also possible to measure one type of load keeping the other constant, and the overall load measured would be an indicator of the modified type of load: extraneous or intrinsic.

6   Final Remarks

The measurement of the cognitive load types envisioned in the Cognitive Load Theory is a critical challenge for its theoretical development and its scientific value. After the literature review conducted in the previous sections, and after the presentation of the critiques that brought to the reconceptualization of the cognitive load types, the reader is left with two possible interpretations. On one hand, germane load is not clearly measurable by a common and standardised way, consequently its theoretical independence is denied, and after its reconceptualisation, it is a function of intrinsic load. On the other hand, there is evidence, triggered by the proposal of novel multiple subjective rating scales [38, 39], that the three types of load are measurable, even the most challenging, namely the germane load. Sweller and colleagues believe that germane load exists but it is not measurable [59]. He suggested that one of the most reliable way to measure the overall cognitive load is the unidimensional subjective scale of Mental Effort [13]. However, the fact that unidimensional scale has been widely employed within Educational Psychology, does not mean it is always the most appropriate. For example, within the discipline of Human Factors (Ergonomics), there exist a plethora of empirical studies that all point to the multi-dimensional nature of the construct of Mental Workload (cognitive load for educational psychologists) [16, 61–65]. There is also an emerging body of knowledge, within Computer Science, that is employing more formal non-linear approaches for modelling mental workload as a multi-dimensional construct [66–68]. Similarly, applications of mental workload as a multi-dimensional concept can be found in Human Computer Interaction [69–72].

Learning is a complex process, it is hard to evaluate it mostly because it is perceived as a subjective one. Similarly, cognitive load it is a complex construct and it is assumed it can be modelled end evaluated through quantitative criteria to satisfy the empirical exigencies of scientific research. This is an existing methodological gap and it is the reason why, so far, there is little evidence of generally applicable subjective measurement techniques and measures for the three types of load and for overall cognitive load. According to Klepsch and colleagues, their informed rating scale is a novelty in CLT research and it seems to be a valid method for measuring the three types of load [39]. They believe it is the most logical approach because if learners are informed, then the evaluation of the experienced load can be done with a higher degree of awareness. However, in our view, this might bring back the issue of circularity, suggesting that we are leading learners to understand Cognitive Load Theory as well as its assumptions and influence them to rate their subjective experience to fit our expectations. Cognitive load is a complex construct and indeed CLT has had a significant impact for instructional design. Circularity is also an important issue that should be avoided in favour of empiricism and falsifiability of measures. We believe that, with advances in technologies and the availability of cheap sensors and non-invasive instruments for gathering responses of the human brain and bodies, physiological measures of mental workload might finally shed further light on the complex but fascinating problem of cognitive load modelling.

References

1. Sweller, J., Van Merrienboer, J.J., Paas, F.G.: Cognitive architecture and instructional design. Educ. Psychol. Rev. **10**(3), 251–296 (1998)
2. Young, M.S., Brookhuis, K.A., Wickens, C.D., Hancock, P.A.: State of science: mental workload in ergonomics. Ergonomics **58**(1), 1–17 (2015). https://doi.org/10.1080/00140139.2014.956151
3. Baddeley, A.: Recent developments in working memory. Curr. Opin. Neurobiol. **8**(2), 234–238 (1998). https://doi.org/10.1016/s0959-4388(98)80145-1

4. Paivio, A.: Mental Representation: A Dual-Coding Approach. Oxford University Press, New York (1986)
5. Hart, S.G., Wickens, C.D.: Workload assessment and prediction. In: Booher, H.R. (ed.) MANPRINT: An Approach to Systems Integration, pp. 257–296. Springer, Dordrecht (2012). https://doi.org/10.1007/978-94-009-0437-8_9
6. Sweller, J.: Element interactivity and intrinsic, extraneous, and germane cognitive load. Educ. Psychol. Rev. **22**(2), 123–138 (2010)
7. Miller, G.A.: The magical number seven, plus or minus two: some limits on our capacity for processing information. Psychol. Rev. **63**(2), 81 (1956)
8. Clark, R.C., Nguyen, F., Sweller, J., Baddeley, M.: Efficiency in learning: evidence-based guidelines to manage cognitive load. Perform. Improv. **45**(9), 46–47 (2006)
9. Mayer, R.E., Moreno, R.: Nine ways to reduce cognitive load in multimedia learning. Educ. Psychol. **38**(1), 43–52 (2003)
10. Mayer, R.E.: Principles for managing essential processing in multimedia learning: segmenting, pretraining, and modality principles. In: The Cambridge Handbook of Multimedia Learning, pp. 169–182 (2005)
11. Kirschner, F., Paas, F., Kirschner, P.A.: Superiority of collaborative learning with complex tasks: a research note on an alternative affective explanation. Comput. Hum. Behav. **27**(1), 53–57 (2011)
12. Chi, M.T.H., Glaser, R., Rees, E.: Expertise in problem solving. In: Sternberg, R. (ed.) Advances in the Psychology of Human Intelligence, pp. 7–75. Lawrence Erlbaum, Hillsdale (1982)
13. Paas, F.G., Van Merriënboer, J.J., Adam, J.J.: Measurement of cognitive load in instructional research. Percept. Mot. Skills **79**(1), 419–430 (1994)
14. Longo, L., Barrett, S.: A computational analysis of cognitive effort. In: Nguyen, N.T., Le, M. T., Świątek, J. (eds.) ACIIDS 2010, Part II. LNCS (LNAI), vol. 5991, pp. 65–74. Springer, Heidelberg (2010). https://doi.org/10.1007/978-3-642-12101-2_8
15. Longo, L., Barrett, S.: Cognitive effort for multi-agent systems. In: Yao, Y., Sun, R., Poggio, T., Liu, J., Zhong, N., Huang, J. (eds.) BI 2010. LNCS (LNAI), vol. 6334, pp. 55–66. Springer, Heidelberg (2010). https://doi.org/10.1007/978-3-642-15314-3_6
16. Longo, L., Leva, M.C.: Human Mental Workload: Models and Applications, vol. 726. Springer, Cham (2017). https://doi.org/10.1007/978-3-319-61061-0
17. Halford, G.S., Maybery, M.T., Bain, J.D.: Capacity limitations in children's reasoning: a dual-task approach. Child Dev. **57**(3), 616–627 (1986). https://doi.org/10.2307/1130340
18. Sweller, J.: Cognitive load theory, learning difficulty, and instructional design. Learn. Instr. **4**(4), 295–312 (1994)
19. Paas, F.G., Van Merriënboer, J.J.: Variability of worked examples and transfer of geometrical problem-solving skills: a cognitive-load approach. J. Educ. Psychol. **86**(1), 122 (1994)
20. Gerjets, P., Scheiter, K.: Goal configurations and processing strategies as moderators between instructional design and cognitive load: evidence from hypertext-based instruction. Educ. Psychol. **38**(1), 33–41 (2003)
21. Miwa, K., Kojima, K., Terai, H., Mizuno, Y.: Measuring cognitive loads based on the mental chronometry paradigm. In: COGNITIVE 2016 : The Eighth International Conference on Advanced Cognitive Technologies and Applications, pp. 38–41 (2016)
22. Meyer, D.E., Osman, A.M., Irwin, D.E., Yantis, S.: Modern mental chronometry. Biol. Psychol. **26**(1–3), 3–67 (1988)

23. Gerjets, P., Scheiter, K., Opfermann, M., Hesse, F.W., Eysink, T.H.S.: Learning with hypermedia: the influence of representational formats and different levels of learner control on performance and learning behavior. Comput. Hum. Behav. **25**(2), 360–370 (2009). https://doi.org/10.1016/j.chb.2008.12.015

24. Corbalan, G., Kester, L., van Merriënboer, J.J.G.: Selecting learning tasks: effects of adaptation and shared control on learning efficiency and task involvement. Contemp. Educ. Psychol. **33**(4), 733–756 (2008). https://doi.org/10.1016/j.cedpsych.2008.02.003

25. Ayres, P.: Using subjective measures to detect variations of intrinsic cognitive load within problems. Learn. Instr. **16**(5), 389–400 (2006)

26. Gerjets, P., Scheiter, K., Catrambone, R.: Can learning from molar and modular worked examples be enhanced by providing instructional explanations and prompting self-explanations? Learn. Instr. **16**(2), 104–121 (2006). https://doi.org/10.1016/j.learninstruc.2006.02.007

27. Hart, S.G., Staveland, L.E.: Development of NASA-TLX (task load index): results of empirical and theoretical research. In: Advances in Psychology, vol. 52, pp. 139–183. Elsevier (1988). https://doi.org/10.1016/s0166-4115(08)62386-9

28. Scheiter, K., Gerjets, P., Catrambone, R.: Making the abstract concrete: visualizing mathematical solution procedures. Comput. Hum. Behav. **22**(1), 9–25 (2006). https://doi.org/10.1016/j.chb.2005.01.009

29. Gerjets, P., Scheiter, K., Catrambone, R.: Designing instructional examples to reduce intrinsic cognitive load: molar versus modular presentation of solution procedures. Instr. Sci. **32**(1/2), 33–58 (2004). https://doi.org/10.1023/b:truc.0000021809.10236.71

30. Galy, E., Cariou, M., Mélan, C.: What is the relationship between mental workload factors and cognitive load types? Int. J. Psychophysiol. **83**(3), 269–275 (2012). https://doi.org/10.1016/j.ijpsycho.2011.09.023

31. Thayer, R.E.: Toward a psychological theory of multidimensional activation (arousal). Motiv. Emot. **2**(1), 1–34 (1978)

32. Leppink, J., Paas, F., Van der Vleuten, C.P.M., Van Gog, T., Van Merriënboer, J.J.G.: Development of an instrument for measuring different types of cognitive load. Behav. Res. Methods **45**(4), 1058–1072 (2013). https://doi.org/10.3758/s13428-013-0334-1

33. Kalyuga, S., Chandler, P., Sweller, J.: Levels of expertise and instructional design. Hum. Factors **40**(1), 1 (1998)

34. Cierniak, G., Scheiter, K., Gerjets, P.: Explaining the split-attention effect: Is the reduction of extraneous cognitive load accompanied by an increase in germane cognitive load? Comput. Hum. Behav. **25**(2), 315–324 (2009). https://doi.org/10.1016/j.chb.2008.12.020

35. Salomon, G.: Television is "easy" and print is "tough": the differential investment of mental effort in learning as a function of perceptions and attributions. J. Educ. Psychol. **76**(4), 647 (1984)

36. Paas, F.G.: Training strategies for attaining transfer of problem-solving skill in statistics: a cognitive-load approach. J. Educ. Psychol. **84**(4), 429 (1992)

37. Leppink, J., Paas, F., van Gog, T., van der Vleuten, C.P.M., van Merriënboer, J.J.G.: Effects of pairs of problems and examples on task performance and different types of cognitive load. Learn. Instr. **30**, 32–42 (2014). https://doi.org/10.1016/j.learninstruc.2013.12.001

38. Zukić, M., Đapo, N., Husremović, D.: Construct and predictive validity of an instrument for measuring intrinsic, extraneous and germane cognitive load. Univ. J. Psychol. **4**(5), 242–248 (2016). https://doi.org/10.13189/ujp.2016.040505

39. Klepsch, M., Schmitz, F., Seufert, T.: Development and validation of two instruments measuring intrinsic, extraneous, and germane cognitive load. Front. Psychol. **8** (2017). https://doi.org/10.3389/fpsyg.2017.01997

40. Rodriguez, M.C., Maeda, Y.: Meta-analysis of coefficient alpha. Psychol. Methods **11**(3), 306 (2006)
41. DeLeeuw, K.E., Mayer, R.E.: A comparison of three measures of cognitive load: Evidence for separable measures of intrinsic, extraneous, and germane load. J. Educ. Psychol. **100**(1), 223–234 (2008). https://doi.org/10.1037/0022-0663.100.1.223
42. Kester, L., Kirschner, P.A., van Merriënboer, J.J.G.: The management of cognitive load during complex cognitive skill acquisition by means of computer-simulated problem solving. Br. J. Educ. Psychol. **75**(1), 71–85 (2005). https://doi.org/10.1348/000709904x19254
43. Van Gog, T., Paas, F.: Instructional efficiency: revisiting the original construct in educational research. Educ. Psychol. **43**(1), 16–26 (2008)
44. Schnotz, W., Kürschner, C.: A reconsideration of cognitive load theory. Educ. Psychol. Rev. **19**(4), 469–508 (2007)
45. De Jong, T.: Cognitive load theory, educational research, and instructional design: some food for thought. Instr. Sci. **38**(2), 105–134 (2010)
46. Gerjets, P., Scheiter, K., Cierniak, G.: The scientific value of cognitive load theory: a research agenda based on the structuralist view of theories. Educ. Psychol. Rev. **21**(1), 43–54 (2009). https://doi.org/10.1007/s10648-008-9096-1
47. Sweller, J., Ayres, P.L., Kalyuga, S., Chandler, P.: The expertise reversal effect. The expertise reversal effect. Educ. Psychol. **38**(1), 23–31 (2003)
48. Popper, K.: The Logic of Scientific Discovery. Routledge, Abingdon (2005)
49. Popper, K.: Conjectures and Refutations: The Growth of Scientific Knowledge. Routledge, Abingdon (2014)
50. Sneed, J.D.: The Logical Structure of Mathematical Physics, vol. 3. Springer, Heidelberg (2012). https://doi.org/10.1007/978-94-009-9522-2
51. Balzer, W., Moulines, C., Sneed, J.: An architectonic for science–the structuralist program. Reidel, Dordrecht (1987). Springer. Traducción al castellano de P. Lorenzano: Una arquitectónica para la ciencia–El programa estructuralista. Universidad Nacional de Quilmes, Bernal (Argentina) (2012)
52. Stegmüller, W.: The Structuralist View of Theories: A Possible Analogue of the Bourbaki Programme in Physical Science. Springer, Heidelberg (2013). https://doi.org/10.1007/978-3-642-95360-6
53. Westermann, R.: Structuralist reconstruction of psychological research: cognitive dissonance. Ger. J. Psychol. **12**(3), 218–231 (1988)
54. Plass, J.L., Moreno, R., Brünken, R.: Cognitive Load Theory. Cambridge University Press, Cambridge (2010)
55. Sweller, J., Cooper, G.A.: The use of worked examples as a substitute for problem solving in learning algebra. Cogn. Instr. **2**(1), 59–89 (1985)
56. Tarmizi, R.A., Sweller, J.: Guidance during mathematical problem solving. J. Educ. Psychol. **80**(4), 424 (1988)
57. Chandler, P., Sweller, J.: Cognitive load theory and the format of instruction. Cogn. Instr. **8**(4), 293–332 (1991). https://doi.org/10.1207/s1532690xci0804_2
58. Mousavi, S.Y., Low, R., Sweller, J.: Reducing cognitive load by mixing auditory and visual presentation modes. J. Educ. Psychol. **87**(2), 319 (1995)
59. Sweller, J., Ayres, P., Kalyuga, S.: Cognitive Load Theory, Explorations in the Learning Sciences, Instructional Systems, and Performance Technologies 1. Springer, New York (2011). https://doi.org/10.1007/978-1-4419-8126-4
60. Sweller, J., Chandler, P.: Evidence for cognitive load theory. Cogn. Instr. **8**(4), 351–362 (1991)

61. Longo, L.: A defeasible reasoning framework for human mental workload representation and assessment. Behav. Inf. Technol. **34**(8), 758–786 (2015)
62. Longo, L.: Formalising human mental workload as a defeasible computational concept. Ph. D. thesis, Trinity College Dublin (2014)
63. Longo, L.: Mental workload in medicine: foundations, applications, open problems, challenges and future perspectives. In: 2016 IEEE 29th International Symposium on Computer-Based Medical Systems (CBMS), pp. 106–111 (2016). https://doi.org/10.1109/cbms.2016.36
64. Wickens, C.D.: Mental workload: assessment, prediction and consequences. In: Longo, L., Leva, M.C. (eds.) H-WORKLOAD 2017. CCIS, vol. 726, pp. 18–29. Springer, Cham (2017). https://doi.org/10.1007/978-3-319-61061-0_2
65. Hancock, P.A.: Whither workload? Mapping a path for its future development. In: Longo, L., Leva, M.C. (eds.) H-WORKLOAD 2017. CCIS, vol. 726, pp. 3–17. Springer, Cham (2017). https://doi.org/10.1007/978-3-319-61061-0_1
66. Rizzo, L., Dondio, P., Delany, S.J., Longo, L.: Modeling mental workload via rule-based expert system: a comparison with NASA-TLX and workload profile. In: Iliadis, L., Maglogiannis, I. (eds.) AIAI 2016. IAICT, vol. 475, pp. 215–229. Springer, Cham (2016). https://doi.org/10.1007/978-3-319-44944-9_19
67. Moustafa, K., Luz, S., Longo, L.: Assessment of mental workload: a comparison of machine learning methods and subjective assessment techniques. In: Longo, L., Leva, M.C. (eds.) H-WORKLOAD 2017. CCIS, vol. 726, pp. 30–50. Springer, Cham (2017). https://doi.org/10.1007/978-3-319-61061-0_3
68. Rizzo, L.M., Longo, L.: Representing and inferring mental workload via defeasible reasoning: a comparison with the NASA Task Load Index and the Workload Profile. In: Proceedings of the 1st Workshop on Advances in Argumentation in Artificial Intelligence co-located with {XVI} International Conference of the Italian Association for Artificial Intelligence (AI*IA 2017), pp. 126–140 (2017)
69. Longo, L., Dondio, P.: On the relationship between perception of usability and subjective mental workload of web interfaces. In: IEEE/WIC/ACM International Conference on Web Intelligence and Intelligent Agent Technology, WI-IAT 2015, Singapore, 6–9 December, vol. I, pp. 345–352 (2015)
70. Longo, L.: Formalising human mental workload as non-monotonic concept for adaptive and personalised web-design. In: Masthoff, J., Mobasher, B., Desmarais, M.C., Nkambou, R. (eds.) UMAP 2012. LNCS, vol. 7379, pp. 369–373. Springer, Heidelberg (2012). https://doi.org/10.1007/978-3-642-31454-4_38
71. Longo, L.: Subjective usability, mental workload assessments and their impact on objective human performance. In: Bernhaupt, R., Dalvi, G., Joshi, A., Balkrishan, D.K., O'Neill, J., Winckler, M. (eds.) INTERACT 2017. LNCS, vol. 10514, pp. 202–223. Springer, Cham (2017). https://doi.org/10.1007/978-3-319-67684-5_13
72. Longo, L.: Experienced mental workload, perception of usability, their interaction and impact on task performance. PLoS ONE **13**(8), e0199661 (2018)

Developing an Objective Indicator of Fatigue: An Alternative Mobile Version of the Psychomotor Vigilance Task (m-PVT)

Michael Scott Evans[1(✉)] , Daniel Harborne[2] ,
and Andrew P. Smith[1]

[1] School of Psychology, Cardiff University,
63 Park Place, Cardiff, Wales CF10 3AS, UK
EvansMS3@cardiff.ac.uk
[2] School of Computer Science and Informatics, Cardiff University,
Cardiff, Wales, UK

Abstract. Approximately 20% of the working population report symptoms of feeling fatigued at work. The aim of the study was to investigate whether an alternative mobile version of the 'gold standard' Psychomotor Vigilance Task (PVT) could be used to provide an objective indicator of fatigue in staff working in applied safety critical settings such as train driving, hospital staffs, emergency services, law enforcements, etc., using different mobile devices. 26 participants mean age 20 years completed a 25-min reaction time study using an alternative mobile version of the Psychomotor Vigilance Task (m-PVT) that was implemented on either an Apple iPhone 6s Plus or a Samsung Galaxy Tab 4. Participants attended two sessions: a morning and an afternoon session held on two consecutive days counterbalanced. It was found that the iPhone 6s Plus generated both mean speed responses (1/RTs) and mean reaction times (RTs) that were comparable to those observed in the literature while the Galaxy Tab 4 generated significantly lower 1/RTs and slower RTs than those found with the iPhone 6s Plus. Furthermore, it was also found that the iPhone 6s Plus was sensitive enough to detect lower mean speed of responses (1/RTs) and significantly slower mean reaction times (RTs) after 10-min on the m-PVT. In contrast, it was also found that the Galaxy Tab 4 generated mean number of lapses that were significant after 5-min on the m-PVT. These findings seem to indicate that the m-PVT could be used to provide an objective indicator of fatigue in staff working in applied safety critical settings such as train driving, hospital staffs, emergency services, law enforcements, etc.

Keywords: Psychomotor Vigilance Task (PVT) · Mental workload · Occupational fatigue · Objective indicator of fatigue · Attention

1 Introduction

In order to be able to meet task demands, there is usually a required amount of operator resources needed, referred to as human mental workload [1]. According to Hart and Staveland [2], human mental workload can be defined as a 'cost incurred by a human

© Springer Nature Switzerland AG 2019
L. Longo and M. C. Leva (Eds.): H-WORKLOAD 2018, CCIS 1012, pp. 49–71, 2019.
https://doi.org/10.1007/978-3-030-14273-5_4

operator to achieve a particular level of performance' and evolves from interactions between task demands, circumstances, skills, behaviour, and perceptions'. Therefore, human mental workload – often referred to as cognitive load – can be intuitively defined as the amount of mental work necessary for a person to complete a task over a given period of time [3, 4]. However, nowadays human mental workload is more generally defined as the measurement of the amount of mental resources involved in a cognitive task [5].

Human mental workload can be measured in real time using a variety of psychological and physiological techniques, which include; subjective psychological self-reported measures e.g., the NASA Task Load Index (NASA-TLX) [2, 6–8] and the NASA-MATB (National Aeronautics and Space Administration Multi-Attribute Task Battery [9] as well as objective physiological measures e.g., heart rate (HR), galvanic skin response (GSR), body temperature, electrocardiogram (ECG), electroencephalogram (EEG), and eye tracking [8, 10–19], and which have been extensively examined in various safety critical environments including; aviation [7, 20], train driving [21], car driving [22–24], and in an operating theater [6] but to name a few.

According to Wickens [25], the greatest value of conducting scientific human mental workload research is to be able to predict the consequences of high mental workload on performance. In other words, to better understand an individual's decision to consciously engage in a safe behaviour or in a potentially dangerous behaviour that could have devastating consequences. As a result, the concept of human mental workload has long been recognised as an important factor in individual performance [26–29]. Xie and Salvendy [29] state that both underload (i.e., low mental workload) and overload (i.e., high mental workload) degrade performance, whereby high and low levels of human mental workload have been shown to lead to operator error [22]. Longo [3] outlines that during low mental workload, individuals are more likely to experience levels of frustration and annoyance when processing information, which could result in an increase in their reaction time (RT). In contract, during high mental workload, individuals could experience confusion, which may result in a decrease in their information processing capacity, which could directly increase the likelihood of errors and mistakes. Therefore, these low and high mental workload information processing stages could have potentially dangerous consequences, especially in safety critical environments. Byrne [30] points out that the main application of mental workload has been to investigate situations where cognitive demand exceeds the acceptable safety tolerance threshold so that workload can be effectively reduced. Therefore, in high risk safety critical environments, the measurement of mental workload is of upmost importance due to its potential implications [31]. However, Xie and Salvendy [29] identified that the effect of fatigue on mental workload is not often considered in human mental workload research. Nevertheless, research carried out by Smith and Smith [32] on conductors/guards and engineers from the rail industry who work in high risk safety critical environments found that workload increased fatigue. However, subjective measures were predominately used in Smith and Smith's study. As a result, there is a need for an alternative mobile objective indicator of fatigue that can be used in high risk safety critical environments. In a controlled laboratory setting, the human Psychomotor Vigilance Task (PVT) [see 33, 34, for review] has become the widely accepted 'gold standard' tool for assessing the impact of fatigue on human cognitive neurobehavioral performance for monitoring temporal dynamic changes in attention [35–38]. The aim of the study was to investigate whether an alternative mobile version of the 'gold standard' Psychomotor Vigilance Task (PVT) could be used to provide an objective indicator of fatigue in staff working in applied safety critical settings, such as train driving, hospital staffs, emergency services, law enforcements, etc.

The rest of the paper is organised as follows. Section 2 describes related work on the Psychomotor Vigilance Task (PVT) while also extracting relevant studies to identify the gaps and rationale for the need of an alternative objective indicator of fatigue in staff working in applied safety critical settings. Section 3 outlines the design and empirical methodology of the proposed alternative mobile Psychomotor Vigilance Task (m-PVT). Section 4 presents the empirical results and discussion of the m-PVT. Finally, Sect. 5 provides a critical conclusion of the proposed alternative m-PVT and suggestions for future work.

2 Related Work

The Psychomotor Vigilance Task (PVT) can be traced back from the early work in simple reaction time (SRT) studies that were carried out by Wilhelm Maximilian Wundt (1832–1920) and continued by James McKeen Cattell (1860–1944) [39]. It is important to note that the modern PVT has been refined several times over the years [40–42] from its original development by Dinges and Powell [33] and has been shown to be sensitive to sleep deprivation, fatigue, drug use, and age. The PVT has also been widely implemented using a handheld device known as the PVT-192 (Ambulatory Monitoring Inc., Ardsley, New York, USA), as well as being extensively validated by various researchers [40, 43–47].

According to Basner, Mcguire, Goel, Rao and Dinges [48] and Basner et al. [49], the PVT-192 records participants' sustained attention based on repeated reaction time (RT) trials to visual stimuli that occur at random inter-stimulus intervals (ISI) that are between 2–10 s, for a standard 10-min period. In summary, the PVT-192 device operated by presenting participants with a stimulus that consisted of a four-digit millisecond counter that appears in a light-emitting diode (LED) dot-matrix display. The response consisted of a left or right button press, which depended on the configuration of the PVT-192 setup. The time difference between the stimulus presentation and the response constituted the participant's reaction time (RT). Each RT value was stored in the device and then uploaded to a personal computer, where the individual RTs are post-processed with the REACT software (Ambulatory Monitoring Inc., Ardsley, New York, USA), or other commercially available software, into summary statistics, such as the mean RT or the mean number of lapses (RTs $\geq$ 500 ms) per session [33, 40, 48, 50, 51]. For example, in Roach, Dawson, and Lamond's study [45], each participant performed either 5 min or 10 min RT sessions spaced at predetermined intervals (e.g., every 2 h) for a prolonged duration (e.g., 28 h), where each session consists of either 50 trials (equivalent to 5 min), or 100 trials (equivalent to 10 min). However, Khitrov et al. [52] tested the average delay of the PVT-192 and found that the recorded delay was greater than what was stated by the PVT-192 manufacturer. The delay recorded by the researchers was on average 2.4 ms greater when compared to the manufacturer's reported delay of 1 ms. Nevertheless, it is important to highlight that Khitrov et al. [52]

did acknowledge the possibility that the difference found could have been due to the non-instantaneous nature of the light detection circuit, or the actual delay associated with the PVT-192, since their experimental design did not permit them to be able to distinguish between these possibilities.

Dinges and Powell [33] have shown that the 10-min PVT is highly reliable. Roach, Dawson and Lamond [45] wanted to investigate whether 90 s could also be sufficiently sensitive enough to detect the effects of fatigue in comparison to their earlier research [see 43, for review], where they were able to find significant fatigue-related impairment during the first 5-min of a 10-min PVT. In this study, the researchers compared participants' neurobehavioral performance using the PVT between three different time durations (90 s, 5-min, and 10-min) to identify whether a shorter PVT could also be sensitive enough to detect the effects of fatigue. They found that it was only possible to implement a 5-min PVT as a substitute of the 10-min PVT, and not a 90 s PVT, thus only further supporting their earlier research [43]. However, it is important to note that analyses of their study were carried out using the mean RT and not the mean speed response (1/RT). Basner and Dinges [43] have identified that the mean RTs should not be the primary measure of alertness, and instead considering using the alternative primary measure of 1/RTs. In a later study, Basner, Mollicone and Dinges [42] aimed to further shorten the 5-min PVT [45] by developing a modified 3-min version of the PVT (PVT-B). They found that this 3-min version could be a useful tool for assessing behavioural alertness in settings where the 'gold standard' 10-min PVT could be more difficult or impractical to implement due to the nature of the study or location. However, further validation is required to determine whether both the 5-min PVT and PVT-B versions could indeed be sensitive enough to detect reduced levels of fatigue. Therefore, this study aimed to investigate a mobile version of the Psychomotor Vigilance Task (m-PVT) that could also be used to provide an objective indicator of fatigue in staff working in applied safety critical settings such as train driving, hospital staffs, emergency services, law enforcements, etc.

3 Design and Methodology

The aim of the study was to investigate whether an alternative mobile version of the 'gold standard' Psychomotor Vigilance Task (PVT) could be used to provide an objective indicator of fatigue in staff working in applied safety critical settings such as train driving, hospital staffs, emergency services, law enforcements, etc. The study received ethics approval from Cardiff University's Ethics Committee (EC.16.02.09.4464R). The study conformed to the seventh amendment of the Declaration of Helsinki 1964 [53] and all participants gave their informed written as well as electronic consent following the explanation of the nature of the study in written form.

3.1 Participants

26 (3 male and 23 female) participants with a mean age of 20 years (SD = 1.66) were recruited as volunteers from Cardiff University via the Experimental Management System (EMS) to take part in the study. The study involved participants attending two

sessions, a morning session (i.e., before 11:00) and an afternoon session (i.e., after 17:00), which were held on two consecutive days and counterbalanced, in exchange for £10. The study lasted 60 min in total for both sessions.

3.2 Materials/Apparatus

The mobile Psychomotor Vigilance Task (m-PVT) was presented to participants on one of two mobile devices: Apple's iPhone 6s Plus running Apple's iOS version 9.3.1 (Apple Inc.) or Samsung's Galaxy Tab 4 (Samsung Electronics Co. Ltd.) running on Android's operating system (OS) version 4.4.2 KitKat (Alphabet Inc.). The m-PVT ran in the following hardware configurations for the iPhone 6s Plus: system chip (Apple A9 APL1022), processor (Dual-core, 1840 MHz, Twister, 64-bit), graphics processor (PowerVR GT7600), and system memory (2048 MB RAM), and for the Samsung Galaxy Tab 4: system chip (Marvell PXA1088), processor (Quad-core, 1200 MHz, ARM Cortex-A7), graphics processor (Vivante), and system memory (1536 MB RAM). The iPhone 6s Plus had the following hardware configurations: the m-PVT was displayed on either a 5.5-in. (diagonal) 1920 × 1080-pixel native resolution at 401 ppi Retina high definition display (iPhone 6s Plus), or a 7-in. (diagonal) 1280 × 800-pixel (WXGA) native resolution at 216 pixels per inch (ppi) liquid crystal display (LCD) display (Samsung Galaxy Tab 4).

The m-PVT was programmed using the client code HTML, and CSS for the page visualisation and layout. JavaScript was also used to initiate the m-PVT, which was run using the Dolphin Web Browser (MoboTap Inc.) on both an Apple's iPhone 6s Plus and Samsung Galaxy Tab 4 (Dolphin Web Browser versions; Apple app version 9.9.0, and Android app version 11.5.6, respectively). The rationale for selecting the Dolphin Web Browser for this study was that it allowed the full screen feature to be enabled across the two different operating systems (OS), Apple iOS and Android OS platforms for both mobile devices. Other more native mobile internet browsers of each OS platform, such as Safari (Apple) and Chrome (Android) including Firefox, to name a few, did not permit full screen. Qualtrics Surveys (Qualtrics Labs, Inc.) were also used to collect demographic information from participants. These surveys were also implemented on both Apple's iPhone 6s Plus (iOS app version 13.28.06) and Samsung Galaxy Tab 4 (Android app version 1.0.38).

3.3 Statistical Analyses

IBM's Statistical Package for the Social Sciences (SPSS) version 23 for Mac was used to analyse the data. A combination of various statistical procedures were carried out on the data; descriptive analyses, mixed-design analysis of variance (ANOVA) and a two-way analysis of variance (ANOVA) to further explore interactions. The level of $\alpha < .05$ was used for all statistical tests of this experiment.

3.4 Design

The experiment employed a $2 \times 2 \times 6$ mixed-design analysis of variance (ANOVA) with mobile device (Apple's iPhone 6s Plus or Samsung's Galaxy Tab 4) as the between-subjects factor, × time of day (Morning or Afternoon) × time on task (1-min; 5-min; 10-min; 15-min; 20 min; or 25-min) as the within-subjects factors. The morning session (i.e., before 11:00) and the afternoon session (i.e., after 17:00) were held on two consecutive days and counterbalanced.

3.5 Procedure

In order to ensure participants were fully aware of the inclusion and exclusion criteria, all participants were contacted using Cardiff University's Experimental Management System (EMS) emailing system 48 h prior to participation and further reminded 24 h before the start, in addition to being provided with brief instructions through EMS. The study was administered using mobile devices. Participants were either assigned to using an iPhone 6s Plus or a Samsung Galaxy Tab 4. To increase validity and standardisation, all instructions were administered to participants in written form for both the morning and the afternoon session. This study consisted of two parts. The first part was the mobile Psychomotor Vigilance Task (m-PVT) reaction time test, which was a modified version of the Dinges and Powell's [33] Psychomotor Vigilance Task. The m-PVT was run on the Dolphin Web Browser mobile application. The second part was the demographic questionnaire that was distributed within Qualtrics Surveys mobile application. In this modified version, the mobile Psychomotor Vigilance Task (m-PVT) (see Fig. 1), participants were presented with on-screen instructions and a button at the end that read 'Start'. In each trial, participants were shown a black screen background, and at the centre of the screen they would be presented with a large red fixation circle. The red fixation circle (i.e., inter-stimulus interval) would remain on the screen for a randomised duration that lasted between 2–10 s, which was then followed by a yellow stimulus counter. As soon as the inter-stimulus interval reached the randomised duration, a yellow stimulus counter appeared counting up in milliseconds from 0–5 s where it would lapse (i.e., error of omission for 0.5 s) and begin the next trial, or until the participant tapped on the screen. Once the participant tapped on the screen, their reaction time (i.e., stimulus) would be displayed for 0.5 s. At the end of each trial, a black background would appear on-screen for 0.5 s. There were 205 trials in total that lasted approximately 25 min. Kribbs and Dinges [54] found that after a maximum of three trials, the practice effect for the PVT was removed. This study conservatively implemented five practice trials to ensure participants were fully aware of the task, which were removed from final analyses. If participants responded prematurely during any trial (i.e., before the timer commenced counting up), the trial would reset. To also ensure participants were made aware of their premature response, the following message in red was displayed on the centre of the screen, 'You clicked too early! This trial will be reset.' A visual illustration of the mobile Psychomotor Vigilance Task (m-PVT) is presented in Fig. 2.

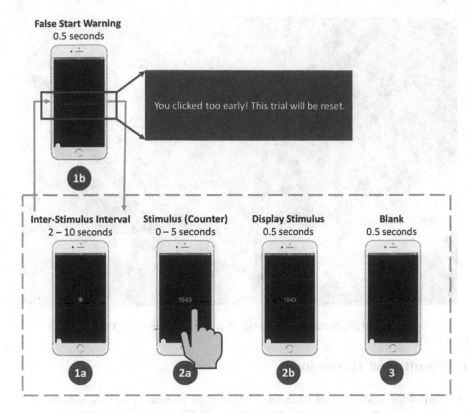

Fig. 1. Mobile Psychomotor Vigilance Task (m-PVT) timeline.

1a. Participants were presented with a large red circle (i.e., inter-stimulus interval), which appeared for a randomised duration between 2–10 s.

1b. If participants responded prematurely, a false start warning message appeared informing them that they clicked too early and that the trial would be reset.

2a. As soon as the inter-stimulus interval reached the randomised duration, a yellow stimulus counter appeared counting up in milliseconds from 0–5 s where it would lapse (i.e., error of omission for 0.5 s) and begin the next trial, or until the participant had tapped on the screen.

2b. Once the participants had tapped on the screen, their reaction time (i.e., stimulus) would be displayed for 0.5 s.

3. At the end of each trial, a black background would appear on-screen for 0.5 s.

Fig. 2. Visual illustration of the mobile Psychomotor Vigilance Task (m-PVT)

4 Results and Discussion

The aim of the study was to investigate whether an alternative mobile version of the 'gold standard' Psychomotor Vigilance Task (PVT) could be used to provide an objective indicator of fatigue in staff working in applied safety critical settings such as train driving, hospital staffs, emergency services, law enforcerments, etc. IBM's Statistical Package for the Social Sciences (SPSS) version 23 for Mac was used to analyse the data. A total of 10,452 test trials were submitted for data analyses, with all 260 practice trials (i.e., 5 practice trials per session) excluded from final analyses. It is important to note that all mobile devices running the online mobile version of the Psychomotor Vigilance Task (m-PVT) were administered through the Dolphin internet browser and were connected using Cardiff University's Eduroam Wi-Fi roaming service. Therefore, on rare occasions when the Wi-Fi connectivity dropped, the participant's trial was lost and thus not recorded. As a result, a total of 1.95% (n = 208) test trials of all 10,660 trials (i.e., 260 practice and 10,400 test) were lost and not recorded. Based on Basner and Dinges [40] recommendations, all 10,452 test trials with reaction time (RTs) < 100 ms (i.e., false start), which accounted for .05% (n = 5) and RTs 500 ms (i.e., number of lapses), which accounted for 31.84% (n = 3,328), were considered for exclusion from the final mean speed response (1/RT) and mean reaction time (RT) analyses. All 31.84% (n = 3,328) of RTs $\geq$ 500 ms (i.e., number of lapses) were analysed separately.

4.1 Mean Speed Response (1/RT) and Reaction Time (RT)

Figure 3 presents the illustrated mean speed responses (1/RTs) across the different conditions while Fig. 4 presents the illustrated mean reaction times (RTs) across the different conditions. Both the 1/RTs and RTs were submitted to a $2 \times 2 \times 6$ mixed-design analysis of variance (ANOVA) with $2 \times$ mobile devices (iPhone 6s Plus or Samsung Galaxy Tab 4) as the between-subjects factor, and $\times 2$ time of day (Morning, or Afternoon) $\times 6$ time on task (1-min; 5-min, 10-min, 15-min, 20 min, or 25-min) as the within-subjects factors. Both the 1/RTs and RTs were significant when comparing the main effect of the two groups using different mobile devices, $F(1, 24)$, 87.21, $p < .001$, $\eta_p^2 = .78$, indicating a large effect size [55, 56] and $F(1, 24)$, 131.85, $p < .001$, $\eta_p^2 = .85$, also indicating a large effect size [55, 56], respectively. In addition, there was a significant main effect of time on task for both the 1/RTs and RTs, Wilks' Lambda = .22, $F(5, 20)$, 14.08, $p < .001$, $\eta_p^2 = .78$, indicating a large effect size [55, 56] and Wilks' Lambda = .24, $F(5, 20)$, 12.66, $p < .001$, $\eta_p^2 = .76$, indicating a large effect size [55, 56], respectively. Furthermore, there was also a significant interaction between mobile devices $\times$ time on task for both the 1/RTs and RTs, Wilks' Lambda = .34, $F(5, 20)$, 7.95, $p < .001$, $\eta_p^2 = .67$, indicating a large effect size [55, 56] and Wilks' Lambda = .43, $F(5, 20)$, 5.23, $p = .003$, $\eta_p^2 = .57$, indicating a moderate effect size [55, 56], respectively. The other main effect (time of day) and interactions (two-way interaction, time of day $\times$ time on task; and three-way interaction, mobile devices $\times$ time of day $\times$ time on task) for both 1/RTs and RTs were not significant.

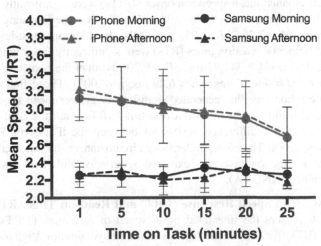

Fig. 3. Mean speed responses (1/RTs) across the different conditions (i.e., morning and afternoon) for both the iPhone 6s Plus and the Samsung Galaxy Tab 4 of the mobile Psychomotor Vigilance Task (m-PVT). *Note:* Mean 1/RTs for both the iPhone 6s Plus and the Samsung Galaxy Tab 4 are presented in bins of 5 min as well as the first minute. Error bars represents standard deviation.

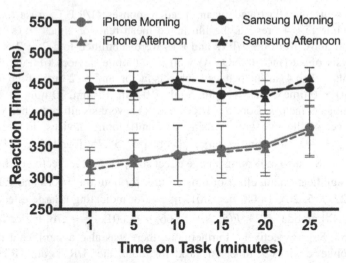

Fig. 4. Mean reaction times (RTs) across the different conditions (i.e., morning and afternoon) for both the iPhone 6s Plus and the Samsung Galaxy Tab 4 of the mobile Psychomotor Vigilance Task (m-PVT). *Note:* Mean RTs for both the iPhone 6s Plus and the Samsung Galaxy Tab 4 are presented in bins of 5 min as well as the first minute. Error bars represents standard deviation.

The main effect of the two groups using different mobile devices was followed by post-hoc tests with Bonferroni correction for multiple comparisons. Post-hoc tests showed that participants' mean speed responses (1/RTs) were significantly greater with the iPhone 6s Plus mobile device ($M = 2.97$, $SE = .05$) than the Samsung Galaxy Tab 4 mobile device ($M = 2.26$, $SE = .05$, $p < .001$). In addition, post-hoc tests also showed that participants' reaction times (RTs) were significantly faster with the iPhone 6s Plus mobile device ($M = 341.92$ ms, $SE = 6.29$ ms) than the Samsung Galaxy Tab 4 mobile device ($M = 444.02$ ms, $SE = 6.29$ ms, $p < .001$). These findings seem to indicate that the iPhone 6s Plus generated significantly greater mean speed responses (1/RTs) and significantly faster mean reaction times (RTs) than the Samsung Galaxy Tab 4, with a mean RT difference of 102 ms between the iPhone 6s Plus and the Samsung Galaxy Tab 4. Therefore, under these circumstances, the interaction between mobile devices × time on task was explored separately with a two-way repeated analysis of variance (ANOVA).

iPhone 6s Plus Mean Speed Response (1/RT) and Reaction Time (RT)
Figures 5 and 6 present the illustrated mean speed of responses (1/RTs) and mean reaction times (RTs) for the iPhone 6s Plus mobile Psychomotor Vigilance Task (m-PVT) across the different conditions. Both the 1/RTs and RTs were submitted to a 2 × 6 two-way repeated analysis of variance (ANOVA) comparing 2 × time of day (Morning, or Afternoon) × 6 time on task (1-min; 5-min, 10-min, 15-min, 20 min, or 25-min). Only the main effect of time on task was significant for both the 1/RTs and RTs, Wilks' Lambda = .12, $F(5, 8)$, 12.02, $p = .001$, $\eta_p^2 = .88$, indicating a large effect

size [55, 56] and Wilks' Lambda = .12, $F(5, 8)$, 11.93, p = .002, η_p^2 = .88, indicating a large effect size [55, 56], respectively. The other main effect (time of day) and inter-actions (two-way interaction, time of day × time on task) for both 1/RTs and RTs were not significant.

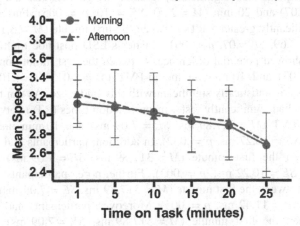

Fig. 5. Mean speed responses (1/RTs) of both the morning session and afternoon session for the iPhone 6s Plus mobile Psychomotor Vigilance Task (m-PVT). *Note:* Mean 1/RTs of both the morning session and afternoon session for the iPhone 6s Plus are presented in bins of 5 min as well as the first minute. Error bars represents standard deviation.

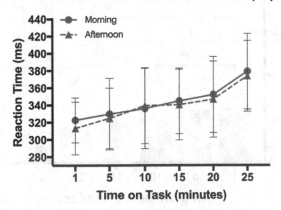

Fig. 6. Mean reaction times (RTs) of both the morning session and afternoon session for the iPhone 6s Plus mobile Psychomotor Vigilance Task (m-PVT). *Note:* Mean RTs of both the morning session and afternoon session are presented in bins of 5 min as well as the first minute. Error bars represents standard deviation.

The main effect of time on task was further explored using Fisher's Least Significant Difference (LSD) post-hoc multiple pairwise comparison, which according to Rovai, Baker and Ponton [57] is used when sample sizes are small. As can be seen from Fig. 7, participants who were assigned to the iPhone mobile device group had significantly greater mean speed responses (1/RTs) between the first minute on the m-PVT ($M = 3.17$, $SE = .07$) and 15-min on the m-PVT ($M = 2.96$, $SE = .09$, $p = .005$). In addition, participants had significantly greater 1/RTs between the first minute ($M = 3.17$, $SE = .07$) and 20-min ($M = 2.90$, $SE = .10$, $p = .005$). Furthermore, participants had significantly greater 1/RTs between the first minute ($M = 3.17$, $SE = .07$) and 25-min ($M = 2.69$, $SE = .07$, $p < .001$). Fisher's LSD post-hoc multiple pairwise comparison also showed potential differences between the first minute on the m-PVT ($M = 3.17$, $SE = .07$) and 10-min on the m-PVT ($M = 3.01$, $SE = .10$, $p = .051$). However, this was not statistically significant with this study size. As can be seen from Fig. 8, participants had significantly faster mean reaction times (RTs) between the first minute on the m-PVT ($M = 317.89$ ms, $SE = 7.09$ ms) and 10-min on the m-PVT ($M = 337.75$ ms, $SE = 10.27$ ms, $p = .032$). In addition, participants had significantly faster RTs between the first minute ($M = 317.89$ ms, $SE = 7.09$ ms) and 15-min ($M = 342.70$ ms, $SE = 10.22$ ms, $p = .003$). Furthermore, participants had significantly faster RTs between the first minute ($M = 317.89$ ms, $SE = 7.09$ ms) and 20-min ($M = 349.52$ ms, $SE = 11.42$ ms, $p = .005$). Moreover, participants had significantly faster RTs between the first minute ($M = 317.89$ ms, $SE = 7.09$ ms) and 25-min ($M = 376.47$ ms, $SE = 9.20$ ms, $p < .001$).

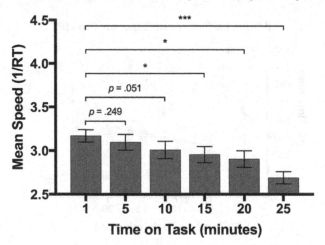

iPhone 6s Plus Mean Speed Response (1/RT)

Fig. 7. *p < .05; **p < .005; ***p < .001. *Note:* Mean speed responses (1/RTs) for the iPhone 6s Plus are presented in bins of 5 min as well as the first minute. Error bars represents standard errors.

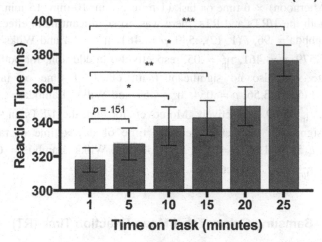

Fig. 8. *p < .05; **p < .005; ***p < .001. *Note:* Mean reaction times (RTs) for the iPhone 6s Plus are presented in bins of 5 min as well as the first minute. Error bars represents standard errors.

Samsung Galaxy Tab 4 Mean Speed Response (1/RT) and Reaction Time (RT)
Figures 9 and 10 present the illustrated mean speed responses (1/RTs) and mean reaction times (RTs) for Samsung Galaxy Tab 4 mobile Psychomotor Vigilance Task (m-PVT) across the different conditions. Both the 1/RTs and RTs were submitted to a

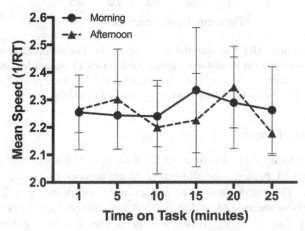

Fig. 9. Mean speed responses (1/RTs) of both the morning session and afternoon session of the Samsung Galaxy Tab 4 mobile Psychomotor Vigilance Task (m-PVT). *Note:* Mean 1/RTs of both the morning session and afternoon session for the Samsung Galaxy Tab 4 are presented in bins of 5 min as well as the first minute. Error bars represents standard deviation.

2 × 6 two-way repeated analysis of variance (ANOVA) comparing 2 × time of day (Morning, or Afternoon) × 6 time on task (1-min; 5-min, 10-min, 15-min, 20 min, or 25-min). For both the 1/RTs and RTs, there was no significant main effect of time of day; Wilks' Lambda = .96, $F(1, 12)$, .530, p = .481, η_p^2 = .04 and Wilks' Lambda = .95, $F(1, 12)$, .579, p = .461, η_p^2 = .05, respectively. In addition, for both the 1/RTs and RTs, there was also no significant main effect of time on task; Wilks' Lambda = .31, $F(5, 8)$, 3.56, p = .054, η_p^2 = .69 and Wilks' Lambda = .31, $F(5, 8)$, 3.53, p = .056, η_p^2 = .69, respectively. Moreover, for both the 1/RTs and RTs, there was also no significant interaction between time of day × time of task; Wilks' Lambda = .61, $F(5, 8)$, 1.05, p = .454, η_p^2 = .40 and Wilks' Lambda = .63, $F(5, 8)$, .954, p = .497, η_p^2 = .37, respectively.

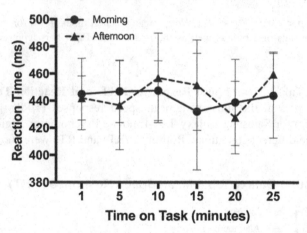

Fig. 10. Mean reaction times (RTs) of both the morning session and afternoon session of the Samsung Galaxy Tab 4 mobile Psychomotor Vigilance Task (m-PVT). *Note:* Mean RTs of both the morning session and afternoon session for the Samsung Galaxy Tab 4 are presented in bins of 5 min as well as the first minute. Error bars represents standard deviation.

4.2   Mean Number of Lapses

From all test trials, a total of 31.84% (n = 3,328) RTs ≥ 500 ms were submitted for data analyses. Figure 11 presents the illustrated mean number of lapses across the different conditions. The mean number of lapses were submitted to a 2 × 2 × 6 mixed-design analysis of variance (ANOVA) with 2 × mobile devices (iPhone 6s Plus or Samsung Galaxy Tab 4) as the between-subjects factor, and × 2 time of day (Morning, or Afternoon) × 6 time on task (1-min; 5-min, 10-min, 15-min, 20 min, or 25-min) as the within-subjects factors. There was a significant main effect of the two groups using different mobile devices, $F(1, 24)$, 131.81, $p < .001$, η_p^2 = .85, indicating a large effect size [55, 56]. In addition, there was a significant main effect of time on task, Wilks' Lambda = .28, $F(5, 20)$, 10.27, $p < .001$, $\eta_p^2 = .72$, indicating a large effect size [55, 56]. Furthermore, there was also a significant interaction between mobile devices × time on task, Wilks' Lambda = .31, $F(5, 20)$, 9.10, $p < .001$, $\eta_p^2 = .70$, indicating a large effect size [55, 56]. The other main effect (time of day, $p = .620$) and interactions (two-way interaction, time of day × time on task, $p = .395$; and three-way interaction, mobile devices × time of day × time on task, $p = .151$) for the mean number of lapses (i.e., RTs $\geq$ 500 ms) were not significant.

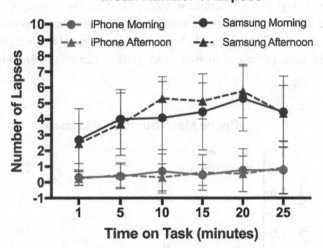

Fig. 11. Mean number of lapses across the different conditions (i.e., morning and afternoon) for both the iPhone 6s Plus and the Samsung Galaxy Tab 4 of the mobile Psychomotor Vigilance Task (m-PVT). *Note:* Mean number of lapses for both the iPhone 6s Plus and the Samsung Galaxy Tab 4 are presented in bins of 5 min as well as the first minute. Error bars represents standard deviation.

The main effect of the two groups using different mobile devices was followed by post-hoc tests with Bonferroni correction for multiple comparisons. Post-hoc tests showed that participants' mean number of lapses were significantly lower for the iPhone 6s Plus mobile device ($M = .54$, $SE = .23$) than the Samsung Galaxy Tab 4 mobile device ($M = 4.31$, $SE = .23$, $p < .001$). These findings seem to indicate that participants assigned to the iPhone 6s Plus recorded significantly less mean number of lapses than the Samsung Galaxy Tab 4. These findings are not too surprising as it was previously found that both the mean speed responses (1/RTs) and mean reaction times (RTs) for the iPhone 6s Plus generated significantly greater 1/RTs and faster RTs than the Samsung Galaxy Tab 4. There was a statistically difference of 102 ms, which would indicate at least for the Samsung Galaxy Tab 4 that there would be significantly more test trials with RTs $\geq$ 500 ms (i.e., number of lapses). As a result, from all

31.84% (n = 3,328) of test trials with RTs ≥ 500 ms, the Samsung Galaxy Tab 4 group represented 90.32% (n = 3,006) and the iPhone 6s Plus group represented 9.68% (n = 322). Therefore, also under these circumstances, the interaction between mobile devices × time on task was explored separately with a two-way repeated analysis of variance (ANOVA).

iPhone 6s Plus Mean Number of Lapses

Figure 12 presents the illustrated mean number of lapses for the iPhone 6s Plus mobile Psychomotor Vigilance Task (m-PVT) across the different conditions. The mean number of lapses were submitted to a 2 × 6 two-way repeated analysis of variance (ANOVA) comparing 2 × time of day (Morning, or Afternoon) × 6 time on task (1-min; 5-min, 10-min, 15-min, 20 min, or 25-min). There was no significant main effect of time of day; Wilks' Lambda = .997, $F(1, 12)$, .04, $p = .846$, $\eta_p^2 = .00$. In addition, there was also no significant main effect of time on task; Wilks' Lambda = .75, $F(5, 8)$, .54, $p = .744$, $\eta_p^2 = .25$. Moreover, there was also no significant interaction between time of task × time of day; Wilks' Lambda = .36, $F(5, 8)$, 2.84, $p = .092$, $\eta_p^2 = .64$.

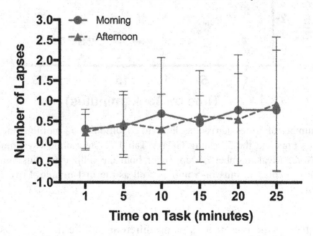

Fig. 12. Mean number of lapses for both the morning session and afternoon session for the iPhone 6s Plus of the mobile Psychomotor Vigilance Task (m-PVT). *Note:* Mean number of lapses for the iPhone 6s Plus are presented in bins of 5 min as well as the first minute. Error bars represents standard deviation.

Samsung Galaxy Tab 4 Mean Number of Lapses

Figure 13 presents the illustrated mean number of lapses for the Samsung Galaxy Tab 4 mobile Psychomotor Vigilance Task (m-PVT) across the different conditions. The mean number of lapses were submitted to a 2 × 6 two-way repeated analysis of variance (ANOVA) comparing 2 × time of day (Morning, or Afternoon) × 6 time on task (1-min; 5-min, 10-min, 15-min, 20 min, or 25-min). Only the main effect of time on task was significant for the mean number of lapses, Wilks' Lambda = .14, $F(5, 8)$, 9.80, $p = .003$, $\eta_p^2 = .86$, indicating a large effect size [55, 56]. The other main effect (time of day, $p = .486$) and two-way interaction (time of day $\times$ time on task, $p = .227$) for the mean number of lapses (i.e., RTs $\geq$ 500 ms) were not significant.

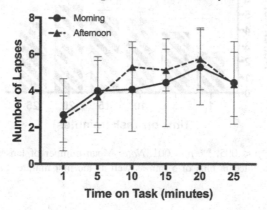

Fig. 13. Mean number of lapses for both the morning session and afternoon session for the Samsung Galaxy Tab 4 of the mobile Psychomotor Vigilance Task (m-PVT). *Note:* Mean number of lapses for the Samsung Galaxy Tab 4 are presented in bins of 5 min as well as the first minute. Error bars represents standard deviation.

The main effect of time on task was further explored using Fisher's Least Significant Difference (LSD) post-hoc multiple pairwise comparison, which according to Rovai, Baker and Ponton [57] is used when sample sizes are small. As can be seen from Fig. 14, participants who were assigned to the Samsung Galaxy Tab 4 mobile device group had significantly less mean number of lapses between the first minute on the m-PVT ($M = 2.58$, $SE = .35$) and 5-min on the m-PVT ($M = 3.85$, $SE = .37$, $p = .001$). In addition, participants also had significantly less mean number of lapses between the first minute on the m-PVT ($M = 2.58$, $SE = .35$) and 10-min on the m-PVT ($M = 4.69$, $SE = .40$, $p < .001$). Furthermore, participants also had significantly less mean number of lapses between the first minute on the m-PVT ($M = 2.58$, $SE = .35$) and 15-min on the m-PVT ($M = 4.81$, $SE = .40$, $p = .001$). Moreover, participants also had a significantly lower mean number of lapses between the first minute on the m-PVT ($M = 2.58$, $SE = .35$) and 20-min on the m-PVT ($M = 5.54$, $SE = .38$, $p < .001$). Finally, participants also had a significantly lower mean number of lapses between the first minute on the m-PVT ($M = 2.58$, $SE = .35$) and 25-min on the m-PVT ($M = 4.42$, $SE = .46$, $p = .008$). These findings seem to indicate that mean number of lapses for mobile devices, that generate on average significantly slower thresholds, due to perhaps hardware configurations than what is typically found in the Psychomotor Vigilance Task (PVT) literature, may not be an accurate representation and comparison from analyses of both the mean speed responses (1/RT) and mean reaction times (RTs). Instead, the analyses of the mean number of lapses may yield far better research insights.

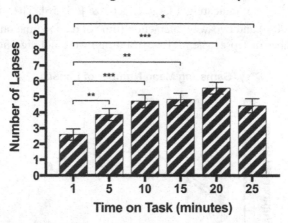

Fig. 14. *p < .05; **p < .005; ***p < .001. *Note:* Mean number of lapses for the Samsung Galaxy Tab 4 are presented in bins of 5 min as well as the first minute. Error bars represents standard errors.

5 Conclusion

The study aimed to investigate whether an alternative online mobile version of the 'gold standard' Psychomotor Vigilance Task (PVT) could be used to provide an objective indicator of fatigue in staff in applied safety critical settings such as train driving, hospital staffs, emergency services, law enforcements, etc. It was found that there was a large significant difference in reaction times (RTs) between the two mobile devices (i.e., Samsung vs. Apple's iPhone). Apple's iPhone 6s Plus generated RTs that were comparable to those found in the literature [33, 34, 40, 42–46, 52]. However, the RTs of the Samsung mobile device were significantly slower than those found in the literature. Findings from this study also support previous research that have identified that an increase in fatigue results in impaired alertness [58, 59], whereby sustained attention, as measured by reaction time, significantly reduces after 10-min of continuous performance using the Psychomotor Vigilance Task (PVT). These findings from this alternative online mobile version of the Psychomotor Vigilance Task (m-PVT) are consistent with previous work, which suggested that sustained attention drops with prolonged duration of the task [60, 61].

This study seems to suggest that an alternative online mobile version of the 'gold standard' 10-min PVT (i.e., m-PVT) could be used to provide an objective indicator of fatigue after 10 min on the m-PVT in staff working in applied safety critical settings such as train driving, hospital staffs, emergency services, law enforcments, etc. However, caution is required when considering implementing an alternative online mobile version (m-PVT) that is running on an internet browser, as only the iPhone 6s Plus was able to generate reaction times that were comparable with the literature. In contrast, there were significantly fewer lapses for the iPhone 6s Plus (n = 322) than the Samsung Galaxy Tab 4 (n = 3,006), which was not surprising when considering that both mean speed responses (1/RTs) and reaction times (RTs) were significantly higher and faster respectively, for the iPhone 6s Plus than for the Samsung Galaxy Tab 4. As a result, perhaps analyses of both the mean speed responses (1/RTs) and mean reaction times (RTs) may not always generate an accurate data representation for analyses based on the hardware differences in mobile manufactures as well as configurations and specifications. Therefore, perhaps using the number of lapses (i.e., RTs $\geq$ 500 ms) may yield richer data for analyses on these circumstances. As a result, this study recommends that pilot studies should be carried out to firstly explore and determine whether the selected mobile device generates RTs that are better suited for either mean RTs and mean 1/RTs, or mean number of lapses analyses. However, there are several factors that could also account for the difference in the mean 1/RTs and mean RTs between the two mobile devices. Firstly, regarding software, both the Apple's iPhone 6s Plus and Samsung Galaxy Tab 4 run on different operating systems (OS). Apple's iPhone 6s Plus run their own native iOS version 9.3.1, while the Samsung Galaxy Tab 4 run on Alphabet's Android KitKat version 4.4.2. Furthermore, even though the same internet browser (Dolphin Web Browser) was used across both mobile devices, the version numbers were different. This may indicate that one may have had more improvement and stability updates than the other (Dolphin Web Browser; Apple\s native iOS app version 9.9.0 vs. Android app OS version 11.5.6). Alternatively, the browser may have been developed for one platform and then expanded to also run on the other platform.

Further research is now needed to determine whether the m-PVT can be used to provide an objective indicator of fatigue in staff working in applied safety critical settings such as train driving, hospital staffs, emergency services, law enforcement, etc. Use of an iPhone 6s Plus is recommended, and further studies with larger samples are required to confirm the length of the task.

Acknowledgment. This work was supported by the Economic and Social Research Council [ES/J500197/1] and Arriva Trains Wales (ATW).

Contributors. MSE designed the experiment, carried out data collection, statistical analysis and writing of the paper. DH programmed the Psychomotor Vigilance Task (m-PVT) under the directions of MSE using the client code HTML, and CSS for the page visualisation and layout. DH also used the JavaScript to initiate the m-PVT. MSE wrote the paper with input from APS. All authors have seen and approved the final version of the paper for publication.

References

1. Eggemeier, F.T., Wilson, G.F., Kramer, A.F., Damos, D.L.: General considerations concerning workload assessment in multi-task environments. In: Damos, D.L. (ed.) Multiple Task Performance, pp. 207–216. Taylor & Francis, London (1991)
2. Hart, S.G., Staveland, L.E.: Development of NASA-TLX (task load index): results of empirical and theoretical research. Adv. Psychol. **52**, 139–183 (1988). https://doi.org/10. 1016/s0166-4115(08)62386-9

3. Longo, L.: Designing medical interactive systems via assessment of human mental workload. In: International Symposium on Computer-Based Medical Systems, pp. 364–365 (2015). https://doi.org/10.1109/cbms.2015.67

4. Longo, L.: Subjective usability, mental workload assessments and their impact on objective human performance. In: IFIP Conference on Human-Computer Interaction, pp. 202–223 (2017). https://doi.org/10.1007/978-3-319-67684-5_13

5. Zammouri, A., Moussa, A.A., Mebrouk, Y.: Brain-computer interface for workload estimation: assessment of mental efforts in learning processes. Expert Syst. Appl. **112**, 138–147 (2018). https://doi.org/10.1016/j.eswa.2018.06.027

6. Byrne, A.J., et al.: Novel method of measuring the mental workload of anaesthetists during clinical practice. Br. J. Anaesth. **105**, 767–771 (2010). https://doi.org/10.1093/bja/aeq240

7. Orlandi, L., Brooks, B.: Measuring mental workload and physiological reactions in marine pilots: building bridges towards redlines of performance. Appl. Ergon. **69**, 74–92 (2018). https://doi.org/10.1016/j.apergo.2018.01.005

8. Shakouri, M., Ikuma, L.H., Aghazadeh, F., Nahmens, I.: Analysis of the sensitivity of heart rate variability and subjective workload measures in a driving simulator: the case of highway work zones. Int. J. Ind. Ergon. **66**, 136–145 (2018). https://doi.org/10.1016/j.ergon.2018.02.015

9. Comstock, J.R.J., Arnegard, R.J.: The Multi-Attribute Test Battery for Human Operator Workload and Strategic Behaviour. National Aeronautics and Space Administration, Hampton (1992)

10. Berka, C., et al.: EEG correlates of task engagement and mental workload in vigilance, learning, and memory tasks. Aviat. Space Environ. Med. **78**, B231–B244 (2007)

11. Borghini, G., Astolfi, L., Vecchiato, G., Mattia, D., Babiloni, F.: Measuring neurophysiological signals in aircraft pilots and car drivers for the assessment of mental workload, fatigue and drowsiness. Neurosci. Biobehav. Rev. **44**, 58–75 (2014). https://doi.org/10.1016/j.neubiorev.2012.10.003

12. Heine, T., Lenis, G., Reichensperger, P., Beran, T., Doessel, O., Deml, B.: Electrocardiographic features for the measurement of drivers' mental workload. Appl. Ergon. **61**, 31–43 (2017). https://doi.org/10.1016/j.apergo.2016.12.015

13. Hogervorst, M.A., Brouwer, A.M., Van Erp, J.B.E.: Combining and comparing EEG, peripheral physiology and eye-related measures for the assessment of mental workload. Front. Neurosci. **8**, 322 (2014). https://doi.org/10.3389/fnins.2014.00322

14. Hsu, B.W., Wang, M.J.J., Chen, C.Y., Chen, F.: Effective indices for monitoring mental workload while performing multiple tasks. Percept. Mot. Skills **121**, 94–117 (2015). https://doi.org/10.2466/22.pms.121c12x5

15. Jimenez-Molina, A., Retamal, C., Lira, H.: Using psychophysiological sensors to assess mental workload during web browsing. Sensors **18**, 458 (2018). https://doi.org/10.3390/s18020458

16. Shaw, E.P., et al.: Measurement of attentional reserve and mental effort for cognitive workload assessment under various task demands during dual-task walking. Biol. Psychol. **134**, 39–51 (2018). https://doi.org/10.1016/j.biopsycho.2018.01.009

17. So, W.K.Y., Wong, S.W.H., Mak, J.N., Chan, R.H.M.: An evaluation of mental workload with frontal EEG. PLoS ONE **12**, e0174949 (2017). https://doi.org/10.1371/journal.pone.0174949

18. Vergara, R.C., Moenne-Loccoz, C., Maldonado, P.E.: Cold-blooded attention: finger temperature predicts attentional performance. Front. Hum. Neurosci. **11**, 454 (2017). https://doi.org/10.3389/fnhum.2017.00454

19. Widyanti, A., Muslim, K., Sutalaksana, I.Z.: The sensitivity of galvanic skin response for assessing mental workload in Indonesia. Work.: J. Prev. Assess. Rehabil. **56**, 111–117 (2017)
20. Blanco, J.A., et al.: Quantifying cognitive workload in simulated flight using passive, dry EEG measurements. IEEE Trans. Cogn. Dev. Syst. **10**, 373–383 (2018). https://doi.org/10. 1109/tcds.2016.2628702
21. Myrtek, M., et al.: Physical, mental, emotional, and subjective workload components in train drivers. Ergonomics **37**, 1195–1203 (1994). https://doi.org/10.1080/00140139408964897
22. Brookhuis, K.A., De Waard, D.: Assessment of drivers' workload: performance and subjective and physiological indexes. In: Hancock, P.A., Desmond, P.A. (eds.) Stress, Workload and Fatigue, pp. 321–333. Lawrence Erlbaum Associates, New Jersey (2001)
23. Foy, H.J., Chapman, P.: Mental workload is reflected in driver behaviour, physiology, eye movements and prefrontal cortex activation. Appl. Ergon. **73**, 90–99 (2018). https://doi.org/ 10.1016/j.apergo.2018.06.006
24. Paxion, J., Galy, E., Berthelon, C.: Mental workload and driving. Front. Psychol. **5**(1344), 2014 (2014). https://doi.org/10.3389/fpsyg.2014.01344
25. Wickens, C.D.: Mental workload: assessment, prediction and consequences. In: Longo, L., Leva, M.C. (eds.) H-WORKLOAD 2017. CCIS, vol. 726, pp. 18–29. Springer, Cham (2017). https://doi.org/10.1007/978-3-319-61061-0_2
26. Gopher, D., Donchin, E.: Workload: an examination of the concept. In: Boff, K.R., Kaufman, L., Thomas, J.P. (eds.) Handbook of Perception and Human Performance. Cognitive Processes and Performance, vol. 2, pp. 1–49. Wiley, Oxford, England (1986)
27. Hancock, P.A., Meshkati, N.: Human Mental Workload. Elsevier Science, Amsterdam (1988)
28. Moray, N.: Mental Workload: Its Theory and Measurement. Plenum, New York (1979)
29. Xie, B., Salvendy, G.: Review and reappraisal of modelling and predicting mental workload in single- and multi-task environments. Work Stress **14**, 74–99 (2000). https://doi.org/10. 1080/026783700417249
30. Byrne, A.: Mental workload as an outcome in medical education. In: Longo, L., Leva, M. Chiara (eds.) H-WORKLOAD 2017. CCIS, vol. 726, pp. 187–197. Springer, Cham (2017). https://doi.org/10.1007/978-3-319-61061-0_12
31. Gaba, D.M., Lee, T.: Measuring the workload of the anesthesiologist. Anesth. Analg. **71** (354–361), 1990 (1990)
32. Smith, A.P., Smith, H.N.: Workload, fatigue and performance in the rail industry. In: Longo, L., Leva, M.C. (eds.) H-WORKLOAD 2017. CCIS, vol. 726, pp. 251–263. Springer, Cham (2017). https://doi.org/10.1007/978-3-319-61061-0_17
33. Dinges, D.F., Powell, J.W.: Microcomputer analyses of performance on a portable, simple visual RT task during sustained operations. Behav. Res. Methods Instrum. Comput. **17**, 652–655 (1985). https://doi.org/10.3758/bf03200977
34. Dinges, D.F., Orne, M.T., Whitehouse, W.G., Orne, E.C.: Temporal placement of a nap for alertness: contributions of circadian phase and prior wakefulness. Sleep **10**, 313–329 (1987)
35. Belenky, G., et al.: Patterns of performance degradation and restoration during sleep restriction and subsequent recovery: a sleep dose-response study. J. Sleep Res. **12**, 1–12 (2003). https://doi.org/10.1046/j.1365-2869.2003.00337.x
36. Dinges, D.F., et al.: Cumulative sleepiness, mood disturbance, and psychomotor vigilance performance decrements during a week of sleep restricted to 4–5 hours per night. Sleep **20**, 267–777 (1997)
37. Jewett, M.E., Dijk, D.J., Kronauer, R.E., Dinges, D.F.: Dose-response relationship between sleep duration and human psychomotor vigilance and subjective alertness. Sleep **22**, 171–179 (1999). https://doi.org/10.1093/sleep/22.2.171

38. Lamond, N., et al.: The impact of a week of simulated night work on sleep, circadian phase, and performance. Occup. Environ. Med. **60**, 1–9 (2003). https://doi.org/10.1136/oem.60.11.e13
39. Davis, C.M., Roma, P.G., Hienz, R.D.: A rodent model of the human psychomotor vigilance test: performance comparisons. J. Neurosci. Methods **259**, 57–71 (2016). https://doi.org/10.1016/j.jneumeth.2015.11.014
40. Basner, M., Dinges, D.F.: Maximizing sensitivity of the psychomotor vigilance test (PVT) to sleep loss. Sleep **34**, 581–591 (2011). https://doi.org/10.1093/sleep/34.5.581
41. Van Dongen, H.P., Dinges, D.F.: Sleep, circadian rhythms, and psychomotor vigilance. Clin. Sport. Med. **24**, 237–249 (2005). https://doi.org/10.1016/j.csm.2004.12.007
42. Basner, M., Mollicone, D.J., Dinges, D.F.: Validity and sensitivity of a brief psychomotor vigilance test (PVT-B) to total and partial sleep deprivation. Acta Astronaut. **69**, 949–959 (2011). https://doi.org/10.1016/j.actaastro.2011.07.015
43. Loh, S., Lamond, N., Dorrian, J., Roach, G., Dawson, D.: The validity of psychomotor vigilance tasks of less than 10-minute duration. Behav. Res. Methods Instrum. Comput. **36**, 339–346 (2004). https://doi.org/10.3758/bf03195580
44. Lamond, N., Dawson, D., Roach, G.D.: Fatigue assessment in the field: validation of a hand-held electronic psychomotor vigilance task. Aviat. Space Environ. Med. **76**, 486–489 (2005)
45. Roach, G.D., Dawson, D., Lamond, N.: Can a shorter psychomotor vigilance task be used as a reasonable substitute for the ten-minute psychomotor vigilance task? Chronobiol. Int. **23**, 379–387 (2006). https://doi.org/10.1080/07420520601067931
46. Dorrian, J., Roach, G.D., Fletcher, A., Dawson, D.: Simulated train driving: fatigue, self-awareness and cognitive disengagement. Appl. Ergon. **38**, 155–166 (2007). https://doi.org/10.1016/j.apergo.2006.03.006
47. Lamond, N., Jay, S.M., Dorrian, J., Ferguson, S.A., Roach, G.D., Dawson, D.: The sensitivity of a palm-based psychomotor vigilance task to severe sleep loss. Behav. Res. Methods **40**, 347–352 (2008). https://doi.org/10.3758/brm.40.1.347
48. Dorrian, J., Rogers, N.L., Dinges, D.F.: Psychomotor vigilance performance: neurocognitive assay sensitive to sleep loss. In: Kushida, C.A. (ed.) Sleep Deprivation: Clinical Issues, Pharmacology and Sleep Loss Effects, pp. 39–70. Marcel Dekker Inc., New York (2005)
49. Basner, M., Mcguire, S., Goel, N., Rao, H., Dinges, D.F.: A new likelihood ratio metric for the psychomotor vigilance test and its sensitivity to sleep loss. J. Sleep Res. **24**, 702–713 (2015). https://doi.org/10.1111/jsr.12322
50. Dinges, D.F., Kribbs, N.B.: Performing while sleepy: effects of experimentally-induced sleepiness. In: Monk, T.H. (ed.) Sleep, Sleepiness and Performance, pp. 97–128. Wiley, Chichester (1991)
51. Warm, J.S., Parasuraman, R., Matthews, G.: Vigilance requires hard mental work and is stressful. Hum. Factors **50**, 43–441 (2008). https://doi.org/10.1518/001872008x312152
52. Khitrov, M.Y., et al.: PC-PVT: a platform for psychomotor vigilance task testing, analysis, and prediction. Behav. Res. Methods **46**, 140–147 (2014). https://doi.org/10.3758/s13428-013-0339-9
53. World Medical Association: World medical association declaration of Helsinki ethical principles for medical research involving human subjects. Jama-J. Am. Med. Assoc. **310**, 2191–2194 (2013). https://doi.org/10.1001/jama.2013.281053
54. Kribbs, N.B., Dinges, D.F.: Vigilance decrement and sleepiness. In: Ogilvie, R.D., Harsh, J. (eds.) Sleep Onset: Normal and Abnormal Processes, pp. 113–125. American Psychological Association, Washington, D.C. (1994)
55. Cohen, J.: Eta-squared and partial eta-squared in fixed factor ANOVA designs. Educ. Psychol. Meas. **33**, 107–112 (1973). https://doi.org/10.1177/001316447303300111
56. Cohen, J.: Statistical Power Analysis for the Behavioral Sciences. Erlbaum, Hillsdale (1988)

57. Rovai, A.P., Baker, J.D., Ponton, M.K.: Social Science Research Design and Statistics: A Practitioner's Guide to Research Methods and IMB SPS Analysis. Watertree Press LLC, Chesapeake (2014)
58. Dorrian, J., Hussey, F., Dawson, D.: Train driving efficiency and safety: examining the cost of fatigue. J. Sleep Res. **16**, 1–11 (2007). https://doi.org/10.1111/j.1365-2869.2007.00563.x
59. Dorrian, J., Baulk, S.D., Dawson, D.: Work hours, workload, sleep and fatigue in Australian Rail Industry employees. Appl. Ergon. **42**, 202–209 (2011). https://doi.org/10.1016/j.apergo.2010.06.009
60. Dinges, D.F., Powell, J.W.: Sleepiness is more than lapsing. J. Sleep Res. **17**, 84 (1988)
61. Dinges, D.F., Powell, J.W.: Sleepiness impairs optimum response capability: it's time to move beyond the lapse hypothesis. J. Sleep Res. **18**, 366 (1989)

Workload Assessment Using Speech-Related Neck Surface Electromyography

Aaron Novstrup[1(✉)], Terrance Goan[1], and James Heaton[2]

[1] Stottler Henke Associates, Inc., Seattle, WA, USA
{anovstrup,goan}@stottlerhenke.com
[2] Massachusetts General Hospital,
Center for Laryngeal Surgery and Voice Rehabilitation, Boston, MA, USA
James.Heaton@mgh.harvard.edu

Abstract. This paper presents preliminary findings of an ongoing effort to evaluate the application of face and neck surface electromyography (sEMG) to real-time cognitive workload assessment. A retrospective analysis of anterior neck sEMG signals, recorded from 10 subjects during a time-pressured mental arithmetic task with verbal responses during a previous study by Stepp et al. [52], suggests that a measure known as neck intermuscular beta coherence (NIBcoh) may be sensitive to cognitive workload and/or error commission in tasks involving speech production, with sub-second temporal resolution. Specifically, the recent reanalysis indicates that subjects exhibited significantly lower NIBcoh when they produced incorrect verbal responses as compared to NIBcoh associated with correct responses. We discuss this promising application of NIBcoh within the context of our continuing research program and introduce future experiments that will shed light on the relationships among face and neck sEMG signals, task demands, performance, cognitive effort/strain, subjective workload measures, and other psychophysiological measures.

1   Introduction

Mental workload researchers have identified a variety of psychophysiological measures that have proven sensitive to cognitive task demands, including indices based on electrocardiography (ECG) [17,44], transcranial Doppler sonography (TCD) [39,53,61], electroencephalography (EEG) [4,14,21], functional near infrared [12,61], and eye tracking [2,5,27,37]. Electromyographic (EMG) measures, based on electrical potentials produced by motor units during muscle contraction, have also demonstrated sensitivity to task demands (e.g., [18,65]), yet *face and neck surface* EMG (sEMG) has received little attention in workload research despite the critical role of face and neck musculature in reflecting and expressing human mental/emotional state (whether through non-verbal cues or spoken expression). The lack of attention is perhaps not surprising given the

© Springer Nature Switzerland AG 2019
L. Longo and M. C. Leva (Eds.): H-WORKLOAD 2018, CCIS 1012, pp. 72–91, 2019.
https://doi.org/10.1007/978-3-030-14273-5_5

obtrusiveness of many existing sEMG sensor designs. However, recent advances in sEMG sensor design/miniaturization and in EMG signal processing technologies are paving the way for a new generation of unobtrusive sEMG sensors that will conform to the skin surface and minimize any negative impact on the wearer. For example, there are new, commercially available miniature differential sensors specifically designed for high-fidelity, wireless recording of facial sEMG signals [41, 42]. These advances have sparked new interest in the application of face/neck sEMG to cognitive workload assessment.

Face and neck sEMG may offer a unique window into human emotional state, complementing or even replacing previously studied psychophysiological measures as sensing modalities in the real-time assessment of cognitive workload. Many facial muscles are situated immediately below the skin surface and are thereby readily accessible for sEMG recording. They have high endurance and show little change in EMG power spectra across repeated facial contractions [57], and a link between emotional responses and high levels of cognitive strain has also been established (e.g., [20]). A study of error-related activity in the corrugator supercilii, a muscle of the upper face (medial eyebrow region) involved in facial expressions, has linked amplified EMG activity to error commission with less than 100 milliseconds of latency [35].

This paper reports findings of an exploratory reanalysis of an existing dataset, originally collected in a previous investigation by Stepp et al. into the modulation of a specific neck sEMG signal, known as neck intermuscular beta coherence (NIBcoh), by speech and non-speech behaviors [52]. In the present work, the authors reanalyzed this dataset to investigate the potential utility of NIBcoh in real-time cognitive workload assessment. Specifically, the sensitivity of NIBcoh to cognitive task demands and the relationships between NIBcoh and task performance were examined. This reanalysis was an initial step in an ongoing program of research intended to shed light on the potential application of face and neck surface EMG to the real-time assessment of cognitive workload.

The paper makes three primary contributions to the sciences of cognitive workload and of EMG-EMG coherence analysis. First, the reanalysis provides limited evidence that NIBcoh is sensitive to variations in task demand (or attention) across similar speech-related tasks. Second, it indicates that NIBcoh may be correlated with error commission within the context of a specific time-pressured mental arithmetic task requiring verbal responses. Finally, the findings offer validation for concerns raised in [45] regarding the common use of full-wave rectification in EMG-EMG coherence analysis.

The rest of the paper is organized as follows. Section 2 provides relevant background concerning EMG and EMG-EMG coherence measures, establishes existing support for a potential connection between cognitive workload and face/neck sEMG, generally, and NIBcoh more specifically, and offers possible advantages of face and neck sEMG as a real-time cognitive workload sensing modality. Section 3 describes the conditions in which the NIBcoh dataset was collected and the methods employed in the recent reanalysis. Section 4 presents and evaluates the results of the analysis. Finally, Sect. 5 concludes by summarizing the key findings and positioning them within the context of ongoing and future research.

2   Related Work

2.1   Human Mental Workload

The general concept of cognitive workload has been recognized and studied for at least 50 years, although no formal, standard definition of the construct has yet to emerge within the research community [9]. This paper defines cognitive workload similarly to the operational definition proposed by O'Donnell and Eggemeier [46], as "the fractional utilization of an individual's limited cognitive resources at a particular moment." As noted above, a number of psychophysiological measures have proven sensitive to variations in cognitive task demands, supporting their potential utility in the measurement of cognitive workload. However, several studies offer evidence of divergence among known psychophysiological workload indices [26,32,38,64]. The hypothesized causes for disassociation among these measures are varied and include both lack of *specificity* (i.e., some measures can be influenced by non-workload factors) and lack of *diagnosticity* (i.e., measures may reflect differing *aspects* of workload, consistent with multi-resource theories (e.g., [40,63]) in which workload is a multi-faceted construct arising from the capacity of and demand for multiple cognitive resources).

In addition to psychophysiological measures, a number of subjective instruments for cognitive workload assessment have been developed and validated [36]. These include both offline, retrospective instruments, such as the NASA Task Load Index (NASA-TLX) [25], the Workload Profile (WP) [56], and the Subjective Workload Assessment Technique (SWAT) [48], and online (real-time) techniques, such as the Instantaneous Self-Assessment of Workload (ISA) [30]. While subjective instruments may help to validate other measures or models of cognitive workload, a valid *objective* measure offers obvious relative benefits, including correspondence to reality uncontaminated by subjectivity and the avoidance of self-assessment procedures that may distract from primary tasks. The assessment of cognitive workload has found applications in a wide variety of human endeavors, including: manual assembly/manufacturing [43], medical education [7], air traffic control [15], and vehicle operation including that of trains [1,47,50], aircraft [8], and motor vehicles [4,55]. Therefore, the development of a robust, objective, real-time measure of cognitive workload can be expected to have widespread benefits.

2.2   Face and Neck Surface Electromyography

Previous research has demonstrated the utility of facial sEMG for recognizing and classifying emotional responses [11,54,58]. In contrast to image-based expression assessment, sEMG has the potential to identify rapid or slight facial expressions, including subtle muscle contractions *below the threshold necessary to generate visible changes in the surface contours of the face* [57]. Further, sEMG may provide greater sensitivity regarding the locations and magnitude of facial contraction when compared to image-based assessment. Automatic video quantification of facial movements is relatively difficult for features aside from high-contrast tissue edges, whereas sEMG can discern a broad combination of facial muscle actions across both high- and low-contrast regions.

Beyond the identification of facial expressions, face/neck sEMG can quantify neuromuscular activity related to the vocalization and articulation of speech, *even for utterances that are not vocalized* (i.e., sub-vocal speech). Several research groups have demonstrated the utility of non-acoustic speech recognition technologies based on surface EMG signals [13,31,41,42], confirming that surface EMG provides ample speech-related information whether speech is spoken aloud or only "mouthed". Because computer-based speech recognition is possible from EMG alone, it is reasonable to suggest that these signals may also change under varying cognitive load conditions in a manner resembling acoustic markers, such as those employed in voice stress analysis. The characteristics of face and neck sEMG make it particularly well suited to specific operational contexts. In noisy environments (such as an aircraft cockpit) in which an acoustic signal might be compromised, for instance, subtle acoustic features relating to cognitive load might be more readily gleaned from activity in the musculature involved in speech articulation than from degraded acoustic signals. The ability to detect subtle contractions associated with sub-vocal speech or slight (perhaps even involuntary) facial expressions could prove beneficial even in tasks that *do not involve significant amounts of speech*. Most facial expression assessment and eye blink tracking is done through image-based data collection, but this approach is problematic when individuals are freely moving and thereby changing head orientation relative to video capture sources. In addition, flight equipment such as helmets, glasses, and face-masks can preclude visualization of facial movements. In contrast, sEMG sensors can reside under headgear [3] or be incorporated into face masks, chin straps, etc. [10].

Finally, the dimensionality of sEMG, particularly when considering signals from multiple locations on the face and neck, offers a distinct advantage over many of the low-dimensional measures that are unobtrusive enough for operational use in real-time workload assessment. If face/neck sEMG can support speech recognition and the classification of emotional responses, perhaps it is also capable, alone or in concert with other measures, of distinguishing cognitive states that are conflated by other physiological signals. That is, it may help to overcome the lack of specificity and diagnosticity noted in Sect. 2.1.

Although sEMG appears to offer distinct advantages over other sensing modalities in some recording contexts, it also has potential drawbacks. Physiological measures typically require some degree of instrumentation, and even though sEMG is less prone to noise from movements and environmental sources compared to electrically weaker EEG, it is perhaps more cumbersome and prone to noise than other measures such as heart and respiration rate. Moreover, while modern sEMG recording systems do not require the use of conductive gels [41,42], the recorded skin surface should nevertheless be clean and free from hair that can impede adequate electrode contact. This precludes some potential speech-related neck/face recording locations in individuals with beards or when proper skin preparation is impractical (e.g., military field deployment, extremely dirty or wet environments, etc.). In addition, the degree to which NIBcoh measurement is potentially degraded by motion artifact or environmental sources of electrical noise in the non-laboratory setting is still unknown.

2.3   Intermuscular Beta Coherence

The present study focuses on a particular measure, known as neck intermuscular beta coherence (NIBcoh), derived from the surface EMG signal at two anterior neck recording locations superior to (above) neck strap muscles involved in speech. Coherence, generally, is a frequency domain measure of the linear dependency or strength of coupling between two processes [24,62]. The coherence function, $|R_{xy}(\lambda)|^2$, can be defined as in Eq. 1 below, where f_{xx} represents the auto-spectra of a time series $x(t)$, f_{yy} the auto-spectra of $y(t)$, and f_{xy} the cross-spectra of the two. *Intermuscular* coherence, the coherence between EMG signals, is a measure of the common presynaptic drive to motor neurons [6].

$$|R_{xy}(\lambda)|^2 = \frac{|f_{xy}(\lambda)|^2}{f_{xx}(\lambda)f_{yy}(\lambda)} \tag{1}$$

Muscle is thought to be driven by a number of different physiological oscillations at varying frequencies (see [23] for a review). The frequencies at which physiological oscillations occur appear to be characteristic of the function of distinct neural circuits and have been categorized into distinct bands such as alpha (8–13 Hz), beta (15–35 Hz), gamma (30–70 Hz), and others. It is generally thought that the beta and low gamma bands originate primarily from the primary motor cortex [23]. The beta band is typically associated with production of static motor tasks and is reduced with movement onset (e.g., [33]). Intermuscular coherence measurements reflect all oscillatory presynaptic drives to lower motoneurons. However, the intermuscular coherence in the beta band has been shown to be qualitatively similar to corticomuscular coherence, both in healthy individuals as well as in individuals with cortical myoclonus [6,33], supporting the hypothesis that *beta-band intermuscular coherence* is due to oscillatory drives originating in the motor cortex and is thereby likely influenced by cognitive state. The coherence of neuromuscular oscillations, whether measured through MEG-EMG, EEG-EMG or EMG-EMG, are affected by concurrent cognitive demands differently across the distinct frequency bands, making measures of coherence potentially useful for detecting changes in cognitive workload. For example, although alpha-band coherence is not dominant during motor tasks, it is known to increase when attention is drawn specifically to motor task execution [19,34]. Beta-band coherence is the dominant signal during synchronized oscillatory discharges of corticospinal or corticobulbar pathways onto lower motor neurons, and is likewise reduced when attention is divided or otherwise drawn away from the motor task at hand [29,34,52]. In addition, beta-band coherence is negatively correlated with motor output errors during concurrent cognitive tasks in young adults [28], suggesting that it may be predictive of both cognitive workload and motor performance in younger individuals. In contrast, beta-band coherence is not necessarily correlated with motor performance in the elderly during divided-attention tasks (61–75 yr; [28]), perhaps due to reduced attentional resources [59] and motor coordination [60] with advancing age.

Measures of neck and face intermuscular beta coherence might be particularly well suited to real-time workload assessment given the bilateral symmetry of contraction typical for neck midline and facial muscles. For example, superficial facial muscles involved in speech articulation and neck midline strap muscles typically contract symmetrically across the right and left sides during speech and swallowing [41], providing an opportunity for coherence measurement during these synchronous contractions. Stepp and colleagues found that NIBcoh measured from ventral neck strap muscles (sternohyoid, sternothyroid, and thyrohyoid) can distinguish not only individuals with disordered (strained, hyperfunctional) versus healthy voice production [51], but also healthy individuals when they mimic a strained voice versus natural speech [52]. Vocal hyperfunction is associated with heightened speaking effort and anxiety [22], which may represent increased cognitive demand during speech and thereby reduce NIBcoh, regardless of whether the hyperfunction is pathological or mimicked. Stepp and colleagues [52] also found that NIBcoh decreases when speech is produced under divided attention (cognitive load imposed by rapid, backwards skip-counting), consistent with prior reports of divided attention effects on beta coherence in different motor systems [29,34]. The goal of the present study was to re-examine the Stepp et al. [52] dataset of NIBcoh during their normal versus divided-attention speaking conditions, with the hypothesis that (1) their finding of reduced NIBcoh under the divided attention condition would be replicated, and (2) the commission of cognitive errors (miss counting) could be detected in the NIBcoh measure as errors occurred during their recordings of running speech (e.g., at a sub-second time resolution). If NIBcoh indeed correlates with cognitive errors, this measure would have important implications for real-time monitoring of cognitive load and performance.

3   Design and Methodology

3.1   Data Collection Procedures

The dataset analyzed in this study consists of simultaneous neck surface EMG (sEMG) and acoustic signals recorded during an earlier investigation by Stepp et al. into the modulation of neck intermuscular beta coherence (NIBcoh) by speech and non-speech behaviors [52]. The signals were recorded under a variety of speech and non-speech task conditions, including a normal speech condition involving both spontaneous and scripted speech and a "divided-attention" condition in which participants were instructed to rapidly skip-count backwards from 100 by 7s. In the present study, these data were reanalyzed (as detailed in Sects. 3.2 and 3.3) to explore the relationships among the neck sEMG signals, the acoustic signal, task demands, and task performance in order to shed more light on the possible relationship between neck sEMG and mental workload. Because this research is ultimately focused on *real-time* workload assessment, the previous analysis was also extended by considering *time-varying* measures and not only summary statistics over the entire time series.

Participants. The participants were ten (10) vocally healthy female volunteers (mean age: 25 years, standard deviation: 2.6 years). They reported no complaints related to their voice, and no abnormal pathology of the larynx was observed during standard digital video endoscopy with stroboscopy performed by a certified speech-language pathologist (SLP). Informed consent was obtained from all participants in compliance with the Institutional Review Board of the Massachusetts General Hospital.

Recording Procedures. As reported by Stepp et al. [52], simultaneous neck sEMG and acoustic signals from a lavalier microphone (Sennheiser MKE2-P-K, Wedemark, Germany) were filtered and digitally recorded at 20 kHz with Delsys hardware (Bagnoli Desktop System, Boston, MA) and software (EMGworks 3.3). The neck of each participant was prepared for electrode placement by cleaning the neck surface with an alcohol pad and "peeling" (exfoliating) with tape to reduce electrode-skin impedance, DC voltages, and motion artifacts. Neck sEMG was recorded with two Delsys 3.1 double differential surface electrodes placed on the neck surface, parallel to underlying muscle fibers. Each electrode consisted of three 10-mm silver bars with interbar distances of 10 mm. Double differential electrodes were chosen instead of single differential electrodes in order to increase spatial selectivity and to minimize electrical cross-talk between the two electrodes.

The two electrodes were placed on the right and left anterior neck surface, as depicted by the schematic in Fig. 1. Electrode 1 was centered approximately 1 cm lateral to the neck midline, as far superior as was possible without impeding the jaw opening, superficial to fibers of the thyrohyoid and sternohyoid muscles, and to some degree the omohyoid. Electrode 2 was centered vertically on the gap between the cricoid and thyroid cartilages of the larynx, and centered 1 cm lateral to the midline contralateral to Electrode 1, superficial to the cricothyroid,

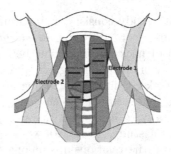

Fig. 1. sEMG electrode placement [52]. Copyright 2011 by the American Speech-Language-Hearing Association. Reprinted with permission.

sternothyroid, and sternohyoid muscles. However, based on previous examinations of sEMG recordings during pitch glides [51], it is doubtful that cricothyroid contraction contributed much energy to the sEMG due to its relatively deep position. The platysma muscle likely contributed to some degree to the activity recorded at both electrode locations. A ground electrode was placed on the superior aspect of the participant's left shoulder. The sEMG recordings were pre-amplified and filtered using the Delsys Bagnoli system set to a gain of 1,000, with a bandpass filter with roll-off frequencies of 20 Hz and 450 Hz. All recordings were monitored by the experimenters in real time to ensure signal integrity, and no recordings included movement artifacts.

Tasks. Participants completed eleven separate speech and non-speech tasks, broadly organized into six task conditions. Only two conditions are relevant to the present study, however: a "normal speech" condition and a "divided attention" condition. The normal speech condition consisted of two tasks—a scripted task in which participants read "The Rainbow Passage" [16], and a spontaneous speech task in which participants produced speech spontaneously in response to a variety of available prompts, selected by participants (e.g., "What did you do last weekend?"). The Rainbow Passage was typically produced for 30–45 s. Spontaneous speech samples were approximately 1 min in length. No participant had any problems completing these speech tasks correctly. In order to collect speech under divided attention, participants were given 60 s to count backwards from 100, aloud, as quickly as possible in decrements of 7. These recordings were typically approximately 45 s in length. Participants uniformly reported this task as difficult, but all were able to produce continuous speech during the recording. The primary cognitive demand in this task is a (non-verbal) one imposed by time pressured arithmetic computation. The production of verbal responses, which imposes modest demands for linguistic processing and motor control resources, can be considered a secondary task. Since EMG-EMG coherence measures have been observed to decrease when attention is diverted from the motor task involving the instrumented muscle, the authors hypothesized that NIBcoh would decrease in response to increased demands of the primary, mental arithmetic task. From this perspective, NIBcoh was expected to function as a measure of secondary task attention.

3.2 Data Analysis

The original data consisted of discrete multivariate time series for ten subjects under five speech-related conditions and one non-speech condition, sampled at a rate of 20 kHz. Each time series included EMG variables from the two anterior neck surface recording locations depicted in Fig. 1 and an acoustic variable. From these "raw" time series, the authors derived several dependent EMG and acoustic measures and down-sampled to a rate of approximately 1.83 Hz (i.e., three samples for every 32,768 samples of the "raw" time series). The derived EMG-based variables were: NIBcoh, average magnitude, and gradient. The acoustic variables were: average amplitude, peak amplitude, spectral roll-off, cepstral peak prominence, and sound intensity.

Two versions of the intermuscular beta coherence measure were computed, with and without full-wave rectification (NIBcoh-rect and NIBcoh, respectively) of the EMG signals. It is common practice in EMG-EMG coherence analysis to apply full-wave rectification as an EMG pre-processing step, and this step was performed in the research in which the NIBcoh dataset originated [52]. Other work, however, has called this practice into question, demonstrating that full-wave rectification may impair the identification of common oscillatory inputs to muscle pairs [45]. Therefore, the present study experimented with both rectified and unrectified EMG signals.

The NIBcoh and NIBcoh-rect time series were computed as follows. First, any DC offset was removed from the raw sEMG signals. In the case of the NIBcoh-rect measure, the resulting signals were then full-wave rectified. The signals were segmented by sliding a 16,384-point ($\approx$820 ms) rectangular window over each of the resulting EMG-EMG bivariate time series, with 50% overlap. Coherence between the two EMG signals, as defined in Eq. 1, was then estimated within each rectangular window using Welch's overlapped averaged periodogram method [62], with sliding 8,192-point ($\approx$410 ms) Hamming windows, a 8,192-point fast Fourier transform, and 50% overlap (i.e., three Hamming windows per rectangular segment). Finally, the beta-band coherence values were computed by averaging the coherence values over the 15–35 Hz frequency range. Based on the findings of Neto and Christou [45] suggesting that oscillatory activity in the 100–150 Hz frequency band of the unrectified signal may drive variations in the beta band of rectified EMG signals, coherence in the 100–150 Hz band was also computed.

In order to associate the acoustic and sEMG signals with time-varying performance metrics, the acoustic signals for the divided-attention condition were manually annotated with labels indicating the participants' verbal responses—each interval i, terminated by the completion of a response, was labeled with the number uttered l_i. Performance in the backwards-skip-counting task is characterized by both speed and accuracy. Accuracy is quantified as a function of error commission, with "errors" defined relative to the most recent element that a subject produced (e.g., 80 was regarded as the correct successor to 87, despite 87 not being an element of the correct sequence) to avoid an error-compounding effect. Speed is quantified by the duration of time required for a subject to produce each element of the sequence (i.e., response time). From the manual response annotations, discrete time series were generated capturing the error commission ϵ and response time r performance metrics. Specifically, the value of the error commission indicator variable ϵ_i for a given labeled interval i reflects whether the response label l_i for the interval is 7 less than the response label l_{i-1} for the previous labeled interval. The value of the response time variable for a given labeled interval is simply the duration of the interval. That is:

$$\epsilon_i = \begin{cases} 1 & \text{if } l_i \neq l_{i-1} - 7 \\ 0 & \text{otherwise} \end{cases} \tag{2}$$

$$r_i = \text{len}(i)$$

The label boundaries did not, in general, align with the $\approx$820 ms segment boundaries used to derive down-sampled time series from the raw EMG and acoustic signals. Therefore, a time-weighted average of the down-sampled time series over each labeled interval was computed to assign a single value of each dependent variable (e.g., NIBcoh) to the interval.

3.3   Statistical Analysis

As an initial step in the present analysis, the authors sought to determine how well a key finding in [52] held up in light of Neto and Christou's [45] criticism of full-wave rectification in EMG-EMG coherence analysis—specifically, Stepp et al. [52] had found a significant effect of task condition on neck intermuscular beta coherence. This result was re-examined by using ANOVA to quantify the effect of condition on four EMG-EMG coherence measures: NIBcoh, NIBcoh-rect, and the corresponding intermuscular coherence measures for the 100–150 Hz frequency band. For consistency with the methods employed in [52], coherence was estimated over each signal as a whole with Welch's overlapped averaged periodogram method [62], with a sliding 16,384-point Hamming window, 16,384-point FFT, and 50% overlap. The recent analysis differs from that of [52] in that their two-factor ANOVA was replaced with a more conservative one-factor repeated measures ANOVA, which makes weaker independence assumptions. The results of this analysis are reported in Table 1, below.

Since the authors' primary interest was in evaluating the coherence measure's utility in workload assessment, a post hoc two-tailed t-test was performed to contrast the cognitively demanding divided-attention condition and the normal speech condition under the assumptions of the ANOVA model, as a means to evaluate the sensitivity of NIBcoh to varying task demands. The relationships between the performance measures for the backwards skip-counting task (defined by Eq. 2) and the measures derived from the EMG and acoustic signals were then investigated. Specifically, associations between response time and each of the EMG/acoustic variables were evaluated by using Student's t-tests to test the null hypotheses that each Pearson's product-moment correlation coefficient was 0 (i.e., $H_0 : \rho_{r,v} = 0$, where $\rho_{r,v}$ denotes the correlation between response time (r) and an EMG/acoustic variable v). Similarly, Student's two sample t-tests were used to evaluate the hypotheses that the distribution of each EMG/acoustic variable had unequal means for correct versus incorrect responses (i.e., $H_0 : \bar{v}_{\epsilon=1} = \bar{v}_{\epsilon=0}$). The results of these statistical tests are shown in Tables 2 and 3, in Sect. 4 below, along with the estimated correlation coefficients and differences in means. The t-tests had 123 degrees of freedom, corresponding to 125 observations (i.e., "responses") across the 10 participants. The reported p-values are *not* adjusted for multiple comparisons, since any such adjustment could itself be misleading due to correlations among several of the variables. In order to statistically control for substantial variability across subjects, both in terms of performance on the skip-counting task and in terms of the EMG/acoustic measures, the EMG/acoustic variables were normalized before computing t-values and correlation coefficients. Specifically, given a value x of a variable for subject s and the within-subject sample mean μ_s and standard deviation σ_s of that variable over the normal speech condition, the standardized value $z(x)$ was computed using Eq. 3. The statistical tests thus reflect the "effects" of performance on the other measures *relative to each subject's "baseline"* from the normal speech condition.

$$z(x) = \frac{x - \mu_s}{\sigma_s} \tag{3}$$

The analysis of the relationships between performance and the EMG/acoustic variables is motivated by the hypothesis that within-subject variations in performance on the skip-counting task result, at least in part, from variations in the difficulty of the task. Given the nature of the task, within-subject variations in cognitive demand might reasonably be expected to be quite small. However, some such variation may arise from differences in the arithmetic problems that each participant encountered while completing the task, especially in subjects with less developed mental arithmetic skills. Some subjects may find it easier to compute $100 - 7 = 93$ than to compute $93 - 7 = 86$, for instance. Whether this was actually the case was examined by comparing mean response times for decrementing numbers with a ones digit of 7, 8, or 9 (which can be computed without regard to the tens digit) versus other numbers (which require "borrowing" from the tens digit). Further, participants were encouraged to count as quickly as possible and to maintain continuous speech during the divided-attention task, which might be expected to lead them to sacrifice accuracy for speed and thereby to experience amplified within-subject variations in cognitive demands. This hypothesis was examined by analyzing the distributions of errors and response times and by comparing mean response times for correct versus incorrect responses within and across subjects. If within-subject variations in performance during the task can be plausibly connected to time-varying cognitive demands, then it is plausible that any observed relationship between performance and a physiological indicator can be interpreted as evidence of a possible relationship between that indicator and cognitive workload (i.e., that task performance acts as a proxy for cognitive workload within the context of this task).

4   Results and Evaluation

Replication analysis (Table 1) confirmed the finding in [52] that the experimental conditions had a significant effect on neck intermuscular beta coherence, despite the use of a more conservative statistical test than that employed by Stepp et al. The results also lend credence to the concerns of [45] regarding the common use of full-wave rectification in EMG-EMG coherence analysis. Rectifying the EMG signals prior to estimating coherence appears to dilute the estimated difference in coherence across conditions, suggesting that full-wave rectification may result in a harmful loss of information—note the difference between the effect sizes and p-values between the unrectified and full-wave rectified beta-band EMG-EMG coherence signals. No significant effect of the task conditions on neck intermuscular coherence in the 100–150 Hz frequency band was found.

Table 1. Summary of replication analysis. Effect of task condition on EMG-EMG coherence measures.

Coherence measure	Size of effect (generalized η^2)	p-value
Full-wave rectified		
Beta band	0.120	0.0715
100–150 Hz	0.0892	0.0905
Unrectified		
Beta band	0.176	**0.0194**[†]
100–150 Hz	0.0651	0.146

[†]Denotes a Huynh-Feldt sphericity-corrected p-value, applied because Mauchly's test for sphericity failed to reach a 5% significance level.

A post hoc comparison of the normal speech and divided-attention conditions revealed a significant difference between the two ($p < 0.001$). The linear model corresponding to the repeated measures ANOVA implied that NIBcoh was lower by an average of 0.0956 in the divided-attention condition, with a standard error of 0.0290. This difference *may* indicate sensitivity of NIBcoh to the change in cognitive demands between the two conditions. Statistical analysis of the performance metrics for the backwards skip-counting task did seem to support the use of these metrics as proxies for cognitive workload within the context of this task. First, it was found that participants tended to compute the successors for numbers with a ones digit of 7, 8, or 9 faster on average, with a mean time of 1.9 s, than for other numbers (3.5 s). This result is consistent with the hypothesis that cognitive demands vary between these two conditions and that the varying cognitive demands are reflected in task performance. Additionally, the data are consistent with the expectation that subjects sacrificed accuracy for speed—time pressure that would tend to amplify the effects of within-subject variations in cognitive demands on accuracy. A full 36% (45 out of 125) of the subjects' responses were erroneous, despite the presumed simplicity of the task. The mean response time was 3.1 s with a standard deviation of 2.8, and the response time distribution was heavily left-skewed with a median response time of only 2.1 s. Furthermore, longer response times were strongly associated with *incorrect* responses both between and within most subjects, indicating that participants took longer to respond when they were struggling but that delayed responses did not generally result in greater accuracy. Analysis of cross-subject variation suggests that standardization of the EMG and acoustic variables, using Eq. 3 as described in the previous section, was justified. Subjects were found to vary substantially, both in terms of their performance on the skip-counting task (the total number of errors committed by each subject ranged from 0 to 10, with a mean of 5 and a median of 4) and on the EMG/acoustic measures (e.g., the mean within-subject standard deviation of NIBcoh was 0.104, while the overall mean was 0.446, overall standard deviation was 0.116, and standard deviation of within-subject means was 0.0497).

Table 2 shows the results of the t-tests comparing the distributions of the standardized EMG and acoustic variables across correct and incorrect responses. NIBcoh, EMG magnitude, sound intensity, average sound amplitude, peak amplitude, and cepstral peak prominence all exhibited significant ($\alpha = 0.05$) differences in estimated means across correct and incorrect responses. The NIBcoh-rect, EMG gradient, and acoustic spectral roll-off measures showed no significant difference across correct and incorrect responses. NIBcoh associated with incorrect responses was lower than NIBcoh associated with correct responses, as may be expected if workload or simply reduced attention to speech reduces intermuscular coherence of oscillatory drives in speech-related muscles during speech. The results for several acoustic measures frequently used in voice stress analysis also accord with expectations.

Table 2. Difference in mean standardized features values for correct vs. incorrect responses.

Measure	Estimated difference	t-statistic	p-value
NIBcoh	0.505	2.81	**<0.006**
NIBcoh-rect	0.078	0.548	0.585
EMG magnitude (site 1)	0.432	−2.22	**0.028**
EMG magnitude (site 2)	0.532	−2.50	**0.014**
EMG gradient (site 1)	0.120	−0.772	0.44
EMG gradient (site2)	0.064	−0.414	0.68
Mean acoustic amplitude	0.852	−2.35	**0.020**
Peak acoustic amplitude	2.52	−2.96	**<0.004**
Sound intensity	0.345	−1.97	0.051
Spectral roll-off	0.276	1.21	0.230
Cepstral peak prominence	0.258	−1.67	0.097

Correlations between response time and the EMG/acoustic variables are shown in Table 3. NIBcoh, peak acoustic amplitude, sound intensity, and cepstral peak prominence exhibited significant ($\alpha = 0.05$) associations with response time.

Table 3. Correlations between response time and the standardized EMG and acoustic features.

Measure	Pearson's r	t-statistic	p-value
NIBcoh	−0.196	−2.22	**0.028**
NIBcoh-rect	−0.078	−0.868	0.387
EMG magnitude (site 1)	−0.176	−1.98	0.050
EMG magnitude (site 2)	0.008	0.084	0.933
EMG gradient (site 1)	0.076	0.849	0.397
EMG gradient (site 2)	0.111	1.24	0.218
Mean acoustic amplitude	−0.139	−1.56	0.122
Peak acoustic amplitude	0.185	2.08	**0.040**
Sound intensity	−0.223	−2.54	**0.012**
Spectral roll-off	−0.005	−0.053	0.958
Cepstral peak prominence	−0.219	−2.49	**0.014**

4.1 Caveats and Limitations

While the results are promising, several caveats must be acknowledged and the exploratory nature of the analysis must be stressed. Because the original experiment in which the data were collected was designed to shed light on the modulation of NIBcoh by speech and non-speech behaviors and *not* to explore the sensitivity of NIBcoh to cognitive demands, the recent reanalysis was necessarily ad hoc. The findings should therefore be considered only suggestive rather than conclusive—robust conclusions will require well controlled experiments in which cognitive demands are manipulated directly (Sect. 5 briefly describes such an experiment, which the authors plan to conduct in the near future).

The small sample size of only 10 participants and the primary focus on the (single) backwards skip-counting task further limit the generalizability of the results. In particular, although the task did require mental arithmetic, the verbal response format makes it impossible to determine from this study whether the NIBcoh measure may offer any insight into cognitive workload in *non-speech-involving tasks*. Additionally, it was found that the statistical hypothesis tests were quite sensitive to outliers—for instance, the omission of one subject in particular, who rapidly produced the entire sequence without errors, changes the p-value for the t-test comparing mean NIBcoh in correct versus incorrect responses from less than 0.006 to 0.074. This lack of robustness underscores the limits of this reanalysis and justifies cautious optimism in interpreting the results.

Finally, it must be noted that several of the EMG and acoustic measures were themselves somewhat correlated (e.g., NIBcoh and peak acoustic amplitude), and the design of the original experiment makes it impossible to infer the causal factors that underlie these correlations. Were NIBcoh and peak acoustic amplitude correlated because of a mutual causal relationship to cognitive demands / workload? It seems intuitively likely that the effect on peak acoustic amplitude is an artifact of the experimental conditions, rather than an indication of any general utility in predicting workload or error commission. Bursts of nervous laughter accompanying high workload might, for instance, contribute to high peak amplitudes in the specific conditions of this experiment, but one would not expect to find the same effect in other settings. Could such an artifact also explain lower intermuscular beta coherence associated with erroneous responses? Questions such as these cannot be addressed adequately with the existing data.

5   Conclusions and Future Work

The data reanalysis reported herein offers some evidence bearing on the utility of neck surface EMG for detecting cognitive strain in real time. Specifically, the analysis demonstrates that time-varying EMG-derived measures, with a sub-second temporal resolution, are correlated with error commission and response time in a backwards skip-counting task. Although the task exhibits only mild variations in task difficulty over the sub-problems that comprise the task, the analysis indicates that a time-varying NIBcoh measure was lower by about half a standard deviation on average during intervals in which subjects produced incorrect responses. Further research is necessary to confirm the effect in a well controlled context, determine whether it is due to a causal relationship with error commission, cognitive demands, and/or workload, investigate whether the effect is limited to tasks involving speech, and generalize the work to other EMG sensing locations on the face/neck surface where other physiological responses to variations in cognitive workload may be detected. A planned study, commencing in 2018, will establish more conclusively whether intermuscular beta coherence or other measures derived from face and neck sEMG signals are sensitive to cognitive task demands by recording these, and other, psychophysiological signals while participants complete tasks with varying levels of difficulty in the NASA Multi-Attribute Task Battery (MATB) [49]. The research will investigate multiple EMG sensing locations on the face and neck surface, relating to muscles involved in facial expression, mastication/jaw clenching, speech articulation, and voice production, and a psychometric analysis will establish relationships to more conventional workload indicators (including subjective workload as measured by the NASA Task Load Index administered within the MATB).

The experiments will employ a novel protocol designed to establish whether a perceived risk of aversive consequences affects the measured psychophysiological responses to cognitive task demands. Specifically, after half of the task blocks, identified to participants *before* and *during* each such block, a series of mildly noxious electrical stimuli will be delivered to participants, with the number of stimuli ostensibly associated with task performance—but *actually* determined by the (manipulated) level of task demand in the block. The protocol will thus test how the presence of perceived risks mediates the relationship between task demands and psychophysiological responses. It is our hope that the technique of employing aversive consequences in order to elevate physiological responses to workload will resolve two key challenges for workload researchers—namely, the risk that muted responses may lead to Type I errors in laboratory studies and the problem that laboratory models may not transfer well into operational environments.

Acknowledgements. This material is based upon work supported by the Defense Advanced Research Projects Agency (DARPA) under Contract No. D17PC00119 (Distribution Statement: approved for public release; distribution unlimited). The views, opinions and/or findings expressed are those of the authors and should not be interpreted as representing the official views or policies of the Department of Defense or the U.S. Government.

References

1. Balfe, N., Crowley, K., Smith, B., Longo, L.: Estimation of train driver workload: extracting taskload measures from on-train-data-recorders. In: Longo, L., Leva, M.C. (eds.) H-WORKLOAD 2017. CCIS, vol. 726, pp. 106–119. Springer, Cham (2017). https://doi.org/10.1007/978-3-319-61061-0_7
2. Beatty, J.: Task-evoked pupillary responses, processing load, and the structure of processing resources. Psychol. Bull. **91**(2), 276–292 (1982). https://doi.org/10.1037/0033-2909.91.2.276
3. Betts, B., Binsted, K., Jorgensen, C.: Small-vocabulary speech recognition using surface electromyography. Interact. Comput. **18**(6), 1242–1259 (2006). https://doi.org/10.1016/j.intcom.2006.08.012
4. Borghini, G., et al.: Assessment of mental fatigue during car driving by using high resolution EEG activity and neurophysiologic indices. In: Proceedings of the Annual International Conference of the IEEE Engineering in Medicine and Biology Society, EMBS, pp. 6442–6445 (2012). https://doi.org/10.1109/EMBC.2012.6347469
5. Brookings, J.B., Wilson, G.F., Swain, C.R.: Psychophysiological responses to changes in workload during simulated air traffic control. Biol. Psychol. **42**, 361–377 (1996). https://doi.org/10.1016/0301-0511(95)05167-8
6. Brown, P., Farmer, S.F., Halliday, D.M., Marsden, J., Rosenberg, J.R.: Coherent cortical and muscle discharge in cortical myoclonus. Brain **122**(3), 461–472 (1999). https://doi.org/10.1093/brain/122.3.461
7. Byrne, A.: Mental workload as an outcome in medical education. In: Longo, L., Leva, M.C. (eds.) H-WORKLOAD 2017. CCIS, vol. 726, pp. 187–197. Springer, Cham (2017). https://doi.org/10.1007/978-3-319-61061-0_12
8. Cahill, J., et al.: Adaptive automation and the third pilot. In: Aircraft Technology. IntechOpen (2018)
9. Cain, B.: A review of the mental workload literature. In: Defence Research and Development Toronto (Canada), pp. 4-1–4-34 (2007). http://www.dtic.mil/cgi-bin/GetTRDoc?Location=U2&doc=GetTRDoc.pdf&AD=ADA474193
10. Chan, A., Englehart, K., Hudgins, B., Lovely, D.: Myo-electric signals to augment speech recognition. Med. Biol. Eng. Comput. **39**(4), 500–504 (2001). https://doi.org/10.1007/BF02345373
11. Cheng, B., Liu, G.: Emotion recognition from surface EMG signal using wavelet transform and neural network. In: Proceedings of The 2nd International Conference on Bioinformatics and Biomedical Engineering (ICBBE), pp. 1363–1366 (2008). https://doi.org/10.1109/ICBBE.2008.670

12. De Joux, N., Russell, P.N., Helton, W.S.: A functional near-infrared spectroscopy study of sustained attention to local and global target features. Brain Cogn. **81**(3), 370–375 (2013). https://doi.org/10.1016/j.bandc.2012.12.003

13. Denby, B., Schultz, T., Honda, K., Hueber, T., Gilbert, J., Brumberg, J.: Silent speech interfaces. Speech Commun. **52**(4), 270–287 (2010). https://doi.org/10.1016/j.specom.2009.08.002

14. Dussault, C., Jouanin, J.C., Philippe, M., Guezennec, C.Y.: EEG and ECG changes during simulator operation reflect mental workload and vigilance. Aviat. Space Environ. Med. **76**(4), 344–351 (2005)

15. Edwards, T., Martin, L., Bienert, N., Mercer, J.: The relationship between workload and performance in air traffic control: exploring the influence of levels of automation and variation in task demand. In: Longo, L., Leva, M.C. (eds.) H-WORKLOAD 2017. CCIS, vol. 726, pp. 120–139. Springer, Cham (2017). https://doi.org/10.1007/978-3-319-61061-0_8

16. Fairbanks, G.: The rainbow passage. In: Voice and Articulation Drillbook, vol. 2 (1960)

17. Fairclough, S.H., Venables, L., Tattersall, A.: The influence of task demand and learning on the psychophysiological response. Int. J. Psychophysiol. **56**(2), 171–184 (2005). https://doi.org/10.1016/j.ijpsycho.2004.11.003

18. Fallahi, M., Motamedzade, M., Heidarimoghadam, R., Soltanian, A.R., Miyake, S.: Effects of mental workload on physiological and subjective responses during traffic density monitoring: a field study. Appl. Ergon. **52**, 95–103 (2016). https://doi.org/10.1016/j.apergo.2015.07.009

19. Feige, B., Aertsen, A.D., Kristeva-Feige, R.: Dynamic synchronization between multiple cortical motor areas and muscle activity in phasic voluntary movements. J. Neurophysiol. **84**(5), 2622–2629 (2000). https://doi.org/10.1152/jn.2000.84.5.2622

20. Fraser, K., Ma, I., Teteris, E., Baxter, H., Wright, B., McLaughlin, K.: Emotion, cognitive load and learning outcomes during simulation training. Med. Educ. **46**(11), 1055–1062 (2012). https://doi.org/10.1111/j.1365-2923.2012.04355.x

21. Gevins, A., Smith, M.E.: Neurophysiological measures of cognitive workload during human-computer interaction. Theor. Issues Ergon. Sci. **4**(1–2), 113–131 (2003). https://doi.org/10.1080/14639220210159717

22. Goldman, S.L., Hargrave, J., Hillman, R.E., Holmberg, E., Gress, C.: Stress, anxiety, somatic complaints, and voice use in women with vocal nodules: preliminary findings. Am. J. Speech-Lang. Pathol. **5**(1), 44–54 (1996). https://doi.org/10.1044/1058-0360.0501.44

23. Grosse, P., Cassidy, M.J., Brown, P.: EEG-EMG. MEG-EMG and EMG-EMG frequency analysis: physiological principles and clinical applications (2002). https://doi.org/10.1016/S1388-2457(02)00223-7

24. Halliday, D., Rosenberg, J., Amjad, A., Breeze, P., Conway, B., Farmer, S.: A framework for the analysis of mixed time series/point process data: theory and application to the study of physiological tremor, single motor unit discharges and electromyograms. Prog. Biophys. Mol. Biol. **64**(2–3), 237–278 (1995)

25. Hart, S.G., Staveland, L.E.: Development of NASA-TLX (task load index): results of empirical and theoretical research. Adv. Psychol. **52**(C), 139–183 (1988). https://doi.org/10.1016/S0166-4115(08)62386-9

26. Horrey, W.J., Lesch, M.F., Garabet, A.: Dissociation between driving performance and drivers' subjective estimates of performance and workload in dual-task conditions. J. Saf. Res. **40**(1), 7–12 (2009). https://doi.org/10.1016/j.jsr.2008.10.011

27. Jacob, R.J., Karn, K.S.: Eye tracking in human-computer interaction and usability research. Ready to deliver the promises. In: The Mind's Eye: Cognitive and Applied Aspects of Eye Movement Research, pp. 531–553. Elsevier, New York (2003). https://doi.org/10.1016/B978-044451020-4/50031-1

28. Johnson, A.N., Shinohara, M.: Corticomuscular coherence with and without additional task in the elderly. J. Appl. Physiol. **112**(6), 970–981 (2012). https://doi.org/10.1152/japplphysiol.01079.2011

29. Johnson, A.N., Wheaton, L.A., Shinohara, M.: Attenuation of corticomuscular coherence with additional motor or non-motor task. Clin. Neurophysiol. **122**(2), 356–363 (2011). https://doi.org/10.1016/j.clinph.2010.06.021

30. Jordan, C., Brennen, S.: Instantaneous self-assessment of workload technique (ISA). Defence Research Agency, Portsmouth (1992)

31. Jou, S., Schultz, T., Walliczek, M., Kraft, F., Waibel, A.: Towards continuous speech recognition using surface electromyography. In: Ninth International Conference on Spoken Language Processing (2006)

32. Kamzanova, A.T., Kustubayeva, A.M., Matthews, G.: Use of EEG workload indices for diagnostic monitoring of vigilance decrement. Hum. Factors **56**(6), 1136–1149 (2014). https://doi.org/10.1177/0018720814526617

33. Kilner, J.M., Baker, S.N., Salenius, S., Jousmäki, V., Hari, R., Lemon, R.N.: Task-dependent modulation of 15–30 Hz coherence between rectified EMGs from human hand and forearm muscles. J. Physiol. **516**(2), 559–570 (1999). https://doi.org/10.1111/j.1469-7793.1999.0559v.x

34. Kristeva-Feige, R., Fritsch, C., Timmer, J., Lücking, C.H.: Effects of attention and precision of exerted force on beta range EEG-EMG synchronization during a maintained motor contraction task. Clin. Neurophysiol. **113**(1), 124–131 (2002). https://doi.org/10.1016/S1388-2457(01)00722-2

35. Lindström, B.R., Mattsson-Mårn, I.B., Golkar, A., Olsson, A.: In your face: risk of punishment enhances cognitive control and error-related activity in the corrugator supercilii muscle. PLOS One **8**(6), e65692 (2013). https://doi.org/10.1371/journal.pone.0065692

36. Longo, L.: Subjective usability, mental workload assessments and their impact on objective human performance. In: Bernhaupt, R., Dalvi, G., Joshi, A., Balkrishan, D.K., O'Neill, J., Winckler, M. (eds.) INTERACT 2017. LNCS, vol. 10514, pp. 202–223. Springer, Cham (2017). https://doi.org/10.1007/978-3-319-67684-5_13

37. Marshall, S.P.: The index of cognitive activity: measuring cognitive workload. In: Proceedings of the 2002 IEEE 7th Conference on Human Factors and Power Plants, pp. 7–9 (2002). https://doi.org/10.1109/HFPP.2002.1042860

38. Matthews, G., Reinerman-Jones, L.E., Barber, D.J., Abich, J.: The psychometrics of mental workload. Hum. Factors: J. Hum. Factors Ergon. Soc. **57**(1), 125–143 (2015). https://doi.org/10.1177/0018720814539505

39. Matthews, G., Warm, J.S., Reinerman-Jones, L.E., Langheim, L.K., Washburn, D.A., Tripp, L.: Task engagement, cerebral blood flow velocity, and diagnostic monitoring for sustained attention. J. Exp. Psychol.: Appl. **16**(2), 187–203 (2010). https://doi.org/10.1037/a0019572

40. McCracken, J., Aldrich, T.B.T.: Analyses of Selected LHX Mission Functions: Implications for Operator Workload and System Automation Goals. Technical report, Anacapa Sciences Inc., Fort Rucker, AL (1984)

41. Meltzner, G.S., Heaton, J.T., Deng, Y., De Luca, G., Roy, S.H., Kline, J.C.: Development of sEMG sensors and algorithms for silent speech recognition. J. Neural Eng. **15**(4), 046031 (2018). https://iopscience.iop.org/article/10.1088/1741-2552/aac965/meta

42. Meltzner, G.S., Heaton, J.T., Deng, Y., De Luca, G., Roy, S.H., Kline, J.C.: Silent speech recognition as an alternative communication device for persons with laryngectomy. IEEE/ACM Trans. Audio Speech Lang. Process. **25**(12), 2386–2398 (2017). https://doi.org/10.1109/TASLP.2017.2740000

43. Mijović, P., Milovanović, M.,Ković, V., Gligorijević, I., Mijović, B., Mačužić, I.: Neuroergonomics method for measuring the influence of mental workload modulation on cognitive state of manual assembly worker. In: Longo, L., Leva, M.C. (eds.) H-WORKLOAD 2017. CCIS, vol. 726, pp. 213–224. Springer, Cham (2017). https://doi.org/10.1007/978-3-319-61061-0_14

44. Mulder, L., De Waard, D., Brookhuis, K.A.: Estimating mental effort using heart rate and heart rate variability. In: Handbook of Human Factors and Ergonomics Methods, pp. 1–20 (2004)

45. Neto, O.P., Christou, E.A.: Rectification of the EMG signal impairs the identification of oscillatory input to the muscle. J. Neurophysiol. **103**(2), 1093–103 (2010). https://doi.org/10.1152/jn.00792.2009

46. O'Donnell, R., Eggemeier, F.: Workload assessment methodology. In: Boff, K.R., Kaufman, L., Thomas, J.P. (eds.) Handbook of Perception and Human Performance, Cognitive Processes and Performance, vol. 2. Wiley, Hoboken (1986)

47. Pickup, L., Wilson, J.R., Sharpies, S., Norris, B., Clarke, T., Young, M.S.: Fundamental examination of mental workload in the rail industry. Theor. Issues Ergon. Sci. **6**(6), 463–482 (2005). https://doi.org/10.1080/14639220500078021

48. Reid, G.B., Nygren, T.E.: The Subjective Workload Assessment Technique: A Scaling Procedure for Measuring Mental Workload, North-Holland, vol. 52 (1988). https://doi.org/10.1016/S0166-4115(08)62387-0

49. Santiago-Espada, Y., Myer, R., Latorella, K., Comstock, J.: The Multi-Attribute Task Battery II (MATB-II) Software for Human Performance and Workload Research: A User's Guide. Technical report, NASA, Chicago (2011)

50. Smith, A.P., Smith, H.N.: Workload, fatigue and performance in the rail industry. In: Longo, L., Leva, M.C. (eds.) H-WORKLOAD 2017. CCIS, vol. 726, pp. 251–263. Springer, Cham (2017). https://doi.org/10.1007/978-3-319-61061-0_17

51. Stepp, C.E., Hillman, R.E., Heaton, J.T.: Use of neck strap muscle intermuscular coherence as an indicator of vocal hyperfunction. IEEE Trans. Neural Syst. Rehabil. Eng. **18**(3), 329–335 (2010). https://doi.org/10.1109/TNSRE.2009.2039605

52. Stepp, C.E., Hillman, R.E., Heaton, J.T.: Modulation of neck intermuscular beta coherence during voice and speech production. J. Speech Lang. Hear. Res. **54**(3), 836–844 (2011). https://doi.org/10.1044/1092-4388(2010/10-0139)

53. Stroobant, N., Vingerhoets, G.: Transcranial Doppler ultrasonography monitoring of cerebral hemodynamics during performance of cognitive tasks: a review (2000). https://doi.org/10.1023/A:1026412811036

54. Tassinary, L.G., Cacioppo, J.T.: Unobservable facial actions and emotion. Psychol. Sci. **3**(1), 28–33 (1992). https://doi.org/10.1111/j.1467-9280.1992.tb00252.x

55. Tong, S., Helman, S., Balfe, N., Fowler, C., Delmonte, E., Hutchins, R.: Workload differences between on-road and off-road manoeuvres for motorcyclists. In: Longo, L., Leva, M.C. (eds.) H-WORKLOAD 2017. CCIS, vol. 726, pp. 239–250. Springer, Cham (2017). https://doi.org/10.1007/978-3-319-61061-0_16

56. Tsang, P.S., Velazquez, V.L.: Diagnosticity and multidimensional subjective workload ratings. Ergonomics **39**(3), 358–381 (1996). https://doi.org/10.1080/00140139608964470

57. Van Boxtel, A., Goudswaard, P., Van der Molen, G., Van Den Bosch, W.: Changes in electromyogram power spectra of facial and jaw-elevator muscles during fatigue. J. Appl. Physiol. **54**(1), 51–58 (1983). https://doi.org/10.1152/jappl.1983.54.1.51

58. Van Boxtel, A.: Facial EMG as a tool for inferring affective states. In: Proceedings of Measuring Behavior, pp. 104–108. Noldus Information Technology Wageningen (2010)
59. Vanneste, S.: Timing in aging: the role of attention. Exp. Aging Res. **25**(1), 49–67 (1999). https://doi.org/10.1080/036107399244138
60. Voelcker-Rehage, C., Stronge, A.J., Alberts, J.L.: Age-related differences in working memory and force control under dual-task conditions. Aging, Neuropsychol. Cogn. **13**(3–4), 366–384 (2006). https://doi.org/10.1080/138255890969339
61. Warm, J.S., Tripp, L.D., Matthews, G., Helton, W.S.: Cerebral hemodynamic indices of operator fatigue in vigilance. In: Handbook of Operator Fatigue, pp. 197–207 (2012)
62. Welch, P.: The use of fast Fourier transform for the estimation of power spectra: a method based on time averaging over short, modified periodograms. IEEE Trans. Audio Electroacoust. **15**(2), 70–73 (1967). https://doi.org/10.1109/TAU.1967.1161901
63. Wickens, C.D.: Multiple resources and mental workload. Hum. Factors **50**(3), 449–455 (2008). https://doi.org/10.1518/001872008X288394
64. Yeh, Y.Y., Wickens, C.D.: Dissociation of performance and subjective measures of workload. Hum. Factors: J. Hum. Factors Ergon. Soc. **30**(1), 111–120 (1988). https://doi.org/10.1177/001872088803000110
65. Zhang, J.Y., Liu, S.L., Feng, Q.M., Gao, J.Q., Zhang, Q.: Correlative evaluation of mental and physical workload of laparoscopic surgeons based on surface electromyography and eye-tracking signals. Sci. Rep. **7**(1), 11095 (2017). https://doi.org/10.1038/s41598-017-11584-4

Analysing the Impact of Machine Learning to Model Subjective Mental Workload: A Case Study in Third-Level Education

Karim Moustafa[1,2] and Luca Longo[1,2(✉)]

[1] School of Computer Science, Technological University Dublin,
Dublin, Republic of Ireland
[2] ADAPT, The Global Centre of Excellence for Digital Content Technology,
Dublin, Republic of Ireland
luca.longo@dit.ie

Abstract. Mental workload measurement is a complex multidisciplinary research area that includes both the theoretical and practical development of models. These models are aimed at aggregating those factors, believed to shape mental workload, and their interaction, for the purpose of human performance prediction. In the literature, models are mainly theory-driven: their distinct development has been influenced by the beliefs and intuitions of individual scholars in the disciplines of Psychology and Human Factors. This work presents a novel research that aims at reversing this tendency. Specifically, it employs a selection of learning techniques, borrowed from machine learning, to induce models of mental workload from data, with no theoretical assumption or hypothesis. These models are subsequently compared against two well-known subjective measures of mental workload, namely the NASA Task Load Index and the Workload Profile. Findings show how these data-driven models are convergently valid and can explain overall perception of mental workload with a lower error.

1 Introduction

Assessing human mental workload is fundamental in the disciplines of Human-Computer Interaction and Ergonomics [13,53]. Through mental workload, human performance can be predicted and used for designing interacting technologies and systems aligned to the limitations of the human mental limited capabilities [26]. However, despite its theoretical utility, and after decades of research, it is still an umbrella construct [12,21,30]. In the last 50 years, researchers and scholars have devoted their effort to the design and development of models of mental workload that can act as a proxy for assessing human performance [9,15,35,47]. Mental Workload (MWL) is a complex psychological construct, believed to be multi-dimensional and composed of several factors. Various approaches have been developed to measure and to aggregate these factors into

© Springer Nature Switzerland AG 2019
L. Longo and M. C. Leva (Eds.): H-WORKLOAD 2018, CCIS 1012, pp. 92–111, 2019.
https://doi.org/10.1007/978-3-030-14273-5_6

an overall index of mental workload [22,28,50]. The vast majority of these are theory-driven, which means that they utilise theoretical hypothesises and beliefs for assessing MWL deductively. Also, even if theoretically sound, these models are rather ad-hoc and they mainly adopt basic operators for aggregating factors together, with the implicit assumption of their linearity and often additivity. However, it is argued that MWL is far from being a linear phenomenon and the application of non-linear computational approaches can advance its modelling. Additionally, instead of using theoretical knowledge, it is argued that data-driven approaches are likely to offer a significant improvement in the development of models of mental workload [56]. In particular, Machine Learning (ML) is one of these approaches that has been recently considered in MWL modelling. For example, researchers have started applying ML techniques using physiological or task performance measures [51,55]. Other studies employing ML have shown promising results as in [38,40,49].

This research study aims at investigating the impact of supervise modelling techniques, hardly borrowed from machine learning, in the creation of models of MWL by employing subjective self-reporting features from humans. In detail, this study compares traditional subjective models of MWL, namely the NASA Task Load Index (NASA-TLX) [14] and the Workload Profile (WP) [50], against data-driven models produced by a number of ML techniques. Concisely, this paper attempts to answer the research question: *Can machine learning techniques help build data-driven models of mental workload that have a better face validity than the Nasa Task Load Index and the Workload Profile?*

The rest of this paper is organised as follows. Section 2 describes related work in the field of MWL measurement, with an emphasis on subjective approaches. It then discusses the gaps in the literature that motivate the need of non-linear modelling methods for mental workload. Section 3 introduces the design of a comparative study and it describes the research methodology adopted for building data-driven models of mental workload. Section 4 presents the findings and critically evaluates them with a rigorous comparison against the selected MWL baseline instruments, namely the NASA-TLX and the Workload Profile. This comparison is performed by computing the convergent and face validity of the induced MWL models from data. Finally, Sect. 5 concludes the paper by highlighting its contribution and suggesting future work.

2 Related Work

The importance of measuring MWL has arisen from the crucial need of predicting human performance [23,25,26]. In turn, human performance plays a central role in the design of interactive technologies, interfaces as well as educational and instructional material [23,24,27,29,31,36,37]. Measuring mental workload is not a trivial task [48]. Various measures exist, with different advantages and disadvantages, and they can be clustered in three main classes:

- subjective measures - this class refers to the subjective perception of the operator who is executing a specific task or interacting with an underlying system. Subjective measures, also referred to as self-reporting measures, rely on a direct estimation of individual differences such as emotional state, level of stress, the effort devoted to the task and its demand. The perception of users usually can be gathered by means of surveys or questionnaires in the post-task phase [13]. This category includes measures such as the NASA Task Load Index (NASA-TLX) [14], the Workload Profile (WP) [50] based on the Multiple Resource Theory [52], and the Subjective Workload Assessment Technique (SWAT) [42];

- task performance measures - this category includes primary and secondary task measures. These measures focus on quantifying the objective performance of humans in relation to a specific task under execution. Example include the number of errors, the time needed and the resources used to accomplish a task or the reaction time to a secondary task [34];
- physiological measures - this class relies on the analysis of the physiological responses of a human executing a task. Examples include the heart rate, EEG brain signals, eye movements and skin conductivity [4, 35].

Self-reporting subjective measures are based upon the assumption that only the human involved with a task can provide accurate and precise judgements about the experienced mental workload. They are often employed post-task and are easy to be administered. For these reasons, they are appealing to many practitioners and are the focus of this paper. However, they contribute to an overall description of the mental workload experienced on a task with no information about its temporal variation. The category of task performance measures is based upon the belief that the mental workload experienced by an individual becomes relevant only if it impacts system performance. Primary task measures are strongly connected to the concept of performance since they provide objective and quantifiable measures of error or human success. Secondary task measures can be gathered during task execution and are more sensitive to mental workload variation. However, they might influence the execution of the primary task and in turn influence mental workload. The class of physiological measures considers responses of the body gathered from the individual interacting with an underlying task/system. The assumption is that they are highly correlated to mental workload. Their utility lies in the interpretation and analysis of psychological processes and their effect on the state of the body over time, without demanding an explicit response by the human. However, they require specific equipment and trained operators minimising their employability in real-world tasks.

2.1   Subjective Measurements Methods

Two out of the several subjective measures of mental workload developed in the last decades are the NASA Task Load Index (NASA-TLX) [14] and the Workload Profile (WP) [50]. Since these have been selected as baselines in this research study, their detailed description follows. NASA-TLX is a mental workload assessment tool developed by the the National Aeronautics and Space Administration agency. It was originally conceived to assess the mental workload of pilots during aviation tasks. Subsequently, it was adopted in other fields and used as a benchmark in many research studies as for instance in [27,43–46]. The original questionnaire behind this instrument can be found in [14]. The NASA-TLX scale is built upon six dimensions and an additional pair-wise comparison among these dimensions. This comparison is used to give weights to the six dimensions as shown in Eq. 1.

$$NASA - TLX_{MWL} = \left(\sum_{i=1}^{6} d_i \times w_i \right) \frac{1}{15} \tag{1}$$

The Workload Profile (WP) is based on the Multiple Resource Theory (MRT) that was introduced by prof. Wickens [52]. The WP index is derived from eight dimensions: perceptual/central processing, response processing, spatial processing, verbal processing, visual processing, auditory processing, manual responses, and speech responses. In WP, the operator is asked to report the proportion of attentional resources elicited during task execution. The final mental workload score is a sum of the eight factors, as shown in Eq. 2.

$$WP_{MWL} = \sum_{i=1}^{8} d_i \tag{2}$$

For a detailed information about the scales used by the two mental workload instruments described above, the reader is referred to [22].

2.2 Machine Learning and Data-Driven Methods for Mental Workload Modeling

Machine learning (ML) is a subfield of Artificial Intelligence that focuses on creating models from data. It can be seen as a method of data analysis for automated analytical model building. It focuses on automatic procedures than can learn from data and identify patterns with minimal human intervention. ML can be supervised, unsupervised or semi-supervised. On one hand, supervised ML aims to build mathematical models from a set of data that contains both the inputs and the desired output (supervisory data). On the other hand, unsupervised ML takes only input data and it is aimed at finding structures, patterns, and groups or clusters in it. Semi-supervised ML employs both the above learning mechanisms and it occurs when not all the inputs have an associated output. A number of research studies have employed ML for mental workload modeling. For example, [16,41] analysed physiological brain signals, gathered by functional Near-Infrared Spectroscopy (fNIRS), with unsupervised ML. [49] and [40] employed supervised ML respectively using speech data and linguistic/keyboard dynamics of the operators to predict her/his mental workload. [8] and [32] adopted supervised ML for mental workload assessment using features extracted from eye movements. Similarly, supervised ML was used to predict levels of cognitive load in driving tasks employing physiological eye movements and primary task measures such as braking, acceleration, and steering angles [55]. Recently, the multi-model approach of combining multiple physiological measures for mental workload assessment has emerged demonstrating an enhancement over using individual techniques separately [1, 20]. Supervised ML has also been employed with subjective self-reporting data [38] and compared against well-known self-reporting measures.

3 Design and Methodology

In order to tackle the research question formalised in Sect. 1, a comparative research study was designed to evaluate the accuracy of data-driven models, built with supervised machine learning versus two subjective baselines models of mental workload, namely the NASA-TLX and the WP, as shown in Fig. 1. Two criteria for evaluating MWL models have been selected, in line to other studies in the literature [22, 43]: convergent [5] and face validity [39]. The definitions of these two forms of validity adopted here are shown in Table 1. Existing data has been used and the CRISP-DM methodology (Cross-Industry Standard Process for Data Mining) has been followed for constructing MWL models [7].

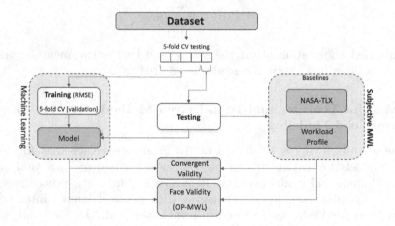

Fig. 1. The design of a comparative study aimed at comparing data-driven models of mental workload, built with supervised machine learning, against two subjective baseline models.

Table 1. Criteria for comparing mental workload models

Name	Description	Statistical tools
Convergent validity	It aims to determine whether different MWL assessment measures are theoretically related	Correlation coefficient of the MWL scores produced my baseline models vs ML models
Face validity	It aims to determine the extent to which a measure can actually grasp the construct of MWL	Error of a MWL model in predicting a self-reported perception of MWL

3.1   Dataset, Context and Participants

The dataset selected for this research study has been formed in an educational context. More specifically, recruited participants were students who attended classes of the *Research Design and Proposal Writing* module, in a master course in the School of Computing, at Dublin Institute of Technology. Four different topics have repeatedly been delivered in four consecutive semesters, from 2015 to 2017. ('Science', 'The Scientific Method', 'Planning Research', 'Literature Review'). These topics were delivered adopting three different instructional formats:

1. The first format focused on the transmission of information with a traditional direct-instruction method – from lecturer to students – by projecting slides on a whiteboard and describing them verbally.
2. The second format included the delivery of the same content, as developed using the first format, as multimedia videos, pre-recorded by the same lecturer. Videos were built by employing the principles of the Cognitive Theory of Multimedia Learning [33]. Further details can be found in [27];
3. The third format included a collaborative activity conducted after the delivery of the video, as developed in the second format. The goal of this activity was to improve the social construction of the information through dialogue among students divided in groups.

The number of classes, their length and the number of students are summarised in Table 2. Students were of 16 nationalities (19–54 years; mean $= 31.7$, std $= 7.5$). For each class, students were randomly split into two groups. They respectively received the questionnaire associated to the NASA-TLX and the WP. In addition to this, students were asked to answer an additional question on overall perception of MWL, hereinafter referred to as the *Overall Perception of Mental Workload (OP-MWL)*, on a discrete scale from 0 to 20 (Fig. 2). Those students who agreed to participate in the experiment received a consent form, approved by the ethics committee of the Dublin Institute of Technology, and a study information sheet. These forms describe the theoretical framework of the study, the confidentiality of the data, and the anonymisation of their personal information. Thus, two sub-datasets were formed, one containing the answers of the NASA-TLX questionnaire, and one related to the answers related to the WP questionnaire, respectively containing 145 and 139 samples.

Table 2. Number of classes for each format, number of students in each class and their length in minutes

Lecture	Format 1			Format 2			Format 3		
	Classes	Students	Mins	Classes	Students	Mins	Classes	Students	Mins
Science	2	14,17	62,60	1	26	18	1	16	60
Scientific method	1	23	46	2	18,18	28,28	1	18	50
Research planning	1	20	54	2	22,22	10,10	1	9	79
Literature review	1	21	55	1	24	19	1	16	77

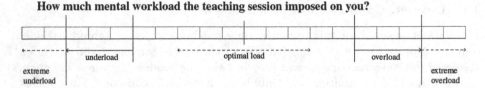

Fig. 2. Scale of the question for measuring the overall perception of mental workload (OP-MWL).

3.2   Machine Learning for Training Mental Workload Models

Supervised machine learning was employed to train models of mental workload from collected data. The dependent feature is the overall perception of mental workload provided by students (OP-MWL) while the independent features are the questions of the NASA-TLX and the WP instruments.

Data Understanding. Three sets of independent features were formed, as described in the summary Table 3. This helped understand the nature of the data and it allowed the investigation of its characteristics, such as the type of features, their values and ranges. The table also shows the normality of the distributions of each feature and its skewness. Figure 3 depicts the distribution of the target variable (the overall perception of mental workload OP-MWL).

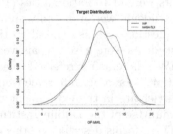

Fig. 3. Distribution of the target variable: the overall perception of mental workload provided by students (OP-MWL).

Data Preparation. The final datasets to be used for training purposes were subsequently constructed. Two datasets were formed:

- *dataset NASA-TLX*: this includes all the NASA-TLX features, in addition to the binary preferences which emerged from the pairwise comparison of the original instrument (Feature sets 1 + 2 of Table 3).
- *dataset WP*: this includes all the eight features of WP (Feature set 3 of Table 3).

The *dataset NASA-TLX* had 41 missing values spotted in 11 records (all in the pair-wise comparison part) so, due to the limited amount of available data, imputation was performed. The *K-Nearest Neighbours* (KNN) algorithm was applied

Table 3. Summary Table (ST) of the dataset features and targets (R = Range, C = Categorical)

	Type	n	Mean	SD	Median	Min	Max	Range	Skew	Kurtosis	SE
Feature set 1: questions of the NASA-TLX											
Mental	R	145	10.04	3.42	10	1	20	19	−0.04	−0.34	0.28
Physical	R	145	6.31	4.19	6	1	20	19	0.63	−0.22	0.35
Temporal	R	145	9.22	3.41	10	1	20	19	−0.01	0.16	0.28
Performance	R	145	8.72	3.73	9	2	17	15	0.17	−0.92	0.31
Frustration	R	145	7.55	3.93	7	1	19	18	0.43	−0.57	0.33
Effort	R	145	9.89	4.02	10	1	20	19	0.13	−0.18	0.33
Feature set 2: pairwise comparisons of the NASA-TLX											
Temporal_vs_frustration	C	145	1.19	0.4	1	1	2	1	1.54	0.37	0.03
Performance_vs_mental	C	145	1.48	0.5	1	1	2	1	0.07	−2.01	0.04
Mental_vs_physical	C	145	1.09	0.29	1	1	2	1	2.84	6.13	0.02
Frustration_vs_performance	C	145	1.81	0.4	2	1	2	1	−1.54	0.37	0.03
Temporal_vs_effort	C	145	1.62	0.49	2	1	2	1	−0.49	−1.77	0.04
Physical_vs_frustration	C	145	1.45	0.5	1	1	2	1	0.21	−1.97	0.04
Performance_vs_temporal	C	145	1.41	0.49	1	1	2	1	0.38	−1.87	0.04
Mental_vs_effort	C	145	1.38	0.49	1	1	2	1	0.49	−1.77	0.04
Physical_vs_temporal	C	145	1.8	0.4	2	1	2	1	−1.48	0.21	0.03
Frustration_vs_effort	C	145	1.79	0.41	2	1	2	1	−1.43	0.05	0.03
Physical_vs_performance	C	145	1.91	0.29	2	1	2	1	−2.84	6.13	0.02
Temporal_vs_mental	C	145	1.7	0.46	2	1	2	1	−0.85	−1.29	0.04
Effort_vs_physical	C	145	1.08	0.28	1	1	2	1	3	7.03	0.02
Frustration_vs_mental	C	145	1.81	0.39	2	1	2	1	−1.6	0.55	0.03
Performance_vs_effort	C	145	1.43	0.5	1	1	2	1	0.26	−1.94	0.04
Feature set 3: questions of the Workload Profile											
Solving_deciding	R	139	11.17	3.93	11	2	20	18	−0.18	−0.51	0.33
Response_selection	R	139	9.92	4.34	10	1	20	19	−0.16	−0.72	0.37
Task_space	R	139	8.74	4.71	9	1	20	19	0.07	−0.96	0.4
Verbal_material	R	139	12.48	3.8	13	2	20	18	−0.57	−0.32	0.32
Visual_resources	R	139	12.24	3.79	13	3	20	17	−0.45	−0.42	0.32
Auditory_resources	R	139	12.78	3.69	13	4	20	16	−0.3	−0.57	0.31
Manual_response	R	139	9.46	5.05	10	1	20	19	−0.03	−0.92	0.43
Speech_response	R	139	8.82	5.03	9	1	20	19	0.14	−0.98	0.43
Dependent features											
$OP - MWL$ (NASA group)	R	145	10.68	3.19	11	2	17	15	−0.41	−0.39	0.27
$OP - MWL$ (WP group)	R	139	10.47	3.37	10	1	18	17	−0.38	−0.19	0.29

to estimate missing values based on the concept of similarity. This algorithm has demonstrated good performance without affecting the quality of data [2,17]. K represents the number of nearest instances to be considered while calculating the missing instance.

Data Modelling. This stage is aimed at inducing models of mental workload by learning from available data rather than making ad-hoc theory-driven models. An assumption made is that the aggregation of those factors believed to model mental workload is non-linear. Tackling the complex problem of MWL modelling, and in the spirit of the *No-Free-Lunch* theorem [54] – stating that there is not one best approach that always outperforms the other – different supervised machine learning algorithms for non-linear regression were chosen. Each learning strategy encodes a distinct set of assumptions, that means different inductive biases. Additionally, a linear method based on probability was also selected for comparison purposes:

- Information-based: Random Forest by Randomization regression (Extra Trees: Extremely Randomized Trees) [11];
- Similarity-based: K-Nearest Neighbours regression [18];
- Error-Based: Support Vector Regression (Radial basis function kernel) [3];
- Probability-based: Bayesian Generalised Linear Model regression [10].

The datasets were randomly split into 5 partitions of equal size, non overlapping. Four of these were used for training purposed (80% of the data) and the held-out set for testing purposes (20%) of the data. The process was repeated 5 times, and at each time, the held-out set was different. The parameters employed in each regression technique have been automatically tuned through a random search approach (number of randomly selected predictors and number of random cuts for extra trees, the number of neighbours for KNN and sigma and regularisation term for SVM) Additionally, 5-fold cross validation has been used in each training phase and the Root Mean Square Error as metric (RMSE) for fitting the overall perception of mental workload (OPMWL). Therefore, one is expected to have 5 *surrogate models*, for each training phase. The best one, that means the one with less RSME, was kept as the *final induced model*. Since, the process was repeated 5 times, as per Fig. 1, one is expected to be left with 5 induced models for each regression technique.

Model Evaluation. In order to evaluate the final induced models from data, the following error metrics are evaluated [6,19]:

- Mean Squared Error (MSE) (Eq. 3). It is the most common metric for the evaluation of regression-based models. The higher the value the worse the model. It is useful if observations contain unexpected value that are important. In case of a single very bad prediction, the squaring will make the error even worse, thus skewing the metric and overestimating the badness of the regression model (range $[0, \infty)$);
- Root Mean Squared Error (RSME) (Eq. 4). It is the square root of the MSE and it has the ability to present the variance on the same scale of the target variable. (range $[0, \infty)$; here $[0, 20]$);
- Mean Absolute Error MAE (Eq. 5). It is a linear score and all the individual differences between expected and predicted outcome are weighted equally in the average. Contrarily to MSE, it is not that sensitive to outliers. (range $[0, \infty)$);

$$MSE = \frac{1}{n} \sum_{i=1}^{n} (y_i - \widehat{y}_i)^2 \tag{3}$$

$$RMSE = \sqrt{\frac{1}{n} \sum_{i=1}^{n} (y_i - \widehat{y}_i)^2} \tag{4}$$

$$MAE = \frac{1}{n} \sum_{i=1}^{n} |(y_i - \widehat{y}_i)| \qquad (5)$$

with y_i is the actual expected value, $\widehat{y}_i$ is the model's prediction.

4 Results and Evaluation

4.1 Accuracy of the Final Induced Models

Figure 4 depicts the box-plots containing the RMSE values for training. According to the previous design, each box plot contains 5 points, one for each final induced model trained with 80% of the data. It can be observed that, in most of the cases, the final induced models, trained with the NASA-TLX features (feature sets $1 + 2$ of Table 3), have always lower RSME than those models built upon the WP features (feature set 3 of Table 3), even if this is not significant. This denotes that the selected regression techniques can train a model similarly and consistently. Also, since it is in the scale $[0, 20]$, it denotes the small error in fitting the target feature (OP-MWL). In fact, errors on average, lies between 1 and 5, across the selected regression techniques, with mean around 3. It can be also noted that the mean of the error of the Bayesian generalised linear models is higher than the others, non-linear model, preliminary confirming the previous hypothesis of non-linearity of the independent features. This means that the non-linear models can better learn the non-linear aggregation of the independent features.

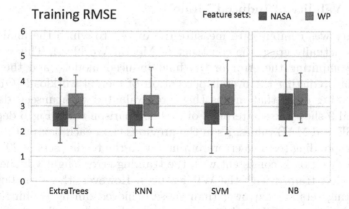

Fig. 4. The distributions of the RSME of the final induced models, grouped by features sets (NASA Task Load Index, Workload Profile). Each bar contains 5 values, one for each model grouped by the regression technique.

4.2 Convergent Validity of the Induced Models

The convergent validity of the induced models is assessed by calculating the Spearman's correlation between their inferred MWL scores, and the scores produced by the baseline models (NASA-TLX, WP) using the testing sets. Figure 5 shows these correlation coefficients in box-plots, each containing 5 values corresponding to the 5 trained models tested with the 5 testing sets of 20% each. The Spearman's correlation statistic was used because the assumptions behind the Pearson's correlation statistics were not met. Generally, a moderate/high positive coefficients have been found (with $p < 0.05$) indicating that the inferences of the induced models, built with machine learning, are valid since they correlate with the baseline models. Also, these results are in line to the recommendation of [5] whereby convergent validities above $\rho = 0.70$ are recommended, whereas those below $\rho = 0.50$ should be avoided.

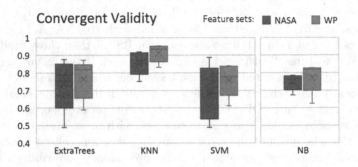

Fig. 5. Convergent validity of the final induced models.

4.3   Face Validity of Induced Models

Face Validity was computed to measure the extent to which the final induced models can actually grasp the construct of Mental Workload. This was determined by computing the error of the final induced models, and the selected baselines, in predicting the overall perception of mental workload (OP-MWL) with the testing data, that means they are evaluated with unseen data. Figures 7, 8 and 9 show the scatterplots of this comparison while Fig. 6 depicts the MSE, RMSE and MAE values. As in the previous case, each box-plot contains 5 values corresponding to the 5 error obtained with the testing sets of 20% each) Firstly, the situation is consistent with the training error: slightly higher for the induced models trained with the WP features. However, the error boundaries for the testing sets are narrower than those achieved during training. In fact, the RSME values, regardless of the regression techniques employed, have mean around 3, with shorter box-plots, suggesting a good degree of generalisability of the induced models. Also it can be seen that the mean of the errors produced by the baseline models is always higher than those produced by the induced models. In other words, the baseline models generate indexes of mental workload that are always more distant to the overall perception of mental workload, reported by subjects, when compared to the distance of the inferences produced by the machine learning models.

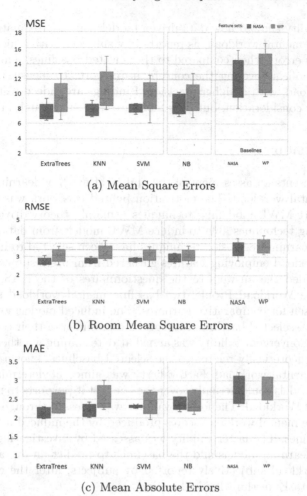

(a) Mean Square Errors

(b) Room Mean Square Errors

(c) Mean Absolute Errors

Fig. 6. The distributions of the errors of the final induced models and baseline models, grouped by features set used (NASA-TLX or Workload Profile). Each bar contains 5 points, one for each model grouped by the regression technique.

4.4   Discussion

Findings are promising and show how subjective mental workload can be modelled with a higher degree of accuracy using data-driven techniques, when compared to traditional subjective techniques, namely the NASA Task Load Index and the Workload Profile, used as baselines. In detail, an analysis of the convergent validity of the data-driven models, learnt from data by employing supervised machine learning regression techniques, against the selected baseline models, show how these are theoretically related. In other words, if we believe that the baseline models actually measure mental workload, so we can do the same with the data-drive models. With this confidence, a subsequent analysis of their face validity showed how data-driven models can approximate the perception of overall mental workload, as reported by subjects, with a higher degree of precision (less error) when compared to the selected baselines. This means that data-driven models covering the concept it purports to measure, that means Mental Workload, with a higher precision. Findings are indeed restricted to the dataset under consideration, but they motivate further research in this space.

5   Conclusion

This work presents an assessment of the ability of machine learning techniques to model mental workload. The motivation behind this work was to shift from state-of-the-art MWL modelling techniques – mainly theory-driven – to automated learning techniques able to induce MWL models from data. Specifically, a number of learning regression techniques have been selected to induce models of mental workload employing features gathered from users subjectively. These features included the answers to the questionnaires of the NASA Task Load Index and the Workload Profile, two baseline mental workload self-reporting measures chosen for comparative purposes. The induced models were compared against the two selected baselines through an assessment of their convergent and face validity. Convergent validity was aimed at determining whether the induced models were theoretically related to the selected baselines, known to model the construct of mental workload. Face validity was aimed at determining whether the induced models could actually cover the concept it purports to measure, that means Mental Workload. The former validity was assessed through a correlation analysis of the mental workload scores produced by the induced models and the selected baselines. The latter validity was assessed by investigating the error of the machine learning models and the baselines to predict an overall perception of mental workload subjectively reported by subjects, after the completion of experimental tasks in third level education.

The findings of this experiment confirm that supervised machine learning algorithms are potential alternatives to traditional theory-driven techniques for modeling mental workload. Machine learning poses itself as a seed for an efficient mechanism that facilitates the understanding of the construct of mental workload, the relationship of its factors and their impact to task performance. A viable direction for future work would be to extend the current experiment with an in depth evaluation of the importance of each feature for predicting the overall perception of mental workload. Subsequently, simpler mental workload models could be created containing the most important features. This can increase the understanding of the complex but fascinating construct of mental workload and contribute towards the ultimate goal of building a highly generalisable model that can be employed across fields, disciplines and experimental contexts.

Appendix

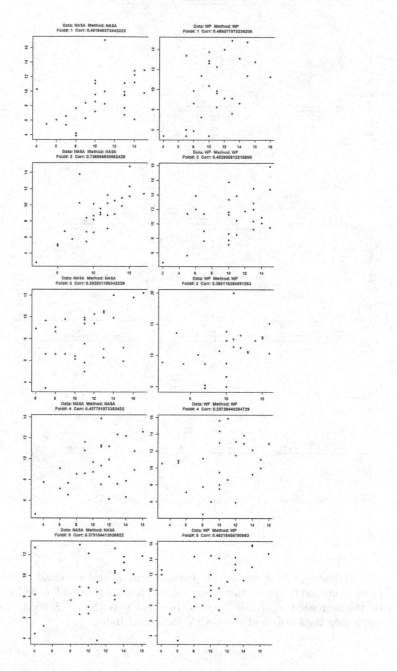

Fig. 7. Scatterplots of the overall perception of mental workload reported by subjects (OP-MWL) (x-axis) and the prediction of the induced models (y-axis) for the NASA-TLX (left) and the Workload Profile (right) grouped by fold

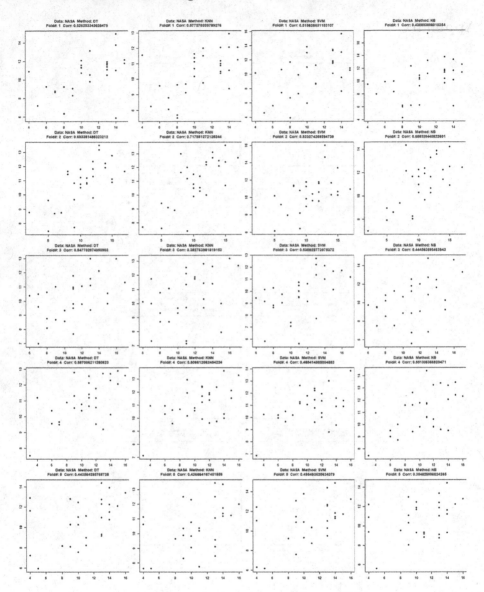

Fig. 8. Scatterplots of the overall perception of mental workload (x-axis), as reported by subjects and the prediction of the induced models (y-axis) for the 5 models produced by the regression algorithms (Extra trees: col 1; KNN: col 2; SVR: col 3; NB: col 4) employing the features of the NASA Task Load Index

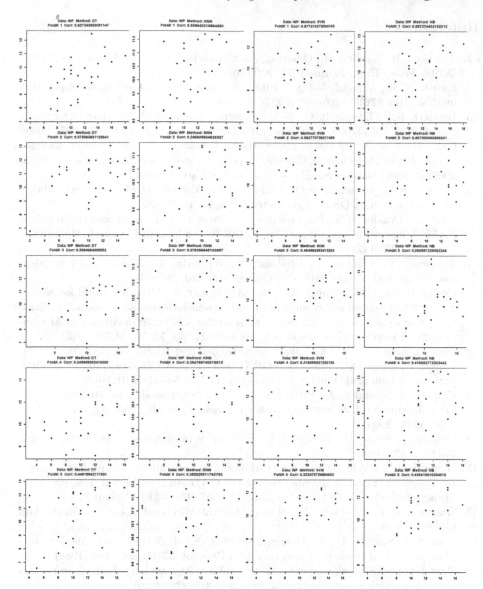

Fig. 9. Scatterplots of the overall perception of mental workload (x-axis), as reported by subjects and the prediction of the induced models (y-axis) for the 5 models produced by the regression algorithms (Extra trees: col 1; KNN: col 2; SVR: col 3; NB: col 4) employing the features of the Workload Profile

References

1. Aghajani, H., Garbey, M., Omurtag, A.: Measuring mental workload with EEG+ fNIRS. Front. Hum. Neurosci. **11**, 359 (2017)
2. Batista, G.E., Monard, M.C.: A study of K-nearest neighbour as an imputation method. HIS **87**(251–260), 48 (2002)
3. Bennett, K.P., Campbell, C.: Support vector machines. ACM SIGKDD Explor. Newsl. **2**(2), 1–13 (2000). http://portal.acm.org/citation.cfm?doid=380995.380999
4. Cain, B.: A review of the mental workload literature. Technical report, Defence Research and Development Canada Toronto Human System Integration Section; 2007. Report Contract No. RTO-TRHFM-121-Part-II (2004)
5. Carlson, K.D., Herdman, A.O.: Understanding the impact of convergent validity on research results. Organ. Res. Methods **15**(1), 17–32 (2012)
6. Chai, T., Draxler, R.R.: Root mean square error (RMSE) or mean absolute error (MAE)?-arguments against avoiding RMSE in the literature. Geosci. Model Dev. **7**(3), 1247–1250 (2014)
7. Chapman, P., Clinton, J., Khabaza, T., Reinartz, T., Wirth, R.: The crisp-dmprocess model. The CRIP–DM Consortium 310 (1999)
8. Cortes Torres, C.C., Sampei, K., Sato, M., Raskar, R., Miki, N.: Workload assessment with eye movement monitoring aided by non-invasive and unobtrusive micro-fabricated optical sensors. In: Adjunct Proceedings of the 28th Annual ACM Symposium on User Interface Software & Technology, pp. 53–54. ACM (2015)
9. Fan, J., Smith, A.P.: The impact of workload and fatigue on performance. In: Longo, L., Leva, M.C. (eds.) H-WORKLOAD 2017. CCIS, vol. 726, pp. 90–105. Springer, Cham (2017). https://doi.org/10.1007/978-3-319-61061-0_6
10. Gelman, A., Jakulin, A., Pittau, M.G., Su, Y.S.: A weakly informative default prior distribution for logistic and other regression models. Ann. Appl. Stat. **2**(4), 1360–1383 (2008)
11. Geurts, P., Ernst, D., Wehenkel, L.: Extremely randomized trees. Mach. Learn. **63**(1), 3–42 (2006)
12. Hancock, P.A.: Whither workload? Mapping a path for its future development. In: Longo, L., Leva, M.C. (eds.) H-WORKLOAD 2017. CCIS, vol. 726, pp. 3–17. Springer, Cham (2017). https://doi.org/10.1007/978-3-319-61061-0_1
13. Hancock, P.A., Meshkati, N.: Human Mental Workload. Elsevier, Amsterdam (1988)
14. Hart, S.G., Staveland, L.E.: Development of NASA-TLX (task load index): results of empirical and theoretical research. Adv. Psychol. **52**(C), 139–183 (1988)
15. Hart, S.G.: NASA-task load index (NASA-TLX); 20 years later. In: Human Factors and Ergonomics Society Annual Meting, pp. 904–908 (2006)
16. Hincks, S.W., Afergan, D., Jacob, R.J.K.: Using fNIRS for real-time cognitive workload assessment. In: Schmorrow, D.D.D., Fidopiastis, C.M.M. (eds.) AC 2016. LNCS (LNAI), vol. 9743, pp. 198–208. Springer, Cham (2016). https://doi.org/10.1007/978-3-319-39955-3_19
17. Jonsson, P., Wohlin, C.: An evaluation of k-nearest neighbour imputation using Likert data. In: 2004 Proceedings of 10th International Symposium on Software Metrics, pp. 108–118, September 2004
18. Kotsiantis, S.B.: Supervised machine learning: a review of classification techniques. Informatica **31**(2), 249–268 (2007). https://books.google.co.in/books?hl=en&lr=&id=vLiTXDHr_sYC&oi=fnd&pg=PA3&dq=survey+machine+learning&ots=CVsyuwYHjo&redir_esc=y#v=onepage&q=survey%20machine%20learning&f=false

19. Kvålseth, T.O.: Cautionary note about R^2. Am. Stat. **39**(4), 279–285 (1985)
20. Liu, Y., Ayaz, H., Shewokis, P.A.: Multisubject "learning" for mental workload classification using concurrent EEG, fNIRS, and physiological measures. Front. Hum. Neurosci. **11**, 389 (2017)
21. Longo, L.: Formalising human mental workload as a defeasible computational concept. Ph.D. thesis, Trinity College, Dublin (2014)
22. Longo, L.: A defeasible reasoning framework for human mental workload representation and assessment. Behav. Inf. Technol. **34**(8), 758–786 (2015)
23. Longo, L.: Designing medical interactive systems via assessment of human mental workload. In: International Symposium on Computer-Based Medical Systems, pp. 364–365 (2015)
24. Longo, L.: Mental workload in medicine: foundations, applications, open problems, challenges and future perspectives. In: 2016 IEEE 29th International Symposium on Computer-Based Medical Systems (CBMS), pp. 106–111. IEEE (2016)
25. Longo, L.: Subjective usability, mental workload assessments and their impact on objective human performance. In: Bernhaupt, R., Dalvi, G., Joshi, A., Balkrishan, D.K., O'Neill, J., Winckler, M. (eds.) INTERACT 2017. LNCS, vol. 10514, pp. 202–223. Springer, Cham (2017). https://doi.org/10.1007/978-3-319-67684-5_13
26. Longo, L.: Experienced mental workload, perception of usability, their interaction and impact on task performance. PloS ONE **13**(8), 1–36 (2018). https://doi.org/10.1371/journal.pone.0199661
27. Longo, L.: On the reliability, validity and sensitivity of three mental workload assessment techniques for the evaluation of instructional designs: a case study in a third-level course. In: Proceedings of the 10th International Conference on Computer Supported Education, CSEDU 2018, Funchal, Madeira, Portugal, 15–17 March 2018, vol. 2, pp. 166–178 (2018). https://doi.org/10.5220/0006801801660178
28. Longo, L., Barrett, S.: Cognitive effort for multi-agent systems. In: Yao, Y., Sun, R., Poggio, T., Liu, J., Zhong, N., Huang, J. (eds.) BI 2010. LNCS (LNAI), vol. 6334, pp. 55–66. Springer, Heidelberg (2010). https://doi.org/10.1007/978-3-642-15314-3_6
29. Longo, L., Dondio, P.: On the relationship between perception of usability and subjective mental workload of web interfaces. In: 2015 IEEE/WIC/ACM International Conference on Web Intelligence and Intelligent Agent Technology (WI-IAT), vol. 1, pp. 345–352. IEEE (2015)
30. Longo, L., Leva, M.C. (eds.): H-WORKLOAD 2017. CCIS, vol. 726. Springer, Cham (2017). https://doi.org/10.1007/978-3-319-61061-0
31. Longo, L., Rusconi, F., Noce, L., Barrett, S.: The importance of human mental workload in web-design. In: 8th International Conference on Web Information Systems and Technologies, pp. 403–409, April 2012
32. Mannaru, P., Balasingam, B., Pattipati, K., Sibley, C., Coyne, J.: Cognitive context detection in UAS operators using eye-gaze patterns on computer screens. In: Next-Generation Analyst IV, vol. 9851, p. 98510F. International Society for Optics and Photonics (2016)
33. Mayer, R.E.: Cognitive theory of multimedia learning, 2nd edn. In: Cambridge Handbooks in Psychology, pp. 43–71. Cambridge University Press, Cambridge (2014)
34. Meshkati, N., Loewenthal, A.: An eclectic and critical review of four primary mental workload assessment methods: a guide for developing a comprehensive model. Adv. Psychol. **52**(1978), 251–267 (1988). http://www.sciencedirect.com/science/article/pii/S0166411508623912

35. Mijović, P., Milovanović, M., Ković, V., Gligorijević, I., Mijović, B., Mačužić, I.: Neuroergonomics method for measuring the influence of mental workload modulation on cognitive state of manual assembly worker. In: Longo, L., Leva, M.C. (eds.) H-WORKLOAD 2017. CCIS, vol. 726, pp. 213–224. Springer, Cham (2017). https://doi.org/10.1007/978-3-319-61061-0_14

36. Mohammadi, M., Mazloumi, A., Kazemi, Z., Zeraati, H.: Evaluation of mental workload among ICU ward's nurses. Health Promot. Perspect. 5(4), 280–7 (2015). http://www.ncbi.nlm.nih.gov/pubmed/26933647, http://www.pubmedcentral.nih.gov/articlerender.fcgi?artid=PMC4772798

37. Monfort, S.S., Sibley, C.M., Coyne, J.T.: Using machine learning and real-time workload assessment in a high-fidelity UAV simulation environment. In: Next-Generation Analyst IV, vol. 9851, p. 98510B. International Society for Optics and Photonics (2016)

38. Moustafa, K., Luz, S., Longo, L.: Assessment of mental workload: a comparison of machine learning methods and subjective assessment techniques. In: Longo, L., Leva, M.C. (eds.) H-WORKLOAD 2017. CCIS, vol. 726, pp. 30–50. Springer, Cham (2017). https://doi.org/10.1007/978-3-319-61061-0_3

39. Nevo, B.: Face validity revisited. J. Educ. Meas. 22(4), 287–293 (1985)

40. Ott, T., Wu, P., Paullada, A., Mayer, D., Gottlieb, J., Wall, P.: ATHENA – a zero-intrusion no contact method for workload detection using linguistics, keyboard dynamics, and computer vision. In: Stephanidis, C. (ed.) HCI 2016. CCIS, vol. 617, pp. 226–231. Springer, Cham (2016). https://doi.org/10.1007/978-3-319-40548-3_38

41. Pham, T.T., Nguyen, T.D., Van Vo, T.: Sparse fNIRS feature estimation via unsupervised learning for mental workload classification. In: Bassis, S., Esposito, A., Morabito, F.C., Pasero, E. (eds.) Advances in Neural Networks. SIST, vol. 54, pp. 283–292. Springer, Cham (2016). https://doi.org/10.1007/978-3-319-33747-0_28

42. Reid, G.B., Nygren, T.E.: The subjective workload assessment technique: a scaling procedure for measuring mental workload. In: Advances in Psychology, vol. 52, pp. 185–218. Elsevier (1988)

43. Rizzo, L., Dondio, P., Delany, S.J., Longo, L.: Modeling mental workload via rule-based expert system: a comparison with NASA-TLX and workload profile. In: Iliadis, L., Maglogiannis, I. (eds.) AIAI 2016. IAICT, vol. 475, pp. 215–229. Springer, Cham (2016). https://doi.org/10.1007/978-3-319-44944-9_19

44. Rizzo, L., Longo, L.: Representing and inferring mental workload via defeasible reasoning: a comparison with the NASA task load index and the workload profile. In: Proceedings of the 1st Workshop on Advances In Argumentation In Artificial Intelligence Co-located with XVI International Conference of the Italian Association for Artificial Intelligence (AI * IA 2017), Bari, Italy, 16–17 November 2017, pp. 126–140 (2017)

45. Rizzo, L., Longo, L.: Inferential models of mental workload with defeasible argumentation and non-monotonic fuzzy reasoning: a comparative study. In: Proceedings of the 2nd Workshop on Advances In Argumentation In Artificial Intelligence Co-located with XVII International Conference of the Italian Association for Artificial Intelligence (AI*IA 2018), Trento, Italy, 20–23 November 2018, pp. 11–26 (2018)

46. Rubio, S., Díaz, E., Martín, J., Puente, J.M.: Evaluation of subjective mental workload: a comparison of swat, NASA-TLX, and workload profile methods. Appl. Psychol. 53(1), 61–86 (2004). https://doi.org/10.1111/j.1464-0597.2004.00161.x

47. Smith, A.P., Smith, H.N.: Workload, fatigue and performance in the rail industry. In: Longo, L., Leva, M.C. (eds.) H-WORKLOAD 2017. CCIS, vol. 726, pp. 251–263. Springer, Cham (2017). https://doi.org/10.1007/978-3-319-61061-0_17

48. Smith, K.T.: Observations and issues in the application of cognitive workload modelling for decision making in complex time-critical environments. In: Longo, L., Leva, M.C. (eds.) H-WORKLOAD 2017. CCIS, vol. 726, pp. 77–89. Springer, Cham (2017). https://doi.org/10.1007/978-3-319-61061-0_5

49. Su, J., Luz, S.: Predicting cognitive load levels from speech data. In: Esposito, A., et al. (eds.) Recent Advances in Nonlinear Speech Processing. SIST, vol. 48, pp. 255–263. Springer, Cham (2016). https://doi.org/10.1007/978-3-319-28109-4_26

50. Tsang, P.S., Velazquez, V.L.: Diagnosticity and multidimensional subjective workload ratings. Ergonomics 39(3), 358–381 (1996)

51. Walter, C., Cierniak, G., Gerjets, P., Rosenstiel, W., Bogdan, M.: Classifying mental states with machine learning algorithms using alpha activity decline. In: 2011 Proceedings of 19th European Symposium on Artificial Neural Networks, ESANN 2011, Bruges, Belgium, April 27–29 (2011). https://www.elen.ucl.ac.be/Proceedings/esann/esannpdf/es2011-35.pdf

52. Wickens, C.D.: Multiple resources and mental workload. Hum. Factors 50(3), 449–455 (2008)

53. Wickens, C.D.: Mental workload: assessment, prediction and consequences. In: Longo, L., Leva, M.C. (eds.) H-WORKLOAD 2017. CCIS, vol. 726, pp. 18–29. Springer, Cham (2017). https://doi.org/10.1007/978-3-319-61061-0_2

54. Wolpert, D.H.: The supervised learning no-free-lunch theorems. In: Roy, R., Köppen, M., Ovaska, S., Furuhashi, T., Hoffmann, F. (eds.) Soft Computing and Industry, pp. 25–42. Springer, London (2002). https://doi.org/10.1007/978-1-4471-0123-9_3

55. Yoshida, Y., Ohwada, H., Mizoguchi, F., Iwasaki, H.: Classifying cognitive load and driving situation with machine learning. Int. J. Mach. Learn. Comput. 4(3), 210–215 (2014)

56. Young, M.S., Brookhuis, K.A., Wickens, C.D., Hancock, P.A.: State of science: mental workload in ergonomics. Ergonomics 58(1), 1–17 (2015)

Measuring the Mental Workload of Operators of Highly Automated Vehicles

Kristen Fernández Medina[(✉)]

TRL, Crowthorne House, Nine Mile Ride, Wokingham RG40 3GA, UK
kfernandez@trl.co.uk

Abstract. As vehicle automation continues to develop, and as the nature of the driver's role begins to shift from vehicle operator to vehicle supervisor, it will be important to understand the task requirements in order to ensure a safe and effective transition between the system and the human operator. As the first to encounter highly automated vehicles, test drivers (the operators being deployed to monitor driverless vehicles being trialed around the world) will present an important case study to better understand the task demand placed on operators when monitoring an automated vehicle, particularly in relation to the workload demands. This study, albeit small scale, presents some of the first evidence relating to the interaction between a driverless system and a human operator in a real-world environment. The study found that test drivers experienced variable levels of subjective workload and that, to some extent, this may relate to their experience of the automated system and exposure to the operator task. Future, more robust, research is recommended to better understand the workload demand and implications on vehicle design and training.

Keywords: Driverless vehicles · Automation · NASA-RTLX ·
Mental workload · Driving task

1 Introduction

Automated vehicles (AV) are quickly becoming a reality. As businesses in countries around the world work hard to develop driverless vehicle systems, services and service models, many questions continue to arise regarding the impact of the deployment of these vehicles on people and society. While much of the current efforts have focused on the technological innovation, rather than the implications of increased vehicle automation, it is clear that the role of the driver (and the driving task) will undergo a significant transformation. This is one of the most discussed potential benefits of increased automation to road safety as research has suggested that over 90% of all vehicle collisions have human error as a contributory factor [1, 2]. The expectation is, therefore (in theory), that by removing the human from the driving task significant safety benefits can be achieved. This said, vehicle technology to be widely adopted at the start of the AV rollout is likely to involve vehicles with conditional (e.g. SAE Level 3) and high (e.g. SAE Level 4) automation that are restricted to perform under specific conditions (and routes) by their operational design domain (ODD). Conditionally automated vehicles will still require an 'operator' to resume control of the vehicle

L. Longo and M. C. Leva (Eds.): H-WORKLOAD 2018, CCIS 1012, pp. 112–128, 2019.
https://doi.org/10.1007/978-3-030-14273-5_7

in situations that are outside of the ODD and in emergencies. Moreover, the current regulatory framework in the United Kingdom has no provision for vehicles to be operated without a human driver. Until then, the Department for Transport has developed a code of practice for real-world testing of driverless vehicles which outlines general safety, insurance, infrastructure and engagement requirements. One such requirements is the use of a 'test driver'; the test driver being the person *"responsible for ensuring the safe operation of the vehicle at all times whether it is in a manual or automated mode."* [3, p. 9].

Although the requirement for a test driver in the UK is expected to change in due course, this requirement has already been relaxed in some countries such as the United States (where states such as California and Arizona have signed executive orders that allow testing of driverless vehicles without a test driver). There is, however, little evidence to shed light on what exactly the role of the test driver (and later, the vehicle 'operator') entails and what mental processes might be involved in the monitoring task as we ease into higher levels of vehicle automation. As such, there are still important questions about the relative safety of making a human operator responsible for an AV, as well as whether the test driver is an important safety mitigation that should be in place until the technology matures.

As the first to experience the technology from an operator's point of view, test drivers will provide an invaluable source of information and evidence in relation to the demands placed on operators of AVs. As such, understanding the experiences and challenges of test drivers, the task requirements, and how it may evolve as technology matures will have important implications on the wider roll-out of vehicles with conditional and high automation.

1.1 Study Aims

Given the limited availability of evidence relating to the changing role of the driver and the relative task complexity for operators of AVs in a real-world environment, the present study sought to undertake an initial assessment of the mental demand placed on test drivers using a sample of operators taking part in one of Europe's first AV public trials.

The research questions of interest were, therefore, as follows:

1. What is the mental workload demand placed on test drivers operating the trial vehicles?
2. How does experience and exposure impact on the perceived task demand?

In order to contextualize the work further, the present paper will start by providing an overview of related work in the field of automation and mental workload, including why mental workload is relevant to this field of study (Sect. 2). Section 3 will describe the sample and method used to undertake the study and the research findings. Lastly, Sect. 4 and Sect. 5 will discuss the research findings in the context of current evidence, before highlighting the limitations to the work and areas for future research in Sect. 6.

2 Related Work

2.1 The Interaction Between Human Drivers and Automated Systems

Currently, prototype AVs being developed will be capable of SAE L3 or L4 automation. Conditional automation (L3) specifically, has received widespread attention as the technology would still require a human to remain in the loop of the driving task. As such, the issues highlighted in the research literature range from the ability to respond to immediate events, to the changing demands of the driving task. Both are briefly discussed in this section.

At a basic level, one important issue that has been discussed in the literature is the notion that the driver would be required to regain control of the vehicle in situations where the vehicle design is limited by its ODD (planned transfer) or where the system is unable to deal with a particular scenario or event (abrupt transfer). The transfer of control can be defined as an activation or deactivation of a function, or a change from a level of automation to another [4]. Simply put, this entails the process by which the vehicle system requires the driver to retake control over the driving task or vice versa. Much research in this area has focused on understanding the skills involved in effectively regaining control of the vehicle after a transition (especially when the driver has been out of the loop) [5].

The reduction in the amount of input required by the driver throughout the driving task may also lead to de-skilling. Conditional automation will still require drivers to retain an acceptable level of skill to enable a safe and effective response to gaps or failures in the automated driving system (ADS) [6]. Reason (1990) [in 6] describes the issue with what he calls the 'catch 22' of increased automation, this is that humans are only present in automated systems to deal with emergencies. This is problematic as research indicates that increased vehicle automation will necessarily result in limited opportunities to practice procedural responses required to undertake the driving task effectively [6, 7].

One of the most significant challenges, however, is the changing demands of the driving task as a result of increased automation; particularly, the change in the role of the driver from vehicle operator to automation supervisor. This change presents a number of challenges to safety, and early research into the relationship between humans and automated systems suggests that humans may be ill-suited to undertake monitoring tasks [6]. Similarly, some research has suggested that human-machine task sharing can be inefficient and lead to poor outcomes. A study by Ensley and Kaber showed decrements in the speed and accuracy of task performance as a result of the human operator being out of the loop during crucial decision-making tasks [8]. Some argue that automation can lead to improved task performance outcomes; for example, Parasuraman [9] (in a paper considering the factors that affect the monitoring of an automated task) presents evidence from the aviation industry to argue that human monitoring can be very effective and lead to a reduction in errors; this is particularly the case when automation is used as an aid to task performance in an increased workload scenario. Nevertheless, the ultimate goal of AVs is not to aid in the driving task (this is more the case of advanced driver assistance systems) rather to eventually take it over completely.

Altogether, overcoming these and other challenges will require extensive research and continuous revision of the changes to the driving task as AV technology continues to advance. A good starting point will be the assessment of the demand placed on operators as they supervise AVs. The study of mental workload, in particular, can provide insights into other fields where automation is widespread (e.g. aviation) and how to design systems and training that will enable humans to interact with AVs safety and effectively [10].

2.2   Mental Workload

Providing a universally accepted definition of the construct of mental workload has been a difficult task [10, 12]. Workload has been defined as *"a hypothetical construct that represents the cost incurred by a human operator to achieve a particular level of performance"* [10]. However, operational definitions used across studies (and fields of study) vary considerably, with some definitions of mental workload referring to a mental process in itself, for example, Eggeimer, Wilson and colleagues [in 11] define it as *"...the portion of operator information processing capacity or resources that is actually required to meet system demands."*; while others seem to characterize workload as an outcome of one or multiple processes, e.g. *"... the cost of performing a task in terms of a reduction in the capacity to perform that use the same processing resource."* [in 11]. Wickens [13] on the other hand, uses the term 'mental workload' and 'effort' interchangeably, in the context of decision-making. Despite these differences, the general consensus seems to indicate that mental workload relates to the relationship between task demand and the relative capacity of a human being to perform the task effectively and within a given period of time; in addition, the current definitions suggest that the relative success in performance will often incur in a mental 'cost'.

The lack of a commonly held definition results in challenges when it comes to empirically measuring mental workload, though a number of strategies are widely applied in research. The three broad categories or workload measurement techniques are self-assessments, performance measures and physiological measures [11, 14, 15]. All of these measurement techniques are regularly applied in transport research, though self-assessment tools such as the NASA-Task Load index (TLX) and NASA - Raw TLX (RTLX) [15, 16] are common in applied research. This is likely to be due to the multidimensionality, sensitivity, ease of administration, and high user acceptability of this previously validated scale [11, 17] and as such, these have been widely applied in research with different road user populations [e.g. 18].

2.3   The Role of Mental Workload for Driving Performance

Driving is a dynamic and continuously changing task [19]. It has generally been assumed that increased vehicle automation will mean a lower task demand (e.g. workload) for drivers (and, later, operators) as they will no longer be required to actively participate in the driving task. For example, in a recent meta-analysis, de Winter and colleagues found that mental workload was significantly reduced in conditions involving high automation [20]; it was found that the unweighted mean of self-reported workload (on the NASA-TRLX) was lowest for highly automated driving (23%), compared to adaptive cruise control (39%) and manual driving (44%). The analysis was based on data from 32 studies.

Another set of studies by Saxby et al. [21], though focused on task-induced fatigue, sought to understand different styles of workload regulation while performing a simulated driving task. The studies, involving over 250 undergraduate students, showed that 'passive' fatigue (defined as that which develops when there is a requirement for system monitoring with either rare or no overt perceptual-motor requirements), as induced by full vehicle automation, corresponded with a decline in task engagement and with cognitive underload. The authors also found that it was passive fatigue that showed an increased crash probability; this was measured as the ability to avoid collision with a parked van that unexpectedly pulled out in front of the participants during the simulation. That said, arguably, the tasks may not be directly comparable from a vehicle automation point of view as the 'active' fatigue (defined as the state change resulting from continuous and prolonged task-related psychomotor adjustment) condition was unrelated to the driving task having been induced by wind gusts.

There is also evidence that supports the notion that increased vehicle automation may lead to cognitive overload. This is particularly the case when drivers are required to regain control of the vehicle in an abrupt or unexpected situation. Young and Stanton state that workload may be increased as a result of an additional tasks placed on the operator to collect (and potentially act upon) information about the automated system state [7].

3   Design and Method

As a new area of research where there are very limited opportunities for the task of interest to be performed and evaluated, a small-scale repeated measures design study was employed to assess self-reported workload of test drivers across three weeks of trial activities. This study involved a small sample (n = 9) of trained test drivers.

3.1   Source of Participants

Study participants were sourced from the GATEway project. GATEway (Greenwich automated transport environment) was an £8 m project partly funded by Government and Industry. The project sought to better understand how automated vehicles can fit into our future urban mobility needs and the barriers we must overcome before these vehicles become a reality on UK roads. The project began in late 2015 and concluded in April 2018.

As part of the GATEway project, four prototype SAE Level 4 shuttles[1] were deployed on a 3.6 km route along the Greenwich Peninsula in London. The route included four designated pod stops where, as the first open trial of AVs, members of the public were able to board or alight the vehicle. A full run of the route consisted on a

---

[1] The Society of Automotive Engineers (SAE) has published a set of definitions for six levels of vehicle automation, from level '0' (No automation) to level '5' (full automation). Level 4 is where the vehicle's driving automation system is designed to function within an operational design domain (ODD); this is, the vehicle is capable of performing autonomously under certain conditions such as geographic, traffic and/or speed limitations.

return trip to/from the starting point (the Intercontinental hotel) and took around 30 min. The vehicle had a four person occupancy (including the test driver) and was wheelchair accessible. The trials ran for four weeks (on week days), with multiple daily operations (from 10:30 am to 5:30 pm).

Research Sample. The sample of interest was the team of trained test drivers who were tasked with operating the vehicles during the public trials. As part of the trial activities, a dedicated team of test drivers was trained in the vehicle operations and maintenance. Test drivers received a day of 'classroom' training as well as various hours (depending on individual need) of supervised hands-on experience with the driverless pods, before receiving formal approval from the vehicle integrators. The classroom training included information about the vehicles, the automated driving system (ADS) and safe operating boundaries, and rules and regulations applicable to them as test drivers.

Once approved, test drivers undertook several 1 or 2 h shifts (with breaks in between) on trial days. During these shifts, test drivers were responsible for one of the trial pods over the 3.6 km route and carrying passengers to/from one of the four designated pod stops.

3.2 Materials

The main data collection tool was the NASA Raw Task Load Index (RTLX) [15]. The RTLX is used to obtain workload estimates from 'operators' while they are performing a task or immediately afterwards [16]. According to a review by Hart in 2006, the range of applications for the NASA-TLX, and the subsequent unweighted version RTLX, has far surpassed its original application. The NASA-TLX has been often used in transport to assess subjective workload in drivers and riders [18, 22].

The RTLX evaluates six factors: mental demands, physical demands, temporal demands, performance, and effort and frustration levels. Each of these factors is scored with a minimum value of 1 and a maximum value of 21. Higher numbers represent higher levels of workload. A brief explanation of each subscale is provided in Table 1.

Table 1. RTLX rating scales and definitions [16]

Rating scale	Scale definition
Mental demand	How much mental and perceptual activity was required (e.g. thinking, deciding, etc.)? Was the task easy or demanding, simple or complex, exacting or forgiving?
Physical demand	How much physical activity was required (e.g. controlling, activating, etc.)? Was the task easy or demanding, slow or brisk, slack or strenuous, restful or laborious?
Temporal demand	How much time pressure did you feel due to the rate or pace at which the task or task elements occurred? Was the pace slow and leisurely or rapid and frantic?

(*continued*)

Table 1. (*continued*)

Rating scale	Scale definition
Effort	How hard did you have to work (mentally and physically) to accomplish your level of performance?
Performance	How successful do you think you were in accomplishing the goals of the task? How satisfied were you with your performance in accomplishing these goals?
Frustration	How insecure, discouraged, irritated, stressed, and annoyed versus secure, gratified, content, relaxed and complacent did you feel during the task?

3.3   Procedure

It is important to note that this research was not the primary objective of the trial activities. As such, some flexibility was required when collecting data from participants who were also trial staff. The research study began during the second week of the trial activities. At the start, participants were provided with an information sheet detailing the purpose of the research and the likely requirements on their time; participants were also informed of their ability to withdraw from the study at any point (the latter was particularly important as the sample was part of the trial staff, and may have felt unduly pressured to take part in the research). They were also provided with a consent form (in both paper and electronic formats) to enable easy access. Participants were asked to complete a weekly assessment of subjective workload using the RTLX. They were also asked to provide the following:

- Information about the number of shifts completed each week
- Any notable features of their experience as a test driver during that week (open text response)

As the task was not being performed for the purpose of this study, the time at which participants completed the assessment was variable. Participants self-completed the assessment during breaks between shifts or at the end of their last shift. Participants completed the assessment either on an electronic or paper copy. Assessments were completed for three of the four trial weeks.

Analysis. Average self-reported workload ratings were assessed. Given the small size of the sample and the gaps in data received from participants from week to week, further statistical analysis was not possible.

4   Results

4.1   Sample

A total of nine participants took part in the study. Five participants provided responses for at least 2 weeks; a further two provided responses for all 3 weeks. Two participants only provided data for one week.

4.2 Workload Ratings

The average workload ratings provided by participants can be seen in Fig. 1.

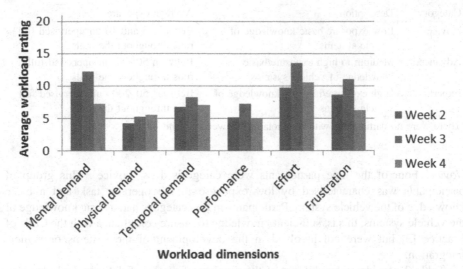

Fig. 1. Workload ratings for all participants (n = 9), by week

Average workload ratings ranged between 4.3 (physical demand) and 10.6 (mental demand) on week 2; for week 3, between 5.2 for physical demand and 13.5 for effort. On week 4, average workload ratings were between 5 (performance) and 10.5 (effort).

Test Driver Categories. As the subjective workload ratings varied significantly between participants, further investigation was undertaken to understand possible differences. As a result, participants were grouped into three categories, depending on their exposure and knowledge of the trial vehicles. As such:

- Exposure was operationalized as participants' self-reported number of unsupervised runs completed throughout the duration of the trials. A run consisted of a full loop of the 3.6 km test route. Runs undertaken during the training process (i.e. supervised runs) were not included in the totals as test drivers would have been accompanied and closely monitored by an instructor;
- Knowledge of the trial vehicles was assessed based on the author's subjective assessment of the test driver's amount of supervised practice and technical expertise.

The categories are described in Table 2.

Table 2. Test driver categories

Category	Description	Average exposure
Novice	Low exposure/basic knowledge of vehicle systems	Between 3 and 10 unsupervised full runs throughout the trials
Advanced	Medium to high exposure/basic knowledge of vehicle systems	Between 50–69[a] unsupervised full runs throughout the trials
Expert	High exposure/in-depth knowledge of vehicle systems	Between 50–200+ unsupervised full runs throughout the trials

[a]There were no participants with runs totaling between 11 and 49 runs.

Novice. Four of the nine participants were categorised as 'novice'. This group of participants was characterised by low exposure to the operator task and a basic knowledge of the vehicle system. Participants in this category had a basic knowledge of the vehicle systems; this is, sufficient knowledge to ensure compliance with the Code of Practice [3] but were not involved in the development of the systems or vehicle integration.

Table 3 provides a breakdown of the number of weeks of data available for participants in this category. As can be seen, three participants provided at least two weeks of data; one provided only 1 week of data.

Table 3. Number of weeks of data provided by 'novice' category participants

	Data provided, per week		
Participant no.	Week 2	Week 3	Week 4
1	X	X	
2	X	X	
3	X		X
7	X		

The average workload ratings for each scale provided by participants in this category can be seen in Fig. 2.

Scores on the physical demand scale had the lowest weekly averages, while mental demand, effort and frustration exhibited the highest scores among this group. As only one participant provided data for week 4, this will not be considered further.

Advanced. Three of the 9 participants were categorised as 'advanced'. This group of participants was characterised by medium to high exposure to the operator task. These participants, similarly to the 'novice' group, had a basic knowledge of the vehicle systems. They were also not involved in the development of the systems or vehicle integration.

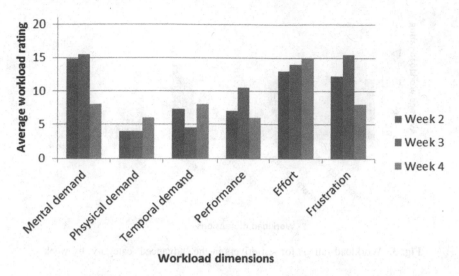

Fig. 2. Workload ratings for test drivers in the 'novice' category, by week

Table 4 provides a breakdown of the number of weeks of data available for participants in this category. As can be seen, two participants provided 3 weeks of data; one provided only 1 week of data.

Table 4. Number of weeks of data provided by 'advanced' category participants

	Data provided, per week		
Participant no.	Week 2	Week 3	Week 4
6	X	X	X
9	X	X	X
8			X

The average workload ratings provided by participants in this category can be seen in Fig. 3.

For this group, scores on the performance scale had the lowest weekly averages, while temporal demand and effort exhibited the highest scores. Overall average workload scores were lower for this group, compared to the novice group. Looking at the data across the three weeks, the self-reported scores seem to indicate a general downward trend in the self-reported workload scores. On the second week, however, the average scores for effort seem to have increased slightly.

Expert. Two of the nine participants were categorised as 'expert'. This group of participants was characterised by very high exposure to the operator task. These participants also had an in-depth and detailed knowledge of the vehicle systems. The average workload ratings provided by participants in this category can be seen in Fig. 4. Due to

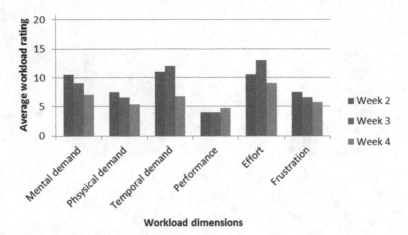

Fig. 3. Workload ratings for test drivers in the 'advanced' category, by week

the pre-existing commitments of delivering the trials, 'expert' participants were only able to provide one week of data (e.g. week 2).

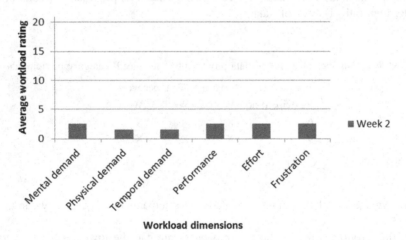

Fig. 4. Workload ratings for test drivers in the 'expert' category, week 2

5 Discussion

The assessment of workload on the task of operating a driverless vehicle is a new concept. While much research has been conducted in aviation (where there are high levels of system automation) throughout the years, little is known about the real-world task demand of operating a highly automated vehicle on humans. This research, albeit limited in design and scope, has provided some initial data about the self-reported workload experienced by a group of trained test drivers. The data provides some support for existing evidence which suggests that operating a driverless vehicle may induce states of both low and high workload. The implications of these findings are briefly discussed in the sections below.

5.1   Overall Workload Ratings

The most interesting evidence emerged from the classification of test drivers based on their exposure and knowledge of the systems. The data showed that participants classified as 'novice' – this is, those with low exposure (fewer unsupervised runs) and with a more basic knowledge of the system - had higher workload scores for most scales of the RTLX. In addition, the findings showed no evidence of a temporal effect on the workload experienced from week 2 to week 3, as scores on most subscales did not decrease from one week to another. Probably unsurprisingly, participants in the 'novice' group experienced higher levels of frustration and mental demand, compared to other groups. Ratings of frustration were likely a result of the reduced experience with the task and thus increased levels of insecurity and stress when performing the task. For the advanced group, the data indicated that there was a tendency towards a reduction of the self-reported workload from week 2 to week 4. Temporal demand and effort, however, remained (and even saw a slight increase) from week 2 to week 3. The expert group, despite only providing 1 week of data, showed the lowest workload scores in all groups.

A visual inspection of these two groups indicates that there is some evidence that exposure may have an impact on self-reported workload, with 'advanced' test drivers exhibiting a trend toward reduction in workload scores from week to week. Despite this, a qualitative assessment of the scores indicates workload scores for advanced and novice test drivers were similar. This may indicate that some demands of the task could not be accounted for by experience of performing the task, at least in the time period that this study could account for. These results have implications in the short and medium term, when considering the testing and deployment of driverless vehicles – particularly SAE L3 (when a driver is still likely to be required to remain in the loop).

5.2   The Test Driver

Test drivers are being deployed in trials all over the world as a key safety mitigation. It is assumed that having a human in the 'driver' seat will help ensure the safety of the vehicles being deployed in trial settings. While the findings of this work do not contradict this notion, it provides useful evidence to support future training requirements. Firstly, it is clear that the perceived task demand is not consistent across test drivers and increased exposure (practice) may only have a limited impact on reducing the perceived workload. Some evidence for this can be derived from the moderate to high perceived workload reported by both novices and advanced test drivers on some subscales (particularly for mental demand and effort).

Mental workload involves tasks such as looking, searching and acting upon emerging information. The vehicles that are being deployed as part of trials around the world are undertaking journeys in public spaces (whether public or private roads or paths) and as such, the operators need to monitor the presence and distance of pedestrians, cyclist and other road users. They also need to maintain the safety of the vehicles as they may still be liable, as vehicle operators, if an incident were to occur while they were 'in control' of the vehicle. Increased workload may also have an impact on fatigue, which must be considered when setting the appropriate duration of test driver shifts. In order to mitigate for this, during the GATEway trials shifts were not to exceed two hours in duration. It is possible that this may need to be monitored more closely, particularly for test drivers that are less experienced with the systems in question.

The data also showed that increased exposure to the task reduced workload. While overload can lead to fatigue, underload can also be problematic when it comes to task performance. Underload, particularly when this occurs as a result of complacency (or overreliance on automation) can also lead to failures in performance. Some research highlights how excessive trust can lead operators to fail to appropriately monitor an automated task; this failure has been implicated in a number of aviation incidents [9]. The author also makes some recommendations for strategies that can help avoid overreliance on automation, for example requiring some level of active operator involvement in the automated processes. Overall, test drivers should not be deployed without consideration for the task demand and the strategies that should be implemented to counteract for issues such as overload, fatigue and possible complacency.

5.3   Transfer of Control

While this research did not directly assess the workload experienced by test drivers during transitions of control, some of the findings may have implications for improving understanding of the mental processes involved in this operation. One of the main findings from the present study is that test drivers, particularly those in the novice and advanced groups, experienced moderate to high levels of self-reported workload. Previous work assessing workload in automation has generally found underload as the most likely effect of increased automation. However, the majority of these studies have taken place in test environments (such as simulation) where vehicle automation was used as a variable that could be modified. In a meta-analysis [20] the authors analyzed the results of 37 studies involving over 1,000 participants. The analysis undertaken showed that highly automated driving, compared to adaptive cruise control and manual driving resulted in the lowest unweighted mean self-reported workload (22%). However, of these 37 studies, 35 were undertaken in a simulator environment. In addition, for many of these studies, additional tasks were required of participants and as such the focus was not solely on the effective operation of the vehicle. The combination of factors probably means that participants would not have felt pressured to maintain an acceptable level of driving task performance.

In the present study, test drivers had received training regarding insurance and liability should an incident occur. As the laws and regulations governing driving in the UK have not yet incorporated changes to account for AVs, test drivers would have been liable for any incident resulting from a failure in monitoring and responding on the part of the test driver. As the vehicles were operating in a public (often busy) environment, full of pedestrians and cyclists and in changing weather conditions, it is likely that the stress of the task would have increased the demand on study participants. When highly automated vehicles are widely introduced, drivers are likely to have some liability for collisions, particularly if the vehicle had transferred control. As such, there will be a requirement to effectively monitor the driving task and ensure safe transitions from one level of automation to another.

Keeping drivers in the loop will be generally challenging for industry and policy makers alike. Much research into public perceptions of driverless vehicles shows that being able to perform other tasks during journeys (such as reading and sleeping) is one of the key benefits expected from this technology. Some research, such as that by de Winter and colleagues has also shown that participants are more likely to undertake non-driving related tasks in highly automated vehicles. As such, and in order to appropriately educate and engage future drivers with the driving task, it will be important to have a detailed understanding of the monitoring tasks requirements; it will also be important to build on this knowledge and develop strategies to support drivers in resuming vehicle control when this is required.

5.4   Limitations

One of the challenges of undertaking this type of assessments in a real-world environment is the lack of control over certain variables of importance. As mentioned earlier, the test drivers were performing the operator task as part of a wider set of trials. This resulted in a number of caveats to the analysis and interpretation of findings.

Firstly, the sample size is very small and the amount of data collected was limited. This limitation is a result of the study subjects (and sampling) being opportunistic in nature. As the study participants were also trial staff, their principal aim was to undertake the tasks required as part of the larger trial activities. This meant that the research had to be designed to allow completion in minimum time so as to not result in a burden to trial staff.

Similarly, and in order to provided added flexibility, the assessments were completed at different points in time after the operator task had been undertaken. While some participants completed the RTLX during breaks, others completed it at the end of the day (and, possibly, on the following day). Therefore, the responses are not anchored on a specific day or experience. This said, there were a total of four pods in operation throughout the trials. In addition, the nature of the automated technology means that vehicles (and ADS) were designed to dynamically interact and react to a changing environment. In this sense, no two journeys were exactly the same from a vehicle operation standpoint. Similarly, journeys (or runs) would have involved transporting between zero and up to four passengers, which would have added (or removed) additional challenges to the operation and supervision of the vehicle (particularly if passengers engaged with the test driver, asked questions, etc.).

As the wider project was of important significance to the transport and other industries, there was also much interest from media and visitors such as Ministers and other professionals. The trial staff was therefore also under increased pressure during some periods of time as the team hosted visits and provided rides for journalists and stakeholders. This may have accounted for some of the variability from one week's assessment to the next. As a last point, it is important to note that the vehicles on trial were prototype technologies. As such, these required occasional manual intervention from test drivers. The vehicles also had some requirement for manual operation, for example, for opening and closing the vehicle doors.

6 Conclusion and Future Work

The evidence provided in the sections above highlights some of the challenges that automation can bring to the operators of automated systems. The literature particularly discusses the functional limitations humans experience when required to undertake a supervisory role. As vehicle automation continues to develop, the technologies we are likely to experience first will involve conditional or highly automated vehicles; with conditional automation in particular, the operator faces challenges in maintaining vigilance, staying in the task loop and acting appropriately when the automated system cannot complete the task. Test drivers, the first formal operators of AVs being trialed in the UK (and further afield) are the first to experience this technology from an operator's perspective and as such can provide valuable insight to enable a better understanding of the task requirements and subjective workload that supervising an AV system entails.

In this light, and despite the clear limitations of this research, the data provides valuable and novel insight into the real-world experiences of operators of highly automated vehicle systems. As vehicle automation continues to develop, and particularly in consideration of the transitional periods where a driver will be required to maintain some level of responsibility over the driving task, it will be important to understand the task requirements in order to ensure a safe and effective transition between the system and the human operator. It will also be important in designing future training and testing protocols for AV operators

Previous research has focused mostly on the impact of low workload as a result of increased automation, while other research has specifically discussed the workload during periods of transition. This research suggests that workload may be an important consideration throughout the monitoring task. This has important implications for the deployment and training of test drivers in the short term, but should also be considered when designing highly automated vehicles. Future research should expand on the sample size and apply a more robust method that allows more consistent data collection and statistical analysis.

References

1. Sabey, B.E., Taylor, H.: The known risks we run: the highway. In: Schwing, R.C., Albers, W.A. (eds.) Societal Risk Assessment, pp. 43–70. Springer, Boston (1980). https://doi.org/10.1007/978-1-4899-0445-4_3
2. National Highway Traffic Safety Administration. Critical Reasons for Crashes Investigated in the National Motor Vehicle Crash Causation Survey. Traffic safety facts. NHTSA, Washington (2015)
3. Department for Transport: The Pathway to Driverless Cars: A Code of Practice for Testing. DfT, London (2015)

4. Lu, Z., Happee, R., Cabrall, C.D., Kyriakidis, M., de Winter, J.C.: Human factors of transitions in automated driving: a general framework and literature survey. Transp. Res. Part F: Traffic Psychol. Behav. **43**, 183–198 (2016). https://doi.org/10.1016/j.trf.2016.10.007
5. Vlakveld, W.: Transition of Control in Highly Automated Vehicles: A Literature Review. SWOV, The Hague (2015)
6. Bainbridge, L.: Ironies of automation. Automatica **19**(6), 775–779 (1983). https://doi.org/10.1016/0005-1098(83)90046-8
7. Young, M.S., Stanton, N.A.: Automotive automation: investigating the impact on drivers' mental workload. Int. J. Cogn. Ergon. **1**(4), 325–336 (1997)
8. Endsley, M.R.: Level of automation effects on performance, situation awareness and workload in a dynamic control task. Ergonomics **42**(3), 462–492 (1999). https://doi.org/10.1080/001401399185595
9. Parasuraman, R., Riley, V.: Humans and automation: use, misuse, disuse, abuse. Hum. Factors **39**(2), 230–253 (1997). https://doi.org/10.1518/001872097778543886
10. Longo, L.: Mental workload in medicine: foundations, applications, open problems, challenges and future perspectives. In: 2016 IEEE 29th International Symposium on Computer-Based Medical Systems (CBMS), pp. 106–111. IEEE, June 2016. http://doi.ieeecomputersociety.org/10.1109/CBMS.2016.36
11. Cain, B.: A review of the mental workload literature. Technical report, Defence Research and Development Canada Toronto, Human System Integration Section, Toronto (2007). 10.1.1.214.7255
12. Rizzo, L., Dondio, P., Delany, S.J., Longo, L.: Modeling mental workload via rule-based expert system: a comparison with NASA-TLX and workload profile. In: Iliadis, L., Maglogiannis, I. (eds.) IFIP International Conference on Artificial Intelligence Applications and Innovations, vol. 475, pp. 215–229. Springer, Cham (2016). https://doi.org/10.1007/978-3-319-44944-9_19
13. Wickens, C.D.: Mental workload: assessment, prediction and consequences. In: Longo, L., Leva, M. (eds.) International Symposium on Human Mental Workload: Models and Applications, vol. 726, pp. 18–29. Springer, Cham (2017). https://doi.org/10.1007/978-3-319-61061-0_2
14. Longo, L.: A defeasible reasoning framework for human mental workload representation and assessment. Behav. Inf. Technol. **34**(8), 758–786 (2015). https://doi.org/10.1080/0144929X.2015.1015166
15. Hart, S.G., Staveland, L.E.: Development of NASA-TLX (Task Load Index): results of empirical and theoretical research. In: Hancock, P.A., Meshkati, N. (eds.) Human Mental Workload. North Holland Press, Amsterdam (1988). https://doi.org/10.1016/s0166-4115(08)62386-9
16. Hart, S.G.: NASA-task load index (NASA-TLX); 20 years later. In: Proceedings of the Human Factors and Ergonomics Society Annual Meeting, vol. 50, no. 9, pp. 904–908. Sage Publications, Los Angeles, October 2006. https://doi.org/10.1177/154193120605000909
17. Paxion, J., Galy, E., Berthelon, C.: Mental workload and driving. Front. Psychol. **5**, 1344 (2014). https://doi.org/10.3389/fpsyg.2014.01344
18. Tong, S., Helman, S., Balfe, N., Fowler, C., Delmonte, E., Hutchins, R.: Workload differences between on-road and off-road manoeuvres for motorcyclists. In: Longo, L., Leva, M. (eds.) International Symposium on Human Mental Workload: Models and Applications, pp. 239–250. Springer, Cham (2017). https://doi.org/10.1007/978-3-319-61061-0_16
19. De Waard, D.: The Measurement of Drivers' Mental Workload. Groningen University, Traffic Research Center, Haren (1996)

20. de Winter, J.C., Happee, R., Martens, M.H., Stanton, N.A.: Effects of adaptive cruise control and highly automated driving on workload and situation awareness: a review of the empirical evidence. Transp. Res. Part F: Traffic Psychol. Behav. **27**, 196–217 (2014). https://doi.org/10.1016/j.trf.2014.06.016

21. Saxby, D.J., Matthews, G., Warm, J.S., Hitchcock, E.M., Neubauer, C.: Active and passive fatigue in simulated driving: discriminating styles of workload regulation and their safety impacts. J. Exp. Psychol. Appl. **19**(4), 287 (2013). https://doi.org/10.1037/a0034386

22. da Silva, F.P.: Mental workload, task demand and driving performance: what relation. Procedia-Soc. Behav. Sci. **162**, 310–319 (2014). https://doi.org/10.1016/j.sbspro.2014.12.212

Applications

Latency Differences Between Mental Workload Measures in Detecting Workload Changes

Enrique Muñoz-de-Escalona[(✉)] and José Juan Cañas

Mind, Brain and Behaviour Research Centre,
University of Granada, Granada, Spain
{enriquemef, delagado}@ugr.es

Abstract. Mental workload has traditionally been measured by three different methods corresponding to its primary reflections: performance, subjective and physiological measures. Although we would expect a certain degree of convergence, research has shown that the emergence of disassociations and insensitivities between measures is very frequent. One possible explanation could be related to the differing latencies between each workload assessment method. We tested this explanation by manipulating task complexity through time spent performing a simulated air-traffic control task. In the experimental session, we collected physiological (pupil size), performance and subjective data. Our results showed two periods of bad performance caused by high traffic density and aircraft configurations. Those periods corresponded to higher mental workload as detected by subjective and physiological measures. However, subjective mental workload reacted sooner than physiological mental workload to task demands. These results suggest that the differences in latency could partially explain mental workload dissociations and insensitivities between measures.

Keywords: Mental workload · Latency · Workload measures · Dissociations · Insensitivities

1 Introduction

There is at present no doubt about the importance of measuring mental workload. Modern society needs some sort of cognitive work measure, and it would be very useful to have a valid and reliable standardised method for assessing it; so far, however, this does not appear possible at present. The study of mental workload poses a series of difficulties, since the mechanisms underlying it are not very well known, which makes evaluation of mental workload difficult. Mental workload is considered a multifaceted construct that cannot be seen directly, but must be inferred from what can be seen or measured [1]. In other words, we do not currently have any objective method to directly measure mental workload as a psychological construct, and we thus have to trust some indirect indicators corresponding to its three primary reflections: (1) performance measures (quantity and quality of performed task); (2) subjective perceptions (questionnaires and scales); and (3) physiological responses (pupil diameter, electrodermal activity, EEG, heart-rate variability, etc.) [2, 3].

© Springer Nature Switzerland AG 2019
L. Longo and M. C. Leva (Eds.): H-WORKLOAD 2018, CCIS 1012, pp. 131–146, 2019.
https://doi.org/10.1007/978-3-030-14273-5_8

We can assume that if the three types of measures reflect the same construct, we would expect a certain degree of convergence between them such that, when a task becomes more complex, the three primary measures would change as follows: (1) lower task performance, (2) subjective perception of higher workload and (3) higher physiological activation responses (taking into account only those physiological variables reflecting physiological activation; other variables such as, e.g. blink rate [4] and heart rate variability [5], have also been shown to decrease during periods of high workload). In other words, we would expect to find associations between task load changes and primary reflections of mental workload, in such a way that we could find positive correlations between measures. However, literature research has shown that this is not always the case, so that the emergence of disassociations, insensitivities and subsequent lack of correlation between measures is more common than we realise [6–8]. An insensitivity occurs when a workload measure does not reflect any change in task load levels, whereas a dissociation takes place when that measure actually changes, but in the opposite direction [6].

Consider, for example, a situation in which a worker is performing a task that becomes more difficult over time. We would expect to find a task performance impairment, higher physiological activation and higher subjective workload perception (associations). We could nevertheless find that the worker is actually showing a stable performance (insensitivity), but a higher physiological activation (association) and a lower subjective workload perception (dissociation). In other words, in this situation it would not be possible to establish positive correlation between workload measures that are supposed to be measuring the same construct. Such situations are very problematic for our science and practice, and understanding these situations represents one of the greatest challenges to be faced in the mental workload research sphere at present [6]. One might well wonder why this occurs with respect to the occurrence of associations, insensibilities and dissociations between mental workload measures. One possible explanation of some disassociations and insensitivities that happen between workload measures is related to the timescale considered between measures. We should consider that each different method for measuring mental workload has its own inherent timescale. While some measures could reflect mental workload within seconds, others could show a longer latency between task load changes and mental workload index reflection. We should therefore take into account such timescale latency differences to avoid considering some disassociations and insensibilities as such when, in fact, they are the result of a methodological misconception [6]. This experiment aims to shed some light on the occurrence of disassociations and insensitivities between mental workload measures due to the differences in timescale between primary workload indexes. We hypothesised that these temporal differences between methods timescale are real, and could explain certain disassociations and/or insensibilities that occur between workload measures.

The rest of the paper proceeds as follows. Section 2 outlines related work about general mental workload, focusing on mental workload measurement techniques and measures. Section 3 describes the design and the methodology followed in conducting the experiment. Section 4 presents the obtained results. Section 5 presents a discussion about our findings, as well as limitations and possible new future work. Section 6 concludes the study, summarising the key findings and its impact on the body of knowledge.

2   Related Work

Mental workload is a complex construct, which has received multiple definitions over the years, but there is no agreed consensus about its definition [9]. However, what does seem clear is its importance to a modern society, which needs some form of cognitive work assessment. High mental workload can result in physical, psychological and social problems [10–12], whereas very low mental workload can lead to the risky situation of being "out of the loop" [13]. Stress and fatigue can be the result of performing highly demanding tasks sustained over time, which would ultimately affect both worker health and performance [14–16]. Poor performance can also lead to dangerous and risky situations in fields such as Air Traffic Control [17, 18] and driving [19–21], increasing the likelihood that accidents will occur. Mental workload management thus appears to be a key issue in supporting increased future cognitive demands. Mental workload is a multi-factorial construct, which depends not only on demanded task resources but also on available resources [22, 23]. For this reason, cognitive models have been developed in order to make it possible to predict mental workload based on a combination of aggregated factors [24–26]. To this effect, computational models have proven appropriate and highly effective in computing the prediction of scientific models in numerous fields [27]. But first, in order to make research possible, validate proposed models and deepen the understanding of mental workload issues, we need reliable methods for assessing it. With this in mind, over the last several decades there has been an exponential increase in the number of studies regarding mental workload measurement techniques and measures [3, 10, 28–30]. There are three main different methodologies for measuring mental workload, which correspond to its three primary reflections:

1. **Performance measures:** this type of methodology is composed of primary task measures (e.g. n° of errors, reaction time, etc.) and secondary task measures (e.g. choice reaction-time tasks, time estimation, memory-search tasks etc.). The aim is to measure objective performance indexes in order to quantify the quantity and the quality of performed tasks.
2. **Subjective measures:** this sort of methodology includes all self-reported measures (e.g. NASA Task Load Index, Instantaneous Self-Assessment, Activation Scale, etc.). The aim is to obtain easy and low-cost subjective data about perceived mental workload.
3. **Physiological measures:** this type of methodology comprises every physiological response to mental workload (e.g. pupil diameter, electrodermal activity, electroencephalogram, etc.). The aim is to collect objective physiological data, which reacts to changes in mental workload [31].

As stated in the section above, presumably, since the three types of measures reflect the same concept, we would expect them to be interrelated. However, as Hancock [6] reports, literature research has found frequent inconsistencies (dissociations and insensitivities) between measures. Although the occurrence of dissociations and insensitivities may be affected by several factors, this study addresses a gap in the literature about temporal differences between methods' timescale, which may partly explain certain inconsistencies between mental workload measures.

3 Design and Methodology

We manipulated two independent variables in this experiment: time on task (TOT) and task complexity, whose effects were tested in an air traffic control (ATC) simulation experiment in which participants were trained and instructed to avoid conflicts between aircraft. This complex and dynamic task would allow us to observe the possible effects of our manipulated independent variables, as well as our measured dependent variables. Participants performed the task for 120 min while their performance, pupil diameter and subjective activation were collected. The hypotheses for the present study are the following:

H1. There exist temporal latency differences between methods.

H2. These temporal latency differences would partly explain certain dissociations and/or insensitivities that occur between mental workload measures.

3.1 Materials and Instruments

^{ATC}**Lab-Advanced Software.** The software used for simulating air traffic control (ATCo) tasks was an air traffic simulator called ^{ATC}Lab-Advanced, which is available for free public download (see Fig. 1) [32]. The ^{ATC}Lab-Advanced software provided a high level of realism (that is, a high level of similarity to real ATC operational scenarios) as well as simplified and easy handling, which allowed it to be used by all participants in several learning sessions. Additionally, the software allowed strong experimental control of air traffic scenarios parameters because its XML code could be modified to develop scenarios consistent with research needs and objectives.

For scenario development, the static characteristics of the simulation environment (control sector size and possible pathways through which aircraft could travel) were defined first. Next, aircraft quantity (density) and initial aircraft parameters (altitude, assigned altitude, speed, time of appearance on stage and planned route) were defined for each aircraft presented in the scenario. Once the structural and dynamic scenario parameters were established, a file that could be launched by the simulator was obtained. This file recorded a .log file with performance data for each participant during simulation.

Finally, we note that the ^{ATC}Lab-Advanced simulator provided participants with all tools needed to carry out the ATCo task, such as the route (the aircraft's fixed route was displayed), distance scale (which allows horizontal aircraft distance measurement) and altitude and speed change tools.

Scenarios. Scenarios used in the study varied according to whether the participant was in the training or the experimental stage. During the training sessions, the standard scenarios provided by the software creator software were used, but a specific scenario was programmed by the experimenters to achieve experimental session goals. This specific scenario was programmed with the following features:

- The purpose of the scenario was to subject participants to a variable complexity task situation, that is, a variable mental workload situation to capture changes in different mental workload indexes.

- The initial number of aircrafts presented was 9, and 6 of these were under participant control.
- Overall, a total of 70 aircraft were presented, with 50 coming from external locations A, D, E, F, W, P, N, L, M and Z and 20 from internal locations C and J. More specifically, 5 aircraft came from each of A, D, E, F, W, P, N, L, M and Z; 12 from J (8 going to P and 4 to A); and 8 from C (2 going to A, D, E and F respectively).

To better understand the set-up, refer to Fig. 1, which represents the initial simulator screen presented to participants; the capital black letters (starting route spots) do not appear on the radar screen.

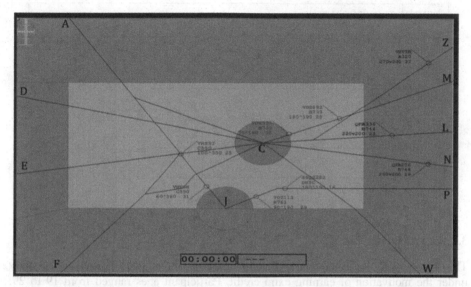

Fig. 1. ATCLab-advanced software initial screenshot presented to participants

Tobii T120 Eyetracker. Pupil diameter measurements were obtained using an infrared-based eye tracker system, the Tobii T120 model marketed by Tobii Video System. This system is characterised by its high sampling frequency (120 Hz). This equipment is completely non-intrusive, has no visible eye movement monitoring system and provides high precision and an excellent head compensatory movement mechanism, which ensures high-quality data collection. In addition, a calibration procedure is completed within seconds, and the freedom of movement it offers participants allows them to act naturally in front of the screen, as though it were an ordinary computer display.

Instantaneous Self-assessmentScale. We used an easy and intuitive instant subjective workload scale called instantaneous self-assessment (ISA), which provides momentary subjective ratings of perceived mental workload during the performance of tasks (see Fig. 2). ISA has been used extensively in numerous domains, including ATC tasks. Participants write down how much mental workload they currently experience on a scale ranging from 1 (no mental workload) to 5 (maximum mental workload), presented from left to right in ascending amount of mental workload experienced. Participants were taught to use the scale just before beginning the experimental stage. While the method is relatively obtrusive to the primary task, it was considered the least intrusive of the available online workload assessment techniques [33, 34].

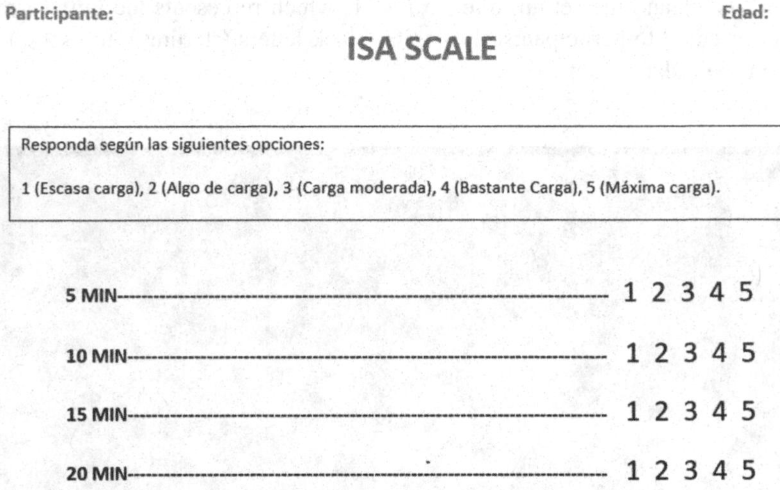

Participante: Edad:

ISA SCALE

Responda según las siguientes opciones:

1 (Escasa carga), 2 (Algo de carga), 3 (Carga moderada), 4 (Bastante Carga), 5 (Máxima carga).

5 MIN--- 1 2 3 4 5

10 MIN--- 1 2 3 4 5

15 MIN--- 1 2 3 4 5

20 MIN--- 1 2 3 4 5

Fig. 2. Instantaneous self-assessment scale

3.2 Participants

Thirty-two psychology students at the University of Granada participated in the study under the motivation of earning extra credit. Participant ages ranged from 19 to 29, with an average of 22.1 and a median of 22. A total of 23 women and 9 men participated. A further requirement was that none of the participants had any previous experience in ATCo tasks.

3.3 Procedure

Participants had to perform the ATCo tasks with the previously described ^{ATC}Lab-Advanced software, so they had to learn how to use it before proceeding through the experimental stage in which the performance data were collected. Thus, we established 2 distinct stages (see Fig. 3):

1. **Training stage:** training took place for a total of 60 min. The main objective of this first stage was for participants to familiarise themselves with the software so that they could handle it comfortably during the experimental stage. The training stage procedure was as follows: during the first day, once informed consent was given by the participants and their main task goal explained (maintaining air traffic security and preventing potential conflicts between aircraft), they started reading a short

manual about the operation of the simulator for about 20 min and were asked to call the researcher once they had finished. Then the participants sat in front of the running simulator while the researcher reviewed the manual in detail with the participants to ensure both correct understanding of the task and assimilation of knowledge through content review. Participants then started using the simulator on their own while the researcher executed a total of six different ATC scenarios in order of difficulty. The participants had free access to both the manual and researcher at all times in case of doubts or questions. The researcher also periodically checked the participants' performance to monitor their learning. Once the training period concluded, participants were ready for the experimental session, which took place the following day.

2. **Data collection stage:** the aim of the data collection stage, which lasted a total of 120 min, was to collect experimental data from participants while they performed ATCo tasks. Both objective (physiological and execution data) and subjective (mental workload subjective index) data were collected. The participants were told the differences between the training and experimental stages, which were as follows: first, they would perform ATCo tasks in front of an eye-tracker system that had been previously calibrated. Secondly, participants were instructed to minimise head and body movements during the session and to fill in the ISA scale every 5 min, when a scheduled alarm sounded. The whole session lasted 2 h. At the end of the session, the participants were thanked and given extra credit.

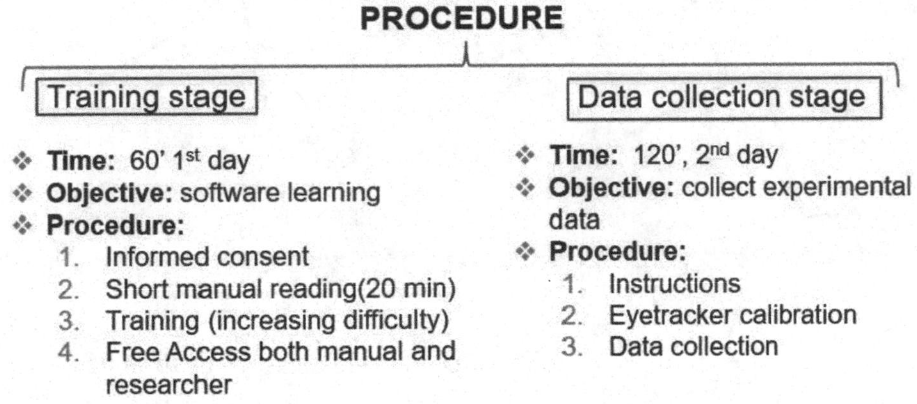

PROCEDURE

Training stage

- ❖ **Time:** 60' 1st day
- ❖ **Objective:** software learning
- ❖ **Procedure:**
  1. Informed consent
  2. Short manual reading(20 min)
  3. Training (increasing difficulty)
  4. Free Access both manual and researcher

Data collection stage

- ❖ **Time:** 120', 2nd day
- ❖ **Objective:** collect experimental data
- ❖ **Procedure:**
  1. Instructions
  2. Eyetracker calibration
  3. Data collection

Fig. 3. Experiment design procedure diagram

3.4 Experimental Room Conditions

Sessions were held in several different rooms, depending on whether the participant was in the training or data collection stage: during the training stage, participants could work in one of three different rooms equipped for training with the simulator, and no special attention to room conditions was needed. However, during the data collection stage, standardising room conditions was essential. Thus, the testing rooms were temperature controlled to 21 °C, and lighting conditions (the main extraneous variable in pupil diameter measurement) were kept constant with artificial lighting and no natural light in the rooms. Moreover, participants always sat in the same place, a comfortable chair spaced 60 cm from the eye-tracker system.

3.5   Variables

Independent Variables

Task Complexity. Complexity of the task is directly related to mental workload: the more complex the task becomes, the higher the mental workload. We manipulated task complexity by modifying aircraft traffic density (occupancy) through the 2 h of the experimental session (see Fig. 4).

Time on Task. TOT was manipulated by setting 5-minute intervals through the 120-minute duration of the experimental session. We thus set a total of 24 intervals from when the first measurement was taken as baseline for pupil diameter, resulting in 23 suitable time intervals.

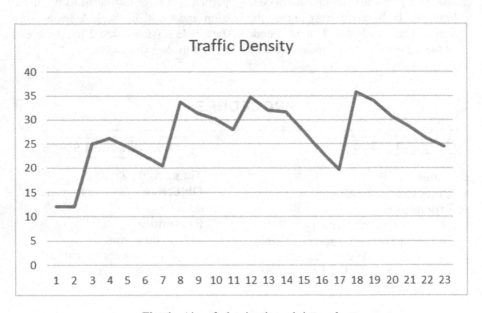

Fig. 4. Aircraft density through intervals

Dependent Variables

Performance. Although performance related to ATCo task can include a wide range of indicators, we found it appropriate to consider conflict rate as our performance indicator, taking into account its well-established correlation with our independent variable, traffic density [35]. However, for the analysis we operationalised this dependent variable by dividing the number of conflicts by the total number of aircraft present in the radar at a given time. We thought that using only the number of conflicts as a performance measurement would not be an appropriate performance indicator, since it largely reflects air traffic density.

Pupil Size. We used pupil diameter as our physiological mental workload indicator, as it effectively reflects mental workload [36–44]. While our eye-tracking system allows continuous sampling rate recording at 120 Hz, we set a total of 24 intervals lasting 5 min each to facilitate subsequent analyses.

Since expressing pupil size in absolute values has the disadvantage of being affected by slow random fluctuations of pupil size (source of noise), we followed the recommendations provided by Sebastiaan Mathôt [45] about baseline correction of pupil-size data. To do this, we took the first interval (5 min) as a reference of standard individual average pupil size, which was then subtracted from the obtained value in each of the remaining 23 intervals, thereby giving a differential standardised value allowing us to reduce noise in our data. Analyses were carried out both for the left and right pupils. A negative value meant that the pupil was contracting while a positive value meant that it was dilating. Finally, we should bear in mind that some participants have larger pupils than others, but such between-subject differences are taken into account statistically, through a repeated measures ANOVA analysis.

Subjective Mental Workload. In order to make it possible to establish comparisons between the three primary workload measures, it was necessary to obtain the subjective momentary ratings continuously throughout the experimental session. With this goal, we used ISA, which is an online subjective workload scale created for this purpose. Ratings were obtained at 5-minute intervals throughout the 2 h of the experimental stage, obtaining a total of 24 intervals, from which we discarded the first interval (used in the physiological scale as a baseline); this left 23 analysable intervals remaining (see Fig. 2). This study was carried out in accordance with the recommendations of the local ethical guidelines of the committee of the University of Granada institution called Comité de Ética de Investigación Humana. The protocol was approved by the Comité de Ética de Investigación Humana. All subjects gave written informed consent in accordance with the Declaration of Helsinki.

4   Results

We used a one-way, within-subject ANOVA to analyse the obtained results. The analyses of participant performance during the experimental scenario confirmed that our task complexity manipulation was successful as, although participants were able to avoid most conflicts, the results showed a significant effect in intervals $F(22, 682) = 42.44$, MSe $= .001$, $p < .001$ on participant performance, due mainly to worse performance in intervals 8 and 18, which correspond to an increase in task demand (see Fig. 5). Left and right pupil diameter also showed the effect of workload at intervals $F(22,682) = 7.98$, MSe $= .005$, $p < .001$, and $F(22,682) = 8.34$, MSe $= .005$, $p < .001$, respectively. Based on our results, we can see that pupil size changes over time, reaching maximum values with increases in task demands; in particular, we can find high pupil size peaks at intervals 9–12 and 19–21 (see Fig. 5).

With regard to the subjective primary measure, we also found a significant main interval effect at $F(22,682) = 25.17$, $MSe = .758$, $p < .001$. Similar to pupil size, we can see how subjective mental workload changes over the intervals, reaching maximum peaks at higher task difficulty and more specifically at intervals 8–12 and 18–21 (see Fig. 5).

Finally, Table 1 reveals that, as expected, there were high positive correlations between left and right pupils .97, $p < .01$. Therefore, taking left pupil as a reference, we found a positive correlation between pupil diameter and subjective workload measure .81, $p < .01$, whereas we could not find a correlation between pupil diameter and performance .27, $p > .05$. Furthermore, we found only a slight correlation between performance and subjective workload measure .26, $p < .05$ (see Table 1).

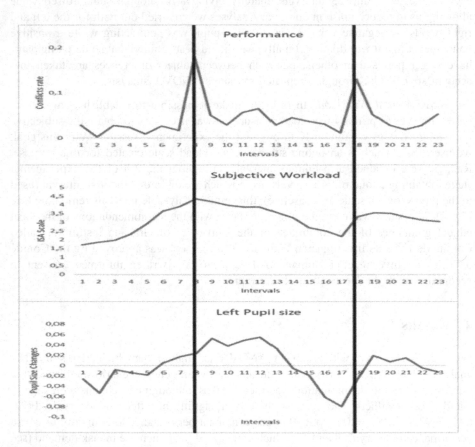

Fig. 5. Participant performance, left pupil and subjective mental workload during task development

Table 1. Correlation chart between measures

		Performance	R. pupil	L. pupil	Subjective
Performance	Pearson	1	.279	.266	.473*
	Sig. (bilateral)		.198	.219	.023
	N	23	23	23	23
R. pupil	Pearson	.279	1	.965**	.870**
	Sig. (bilateral)	.198		.000	.000
	N	23	23	23	23
L. pupil	Pearson	.266	.965**	1	.808**
	Sig. (bilateral)	.219	.000		.000
	N	23	23	23	23
Subjective	Pearson	.473*	.870**	.808**	1
	Sig. (bilateral)	.023	.000	.000	
	N	23	23	23	23

*$p < .05$, **$p < .01$

5 Discussion

To synthesise our data, our performance results revealed two lower performance peaks at intervals 8 and 18 (higher task demand), which correspond with physiological and subjective measures reaching maximum values (with different latencies). We should consider that, despite aircraft density reaching 4 high-density peaks at intervals 4, 8, 12 and 18, we only found 2 real high-complexity peaks reflected as bad performance peaks at intervals 8 and 18. In that respect, even though it seems from the literature that traffic density strongly influences complexity and so mental workload [46], complexity of ATCo scenarios are not only dependent on this factor but on others such as traffic configuration and aircraft evolution [25, 46, 47]. In that sense, by analysing the recorded scenario, we can actually verify that task demand does in fact become much higher at intervals 8 and 18, not only because of traffic density but also because of traffic evolution and configuration. That is the reason why there is not a comparable increase in mental workload reflections at interval 4 and 12 as were observed at 8 and 18.

The first important finding from our data is that pupil size and subjective workload measures follow a similar pattern: they increase at high-imposed task load, and they decrease when task demands become lower. Taking into account that both workload responses track to external task load, showing a positive correlation between each other (.87), our data revealed what has been called a double association [6]. A key finding should be emphasised. We found that at highest demand peaks (8 and 18), subjective mental workload measures reacted sooner than physiological response, even taking into account that subjective measures take some time for administration. In other words, subjective mental workload reflection responded with a lower latency than physiological measures, only at high–task load peaks. As we can see in the results, higher pupil size peaks are reached one interval after the highest demand peaks (intervals 9–12 and 19–21), whereas higher subjective workload responses were achieved immediately: at the first high demand peak at interval 8, and at the second high demand peak at intervals 18–19. Therefore, although these correlations showed associations among our physiological and subjective measures, this collected data also suggested some indications of dissociations in line with the explanations provided by Hancock [6] about disassociations and insensitivities between mental workload measures: "there is strong reason to believe that each of these methods (and each of their component elements) possess their own inherent timescale and that certain, if not many, of the associations, dissociations and insensitivities are contingent upon such temporal differences" (p. 8). In other words, in our results there were some indications of the existence of different timescales for physiological and subjective measures. Further research is therefore necessary to explore this relation between insensitivities, dissociations and timescales.

The performance measure correlated only slightly with the subjective measure (.47), whereas it did not correlate with the physiological measure (.27). We think that these poor correlation results between performance and the rest of the primary indicators may be due to the low variability obtained on the performance variable (ceiling effect): participants were able to solve the vast majority of conflicts, and their performance was nearly perfect, so that variance was not particularly measurable. In any case, we believe that, in the absence of this ceiling effect, this lack of correlation would not have occurred.

It is worth noting an unexpected finding in our data that is not related to our main objective in this study: the effects of task learning on mental workload. At the first high-demand period, we found participants were experiencing more cognitive load, as they were not used to solving conflicts in that particular scenario. However, the more the participants practiced with the experimental scenario, the lower the cognitive demands as new cognitive strategies were being developed. We could therefore say that changing from a more consciously controlled to a more automated task would ultimately decrease mental workload. Our results showed up a mental workload decline at high demand peaks with TOT, which was reflected by the performance, subjective and physiological primary measures. This evidence is consistent with findings by Foroughi et al., who found that trial completion times and maximum pupil size significantly reduced across trials performing a cognitive task that required individuals to orient themselves in space relative to a target [48]. Furthermore, these results are also in line with cognitive load theory, which postulates that individuals would shift from learned procedures to automatic processes over time practising a new task [49].

In summary, by looking at our results, we could assume that differences in latency may partially explain mental workload dissociations and insensitivities between measures at high mental workload peak experiences. Moreover, mental workload decline over time could be explained by the effects of learning on cognitive efficiency, as literature research has shown. Several limitations must be addressed. First, we think it would be necessary to deepen the study of this phenomenon with other physiological measures, such as electrodermal activity, heart-rate variability and EEG. Dissociations and insensibilities have been found not only between the three primary measures of workload, but also within different indicators of each kind of primary measure. In that sense, we are convinced that each different physiological indicator would have its own particular timescale, and further research is thus needed to untangle the issue. Another point to note is the granularity of the timescale considered on collected data. Intervals were defined in our experiment as every 5 min. We think it would be interesting to consider shorter intervals in order to obtain better granularity on data analysis. It is important to bear in mind, however, the related level of intrusiveness created by shorter data collection intervals: for example, an online subjective workload measure collected every 30 s would strongly interfere with both primary task development and experienced mental workload. Finally, it also needs to be noted that we conducted this research with students under simulated conditions, and we think it would be necessary to replicate this experiment under real conditions to improve the validity of our findings.

6 Conclusions

Cognitive mental workload assessment is fundamental to the development of modern society and has been one of the greatest challenges for the last several decades. Hundreds of studies have been conducted for measuring mental workload in its three main axes: performance, subjective and physiological measures [3]. Although we would expect a certain degree of convergence between different mental workload measures, the literature has shown that associations do not always occur. In this study, we explored the occurrence of disassociations and insensitivities across the different methods of measuring mental workload. A possible explanation for this might be related to the inherent timescale of each of these different methods. That is, each of the different methods for assessing a mental workload primary reflection possesses its own timescale, so that some show longer response latency to task demand changes than others [6].

Our findings suggest that dissociations and insensitivities may appear at high mental workload peak experiences due to latency differences between measures: subjective measure showed lower latency response than physiological response (pupil size). One important implication of this finding is that latency response in mental workload measures might vary depending on task demand levels. Thus, mental workload measures may correlate at low- and medium medium-task-demand levels, but when the situation becomes very complex (high cognitive-demand- peaks), dissociations and insensitivities between measures may appear. In other words, a worker experiencing moderate task demands may be reflecting moderate mental workload levels through physiological and subjective responses equally, but if the situations suddenly become much more difficult, we might better rely on subjective measures to reflect mental workload changes, rather than relying on physiological responses (at least those physiological variables reflecting physiological activation). Another interesting finding, in line with literature research, are the effects of task learning on cognitive efficiency, which was reflected as a mental workload decline with TOT. However, due to methodological limitations, explained in the previous section, these promising findings must be taken cautiously before generalising them. Further research should be undertaken to map the intrinsic timescale of the measurement problem, which will bring us closer to achieving a better understanding of associations, insensitivities and dissociations among mental workload responses.

References

1. Crevits, I., Debernard, S., Denecker, P.: Model building for air-traffic controllers' workload regulation. Eur. J. Oper. Res. **136**(2), 324–332 (2002). https://doi.org/10.1016/S0377-2217 (01)00119-9
2. Moray, N.: Mental Workload: Its Theory and Measurement. Plenum Press, New York (1979). https://doi.org/10.1007/978-1-4757-0884-4_2
3. Wickens, C.D.: Mental workload: assessment, prediction and consequences. In: Longo, L., Leva, M. (eds.) H-WORKLOAD 2017. CCIS, vol. 726, pp. 18–29. Springer, Cham (2017). https://doi.org/10.1007/978-3-319-61061-0_2
4. De Alwis Edirisinghe, V.: Estimating mental workload of university students using eye parameters, Master's thesis, NTNU (2017)
5. Murai, K., Hayashi, Y., Okazaki, T., Stone, L.C.: Evaluation of ship navigator's mental workload using nasal temperature and heart rate variability. In: 2008 IEEE International Conference on Systems, Man and Cybernetics, pp. 1528–1533. IEEE, New York (2008). https://doi.org/10.1109/icsmc.2008.4811503
6. Hancock, P.A.: Whither workload? Mapping a path for its future development. In: Longo, L., Leva, M. (eds.) H-WORKLOAD 2017. CCIS, vol. 726, pp. 3–17. Springer, Cham (2017). https://doi.org/10.1007/978-3-319-61061-0_1
7. Yeh, Y.H., Wickens, C.D.: The dissociation of subjective measures of mental workload and performance (final report). (No. NASA-CR-176609; NAS 1.26:176609; EPL-84-2/NASA-84-2) (1984)
8. Casper, P.A.: Dissociations among measures of mental workload: effects of experimenter-induced inadequacy (1988)
9. Moray, N.: Mental Workload: Its Theory and Measurement, vol. 8. Springer, Heidelberg (2013). https://doi.org/10.1007/978-1-4757-0884-4
10. Longo, L., Leva, M.C. (eds.): H-WORKLOAD 2017. CCIS, vol. 726. Springer, Cham (2017). https://doi.org/10.1007/978-3-319-61061-0
11. Dawson, D., Ian Noy, Y., Härmä, M., Åkerstedt, T., Belenky, G.: Modelling fatigue and the use of fatigue models in work settings. Accid. Anal. Prev. **43**(2), 549–564 (2011). https://doi.org/10.1016/j.aap.2009.12.030
12. Jorna, P.G.: Spectral analysis of heart rate and psychological state: a review of its validity as a workload index. Biol. Psychol. **34**(2), 237–257 (1992). https://doi.org/10.1016/0301-0511 (92)90017-O
13. Endsley, M.: From here to autonomy: lessons learned from human–automation research. Hum. Factors **59**(1), 5–27 (2017). https://doi.org/10.1177/0018720816681350
14. Josten, E.J., Ng-A-Tham, J.E., Thierry, H.: The effects of extended workdays on fatigue, health, performance and satisfaction in nursing. J. Adv. Nurs. **44**(6), 643–652 (2003). https://doi.org/10.1046/j.0309-2402.2003.02854.x
15. Taylor, A.H., Dorn, L.: Stress, fatigue, health, and risk of road traffic accidents among professional drivers: the contribution of physical inactivity. Ann. Rev. Publ. Health **27**, 371–391 (2006). https://doi.org/10.1146/annurev.publhealth.27.021405.102117
16. Fan, J., Smith, A.: The impact of workload and fatigue on performance. In: Longo, L., Leva, M. (eds.) H-WORKLOAD 2017. CCIS, vol. 726, pp. 90–105. Springer, Cham (2017). https://doi.org/10.1007/978-3-319-61061-0_6
17. Sawaragi, T., Horiguchi, Y., Hina, A.: Safety analysis of systemic accidents triggered by performance deviation. 제어로봇시스템학회 국제학술대회 논문집, pp. 1778–1781 (2006). https://doi.org/10.1109/sice.2006.315635

18. Edwards, T.E., Martin, L., Bienert, N., Mercer, J.: Workload and performance in air traffic control: exploring the influence of levels of automation and variation in task demand (2017). https://doi.org/10.1007/978-3-319-61061-0_8
19. Brookhuis, K.A., de Waard, D.: Monitoring drivers' mental workload in driving simulators using physiological measures. Accid. Anal. Prev. **42**(3), 898–903 (2010). https://doi.org/10.1016/j.aap.2009.06.001
20. da Silva, F.P.: Mental workload, task demand and driving performance: what relation? Proc.-Soc. Behav. Sci. **162**, 310–319 (2014). https://doi.org/10.1016/j.sbspro.2014.12.212
21. Paxion, J., Galy, E., Berthelon, C.: Mental workload and driving. Front. Psychol. **5**, 1344 (2014). https://doi.org/10.3389/fpsyg.2014.01344
22. Wickens, C.D.: Multiple resources and performance prediction. Theor. Issues Ergon. Sci. **3** (2), 159–177 (2002). https://doi.org/10.1518/001872008X288394.200850:449
23. Munoz-de-Escalon, E., Canas, J.: Online measuring of available resources. In: H-Workload 2017 The First International Symposiumon Human Mental Workload, Dublin Institute of Technology, Dublin, Ireland, 28–30 June (2017). https://doi.org/10.21427/d7dk96
24. Cañas, J.J., Ferreira, P.N.P., Puntero, E., López, P., López, E., Gomez-Comendador V.F.: An air traffic controller psychological model with automation. In: 7th EASN International Conference "Innovation in European Aeronautics Research", Warsaw, Poland (2017). https://doi.org/10.3390/s180515864
25. Majumdar, A., Ochieng, W.: Factors affecting air traffic controller workload: multivariate analysis based on simulation modeling of controller workload. Transp. Res. Rec. **1788**, 58–69 (2002). https://doi.org/10.3141/1788-08
26. Wu, C., Liu, Y.: Queuing network modeling of driver workload and performance. IEEE Trans. Intell. Transp. Syst. **8**(3), 528–537 (2007). https://doi.org/10.1109/TITS.2007.903443
27. Sozou, P.D., Lane, P.C., Addis, M., Gobet, F.: Computational scientific discovery. In: Magnani, L., Bertolotti, T. (eds.) Springer Handbook of Model-Based Science. SH, pp. 719–734. Springer, Cham (2017). https://doi.org/10.1007/978-3-319-30526-4_33
28. Moustafa, K., Luz, S., Longo, L.: Assessment of mental workload: a comparison of machine learning methods and subjective assessment techniques. In: Longo, L., Leva, M. (eds.) H-WORKLOAD 2017. CCIS, vol. 726, pp. 30–50. Springer, Cham (2017). https://doi.org/10.1007/978-3-319-61061-0_3
29. Rizzo, L., Longo, L.: Representing and inferring mental workload via defeasible reasoning: a comparison with the NASA task load index and the workload profile. In: 2017 1st Workshop on Advances in Argumentation in Artificial Intelligence, Bari, Italy (2017)
30. Rizzo, L., Dondio, P., Delany, S., Longo, L.: Modeling mental workload via rule-based expert system: a comparison with NASA-TLX and workload profile. In: Iliadis, L., Maglogiannis, I. (eds.) AIAI 2016. IAICT, vol. 475, pp. 215–229. Springer, Cham (2016). https://doi.org/10.1007/978-3-319-44944-9_19
31. Marinescu, A.C., Sharples, S., Ritchie, A.C., Sánchez López, T., McDowell, M., Morvan, H. P.: Physiological parameter response to variation of mental workload. Hum. Factors **60**(1), 31–56 (2018). https://doi.org/10.1177/0018720817733101
32. Fothergill, S., Loft, S., Neal, A.: ATC-labAdvanced: an air traffic control simulator with realism and control. Behav. Res. Methods **41**(1), 118–127 (2009). https://doi.org/10.3758/BRM.41.1.118
33. Brennan, S.D.: An experimental report on rating scale descriptor sets for the instantaneous self-assessment (ISA) recorder. DRA Technical Memorandum (CAD5) 92017, DRA Maritime Command and Control Division, Portsmouth (1992)
34. Jordan, C.S.: Experimental study of the effect of an instantaneous self-assessment workload recorder on task performance. DRA Technical Memorandum (CAD5) 92011, DRA Maritime Command Control Division, Portsmouth (1992)

35. Prandini, M., Piroddi, L., Puechmorel, S., Brázdilová, S.L.: Toward air traffic complexity assessment in new generation air traffic management systems. IEEE Trans. Intell. Transp. Syst. **12**(3), 809–818 (2011). https://doi.org/10.1109/TITS.2011.2113175

36. Matthews, G., Middleton, W., Gilmartin, B.Y., Bullimore, M.A.: Pupillary diameter and cognitive and cognitive load. J. Psychophysiol. **5**, 265–271 (1991)

37. Backs, R.W., Walrath, L.C.: Eye movement and pupillary response indices of mental workload during visual search of symbolic displays. Appl. Ergon. **23**, 243–254 (1992). https://doi.org/10.1016/0003-6870(92)90152-l

38. Hyönä, J., Tommola, J., Alaja, A.: Pupil dilation as a measure of processing load in simultaneous interpreting and other language tasks. Q. J. Exp. Psychol. **48**, 598–612 (1995). https://doi.org/10.1080/14640749508401407

39. Granholm, E., Asarnow, R.F., Sarkin, A.J., Dykes, K.L.: Pupillary responses index cognitive resource limitations. Psychophysiology **33**, 457–461 (1996). https://doi.org/10.1111/j.1469-8986.1996.tb01071.x

40. Iqbal, S.T., Zheng, X.S., Bailey, B.P.: Task evoked pupillary response to mental workload in human-computer interaction. In: Proceedings of the ACM Conference on Human Factors in Computing Systems, pp. 1477–1480. ACM, New York (2004). https://doi.org/10.1145/985921.986094

41. Verney, S.P., Granholm, E., Marshall, S.P.: Pupillary responses on the visual backward masking task reflect general cognitive ability. Int. J. Psychophysiol. **52**, 23–36 (2004). https://doi.org/10.1016/j.ijpsycho.2003.12.003

42. Porter, G., Troscianko, T., Gilchrist, I.D.: Effort during visual search and counting: insights from pupillometry. Q. J. Exp. Psychol. **60**, 211–229 (2007). https://doi.org/10.1080/17470210600673818

43. Privitera, C.M., Renninger, L.W., Carney, T., Klein, S., Aguilar, M.: Pupil dilation during visual target detection. J. Vis. **10**, 1–14 (2010). https://doi.org/10.1167/10.10.3

44. Reiner, M., Gelfeld, T.M.: Estimating mental workload through event-related fluctuations of pupil area during a task in a virtual world. Int. J. Psychophysiol. **93**(1), 38–44 (2014). https://doi.org/10.1016/j.ijpsycho.2013.11.002

45. Mathôt, S., Fabius, J., Van Heusden, E., Van der Stigchel, S.: Safe and sensible preprocessing and baseline correction of pupil-size data. Behav. Res. Methods **50**(1), 94–106 (2018). https://doi.org/10.3758/s13428-017-1007-2

46. Mogford, R.H., Guttman, J.A., Morrow, S.L., Kopardekar, P.: The complexity construct in air traffic control: a review and synthesis of the literature. CTA INC., McKee City, NJ (1995)

47. Athènes, S., Averty, P., Puechmorel, S., Delahaye, D., Collet, C.: ATC complexity and controller workload: trying to bridge the gap. In: Proceedings of the International Conference on HCI in Aeronautics, pp. 56–60. AAAI Press, Cambridge (2002)

48. Foroughi, C.K., Sibley, C., Coyne, J.T.: Pupil size as a measure of within-task learning. Psychophysiology **54**(10), 1436–1443 (2017). https://doi.org/10.1111/psyp.12896

49. Sweller, J.: Cognitive load theory, learning difficulty, and instructional design. Learn. Instr. **4**(4), 295–312 (1994). https://doi.org/10.1016/0959-4752(94)90003-5

Mental Workload and Other Causes of Different Types of Fatigue in Rail Staff

Jialin Fan[✉] ⓘ and Andrew P. Smith ⓘ

Centre for Occupational and Health Psychology, School of Psychology,
Cardiff University, 63 Park Place, Cardiff CF10 3AS, UK
{FanJ12,SmithAP}@cardiff.ac.uk

Abstract. Workload and shift work have been addressed as causes of occupational fatigue in previous research. Fatigue in the workplace has usually been investigated as a single outcome. However, taking into account separate kinds of energy resources, there are different types of fatigue. The present study investigated mental workload and other causes of physical fatigue, mental fatigue, and emotional fatigue in a rail company. Overall, the results confirm the importance of mental workload for different types of work fatigue and reveal other specific causes for each type of fatigue. Prolonged work and insufficient rest resulted in physical fatigue, while poor shift patterns caused mental and emotional fatigue.

Keywords: Workload · Occupational fatigue · Rail industry ·
Physical fatigue · Mental fatigue · Emotional fatigue

1 Introduction

Occupational fatigue refers to extreme tiredness and reduced functional capacity experienced during and after work. Resulting in the deterioration of attention and impaired performance in the workplace, fatigue brings an increased risk of danger to rail staff, as many of their jobs are safety-critical. It also affects well-being of rail staff both at work and outside work [1]. Fatigue has generally been discussed as a single entity. However, taking into account the separate energy resources, it is clear that there are different types of fatigue, including physical fatigue, mental fatigue, and emotional fatigue. The physical fatigue resulting from the depletion of muscular energy represents physical tiredness and the incapacity to engage in physical activity, while mental fatigue resulting from the depletion of cognitive energy represents tiredness and the incapacity to engage in mental activity. Recently, in addition to these two types of fatigue, emotional fatigue has received growing amount of attention [2, 3]. This kind of fatigue results from the depletion of emotional energy and represents tiredness and the incapacity to engage in emotional activity. Frone and Tidwell [4] proposed the Three-Dimensional Work Fatigue Inventory (3D-WFI), suggesting that the measure of work fatigue should be multidimensional, with separate assessments of physical, mental, and emotional fatigue. The psychometric quality and construct of 3D-WFI was then validated in a large-scale national survey in the US [4]. In the railway industry, however, research that measures the three different types of work fatigue separately is still

L. Longo and M. C. Leva (Eds.): H-WORKLOAD 2018, CCIS 1012, pp. 147–159, 2019.
https://doi.org/10.1007/978-3-030-14273-5_9

lacking, and the causes of different types of fatigue are still unclear. The Demands, Resources, and Individual Effects (DRIVE) model has been used as a framework for assessing fatigue in previous fatigue studies (e.g. [1, 5, 6]). In basic terms, this model proposes that high job demands, low job resources (support and control), and individual differences (e.g., negative personality or coping type) predict high levels of fatigue [7]. The DRIVE model was used in the present study to assess different types of fatigue.

The main goal of this study was to investigate the causes of different types of fatigue among rail staff. Toward this end, we began by reviewing the related work on risk factors of occupational fatigue. We then presented the aims, methods, and findings of present study aimed at identifying the stressors of physical, mental and emotional fatigue. It was followed by the discussion and the conclusions in the final two sections of this paper.

2 Related Work

Workload has been identified as one of the essential stressors of occupational fatigue, with high workload leading to a greater subjective feeling of fatigue [8, 9]. Workload is a multi-dimensional concept which involves time, the input load of mental and physical tasks [10], operator effort, and outcomes (i.e., performance or other results) [11]. In the domain of occupational fatigue, workload is often equated with job demands. Edwards and her colleagues [12] suggested that workload was affected by task demands variation, as well as the level of automation in the workplace. Smith and Smith [5] mentioned that in interviews, rail staff members generally believed that the level of effort required to complete work tasks was the major component of workload. These confirmed that the perception of the task load (i.e., subjective job demands) and effort are the core to understanding workload [13].

In the modern railway industry, jobs have placed more emphasis on mental workload, while the traditional physical workload has diminished due to the increasing level of automation in operating systems [14]. Mental workload is also complex and multi-dimensional which frequently is described by terms of mental effort or emotional strain [15–17]. It reflects the capacity or resources that are actually required to meet task demands [18], involving the time pressure and the effort exerted for the execution of the task [19, 20]. There has been considerable interest in mental workload [13, 20, 21] which has led to the development of models of mental workload and application to real-world problems (see [22–25]). Cain [26] reviewed the mental workload literature and claimed that it can be summarised as the total cognitive load required to accomplish a task under specific environmental and operational conditions (e.g., in a finite period of time). The majority jobs in rail transport, such as being a train driver, signaller (i.e., controller), and conductor (i.e., guard), require sustained vigilance. In addition, the engineer may be exposed to heavy time pressure which may result in heavy mental workload and increased feelings of fatigue.

Other than workload, risk factors such as shift work, sleep and rest, and individual differences have also been found to be associated with fatigue. Based on the timing to work, shift work includes day, night, and early morning (i.e., begins before 4 a.m.)

shifts. The night and early morning shifts have been found to result in fatigue [27]. Such shifts also disrupt the sleep–wake cycle and make recovery from fatigue more difficult [28]. Individual differences, such as a healthy lifestyle and positive personality, have been found to play a buffing role in increased fatigue [1]. Fan and Smith [6] systematically reviewed previous research on fatigue among rail staff, and found that workload, length of work, timing of the work (i.e., shift work), insufficient rest and sleep, poor sleep quality, job roles, and individual differences were associated with fatigue. An Australian study [29] suggested that the sleep/wake cycle, work hours and workload influenced rail staff's fatigue. Later, a large-scale fatigue survey covering all the job roles among rail staff [30] showed that train crew fatigue was predicted by heavy mental workload, low job control and support, shift work, noisy working environment, unhealthy lifestyle, and negative personality.

3   Aims

The main aim of the present study described in this paper was to investigate the causes of physical fatigue, mental fatigue, and emotional fatigue in a rail company in the UK. It separately measured the different types of fatigue, as well as types of job demands (i.e., physical demands, mental demands, and emotional demands). The study also aimed to build a more detailed picture of the relationships regarding mental workload, other risk factors, and different types of fatigue using the DRIVE model. The survey covered most of the potential risk factors of fatigue which were mentioned in previous literature, such as workload, timing to work, working hours, rest during work, sleep time and quality, and other activities that may influence fatigue. In addition, the current study aimed to determine whether an online version of such subjective measurements was as reliable as the offline one [30], and whether the online version can be used in future research (e.g., an online diary study).

4   Methods

4.1   Participants

A total of 246 participants completed an online questionnaire. Most of the participants were male (N = 173, 70.3%), with a mean age of 43.21 years (SD = 10.458, minimum 19.5yr, maximum 65.42yr). There were 66.9% of them who worked in South Wales, UK, while the rest worked in North Wales. The School of Psychology Research Ethics Committee at Cardiff University reviewed and approved this online study.

4.2   Materials

This online survey ran in the spring of 2017. The questionnaire consisted of 39 questions, the majority of which were on a 10-point scale and the rest were Yes/No answers. Data collection was performed on the Qualitrics online survey platform. The survey used single-item subjective measures which were valid and reliable [31] and have been used in previous fatigue studies (e.g., [5, 30]). It investigated the details of working hours, shift work, workload, and the potential risk factors outside work (e.g., sleep quality, other activity), and assessed the six predictors of train crew fatigue confirmed in a previous study [30]. The survey asked participants not only about the causes of their own fatigue, but also of that of their colleagues, which provided relatively objective observation data for assessing the risk factors of fatigue. Frone and Tidwell [4] claimed that the measure of work fatigue should be multidimensional with separately assessing physical, mental and emotional fatigue. Given their suggestion, in this questionnaire, work fatigue and job demands were measured alongside physical, mental, and emotional dimensions.

4.3   Analysis

Data analysis was carried out using SPSS 23. The data were analysed using descriptive analysis, exploratory factor analysis, correlation analysis, and regressions. The approach of exploratory factor analysis used here was principal components analysis (PCA) with Direct Oblimin rotation, with an oblique rotation to extract eigenvalues equalling or exceeding the threshold of 1.

5   Results

5.1   Descriptive

The primary job types participants reported were managers (21.7%), conductors (20.9%), administrators (20.9%), and train drivers (19.1%), followed by engineers (11.9%) and station workers (5.3%). There were two participants with missing job type data. There were 67.9% of participants doing shift-work. The sample generally reported personality (73.3%), efficiency (91.4%), and effort (95.5%) toward the positive end (all with threshold = 6).

5.2   Factor Analysis

Principal components analysis (PCA) with the Direct Oblimin rotation was conducted, and the factor scores (i.e., component scores) were created using the regression method. The components and factor loadings are described in Table 1.

In total, there were 11 components, including 10 independent factors and one outcome. Independent factors included negative work characteristics, positive work and individual characteristics, job demands, length of shift, overtime work, timing of shift, mental workload, effort, positive sleep factor, and other activities. The outcome component was three-dimensional fatigue (3D-fatigue). It should be noted that, based on factor loading, the contribution of physical demands on three-dimensional work demands (3D-demands, originally component 7) was found to be much smaller than that of either mental or emotional demands; thus, component 7 was renamed as mental workload.

Table 1. Summary of the factor loading of PCA with Oblimin rotation.

	Factor loading	Initial eigenvalue	Cumulative variance (%)
Predictors		1.657	68.1
Component 1: negative work characteristics			
Shift work	.882		
Exposure to noise and vibration	.859		
Component 2: positive work and individual characteristics			
Positive personality	.811		
Healthy behaviours	.667		
Job control and support	.580		
Component 3: job demands			
Job demands	.934		
Causes of fatigue		3.058	68.4
Component 4: length of shift			
Length of shift (colleagues)	.808		
Length of shift (self)	.805		
Component 5: overtime work			
Overtime	.829		
Number of shifts before rest day (colleagues)	.695		
Overtime (colleagues)	.613		
Number of shifts before rest day (self)	.544		
Component 6: timing of shift			
Timing of shift (self)	.828		
Timing of shift (colleagues)	.822		
Workload		2.109	63.5
Component 7: mental workload			
Hurried or rushed	.845		
Frustrating	.782		
Mental demands	.750		
Physical demands	.462		
Component 8: effort			
Effort	.960		
Activity outside work		1.585	72.4
Component 9: positive sleep factor			
Sleep length (hours)	.874		
Quality of sleep	.870		
Component 10: other activities			
Activities outside work (colleagues)	.826		
Activities outside work (self)	.816		
Outcome		2.021	67.4
Component 11: 3D-fatigue			
Emotional fatigue	.876		
Mental fatigue	.859		
Physical fatigue	.717		

5.3   Bivariate Analysis

Associations Between Fatigue, Efficiency, and Working Hours. The associations between the three different types of fatigue, efficiency, and six working hours-related variables were investigated using a Pearson correlation (shown in Table 2). The three dimensions of fatigue were significantly correlated with each other ($p < .01$). Physical fatigue showed a significant positive correlation with shift length and the frequency of rest and breaks during work (r from .26 to .27, $p < .01$). Mental fatigue showed a significant correlation with the start time of shift work (r (222) = −.20, $p < .01$), with higher levels of mental fatigue associated with earlier shift work start times (i.e., early morning shift work). Mental fatigue, emotional fatigue, and efficiency were significantly correlated with the numbers of shifts taken before a rest day, with correlation coefficients between .13 and .15, both $p < .05$. In addition, higher efficiency was found to be significantly associated with longer break length, (r (219) = .17, $p < .05$).

Table 2. Correlations between three different types of fatigue, efficiency, and working hour-related independent variables (IV).

Variables	(1)	(2)	(3)	(4)	(5)	(6)	(7)	(8)	(9)	(10)
Physical fatigue (1)	1									
Mental fatigue (2)	.40**	1								
Emotional fatigue (3)	.44**	.67**	1							
Efficiency (4)	−.02	−.09	−.12	1						
Shift length (5)	.26**	.11	.09	−.12	1					
Number of shifts before rest day (6)	.02	.13*	.15*	.15*	−.31**	1				
Start time of shift (7)	−.10	−.20**	−.08	−.11	.18**	−.27**	1			
Overtime work (8)	.11	.03	.07	.13	−.09	.15*	−.13	1		
Frequency of break during work (9)	.27**	.02	.03	.06	.18*	−.09	−.10	−.05	1	
Break length (10)	−.06	−.08	−.10	.17*	.09	.01	.03	.04	−.02	1

$^{*}p < 0.05$, $^{**}p < 0.001$

Associations Between 3D-Fatigue and Independent Factors. The associations between 3D-fatigue and 10 independent components were analysed using their factor scores. The results are summarised in Table 3. As the components of fatigue predictors, job demands and negative work characteristics showed a significant positive correlation with 3D-fatigue, while positive work and individual characteristics showed significant negative correlations with fatigue (all $p < 0.01$). 3D-fatigue positively correlated with length of shift, overtime work, and timing of shift (r from .20 to .32, $p < .01$). Considering the components of the factor mental workload, 3D-fatigue showed a significant positive correlation with emotional and mental demands, r (217) = .66, $p < .01$, with a higher level of fatigue associated with a higher level of emotional and mental demands. Meanwhile, fatigue showed a negative correlation with effort, indicating that poorer effort was associated with a higher level of fatigue. In terms of the activities outside of work, fatigue showed a significant correlation with the sleep factor, $r(195) = -.260$, $p < 0.01$, with a higher level of fatigue associated with a poorer sleep experience. There was no significant association between fatigue and other activities.

Table 3. Correlation between 3D-fatigue and factor IVs.

Factor	3D-fatigue
Negative work characteristics	$.35^{**}$
Positive work and individual characteristics	$-.24^{**}$
Job demands	$.47^{**}$
Length of shift	$.32^{**}$
Overtime work	$.31^{**}$
Timing of shift	$.20^{**}$
Mental workload	$.66^{**}$
Effort	$-.17^{*}$
Sleep factor	$-.26^{**}$
Other activity	$.02$

$^{*}p < 0.05$, $^{**}p < 0.001$

5.4   Regression

Regression analyses were carried out to investigate the associations of multiple independent variables with fatigue. First, a linear regression was run using the factor scores of the independent components and 3D-fatigue. As shown in Table 4, mental work, positive work and individual characteristics, and job demands were the strongest predictors of 3D-fatigue by beta weight, followed by overtime work. The regressions account for 51.3% of the variance in 3D-fatigue.

Table 4. Regression predicting 3D-fatigue.

Variables	B	S. E	β	t	Sig.
Negative work characteristics	.099	.071	.100	1.384	0.168
Positive work and individual characteristics	−.172	.064	−.173	−2.680	<0.01
Job demands	.178	.080	.171	2.231	<0.05
Length of shift	.048	.066	.050	.727	0.468
Overtime work	.123	.058	.123	2.109	<0.05
Timing of shift	.079	.065	.080	1.216	0.226
Mental workload	.425	.084	.418	5.042	<0.001
Effort	−.047	.067	−.045	−.700	0.485
Sleep factor	−.081	.058	−.083	−1.408	0.161
Other activities	.040	.057	.041	.702	0.484

However, given that the risk factors for different dimensions of fatigue can be different, separate analyses of the physical, mental, and emotional fatigue variables were needed. Therefore, binary logistics regression analyses (using enter method) were run, using the original fatigue variables as the outcomes, and dichotomised factors as the predictors. The dependent variables used here were physical fatigue, mental fatigue, and emotional fatigue, which were dichotomised into high/low groups using median splits (M $_{Physical\ Fatigue}$ = 6, M $_{Mental\ Fatigue}$ = 7, M $_{Emotional}$ Fatigue = 6). The independent variables were the 10 independent factors, which were dichotomised though median splitting the factor scores. The results are presented in Tables 5, 6 and 7.

Analysing Predictors of Physical Fatigue. In the regression analysis, negative work characteristics, long length of shifts, and overtime work were found to be associated with physical fatigue at a significant level ($p < .05$). The strongest predictor of reporting a physical fatigue problem in this model was the length of shift work, recording an odds ratio (OR) of 4.5, indicating that participants working long shifts were 4.5 times more likely to report physical fatigue problems ($p < 0.001$) than those with shorter shifts. This was followed by overtime work, recording an OR of 3.1, and negative work characteristics, recording an OR of 2.6. High mental workload and high job demands showed a trend toward significance in predicting physical fatigue (p $_{Mental\ workload}$ = 0.069, p $_{Job\ Demands}$ = 0.084, both OR = 2.1). There was no significant association between other factors and physical fatigue in this model. The account of explanatory power of this model was 39.5% of the variance, and the classification accuracy was 75.0%. The full model containing all predictors, was statistically significant, X^2 (1, N = 172) = 59.972, $p < 0.001$, indicating that the model was able to distinguish between participants who reported and those who did not report a physical fatigue problem.

Table 5. Odds ratio of each IV on physical fatigue.

Variables	Odds ratio	95% CI for odds ratio
Negative work characteristics (high)	2.630[*]	[1.189, 5.820]
Positive work and individual characteristics (low)	2.080	[0.907, 4.771]
Job demands (high)	1.888	[0.856, 4.165]
Length of shift (long)	4.468[**]	[1.929, 10.347]
Overtime work	3.122[*]	[1.433, 6.804]
Timing of shift (poor)	0.909	[0.420, 1.969]
Mental workload (high)	2.105	[0.943, 4.702]
Effort (high)	1.239	[0.563, 2.729]
Sleep factor (negative)	1.489	[0.682, 3.250]
Other activities	1.769	[0.808, 3.874]

[*]$p < 0.05$, [**]$p < 0.001$

Analysing Predictors of Mental Fatigue. Job demands, mental workload, and overtime work were found to influence mental fatigue significantly ($p < .01$). The strongest predictor of mental fatigue was job demands, recording an OR of 5.4, indicating that participants working with high job demands were 5.4 times more likely to report a mental fatigue problem ($p < 0.001$) than those with low job demands. This was followed by mental workload (OR = 3.0) and overtime work (OR = 2.9). No significant association between other factors and mental fatigue was found in this model. The model of mental fatigue accounted for 40.0% of the variance and correctly classified 75.7% of cases. The full model containing all predictors, was statistically significant (X^2 (1, N = 173) = 61.131, $p < 0.001$), indicating that the model was able to distinguish between participants who reported and those who did not report a mental fatigue problem.

Table 6. Odds ratio of each IV on mental fatigue.

Variable	Odds ratio	95% CI for odds ratio
Negative work characteristics (high)	1.658	[0.728, 3.777]
Positive work and individual characteristics (low)	1.253	[0.549, 2.857]
Job demands (high)	5.403**	[2.465, 11.840]
Length of shift (long)	0.807	[0.337, 1.932]
Overtime work	2.899*	[1.324, 6.345]
Timing of shift (poor)	1.066	[0.478, 2.378]
Mental workload (high)	2.959*	[1.311, 6.679]
Effort (high)	1.788	[0.808, 3.954]
Sleep factor (negative)	1.819	[0.817, 4.051]
Other activities	0.951	[0.440, 2.058]

* $p < 0.05$, ** $p < 0.001$

Analysing Predictors of Emotional Fatigue. Emotional fatigue was significantly predicted by positive work and individual characteristics, job demands, length of shift, overtime work, timing of shift, and mental workload. Overtime work was the strongest predictor of reporting emotional fatigue, recording an OR of 4.2, $p < 0.001$. This was followed by length of shift (OR = 3.9, $p < .01$), low scores for positive work and individual characteristics (OR = 3.8, $p < .01$), and high job demands (OR = 3.6, $p < .01$). Mental workload and the timing of shift were also the important predictors of emotional fatigue, both recording ORs of 2.7, $p < .05$. The model of emotional fatigue accounted for 42.1% of the variance and correctly classified 76.3% of cases. The full model containing all predictors, was statistically significant (X^2 (1, N = 173) = 65.407, $p < 0.001$), indicating that the model was able to distinguish between participants who reported and those who did not report an emotional fatigue problem.

Table 7. Odds ratio of each IV on emotional fatigue.

Variable	Odds ratio	95% CI for odds ratio
Negative work characteristics (high)	1.478	[0.636, 3.434]
Positive work and individual characteristics (low)	3.809*	[1.635, 8.875]
Job demands (high)	3.603*	[1.604, 8.093]
Length of shift (long)	3.883*	[1.591, 9.473]
Overtime work	4.180**	[1.851, 9.436]
Timing of shift (poor)	2.804*	[1.197, 6.568]
Mental workload (high)	2.809*	[1.248, 6.323]
Effort (high)	1.541	[0.703, 3.381]
Sleep factor (negative)	1.378	[0.630, 3.014]
Other activities	1.776	[0.799, 3.948]

*$p < 0.05$, **$p < 0.001$

6 Discussion

The present study confirmed that mental workload is an essential cause of fatigue among rail staff. Although other risk factors were also found to be associated with fatigue, only positive work and individual characteristics, job demands, overtime work, and mental workload predicted fatigue as a single outcome, which is consistent with previous studies [6, 30]. The findings provided more specific information on mental workload and other causes of different types of fatigue. When different types of fatigue were analysed separately, mental workload, job demands, and overtime work were still found to predict fatigue in all its three dimensions. Physical fatigue was also associated with longer length of shift work, negative work characteristics, and less frequent breaks during work. Moreover, the findings provide evidence that poor shift patterns result in mental and emotional fatigue. Both mental and emotional fatigue were associated with poor timing of shifts and a greater number of shifts taken before a day of rest. Emotional fatigue was also predicted by positive work and individual characteristics, which means that high job supports and control, healthy lifestyle, and positive personality helped to reduce emotional fatigue. Although the effects of positive work and individual characteristics were in line with a previous large-scale study [1] that showed they play a buffering role in fatigue, they only influenced emotional fatigue, not mental fatigue. These findings support the idea that the jobs of rail staff place greater emphasis on the mental workload. In the factor analysis, the contribution of physical job demands to 3D-demands was much smaller than that of mental and emotional demands. This supported the view from previous research [14] that currently, work in the railway industry imposes more cognitive demands than physical demands. Moreover, the predictive ability of job demands was consistent with those of mental workload. It predicted all three different types of fatigue, as well as fatigue as a whole, while the effect of effort was not found to be significant. It was the mental workload and overtime work that resulted in all different types of fatigue among train crew. "More work over longer times from fewer people" is a dangerous strategy which can make the train staff more fatigued. Currently, fatigue is conceptualised in terms of working hours in rail transport. This suggests that future fatigue study of the railway staff should develop an appropriate mental workload measurement. Subjective measure of the mental workload will be sufficient [16, 26], despite the fundamental research required to compare subjective and objective workload in the industry. Based on data gathered through an online survey, the results of the current study are in line with those of previous studies (e.g., [5, 6, 30]). Furthermore, the results showed a bias towards having a positive personality, efficiency, and effort, which also appeared in the offline survey [30]. These suggests that the online survey was as reliable as the offline version, and in the future, online studies can be carried out.

In future research, measuring different types of fatigue separately will be useful to better understand job role differences. Although the high mental workload and overtime work cannot be avoided in many industries, a better understanding of the causes of different types of fatigue among workers will help with fatigue management in the workplace. It is suggested that sufficient opportunities to take breaks during work should be provided to control physical fatigue, and that shift patterns should be well arranged to reduce the risk of mental and emotional fatigue.

7 Conclusion

Fatigue has usually been investigated as a single outcome, but there are different types of fatigue taking into account separate kinds of energy resources. This study explored the causes of physical, mental, and emotional fatigue among rail staff. The finding indicated that mental workload and overtime work were the essential causes of all these types of fatigue among rail staff. Alongside these two causes, these three dimensions of fatigue were influenced by different factors. Physical fatigue resulted from prolonged shift work, insufficient rest during work, and negative work characteristics, while mental and emotional fatigue resulted from poorly arranged shift patterns, including poor timing of shifts and working more shifts before taking a regular rest day. Positive work and individual characteristics played a buffering role only for emotional fatigue, but not for mental fatigue. This suggested that to recovery from physical and mental fatigue, appropriate rests and breaks and better arranged shift patterns were needed. In future research, measuring different types of fatigue separately will be useful to better understand job role differences and benefit fatigue management.

References

1. Fan, J., Smith, A.P.: The mediating effect of fatigue on work-life balance positive well-being in railway staff. Open J. Soc. Sci. **6**, 1–10 (2018). https://doi.org/10.4236/jss.2018.66001
2. Shirom, A., Melamed, S.: A comparison of the construct validity of two burnout measures in two groups of professionals. Int. J. Stress Manag. **13**(2), 176–200 (2006). https://doi.org/10.1037/1072-5245.13.2.176

3. Australian Safety and Compensation Council. Work-related fatigue: summary of recent indicative research. https://www.safeworkaustralia.gov.au/doc/work-related-fatigue-summary-recent-indicative-research-archived

4. Frone, M.R., Tidwell, M.C.O.: The meaning and measurement of work fatigue: development and evaluation of the three-dimensional work fatigue inventory (3D-WFI). J. Occup. Health Psychol. **20**(3), 273–288 (2015). https://doi.org/10.1037/a0038700

5. Smith, A.P., Smith, H.N.: Workload, fatigue and performance in the rail industry. In: Longo, L., Leva, M.C. (eds.) H-WORKLOAD 2017. CCIS, vol. 726, pp. 251–263. Springer, Cham (2017). https://doi.org/10.1007/978-3-319-61061-0_17

6. Fan, J., Smith, A.P.: A preliminary review of fatigue among rail staff. Front. Psychol. **9**, 634 (2018). https://doi.org/10.3389/fpsyg.2018.00634

7. Mark, G.M., Smith, A.P.: Stress models: a review and suggested new direction. In: Houdmont, J., Leka, S. (eds.) Occupational Health Psychology: European Perspectives on Research, Education and Practice, pp. 111–144. Nottingham University Press, Nortingham (2008)

8. Robert, G., Hockey, J., Wiethoff, M.: Assessing patterns of adjustment to the demands of work. In: Puglisi-Allegra, S., Oliverio, A. (eds.) The Psychobiology of Stress, vol. 54, pp. 231–240. Springer, Dordrecht (1990). https://doi.org/10.1007/978-94-009-1990-7_21

9. Dorrian, J., Baulk, S.D., Dawson, D.: Work hours, workload, sleep and fatigue in australian rail industry employees. Appl. Ergon. **42**(2), 202–209 (2011). https://doi.org/10.1016/j.apergo.2010.06.009

10. Wickens, C.D.: Engineering Psychology and Human Performance, 2nd edn. HarperCollins Publishers Inc., New York (1992). https://doi.org/10.1146/annurev.ps.27.020176.001513

11. Jahns, D.W.: A concept of operator workload in manual vehicle operations. Research Institute Anthropotechnology, Meckenheim (1973)

12. Edwards, T., Martin, L., Bienert, N., Mercer, J.: The relationship between workload and performance in air traffic control: exploring the influence of levels of automation and variation in task demand. In: Longo, L., Leva, M.C. (eds.) H-WORKLOAD 2017. CCIS, vol. 726, pp. 120–139. Springer, Cham (2017). https://doi.org/10.1007/978-3-319-61061-0_8

13. Hancock, P.A., Caird, J.K.: Experimental evaluation of a model of mental workload. Hum. Factors **35**, 413–429 (1993). https://doi.org/10.1177/001872089303500303

14. Young, M.S., Brookhuis, K.A., Wickens, C.D., Hancock, P.A.: State of science: mental workload in ergonomics. Ergonomics **58**(1), 1–17 (2015). https://doi.org/10.1080/00140139.2014.956151

15. Longo, L.: Formalising human mental workload as a defeasible computational concept. Ph. D. thesis, Trinity College Dublin (2014)

16. Longo, L.: A defeasible reasoning framework for human mental workload representation and assessment. Behav. Inf. Technol. **34**(8), 758–786 (2015). https://doi.org/10.1080/0144929X.2015.1015166

17. Reid, G.B., Nygren, T.E.: The subjective workload assessment technique: a scaling procedure for measuring mental workload, vol. 52. North-Holland (1988). https://doi.org/10.1016/s0166-4115(08)62387-0

18. Eggemeier, F.T., Wilson, G.F., Kramer, A.F., Damos, D.L.: Workload assessment in multi-task environments. In: Damos, D.L. (ed.) Multiple Task Performance, pp. 207–216. Taylor & Francis, London (1991)

19. Hancock, P.A., Chignell, M.H.: Mental workload dynamics in adaptive interface design. IEEE Trans. Syst. Man Cybern. **18**(4), 647–658 (1988). https://doi.org/10.1109/21.17382

20. Wickens, C.D.: Mental workload: assessment, prediction and consequences. In: Longo, L., Leva, M.C. (eds.) H-WORKLOAD 2017. CCIS, vol. 726, pp. 18–29. Springer, Cham (2017). https://doi.org/10.1007/978-3-319-61061-0_2

21. Hancock, P.A.: Whither workload? Mapping a path for its future development. In: Longo, L., Leva, M.Chiara (eds.) H-WORKLOAD 2017. CCIS, vol. 726, pp. 3–17. Springer, Cham (2017). https://doi.org/10.1007/978-3-319-61061-0_1

22. Rizzo, L., Dondio, P., Delany, S.J., Longo, L.: Modeling mental workload via rule-based expert system: a comparison with NASA-TLX and workload profile. In: Iliadis, L., Maglogiannis, I. (eds.) AIAI 2016. IAICT, vol. 475, pp. 215–229. Springer, Cham (2016). https://doi.org/10.1007/978-3-319-44944-9_19

23. Longo, L.: Mental workload in medicine: foundations, applications, open problems, challenges and future perspectives. In: 2016 IEEE 29th International Symposium on Computer-Based Medical Systems (CBMS), pp. 106–111. IEEE (2016). https://doi.org/10.1109/cbms.2016.36

24. Byrne, A.: Mental workload as an outcome in medical education. In: Longo, L., Leva, M.C. (eds.) H-WORKLOAD 2017. CCIS, vol. 726, pp. 187–197. Springer, Cham (2017). https://doi.org/10.1007/978-3-319-61061-0_12

25. Guastello, S.J., Marra, D.E., Correro, A.N., Michels, M., Schimmel, H.: Elasticity and rigidity constructs and ratings of subjective workload for individuals and groups. In: Longo, L., Leva, M.C. (eds.) H-WORKLOAD 2017. CCIS, vol. 726, pp. 51–76. Springer, Cham (2017). https://doi.org/10.1007/978-3-319-61061-0_4

26. Cain, B.: A review of the mental workload literature. RTO-TR-HFM-121-Part II, NATO report, pp. 4-1–4-34. Defence Research and Development, Toronto, Canada (2007)

27. Dorrian, J., Baulk, S.D., Dawson, D.: Work hours, workload, sleep and fatigue in Australian Rail Industry employees. Appl. Ergon. 42, 202–209 (2011). https://doi.org/10.1016/j.apergo.2010.06.009

28. Ferguson, S.A., Lamond, N., Kandelaars, K., Jay, S.M., Dawson, D.: The impact of short, irregular sleep opportunities at sea on the alertness of marine pilots working extended hours. Chronobiol. Int. 25(2–3), 399–411 (2008). https://doi.org/10.1080/07420520802106819

29. Dorrian, J., Baulk, S.D., Dawson, D.: Work hours, workload, sleep and fatigue in Australian Rail Industry employees. Appl. Ergon. 42(2), 20–209 (2011). https://doi.org/10.1016/j.apergo.2010.06.009

30. Fan, J., Smith, A.P.: The impact of workload and fatigue on performance. In: Longo, L., Leva, M.C. (eds.) H-WORKLOAD 2017. CCIS, vol. 726, pp. 90–105. Springer, Cham (2017). https://doi.org/10.1007/978-3-319-61061-0_6

31. Williams, J., Smith, A.P.: Stress, job satisfaction and mental health of NHS nurses. In: Contemporary Ergonomics and Human Factors 2013: Proceedings of the International Conference on Ergonomics and Human Factors 2013, Cambridge, UK, 15–18 April 2013, p. 95. Taylor & Francis, London (2013). https://doi.org/10.1201/b13826-22

On the Mental Workload Assessment of Uplift Mapping Representations in Linked Data

Ademar Crotti Junior[1]($\boxtimes$) (ID), Christophe Debruyne[1] (ID),
Luca Longo[2] (ID), and Declan O'Sullivan[1] (ID)

[1] ADAPT Centre, Trinity College Dublin, Dublin 2, Ireland
{ademar.crotti, christophe.debruyne,
declan.osullivan}@adaptcentre.ie
[2] ADAPT Centre, Dublin Institute of Technology, Dublin 8, Ireland
luca.longo@dit.ie

Abstract. Self-reporting procedures have been largely employed in literature to measure the mental workload experienced by users when executing a specific task. This research proposes the adoption of these mental workload assessment techniques to the task of creating uplift mappings in Linked Data. A user study has been performed to compare the mental workload of "manually" creating such mappings, using a formal mapping language and a text editor, to the use of a visual representation, based on the block metaphor, that generate these mappings. Two subjective mental workload instruments, namely the NASA Task Load Index and the Workload Profile, were applied in this study. Preliminary results show the reliability of these instruments in measuring the perceived mental workload for the task of creating uplift mappings. Results also indicate that participants using the visual representation achieved smaller and more consistent scores of mental workload.

Keywords: Mental workload · Uplift mapping representations · Linked Data

1 Introduction

Human mental workload (MWL) is a fundamental design concept used to investigate the interaction of human with computers and other technological devices [22]. MWL instruments measure the cognitive load experienced by users when executing a specific task [5]. Literature suggests that both mental overload and underload can affect performance [22]. This study employs human mental workload instruments to the task of creating uplift mappings in Linked Data. Linked Data refers to a set of best practices for publishing and interlinking data on the Web [4]. The standard data model used in Linked Data is the Resource Description Framework[1] (RDF). Uplift mappings are responsible for expressing how non-RDF data should be transformed to RDF [8]. A significant part of the Linked Data web is achieved by such conversion process.

The uplift process is often express through mapping languages. The W3C Recommendation mapping language R2RML [9] (RDB to RDF mapping language) is an example of a formal language used to express mappings that transform relational

---

[1] http://www.w3.org/TR/rdf11-concepts/.

L. Longo and M. C. Leva (Eds.): H-WORKLOAD 2018, CCIS 1012, pp. 160–179, 2019.
https://doi.org/10.1007/978-3-030-14273-5_10

databases into RDF. These mappings can be created "manually", trough text editors or by applications that support user involvement in the mapping process. Such applications may make use of visual representations to alleviate the knowledge required by mapping languages [31]. An example of a visual representation is the Jigsaw Puzzles for Representing Mappings (Juma) [18]. Juma is based on the block metaphor, which has become popular with visual programming languages (see Sect. 2.3). It is assumed that the creation of mappings using different uplift mapping representations require different cognitive processing resources. And that the assessment of the cognitive workload of uplift mapping representations can be used to evaluate and improve the interaction between users and these representations. Thus, this paper extends the application of MWL instruments by evaluating the perceived mental workload of users when performing an uplift mapping task. The user experiment presented in this paper assesses the cognitive load of creating uplift mappings using the two aforementioned mapping representations, R2RML and Juma. Two subjective mental workload instruments were applied in this study, namely the Workload Profile and the Nasa Task Load Index. To the authors knowledge, this paper presents the first evaluations considering the cognitive load of creating uplift mappings in Linked Data.

The remainder of this paper is structured as follows: Sect. 2 discusses the background knowledge, which contains a brief description of mappings applied in the Linked Data domain. Section 3 presents the two mental workload assessment instruments used in this study. Section 4 introduces the design of a novel primary research at the intersection of mental workload and uplifting mapping tasks. Results and their analysis are presented in Sect. 5. Related work is presented in Sect. 6. Section 7 concludes the paper and suggests future work.

2 Background

2.1 Mappings in Linked Data

The term Linked Data refers to a set of best practices for publishing and interlinking data on the Web [4]. A Linked Data dataset is structured information encoded using the Resource Description Framework (RDF), that are linked to other datasets, and accessible via HTTP. RDF is a graph data model that provides one means to describe, annotate and exchange information such that machines can process them [4]. The Linking Open Data project has the goal of publishing open datasets as Linked Data. These open datasets are freely accessible and collectively known as the Linked Open Data cloud[2]. A significant part of the Linked Data cloud is achieved by converting resources to RDF, often through mappings. In a general context, a mapping defines a relation between source and target elements [12]. The properties of a mapping are represented in a structured format using mapping languages [8]. Mappings that express how non-RDF data is transformed to RDF are called uplift mappings. An example of a transformation from a relational database to RDF is presented in Fig. 1. In this example, the table *person* is transformed into the graph-based RDF data model.

---

[2] http://lod-cloud.net/

Fig. 1. Example of a transformation from a relational database to RDF

The R2RML mapping language, which can be used to express these transformations, is presented in Sect. 2.2. Juma, a visual representation that can be used to generate such mappings, is presented in Sect. 2.3.

2.2　R2RML

The RDB to RDF mapping language (R2RML) [9] is the W3C Recommendation mapping language used to express mappings between relational databases and RDF. R2RML's vocabulary defines that each mapping consists of one or more *triples maps*. A triples map has (1) one *logical table*, (2) one *subject map* and (3) zero or more *predicate object maps*, where:

1. **Logical Table**: a table or an SQL query from which RDF will be generated.
2. **Subject Map**: subject maps define the subjects of the RDF triples. These subjects can be IRIs or blank nodes. One also may specify zero or more URI class types.
3. **Predicate Object Map**: each predicate object map defines the predicates, using predicate maps, and objects, using object maps, of the RDF triples. Each predicate object map must have at least one predicate map and one object map. Predicates must be valid IRIs. Objects can be IRI's, blank nodes or literal values. For literal values, it is possible to define a data type or a language. One may link triples maps using *parent triples map*. A parent triples map can have zero or more join conditions.

Listing 1 shows an example the transformation presented in Fig. 1 expressed using the R2RML mapping language.

```
<#TripleMap1>
  rr:logicalTable [
   rr:tableName "person";
  ];

  rr:subjectMap [
    rr:template "http://example.org/person/{id}";
    rr:class foaf:Person;
  ];

  rr:predicateObjectMap [
    rr:predicateMap [ rr:constant foaf:name; ];
    rr:objectMap [ rr:column "name"; ];
  ]; .
```

Listing 1. R2RML mapping definition

In this mapping, the logical table is defined as *person*. Using one triples map, we define the subjects to have the following URI `http://example.org/person/{id}`. *Id* is an attribute coming from the table *person*. In this sense, for row with *id* equals to 1, this mapping would generate triples with the subject as `http://example.org/person/1`, and so on. A class definition construct is used to define that these subjects are instances of the class `foaf:Person`, which is declared in the FOAF[3] vocabulary. A predicate object map defines the predicate of the triples to be `foaf:name`, and the object of the triples to be come from the attribute *"name"* of the declared logical table *person*. The output of this mapping, considering that the fictional table *person* has only one record with the attribute *id* as an integer with value *1* and attribute *name* as a string with value *"Ana"*, is shown in RDF Turtle syntax in Listing 2.

```
<http://example.org/person/1>
    a          <http://xmlns.com/foaf/0.1/Person> ;
    <http://xmlns.com/foaf/0.1/name>
               "Ana" .
```

Listing 2. RDF output from executing the mapping presented in Listing 1

2.3 Juma

Juma is a method for visually representing mappings in Linked Data. Juma is based on the block (or jigsaw) metaphor that has become popular with visual programming languages – where it is called the block paradigm – such as Scratch[4]. This metaphor allows users to focus on the logic instead of the language's syntax. In addition, the block metaphor has been successfully used in other domains [3, 6]. The implementation of Juma applied to uplift languages used in this study is called Juma Uplift [19]. In Juma Uplift, each mapping defines an input source that is associated to 0 or more vocabularies. These vocabularies are then used in the mapping definitions. A mapping is also associated with 0 or more subject definitions. These subject definitions express how subjects are generated from the input data. Each subject definition has associated predicate object definitions. Subject definitions can also declare these to be instances of 0 or more classes, to be a blank node, and associate triples to a named graph. For more information about Juma Uplift the reader is referred to [19]. Figure 2 shows the mapping from Listing 1 represented using the Juma Uplift representation. The RDF output of this mapping was presented in Listing 2.

---

[3] http://xmlns.com/foaf/0.1/

[4] https://scratch.mit.edu/, last accessed May 2018

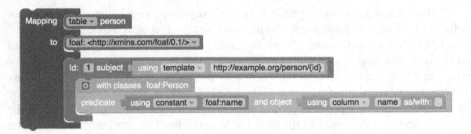

Fig. 2. Juma Uplift mapping representation

3   Mental Workload Self-reporting Assessment Instruments

Human mental workload (MWL) is a fundamental design concept used to investigate the interaction of human with computers and other technological devices [22]. It can be intuitively described as the amount of work necessary for users to complete a task [5]. MWL measurements can be classified into three broad categories:

- subjective measures: subjects auto-assess their mental workload by rating a set of dimensions, within pre-defined scales, in relation with the execution of a task performed immediately before;
- performance measures: subjects have some physiological characteristics measured while performing a task. As, for instance, eye activity and heart rate;
- physiological measures: subjects' mental workload is assessed according with the performance reached in a primary or for a secondary task (e.g. error rates; task completion time).

This paper focuses on two subjective mental workload assessment techniques: the Workload Profile and the NASA Task Load Index.

3.1   Workload Profile

The Workload Profile (WP) assessment procedure [42] is built upon the Multiple Resource Theory proposed in [45, 46]. In this theory, individuals are seen as having different capacities or 'resources' related to:

- stage of information processing: perceptual/central processing and response selection/execution;
- code of information processing: spatial/verbal;
- input: visual and auditory processing;
- output: manual and speech output.

Each dimension is quantified through subjective rates and subjects, after task completion, are required to rate the proportion of attentional resources used for performing a given task with a value in the range $0..1 \in \Re$. A rating of 0 means that the task placed no demand while 1 indicates that it required maximum attention. The questionnaire is presented in Table 7. The aggregation strategy is a simple sum of the 8 rates d (averaged here, and scaled in $[1..100 \in \Re]$ for comparison purposes):

$$WP:[0..100] \in \Re$$

$$WP = \frac{1}{8} \sum_{i=1}^{8} d_i * 100$$

3.2 NASA Task Load Index

The NASA Task Load Index (NASA-TLX) instrument [16] belongs to the category of self-assessment measures. It has been validated in the aviation industry and other contexts in Ergonomics [16, 36] with several applications in many socio-technical domains. It is a combination of six factors believed to influence MWL (full questionnaire in Table 8). Each factor is quantified with a subjective judgement coupled with a weight computed via a paired comparison procedure. Subjects are required to decide, for each possible pair (binomial coefficient, $\binom{6}{2} = 15$) of the 6 factors, 'which of the two contributed the most to mental workload during the task', such as 'Mental or Temporal Demand?', and so forth. The weights w are the number of times each dimension was selected. In this case, the range is from 0 (not relevant) to 5 (more important than any other attribute). The final MWL score is computed as a weighted average, considering the subjective rating of each attribute d_i and the correspondent weights w_i:

$$NASATLX:[0..100] \in \Re$$

$$NASATLX = \left(\sum_{i=1}^{6} d_i * w_i \right) \frac{1}{15}$$

Alternatively, it is possible to calculate the MWL scores eliminating the weighted procedure, which is called *Raw TLX*.

4 Design and Methodology

A primary research study has been designed to assess the mental workload of creating uplift mappings in Linked Data using two different mapping representations. This experiment compares the "manual" creation of uplift mappings with R2RML using the RDF TURTLE notation[5] (which is in essence a text file) to the visual mapping representation Juma. For the remainder of this paper, R2RML mappings refers to

---

[5] TURTLE is only one of the many standardized RDF representations. TURTLE was chosen as it is terse, and one of the more usable and easier to read representations. Even the R2RML W3C Recommendation uses TURTLE for their examples.

mappings in R2RML using RDF TURTLE syntax, and Juma refers to mappings represented using the Juma Uplift representation.

The research hypotheses related to this experiment are:

- **Hypothesis H1**: the perceived mental workload of users interacting with Juma for the creation of uplift mappings is expected to be lower than the perceived mental workload experienced by users that crafted the same mappings manually, according to the NASA-TLX and WP mental workload measures.
- **Hypothesis H2**: the NASA-TLX and WP mental workload measures have high reliability.

4.1 Participants and Procedure

A number of students enrolled in a third-level class from a MSc module in Information and Knowledge Architecture in Trinity College Dublin, Ireland, in 2017, have been approached for this experiment. The experiment was executed in week 10 of a 12-week module. At that time, the course on Knowledge Engineering and Semantic Web technologies had covered OWL modeling, RDF, and SPARQL (amongst others). Participants also had one class, a week before the experiment, on R2RML, which included exercises. This highlights the pre-training on R2RML that the participants have received prior to this research experiment. Note that participants had no knowledge of Juma prior to the experiment. In order to evaluate the Juma and R2RML mapping representations for the task of creating uplift mappings, participants were split into two groups. Students in one group were exposed to the Juma visual representation – which, for the remainder of the paper, we refer to as the Juma group. Participants in the second group were able to use their preferred text editor to create uplift mappings manually, using R2RML – referred as the R2RML group for the remainder of the paper. The study was executed with 26 participants, 12 in the Juma group and 14 in R2RML group. The experiment was executed with participants in a classroom; and lasted for 50 min. The first 10 min were used to explain the experiment to participants, and for participants to examine the material provided. Note that participants still did not have access to the uplift mapping task at this point. Participants were also asked to fill in, read, and consent to the study information sheet, to be able to participate in the experiment. All participants had exactly 30 min for the execution of the task. Finally, in the last 10 min, participants were asked to fill in the questionnaires associated to the WP and NASA-TLX mental workload assessment instruments. Note that the question of the NASA-TLX related to 'physical demand' (NT_2 in Table 8) was set to 0, as there is no physical load related to the task assessed in this experiment. In detail, the evaluation was structured in four parts, as also depicted in Fig. 3:

1. **Technical debriefing:** all participants had the opportunity to watch videos about R2RML[6] prior to executing the uplift mapping task. The group using the Juma

---

[6] Available at https://www.scss.tcd.ie/∼crottija/juma/r2rml.pdf and https://www.youtube.com/watch?v=fn5mKGGj2us.

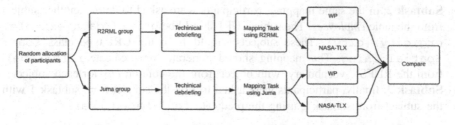

Fig. 3. Experiment design diagram

method also had a presentation and a video about the visual representation[7]. The material was also available during the execution of the task.

2. **Mapping task:** in the main part of this study, participants were asked to create a specific uplift mapping (described in Sect. 4.2). Participants could ask questions for clarifying any doubts about the experiment.

3. **Post-task questionnaire:** after completion of the task, participants were asked to fill in the WP and NASA-TLX mental workload questionnaires.

4.2 Mapping Task

This user study was built on top of the Microsoft Access 2010 Northwind sample database that has been ported to MySQL[8]. Participants were asked to create one R2RML mapping divided in three subtasks. For each subtask, a sample RDF output was shown to participants. In addition, they could run the mapping, by using an R2RML processor, and compare the output of their mapping execution to the sample provided. In this sense, an R2RML processor [10] was integrated to Juma. Participants creating the mappings using a text editor had access to a compacted folder with the same engine and the command line instruction that runs it. By executing the mappings, participants were able to validate the correctness of the output. A summary of the mapping task, separated into its subtasks, is shown below:

- **Subtask 1**: participants had to define a mapping with one subject per row of the table *employees*. The subject URI for the triples should be http://data.ex-ample.org/employee/{id}. These subject should also have the URI type class foaf:Person from the FOAF[9] vocabulary. The mapping definition should also create, for these subjects, the predicate foaf:givenName with object from the column *first_name*. The predicate foaf:familyName with object from the column *last_name*. Finally, the predicate foaf:name should have the concatenation of the columns *last_name* and *first_*name separated by comma as object.

- **Subtask 2**: in the same mapping, participants were asked to define another subject from the table *employees*. The subject URI should be `http://data.example.org/city/{city}`. These subjects should have the URI type class `foaf:Spatial_Thing`. The mapping should generate the predicate `rdfs:label`, from the RDFS[10] vocabulary, with object from the column *city* for each subject.
- **Subtask 3**: finally, participants were asked to link the subject from subtask 1 with the subject from subtask 2 using the predicate `foaf:based_near`.

Some elements of the task could be achieved in different ways. For example, since not all attributes are mapped, participants could map an SQL query instead of the whole table. Concatenating could be implemented using a template construct, an SQL query, or through the use of the data transformation function called 'concatenating' - for participants using Juma Uplift. The template construct would be the expected solution to concatenating. Subtask 3 asked participants to relate the subjects created in subtask 1 and subtask 2. This could be achieved by mapping using an SQL query with a join, a template construct - since this value comes from the same table – or with a parent triples map (for users creating mappings manually) or the linking block (for participants using Juma Uplift). For subtask 3, parent triples map or the linking block would be the expected solution. The task performance, as it is defined in this paper, is the number of correct triples found in the RDF output generated from the participants' mappings. Note that the performance takes the output of the mapping into account and not the mapping itself, as there are multiple possible correct solutions, but only one correct output. The Jena API[11] was used to compare the RDF models and count the triples. Table 1 shows the challenges associated to the task.

Table 1. Challenges associated to the task

Subtask	Short description	Challenge/Non-trivial aspects
#1	Map and type entities to a class with three attributes	One attribute mapping is the concatenation of other two attributes. This requires mapping using a SQL query, the use of a template construct or the data transformation function 'concatenating' - for participants using Juma Uplift
#2	Map and type another entity with one attribute	Map cities as a second entity from the same table using another triples map
#3	Linking the subjects created in the previous subtasks	Linking subjects created in subtasks 1 and 2. This requires the use of a template construct, a SQL query with a SQL join, the R2RML parent triples map construct for mappings created manually, or the linking block for participants using Juma Uplift

---

[10] http://www.w3.org/2000/01/rdf-schema.

[11] https://jena.apache.org/, accessed May 2018.

5 Results and Analysis

In this section, we present the results and analysis of the experiment described in Sect. 4. As stated in the previous section, in order to test the research hypothesis **H1**, the WP and NASA-TLX instruments were applied. Table 2 shows the perceived mental workload of both instruments for the R2RML group. Table 3 shows the same scores for the Juma group.

Table 2. Perceived mental workload scores for the R2RML group

Participant	WP	NASA-TLX
#1	45.86	65.6
#2	37.86	64.8
#3	41.28	37.8
#4	73.13	51.4
#5	27.86	35.6
#6	32.43	51.6
#7	75.29	56.8
#8	46.29	42
#9	71.13	62.8
#10	16.13	34
#11	58.43	54.4
#12	63.56	56
#13	63.13	73.2
#14	49.56	61.6
AVG	**50.14**	**53.40**
STD	**18.08**	**12.14**

Table 3. Perceived mental workload scores for the Juma group

Participant	WP	NASA-TLX
#1	46.86	52.6
#2	41.29	47
#3	36.57	31.2
#4	54.57	51.2
#5	54.72	48
#6	45.56	61.8
#7	57.87	57.4
#8	46	34.4
#9	54.86	52.4
#10	64.13	48.2
#11	28.43	26.4
#12	43.29	37
AVG	**47.85**	**45.63**
STD	**9.92**	**10.95**

The Anderson-Darling normality test was applied to the R2RML and Juma groups. Table 4 shows the A values and p-values resulting from this test. Figure 4 shows histograms for the same data.

Table 4. Anderson-Darling normality test per group

MWL	R2RML		Juma	
	A	p-value	A	p-value
WP	0.20	0.84	0.23	0.47
NASA-TLX	0.33	0.74	0.39	0.33

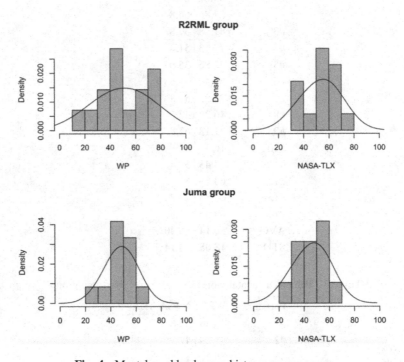

Fig. 4. Mental workload score histograms per group

In order to compare the scores between the groups, we have applied the Welch T-Test and the Wilcoxon test. These tests are used to compare whether two samples are statistically different. The main difference between these tests is that the Welch T-Test assumes normality of the data. The Wilcoxon Test, however, is considered an alternative test when the data does not follow a normal distribution. Considering that the Anderson-Darling test indicates that the data in both groups is normal, the Welch T-Test should be sufficient. For clarity, we have also applied the Wilcoxon test. The results of the independent two sample Welch T-Test and Wilcoxon test are presented in Table 5.

Table 5. Mental workload test between groups

MWL	Welch Test		Wilcoxon Test	
	T	p-value	W	p-value
WP	−0.41	0.69	75.5	0.68
NASA-TLX	−1.72	0.10	50	0.08

As mentioned in Sect. 4.2, the performance of participants was calculated by counting the correct triples in the output of the execution of the mappings created by each participant. In this sense, the R2RML group achieved task performance of 35.98%; while the Juma group achieved 93.08%. Figure 5 shows a scatterplot between performance and the MWL scores. In this plot, the correlation between performance and mental workload scores in the R2RML group seems to be multi modal, while the distribution in the Juma group seems to be unimodal. These plots and the smaller standard deviation indicate that the mental workload scored perceived by participants in the Juma group are more consistent than the ones found in the R2RML group.

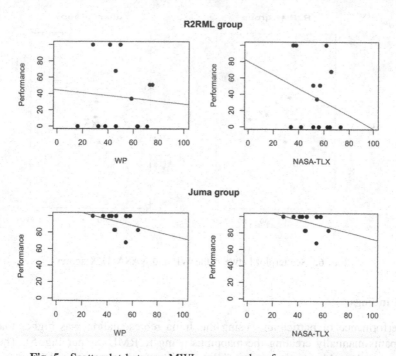

Fig. 5. Scatterplot between MWL scores and performance per group

5.1 Reliability

In order to test the research hypothesis **H2**, the Cronbach's alpha coefficient was applied. Cronbach's alpha is a commonly used measure of reliability within questionnaires. Cronbach's alpha should coefficients should be higher than 0.70, as it is suggested in the literature [30]. Table 6 shows the Cronbach's alphas for the WP and NASA-TLX mental workload instruments. These results highlight a strong internal consistency of the items (questions) in these instruments. They also suggest that these instruments are reliable measures of mental workload.

Table 6. Cronbach's alpha index for WP and NASA-TLX

MWL	Alpha index
WP	0.78
NASA-TLX	0.85

Figure 6 shows a scatterplot between WP and NASA-TLX scores per group. This plot suggests a positive linear relation between the MWL instruments WP and NASA-TLX. It also indicates that when WP increases, so does the NASA-TLX score.

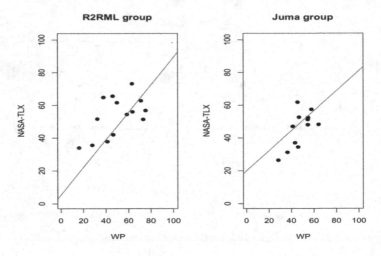

Fig. 6. Scatterplot between the WP and NASA-TLX scores

5.2 Findings

The performance of participants using the Juma representation was higher than for participants manually creating the mappings using R2RML (as per Fig. 5). The perceived mental workload scores were slightly smaller for Juma, for the WP and NASA-TLX instruments (Fig. 4). It is important to note that the performance achieved by the Juma group is almost three times the performance achieved by the R2RML group, and that the mental workload scores in the Juma group are slightly smaller. The standard deviation in the Juma group is also smaller than the standard deviation found in the R2RML group. This suggests that these mental workload scores are more consistent in the Juma group, which can also be seen in Fig. 5. However, the difference between the mental workload scores' groups was found not to be statistically significant, through the independent two sample Welch T-Test and Wilcoxon test, with NASA-TLX presenting the p-value nearest to the threshold of 0.05. Nonetheless, we argue that these results indicate that the hypothesis **H1** is true. However, since the Welch T-Test and Wilcoxon test did not find the differences between the groups to be statistically significant, maybe due to the small sample size, our conclusion is that more experimentation is needed to confirm the hypothesis **H1**. Cronbach's alpha showed that the MWL through WP and NASA-TLX are reliable instruments for measuring mental workload, thus the research hypothesis **H2** can be accepted and findings reliably considered. Figure 6 also suggests evidence for the validity of MWL instruments, showing a high correlation between WP and NASA-TLX scores for both groups, which is expected.

6 Related Work

6.1 Uplift Mapping Representations

Several mappings languages have been proposed in literature. R2RML [9] is the W3C Recommendation mapping language to map relational databases to RDF. Examples of R2RML implementations are db2triples[12], and morph [32]. Sparqlification Mapping Language [40] is another mapping language based on SQL CREATE VIEWS and SPARQL CONSTRUCT queries with support for relational databases and CSV files. SPARQL-Generate [21] is another SPARQL-based mapping language with support for multiple input data formats. A number of tools provide different visual representations for uplift mappings in order to support user engagement. Karma [20] is an example a web-based visual application for uplift mappings where data is loaded before it can be mapped to RDF. Karma presents the ontologies used during the mapping process in a tree structure and the data being mapped as a table. The mapping is represented using a graph. Map-On [38] is another visual web-based editor where the input data and ontologies being mapped are shown as graphs. Assertions between these graphs are used to generate the uplift mapping. Juma [18], as explained in Sect. 2.3, is a method that uses the block metaphor in the representation of mappings.

6.2 Mental Workload Applications

Self-assessment measures of MWL include multidimensional approaches such as the NASA's Task Load Index [16], the Subjective Workload Assessment Technique [33], the Workload Profile (WP) [42] as well as unidimensional measures such as the Copper-Harper scale [7], the Rating Scale Mental Effort [47], the Subjective Workload Dominance Technique [44] and the Bedford scale [34]. These procedures have low implementation requirements, low intrusiveness and high subject acceptability. Mental workload assessment is typically conducted to evaluate the cognitive capabilities related to a certain task. This task may be related to operating vehicles [2, 15, 39, 41],

---

[12] https://github.com/antidot/db2triples, accessed in May 2018.

user interfaces [23, 24, 26, 27, 37], teaching [35], emergency response [13], amongst others. The NASA-TLX has been used for evaluating user interfaces in health-care [23, 24, 26, 27] or in e-commerce, along with a dual-task objective methodology for investigating the effects on user satisfaction [37]. The NASA-TLX instrument has also been used in an educational context to evaluate teaching methods [35]. Tracy and Albers adopted three different techniques for measuring MWL in web-site design: NASA-TLX, the Sternberg Memory Test and a tapping test [1, 43]. They proposed a technique to identify sub-areas of a web-site in which end-users manifested a higher mental workload during interaction, allowing designers to modify those critical regions. Similarly, [11] investigated how the design of query interfaces influence stress, workload and performance during information search. Here stress was measured by physiological signals and a subjective assessment technique - Short Stress State Questionnaire. Mental workload was assessed using the NASA-TLX and log data was used as objective indicator of performance to characterize search behavior. In [28], the author investigates the relation between usability, mental workload and human performance. A comparison between machine learning techniques used to predict MWL to the NASA-TLX and the Workload Profile instruments is presented in [29]. In the Linked Data domain, MWL instruments have been used to assess ontology visualizations for semantic mappings [14], and exploratory search over Linked Data [17]. As it can be seen in this section, several studies have assessed the mental workload, including in Web systems, such as the work presented in [25], which is the case of the Juma Uplift tool evaluated in this paper. The evaluation of performance and usability of uplift mapping representations can be found in various studies, including for Juma [18]. However, to the author's knowledge, this paper presents the first attempt at evaluating the mental workload of creation and editing uplift mapping representations.

7   Conclusions and Future Work

This study extends the application of MWL instruments by showing how these can be employed for the task of creating uplift mappings in Linked Data. These instruments can guide developers and researchers in creating tools that find the optimal cognitive load on users. A primary research has been designed and performed to compare the cognitive load of two different approaches that can be used to create uplift mappings. From the many uplift representations available, the W3C-Recommended mapping language to express mappings from relational databases to RDF, R2RML, and Juma, a visual representation for mappings based on the block metaphor, were selected for this study.

The experiment presented in this paper separated participants into two groups, one creating mappings "manually" in R2RML, and another using Juma Uplift to create the same mapping. After the time allocated to execute this task, two mental workload instruments were applied to participants, namely the Workload Profile and NASA Task Load Index. Results have shown that participants using Juma Uplift achieved higher performance with slightly smaller, and more consistent, perceived mental workload scores, when compared to participants creating mapping manually. This may suggest that users interact better with the Juma representation, and that it has a smaller learning curve for the task of creating uplift mappings. Cronbach's alpha showed a strong internal consistency of the items of the questionnaires associated to the two selected mental workload instruments, suggesting that these are reliable. As it was shown in Sect. 6, uplift mapping representations are commonly evaluated based on the performance and usability of participants, while the mental workload of performing tasks involving these mapping representations is neglected. The findings of this paper show that the cognitive load is a reliable instrument that can be used to compare, and improve, uplift mapping representations.

Future work might include a comprehensive user study to evaluate performance and usability, together with the cognitive load measurements presented in this study, for the task of creating uplift mappings in Linked Data. Future work might also include the evaluation of the interpretability of uplift mapping representations in Linked Data as an additional task performance measure jointly with other self-reporting MWL instruments.

Acknowledgements. This paper was supported by CNPQ, National Counsel of Technological and Scientific Development – Brazil and by the Science Foundation Ireland (Grant 13/RC/2106) as part of the ADAPT Centre for Digital Content Technology (http://www.adaptcentre.ie/) at Trinity College Dublin.

Appendix A: MWL Questionnaires

Table 7. The Workload Profile questionnaire

Label	Question
WP_1	How much attention was required for activities like remembering, problem-solving, decision-making, perceiving (detecting, recognizing, identifying objects)?
WP_2	How much attention was required for selecting the proper response channel (manual - keyboard/mouse, or speech - voice) and its execution?
WP_3	How much attention was required for spatial processing (spatially pay attention around)?
WP_4	How much attention was required for verbal material (e.g. reading, processing linguistic material, listening to verbal conversations)?
WP_5	How much attention was required for executing the task based on the information visually received (eyes)?
WP_6	How much attention was required for executing the task based on the information auditorily received?
WP_7	How much attention was required for manually respond to the task (e.g. keyboard/mouse)?
WP_8	How much attention was required for producing the speech response (e.g. engaging in a conversation, talking, answering questions)?

Table 8. The NASA Task Load Index questionnaire

Label	Question
NT_1	How much mental and perceptual activity was required (e.g. thinking, deciding, calculating, remembering, looking, searching, etc.)? Was the task easy or demanding, simple or complex, exacting or forgiving?
NT_2	How much physical activity was required (e.g. pushing, pulling, turning, controlling, activating, etc.)? Was the task easy or demanding, slow or brisk, slack or strenuous, restful or laborious?
NT_3	How much time pressure did you feel due to the rate or pace at which the tasks or task elements occurred? Was the pace slow and leisurely or rapid and frantic?
NT_4	How hard did you have to work (mentally and physically) to accomplish your level of performance?
NT_5	How successful do you think you were in accomplishing the goals, of the task set by the experimenter (or yourself)? How satisfied were you with your performance in accomplishing these goals?
NT_6	How insecure, discouraged, irritated, stressed and annoyed versus secure, gratified, content, relaxed and complacent did you feel during the task?

References

1. Albers, M.: Tapping as a measure of cognitive load and website usability. In: Proceedings of the 29th ACM International Conference on Design of Communication, pp. 25–32 (2011). https://doi.org/10.1145/2038476.2038481
2. Balfe, N., Crowley, K., Smith, B., Longo, L.: Estimation of train driver workload: extracting taskload measures from on-train-data-recorders. In: Longo, L., Leva, M.C. (eds.) H-WORKLOAD 2017. CCIS, vol. 726, pp. 106–119. Springer, Cham (2017). https://doi.org/10.1007/978-3-319-61061-0_7
3. Bart, A.C., Tibau, J., Kafura, D., Shaffer, C.A., Tilevich, E.: Design and evaluation of a block-based environment with a data science context. IEEE Trans. Emerg. Top. Comput. (2017). https://doi.org/10.1109/TETC.2017.2729585
4. Bizer, C., Heath, T., Berners-Lee, T.: Linked data-the story so far. Int. J. Semant. Web Inf. Syst. **5**(3), 1–22 (2009). https://doi.org/10.4018/jswis.2009081901
5. Cain, B.: A review of the mental workload literature. Technical report, Defence Research & Development, Canada, Human System Integration (2007)
6. Ceriani, M., Bottoni, P.: SparqlBlocks: using blocks to design structured linked data queries. J. Vis. Lang. Sentient Syst. **3**, 1–21 (2017)
7. Cooper, G.E., Harper, R.P.: The use of pilot ratings in the evaluation of aircraft handling qualities. Technical report AD689722, 567, Advisory Group for Aerospace Research & Development (1969)
8. Crotti Junior, A., Debruyne, C., Brennan, R., O'Sullivan, D.: An evaluation of uplift mapping languages. Int. J. Web Inf. Syst. **13**(4), 405–424 (2017). https://doi.org/10.1108/IJWIS-04-2017-0036
9. Das, S., Sundara, S., Cyganiak, R.: R2RML: RDB to RDF Mapping Language (2012). https://www.w3.org/TR/r2rml/
10. Debruyne, C., O'Sullivan, D.: R2RML-F: towards sharing and executing domain logic in R2RML mappings. In: Workshop on Linked Data on the Web (LDOW 2016)

11. Edwards, A., Kelly, D., Azzopardi, L.: The impact of query interface design on stress, workload and performance. In: Hanbury, A., Kazai, G., Rauber, A., Fuhr, N. (eds.) ECIR 2015. LNCS, vol. 9022, pp. 691–702. Springer, Cham (2015). https://doi.org/10.1007/978-3-319-16354-3_76
12. Euzenat, J., Shvaiko, P.: Ontology Matching, vol. 18. Springer, Heidelberg (2007). https://doi.org/10.1007/978-3-540-49612-0
13. Fan, J., Smith, A.P.: The impact of workload and fatigue on performance. In: Longo, L., Leva, M. (eds.) H-WORKLOAD 2017. CCIS, vol. 726, pp. 90–105. Springer, Cham (2017). https://doi.org/10.1007/978-3-319-61061-0_6
14. Fu, B., Noy, N.F., Storey, M.-A.: Indented tree or graph? A usability study of ontology visualization techniques in the context of class mapping evaluation. In: Alani, H., et al. (eds.) ISWC 2013. LNCS, vol. 8218, pp. 117–134. Springer, Heidelberg (2013). https://doi.org/10.1007/978-3-642-41335-3_8
15. Guastello, S.J., Marra, D.E., Correro, A.N., Michels, M., Schimmel, H.: Elasticity and rigidity constructs and ratings of subjective workload for individuals and groups. In: Longo, L., Leva, M. (eds.) H-WORKLOAD 2017. CCIS, vol. 726, pp. 51–76. Springer, Cham (2017). https://doi.org/10.1007/978-3-319-61061-0_4
16. Hart, S.G.: Nasa-task load index (NASA-TLX); 20 years later. In: Human Factors and Ergonomics Society Annual Meeting, vol. 50. Sage Journals (2006). https://doi.org/10.1177/154193120605000909
17. Hoefler, P., Granitzer, M., Veas, E.E., Seifert, C.: Linked data query wizard: a novel interface for accessing SPARQL endpoints. In: Workshop on Linked Data on the Web (LDOW 2014) (2014)
18. Junior, A.C., Debruyne, C., O'Sullivan, D.: Using a block metaphor for representing R2RML mappings. In: Proceedings of the 3rd International Workshop on Visualization and Interaction for Ontologies and Linked Data (VOILA@ISWC 2017) (2017)
19. Junior, A.C., Debruyne, C., O'Sullivan, D.: Juma uplift: using a block metaphor for representing uplift mappings. In: 12th IEEE International Conference on Semantic Computing (ICSC 2018). https://doi.org/10.1109/ICSC.2018.00037
20. Knoblock, C.A., et al.: Semi-automatically mapping structured sources into the semantic web. In: Simperl, E., Cimiano, P., Polleres, A., Corcho, O., Presutti, V. (eds.) ESWC 2012. LNCS, vol. 7295, pp. 375–390. Springer, Heidelberg (2012). https://doi.org/10.1007/978-3-642-30284-8_32
21. Lefrançois, M., Zimmermann, A., Bakerally, N.: A SPARQL extension for generating RDF from heterogeneous formats. In: Blomqvist, E., Maynard, D., Gangemi, A., Hoekstra, R., Hitzler, P., Hartig, O. (eds.) ESWC 2017. LNCS, vol. 10249, pp. 35–50. Springer, Cham (2017). https://doi.org/10.1007/978-3-319-58068-5_3
22. Longo, L.: A defeasible reasoning framework for human mental workload representation and assessment. Behav. Inf. Technol. 34(8), 758–786 (2015). https://doi.org/10.1080/0144929X.2015.1015166
23. Longo, L., Dondio, P.: On the relationship between perception of usability and subjective mental workload of web interfaces. In: IEEE/WIC/ACM International Conference on Web Intelligence and Intelligent Agent Technology, WI-IAT 2015 (2015). https://doi.org/10.1109/WI-IAT.2015.157
24. Longo, L.: Designing medical interactive systems via assessment of human mental workload. In: 28th IEEE International Symposium on Computer-Based Medical Systems, CBMS 2015 (2015). https://doi.org/10.1109/CBMS.2015.67

25. Longo, L.: Formalising human mental workload as non-monotonic concept for adaptive and personalised web-design. In: Masthoff, J., Mobasher, B., Desmarais, M.C., Nkambou, R. (eds.) UMAP 2012. LNCS, vol. 7379, pp. 369–373. Springer, Heidelberg (2012). https://doi.org/10.1007/978-3-642-31454-4_38

26. Longo, L.: Human-computer interaction and human mental workload: assessing cognitive engagement in the world wide web. In: Campos, P., Graham, N., Jorge, J., Nunes, N., Palanque, P., Winckler, M. (eds.) INTERACT 2011. LNCS, vol. 6949, pp. 402–405. Springer, Heidelberg (2011). https://doi.org/10.1007/978-3-642-23768-3_43

27. Longo, L.: Mental workload in medicine: foundations, applications, open problems, challenges and future perspectives. In: 29th IEEE International Symposium on Computer-Based Medical Systems, CBMS 2016, (2016). https://doi.org/10.1109/CBMS.2016.36

28. Longo, L.: Subjective usability, mental workload assessments and their impact on objective human performance. In: Bernhaupt, R., Dalvi, G., Joshi, A., Balkrishan, D.K., O'Neill, J., Winckler, M. (eds.) INTERACT 2017. LNCS, vol. 10514, pp. 202–223. Springer, Cham (2017). https://doi.org/10.1007/978-3-319-67684-5_13

29. Moustafa, K., Luz, S., Longo, L.: Assessment of mental workload: a comparison of machine learning methods and subjective assessment techniques. In: Longo, L., Leva, M.C. (eds.) H-WORKLOAD 2017. CCIS, vol. 726, pp. 30–50. Springer, Cham (2017). https://doi.org/10.1007/978-3-319-61061-0_3

30. Nunnally, J.C.: Psychometric Theory, 2nd edn. McGraw-Hill, New York (1978)

31. Pinkel, C., Binnig, C., Haase, P., Martin, C., Sengupta, K., Trame, J.: How to best find a partner? An evaluation of editing approaches to construct R2RML mappings. In: Presutti, V., d'Amato, C., Gandon, F., d'Aquin, M., Staab, S., Tordai, A. (eds.) ESWC 2014. LNCS, vol. 8465, pp. 675–690. Springer, Cham (2014). https://doi.org/10.1007/978-3-319-07443-6_45

32. Priyatna, F., Corcho, O., Sequeda, J.: Formalisation and experiences of R2RML-based SPARQL to SQL query translation using morph. In: 23rd International World Wide Web Conference, WWW 2014, Seoul, Republic of Korea, pp. 479–490 (2014). https://doi.org/10.1145/2566486.2567981

33. Reid, G.B., Nygren, T.E.: The subjective workload assessment technique: a scaling procedure for measuring mental workload. In: Hancock, P.A., Meshkati, N. (eds.) Human Mental Workload, Advances in Psychology, vol. 52, chap. 8, pp. 185–218, North-Holland (1988). https://doi.org/10.1016/S0166-4115(08)62387-0

34. Rizzo, L., Dondio, P., Delany, S.J., Longo, L.: Modeling mental workload via rule-based expert system: a comparison with NASA-TLX and workload profile. In: Iliadis, L., Maglogiannis, I. (eds.) AIAI 2016. IAICT, vol. 475, pp. 215–229. Springer, Cham (2016). https://doi.org/10.1007/978-3-319-44944-9_19

35. Rizzo, L., Longo, L.: Representing and inferring mental workload via defeasible reasoning: a comparison with the NASA task load index and the workload profile. In: Proceedings of the 1st Workshop on Advances in Argumentation in Artificial Intelligence Co-located with XVI International Conference of the Italian Association for Artificial Intelligence (AI*IA 2017) (2017)

36. Rubio, S., Diaz, E., Martin, J., Puente, J.M.: Evaluation of subjective mental workload: a comparison of swat, NASA-TLX, and workload profile methods. Appl. Psychol. 53(1), 61–86 (2004). https://doi.org/10.1111/j.1464-0597.2004.00161.x

37. Schmutz, P., Heinz, S., Metrailler, Y., Opwis, K.: Cognitive load in ecommerce applications: measurement and effects on user satisfaction. Adv. Hum.-Comput. Interact. (2009). https://doi.org/10.1155/2009/121494

38. Sicilia, Á., Nemirovski, G., Nolle, A.: Map-on: a web-based editor for visual ontology mapping. Semant. Web J. 8(6), 969–980 (2017). https://doi.org/10.3233/SW-160246

39. Smith, A.P., Smith, H.N.: Workload, fatigue and performance in the rail industry. In: Longo, L., Leva, M.C. (eds.) H-WORKLOAD 2017. CCIS, vol. 726, pp. 251–263. Springer, Cham (2017). https://doi.org/10.1007/978-3-319-61061-0_17
40. Stadler, C., Unbehauen, J., Westphal, P., Sherif, M.A., Lehmann, J.: Simplified RDB2RDF mapping. In: Workshop on Linked Data on the Web (LDOW 2015) (2015)
41. Tong, S., Helman, S., Balfe, N., Fowler, C., Delmonte, E., Hutchins, R.: Workload differences between on-road and off-road manoeuvres for motorcyclists. In: Longo, L., Leva, M.C. (eds.) H-WORKLOAD 2017. CCIS, vol. 726, pp. 239–250. Springer, Cham (2017). https://doi.org/10.1007/978-3-319-61061-0_16
42. Tsang, P.S., Velazquez, V.L.: Diagnosticity and multidimensional subjective workload ratings. Ergonomics **39**(3), 358–381 (1996). https://doi.org/10.1080/00140139608964470
43. Tsang, P.S.: Mental workload. In: Karwowski, W. (ed.) International Encyclopedia of Ergonomics and Human Factors (2nd ed.), vol. 1, chap. 166. Taylor & Francis (2006)
44. Vidulich, M.A., Ward Frederic, G.F., Schueren, J.: Using the subjective workload dominance (sword) technique for projective workload assessment. Hum. Factors Soc. **33** (6), 677–691 (1991). https://doi.org/10.1177/001872089103300605
45. Wickens, C.D., Hollands, J.G.: Engineering Psychology and Human Performance, 3rd edn. Prentice Hall, Upper Saddle River (1999)
46. Wickens, C.D.: Multiple resources and mental workload. Hum. Factors **50**(2), 449–454 (2008). https://doi.org/10.1518/001872008X288394
47. Zijlstra, F.R.H.: Efficiency in work behaviour. Doctoral thesis, Delft University, The Netherlands (1993)

An Empirical Approach to Workload and Human Capability Assessment in a Manufacturing Plant

Lorenzo Comberti[1]([⊠]), Maria Chiara Leva[2], Micaela Demichela[1], Stefano Desideri[3], Gabriele Baldissone[1], and Franco Modaffari[4]

[1] DISAT, Politecnico di Torino,
Corso Duca degli Abruzzi, 24, 10129 Torino, Italy
lorenzo.comberti@polito.it
[2] School of Food Science and Environmental Health,
Dublin Institute of Technology, DIT Kevin Street,
Dublin 2 D08 X622, Ireland
[3] IVECO Spa, Suzzara-MN, Italy
[4] CNH Industrial, Via Puglia, 35, 10156 Torino, Italy

Abstract. The Human Factors contribution in the scope of the industrial process optimization presented in this case study had to deal with considerations regarding the physical and mental workload requirements of different workstations and the capabilities of the operators assigned to them. The scope was to provide the industrial management with a better way to allocate human resources to tasks requiring different operational skills. The model developed and customised showed promises results for the case study in which it was applied but offers also a generalizable feature that can extend to other contexts and situations. The assessment performed can contribute to consider necessary areas of improvement in terms of technical measures, procedure optimizations and improved work organization, to reduce defects and waste generation. The paper presents a brief description of the theoretical and empirical approach used to assess the workload of complex tasks in assembly lines and the matching operators' skillsets; furthermore, it also discusses some of the preliminary results of its application.

Keywords: Human Factor · Workload · Human Performance · World class manufacturing

1 Introduction

The main purpose of process optimization in manufacturing is to improve production efficiency and economic benefits. To reach these goals process optimization works through several areas: technical measures upgrading, work organization procedures designing, and, energy saving. There is growing interest in addressing Human Factors as part of these areas [1]. The discipline of Human Factors in fact, has a very relevant role to play, despite the ever-increasing level of automation and the standardization of working-procedures [2]. Quality managers focused their attention to human behaviour

© Springer Nature Switzerland AG 2019
L. Longo and M. C. Leva (Eds.): H-WORKLOAD 2018, CCIS 1012, pp. 180–201, 2019.
https://doi.org/10.1007/978-3-030-14273-5_11

and try to analyse the causes of deviations from procedures where errors are detected [3]. Safety experts included HF into accidents precursor analysis [4, 5] and into ex-post events analysis [6] with the aim of reducing their repetition. HF considerations are used in the area of work organization to reduce operational risks and improve task-time optimization [7]. HF influence has been modelled and measured differently depending on the characteristics of each application. Human Performance modelling is a complex system, where behaviour, cognition, physiology and working condition deeply interact [7, 8]. However the topic of Human reliability analysis and modelling, was initially developed for safety critical industries such as nuclear and aviation and was not widely applied to manufacturing even where humans are still at the forefront of production process that are not completely automated. Automotive for instance is a sector where production systems are based on assembly lines that are required a cross interaction between highly automated workstations and highly trained human resources too. Different operators are needed to contribute towards the final products, which calls for different capabilities for analysing information, recalling items from memory, making decision etc. while performing time constrained tasks. An empirical way to assess human performance, such as the reliability of individuals to perform specific tasks can be a very useful element in the process of allocating human resources to various workstations in an assembly line, as different workstations will present different elements of complexity, ultimately affecting the frequency of defects, human errors [9] and potential unsafe acts [9, 10]. The design of such a system requires an interaction between **task complexity in terms of both mental and physical workload**, and the assessment of the **required human capabilities to cope with it**. The main part of the plant considered as a case study is organised into heavy vehicles assembly lines, which include a sequence of workstations. The level of robotic application is relatively low, most of the tasks are still manually performed As a consequence the impact of human performance on production efficiency is significant; human errors, expressed in term of defects and error of assembly, represent both an increase in cost and waste. The aim of this study was to deliver a Human Performance (HP) modelling capability able to identify areas of improvement in the industrial process so as to produce measurable impact on the rate of human errors. Within the scope of the work was the cooperation with the Management of the manufacturing plant, so as to deliver a practical operational model that could be applied by the plant managers themselves.

Section 2 summarises related work to this paper, while Sect. 3 presents the designing process of the Model. Section 4 shows the model application and Sect. 5 provides an overview of the results and of the future developments for model validation.

2 Related Work

This type of assessment demands a multidisciplinary approach [11] supported by research in the field of Engineering, Psychology and Ergonomics [12]. This work was intended to provide a both a theoretical and an empirical validated approach, and ultimately offer a contribution to the study of human performance optimization in manufacturing. The proposed model is based on previous work presented by the authors where fundamental hypothesis was that Human Performance HP could be represented as directly dependent from two macro-factors [13]:

- Workload (WL): it represents all the factors contributing to the physical and mental demands to execute a given operative task, including work environmental factors [14, 15].
- Human capability (HC): it represents the resources of workers under the real working conditions and includes the physical, mental and cognitive abilities of each worker. As a contribution the authors considered some key hypothesis for the concept of mental workload and how it can be operationalized for practical assessments [16, 17].

3   Design and Methodology

The methodology used to estimate Human Performance in the assembly line can be broken down into five steps (as it is showed in Fig. 1). First step was focused on the "Conceptual Model" designing. This step began with understanding the variables having an influence on Workload and Human Capabilities. Those variables have been initially selected through a literature review balanced by an appraisal of the working conditions of the different workstation and a task analysis [1, 3, 4] of the key activities of the workstations considered for the study in the assembly line. The second step consisted in characterizing the conceptual model to suit the actual empirical situation found in the case study. This process identified, with the support of task analysis method [18], the actual empirical data sources and or proxies to assess the variables of the conceptual model identified from the literature review, so as to be connected with one or more observable and measurable quantities. This process lead to a simplification of the initial conceptual model into a version applicable to the data availability and the needs expressed for the case study. Data-Field collection was dedicated to empirical measurements of all quantities defined in the operative model structure: results were used for Human Performance Assessment involving the assessment of the workload element together with operator's capabilities. The results obtained from the Data-Field collection campaign lead to the Human Performance (HP) assessment, and that is used to plan interventions on the human resources management of the assembly line. A validation period during which results, expressed in term of production efficiency, will be monitored would allow a validation of the proposed model.

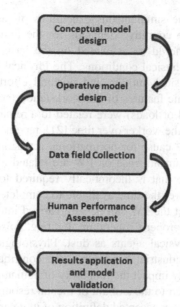

Fig. 1. Project development

3.1 Conceptual Model

The conceptual model is based on the Model developed by Rash [19] In the Rasch model, the probability of a specified outcome (e.g. right/wrong results) is a logistic function of the difference between the person and item difficulty parameter. Let X_{ni} be a dichotomous random variable with binary values where, for example, $X_{ni} = 1$ denotes a correct response and an $X_{ni} = 0$ an incorrect response to a given assessment item. In the Rasch model for dichotomous data, the probability of the outcome is given by the formula provided in Eq. (1):

$$Pr(X_{ni} = 1) = e^{\beta_n - \delta_i} / 1 + e^{\beta_n - \delta_i} \tag{1}$$

where β_n the ability of person n and δ_i the difficulty of item i.

The model needs to be radically enhanced to take into account an assessment of performance that is not dichotomous and feed into the interaction between two macro factors:

- Human Capability (HC): summarising the skills, training and experience of the people facing the tasks, representing a synthesis of their physical and cognitive abilities to verify whether or not they match the task requirements.
- Workload (WL) summarising the contribution of two main factors [15, 16]: "Mental Workload" (MW) and "Physical Workload" (PW), both associated to each activity identified and analysed in the assembly line.

The reason why we consider mental workload and physical workload together for these type of manufacturing tasks is because recent sensorised EEG experimental studies have shown that the simultaneous executions of tasks, whether physical or cognitive, tends to increase cognitive demands for the human brain [20]. Similarly then, operator capability should be estimated on the basis of the operators' set of cognitive capabilities and physical conditions. The Physical Workload (PW) factor is easily relatable to the physical, motion and postural efforts required to perform a specific task. Poor ergonomic features of the workstation (such as the need to sustain uncomfortable postures and or loads) were related to a remarkable decreasing of performance for discomfort of the worker over time [21], repetitive motions and static task were observed as additional cause for occupational accidents and lower performance [22]. Other factors having an influence on PW are related to the Saturation time: the percentage of the takt-time that is theoretically required to complete the task. The higher the saturation the lower the time available to complete a task. In addition, some general factors able to affect the PW can be summarized into environmental variables [22, 23] which included improper temperature, lighting, noise, vibration and exposure to chemical agents and physical agents as dust. Physiological effects of these environmental factors, under industrial conditions, can contribute to an increase of the stress level and consequently impact the reliability of human performance [24]. Mental Workload is generally related to the amount of mental resources imposed by a specific task [25] but there is no widely accepted definition of it, it can be seen as an interaction between the demands of the task and the performance of the operator [26] or according to Kahneman [27] as: "a factor directly related to the proportion of the mental capacity of an operator spends on task performance". In the literature several methodologies were developed to assess it such as objective physiological measures [28], subjective cognitive analysis [29] and combined multivariate approaches [30]. Generally research in MW assessment have been performed in normative condition, with a simple standardized task and under controlled environmental condition that are not the one faced on the shop floor of the assembly line chosen for this application. However the literature offers more and more empirical studies performed in manufacturing plants [31] related the MW assessment considering ergonomic factors and task complexity on the shop floor and it has also offered recent papers on the effect of task variability over mental workload demands [31, 32]. For the purpose of the empirical study performed MW was assessed on the basis of a combination of subjective measurement and indirect task-related variable quantification, as physiological measurement and cognitive normative test were not approved as a feasible mean of assessment by the industrial partner. As a result of literature review and task analysis performed with plant managers a set of variables relatable to WL were identified. Figure 2 summarizes all variables selected to model WL for the case study.

MW has been assessed on the basis of the following variables (see Fig. 2):

- Task variability: this variable takes into account the effects of parts and product variability and consequently the need to identify and evaluate the appropriate procedural variations for each workstation in the assembly line.
- Task complexity: it represents the effects of remembering how to perform the task.
- Each task is composed by a sequence of simple operations. The higher the number of operations composing the task the bigger is the mental effort required to remember them.

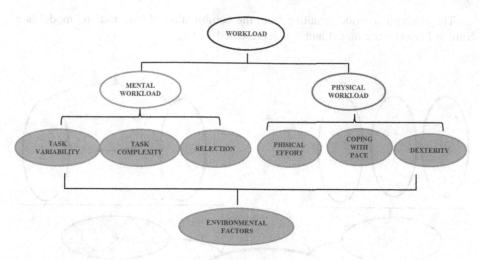

Fig. 2. WL conceptual model

– Selection: some tasks may require a certain degree of decision-making in choosing the right approach during performance that contributes to affect mental workload demand.

PW has been assessed on the basis of the following variables:

– Physical effort: tasks may differ depending to the physical and postural effort required to perform them.
– Coping with pace: in the assembly line all tasks have to be performed in a fixed short period called "takt time". Tasks may differ depending on the percentage of takt-time allocated to complete the task: The higher the saturation the lower the time available to complete a task.
– Dexterity: this variable is intended to measure the manual precision requested by the task characteristics.

Environmental factors take into account all the variables such as: lighting, humidity, noise and temperature that have an impact both on MW and PW. Human Capability (HC), as mentioned in the previous section, represents the total amount of resources that a worker can offer to execute tasks under given environmental working condition. Several human skills have been considered as solicited by the WL associated to each specific task. Human skills that have been considered to model the HC are:

– Manual skill: skills like precision, manual handling, and coordination are solicited continuously during an assembly task.
– Memory: remembering the sequence of operations and parts to be assembled can differ considerably from task to task.
– Physical: the ability of maintaining a constant performance during the shift and coping with pace.

The conceptual model resulting from the combination of WL and HC model is a Human Performance model and it is represented in Fig. 3.

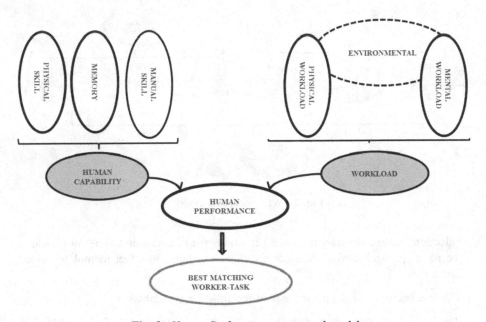

Fig. 3. Human Performance conceptual model

The part of the conceptual model shown in Fig. 3 is to highlight that the variables used to assess WL and HC to assess human performance in relation to each activity analysed for the assembly line. WL is assessed for each activity while the factors chosen to assess Human Capability are specific to each worker. This model provides an estimate of HP index and can be used to identify worker-task matching. This effort is aimed at improving global performance of the assembly line in terms of probability of human error and unsafe acts occurrence.

3.2 Operational Model

The Conceptual model defined in the previous section represented the starting point to define the operative model. To shift from a purely conceptual model to an operational one it was necessary to identify a set of actual observable and measurable quantities to estimate/assess the model variables. In addition to this, a common scale of evaluation for all quantities was adopted so as to allow a quantitative comparison between Human Capabilities (HC) against Workload (WL) requirements. The WL operational model was defined using a task analysis of each workstation activity plus an observation protocol to score the whole assembly line. A participatory approach involved both academic and industry professionals operating in the various management areas: Safety, Work Analysis, Quality, Work-Organization.

Workload Operational Model

Figure 4 shows results of this process with reference to WL operational definition. With reference to Fig. 4 the shift from a conceptual to an operational model implied the exclusion of the "Environmental factors" variable as it was the same for all the workstation and did not appear to have changes and or influence on the overall performance. The environmental conditions were in fact of good quality and therefore did not have an observable impact on performance, furthermore the environmental factors were approximately constant along the production line therefore their effect was not observable in this specific case study. With the exception of the environmental ones all the other variables identified in the conceptual model were matched by one or more observable quantities. Each quantity had a different measurement-unit therefore to adopt a common scale, the indicators were scored according to calibrated Likert scales from 1to 10. Each Likert scale was calibrated according to the original unit measurements of the observable variables.

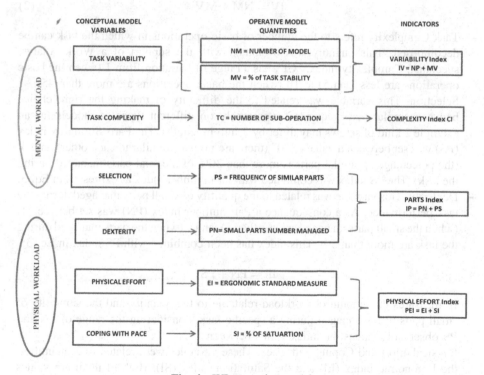

Fig. 4. WL operative model

The choices made to operationalize the conceptual model can be summarised as follow:

– Task Variability was measured considering the following aspect: the assembly line is a sequence of working-places where a shell is moved automatically from a workstation to the next following a certain rate called takt-time. In all working-place a task is performed on the shell according to a specific well defined procedure. Each task is composed by several operations that can change or remaining constant depending on the kind of product being assembled. To assess this variability two quantities were identified: number of models (NM) represents the number of task variation required by different shell-types in each workstation; NM was assessed between 1 (when the task does not vary following a shell-type variation) and 6 (when there are more than 5 possible task differences following different shell-types). The other factor considered is MV (task stability), which represents the percentage of variations observed in each workstation. MV varied between 0 (when there are no variations depending on the shells being assembled, 100% of tasks in the same type) and 4, when the percentage of the most frequent activities for shell type is only about 60% of the total amount of assembly activities performed during the working day. The combination of this two quantities leads to definition of a numerical index called "Variability index".

The relation defined to relate these two quantities is expressed by the following equation:

$$IV = NM + MV \tag{2}$$

- Task Complexity refers to the number of basic operations in which the task can be decomposed. This quantity was evaluated with the support of a Work Analyst specialist. Complexity index, "CI", has a range of variation from 1 (when the basic operations are less than 5) to 10 (when the basic operations are more than 45).
- Selection. This variable was related to the difficulty of making the right choice between similar parts required for assembly on different types of models (as an example 2 kind of screws may differ by 2 mm in length). The Parts Similarity index (PS) was set between a value of "0" (there are no parts similar to each other), and 3, (the percentage of similar parts is more than 30% of the total parts managed during the task). The PS index was combined with Part number index as expressed in Eq. 3.
- Dexterity. This variable was related to the quantity of small parts managed during the task performance. As a consequence a Part number index (PN) was set between 1, (when the small parts managed are less than 5), and 7 (when the parts managed during the task are more than 50). This index has been combined with PS index in Eq. 3:

$$IP = PN + PS \tag{3}$$

IP measures the amount of workload relatable to the quantity and the similarity of small parts to be managed during a specific task, considering the range of PN and PS observable values the index varies between 1 and 10.

- Physical effort and Coping with pace. These variables were related to 2 quantities: the Ergonomic index (EI) and the Saturation index (SI). Both of them are values varying between 1 and 5 depending on the ergonomics assessment of the various workstations (evaluated with a standardized methodology called OCRA [33]) and to the level of saturation of takt-time defined by Work analysis. As a consequence of this the Physical Effort index (PEI) was defined as expressed by Eq. 4:

$$PEI = EI + SI \tag{4}$$

In summary as a consequence of the operational model each workstation would be analysed in term of Physical Workload (PW) and Mental workload (MW) using 4 indicators: IV, CI, IP and PEI.

Human Capability Operational Model

HC represents the total amount of resources that a worker potentially can provide to perform a given task. According to the kind of tasks involved into the assembly line, the HC conceptual model identified 3 set of measurable capabilities: Manual skills, Memory and Physical skill. In order to assess these skills a set of empirical tests were designed. The key conditions considered for the test design process were the followings:

1. The tests have to represents or simulate frequents operations close to the ones performed in the assembly line.
2. The tests have to be performed by workers during the working activity, as a consequence the time requested to perform them needs to be below 10 min.

Considering the above conditions four test were defined:

1. Memory test: sequences of geometric schemes were shown to the worker for few second. The worker was then asked to replicate them on a piece of paper. During this test the time to complete the task and its accuracy were recorded.
2. Precision test: it consists in moving an iron circle along a not linear contour without touching the line. This test is related to the manual precision required in many tasks. During this test the time to complete the path and the number of errors were recorded.
3. Coordination test: In this test the worker is required to use both hands to perform simple actions. Time and precision of coordinate movements were recorded.
4. Methodology test: During this test the worker have to decide and to complete a set of simple assembly steps with small parts. Time and errors were recorded.

Results of these tests have been used to assess the part of the model related to human capability (HC) as reported in Fig. 5.

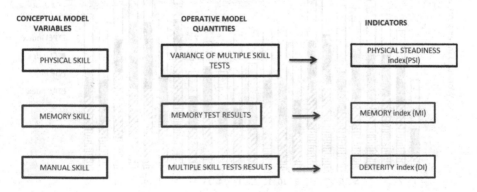

Fig. 5. Human capability operative model

The variables identified in the HC Conceptual model and reported in Fig. 5 are follows:

1. Physical skills: assessed considering the variance in performance on all the tests performed by a single worker. The variance was considered as a proxy of Physical Steadiness. This indicator is express in a scale from 1 to 10, where 10 indicates the capability to attain best consistency in good work performance.
2. Memory skill was associated to the result of the memory test. A memory index was introduced within the 1 to 10 Likert scale.
3. Manual skill was associated to the results of the Precision, Coordination and Methodology tests. All of them represent a measure of dexterity and consequently it was defined as a Dexterity index.

As a consequence of the operational model developed, each worker of the assembly line would be characterized in term of HC with a set of the 3 indicators (PSI, MI, DI) mentioned above.

3.3   Data Field Collection

On the basis of the Operational model and the variable identified it was possible to perform the field data collection campaign. An assembly line of 23 work-stations was selected as test-line. Therefore 23 different WL were calculated according to the indicators reported in Fig. 4. The results of this activity are summarized in Fig. 6. Figure 6 highlights how the WL differs along the assembly line. Workstation 1 for instance has a WL index not far from Workstation 16, while the workstation reporting the highest WL value (with an overall score of 28) is the one marked as number 17.

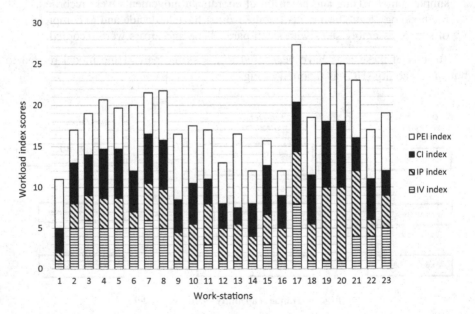

Fig. 6. Work stations workload assessment

The HC assessment campaign with the tests involved directly 50 workers employed in the selected assembly line. The tests were planned so as to minimize the impact on the working activity of the assembly line itself and the average time of execution was between 7–9 min. To perform the tests each worker was given a short break, for the time strictly necessary, and replaced by a substitute. This configuration allowed the tests to be repeated 3 times during the whole shift for all the workers. All test results showed a good discrimination of workers skills highlighting a wide range of variation in performances. The HC indicators were all reported in a numerical scale 1–10 in relation to test results. The test measures 2 quantities: the amount of time spent to complete the test and the number of errors committed during its execution. The two quantities were combined in a single index as reported in Eq. (5). Considering the results of each individual skill test, time and errors observed in the text were linearly combined in a common quantity named "Modified Time" (MT) according to the following equation:

$$MT = Time[s] + Errors \times 3[s] \tag{5}$$

Where each error was transformed in an additional amount of time of 3 s. On the basis of the MT distribution the correspondent HC indicator was assessed. Figure 7 shows the results measured in term of Time and number of errors for 25 workers and Fig. 8 highlights the corresponding MT distribution.

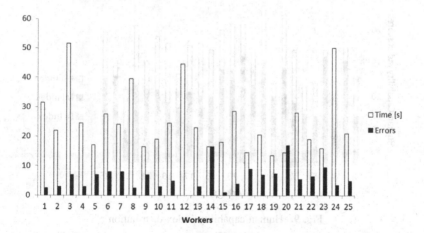

Fig. 7. Precision-test results: time to complete test expressed in second and number of errors

Figure 7 highlights the capacity of the Precision test of discriminating between different skill-levels among workers. The MD assessment (Fig. 8) revealed a wide range of performance variation, from a minimum of 21 s to a maximum of 70 s. On the basis of this range of variation, each MD value was scaled into a numerical index.

This process was repeated for all tests' results, leading to the definition of the required HC indicators for all the workers involved. Figure 9 summarizes the HC distribution.

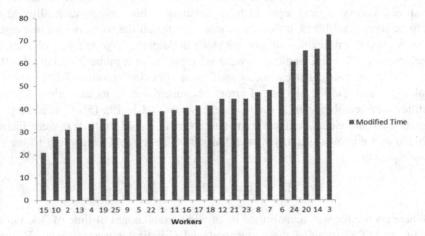

Fig. 8. Modified Time (MT) distribution

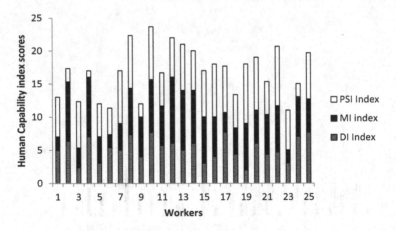

Fig. 9. Human capability index distribution

Figure 9 highlights how HC change even significantly from operator to operator. For each worker it is possible to consider the overall score for HC or the score of each specific skill. For example worker number 6 has the following indicators: PSI = 5, DI = 5 and MI equal to 10 for a total of recorded HC of 20 which is in the highest percentile of the HC values recorded for the overall population. This information suggests that this worker may be better allocated to a workstation where Memory is a key requirement. The effects of HC and WL assessment, with the set of Indicators defined in the Operational model, will be discussed in the next section.

4 Human Performance Assessment

The HP assessment was defined according to the scheme proposed in the Conceptual model (Fig. 3) and in compliance with the operational evaluation process defined for HC and WL. The HP calculation therefore is outlined as follow (see Fig. 10): for each possible matching worker/workstation the combination of the 3 HC index (MI, DI, PSI) with 4 WL index (PEI, IP, CI and IV) lead to an overall matching index reported in Eq. (6):

$$HC_{worker} - WL_{workingplace} - HP \tag{6}$$

The Matching-index assesses the level of adequacy of human capability to the workload determined for each workstation.

Figure 10 outlines an example where the Matching is characterized by:

- Two negatives value due to MI-IV and to DI-PI. These represent a negative matching worker-workstation as the variability (IV) and dexterity required by the task are not well matched by the memory and dexterity scores of the worker.
- Two positive indices representing a favourable matching.

On the basis of the Matching index, two Human Performance assessment indices were defined:

- HPminus: represents the sum of all negatives matching index.
- HPplus: represents the sum of all positive values of matching index.

With these two indexes it is possible to quantify the potential goodness of fit, in term of all the possible matching of workers and workstations.

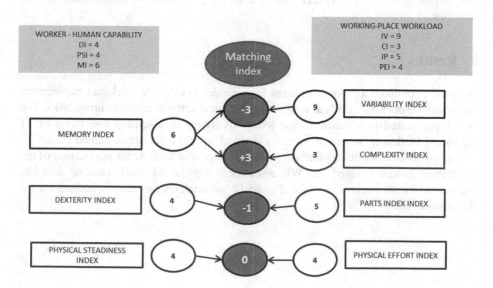

Fig. 10. Human Performance scheme of calculation

This matching index is a predictor of human performance, as the lower the value of HPminus the higher is the probability of human error for that combination. On the basis of this systematic assessment of HPminus and HPplus, for all the possible combination workers/workstation a matrix of matching combination is defined.

Figure 11 summarises the results of this approach showing, as an example the matrix of combinations obtained for 5 workstations and 25 workers (with all their relative HP assessment index). The score of the 25 workers are reported for each workstation in a decreasing order (the workers are in the upper row, and the HP index in the lower row).

1	Workers	AC	AV	AJ	AT	AG	AA	AN	AO	AP	AH	AW	AQ	AE	AF	AI	AU	AA	AD	AK	AL	AM
	HP	23	18	18	13	12	10	8	-1	-1	-2	-2	-3	-3	-3	-3	-3	-5	-5	-6	-7	-7
2	Workers	AC	AV	AJ	AX	AG	AA	AT	AN	AH	AP	AR	AS	AW	AE	AU	AQ	AD	AA	AL	AM	AK
	HP	16	12	11	-1	-2	-3	-3	-3	-4	-5	-5	-6	-7	-8	-9	-9	-11	-11	-11	-11	-13
3	Workers	AC	AV	AJ	AX	AG	AA	AT	AN	AH	AP	AR	AS	AW	AE	AU	AQ	AD	AA	AL	AM	AK
	HP	10	9	9	-1	-2	-3	-3	-3	-4	-5	-5	-6	-7	-8	-9	-9	-11	-11	-11	-11	-13
4	Workers	AV	AJ	AX	AT	AG	AP	AR	AC	AE	AF	AI	AO	AS	AW	AQ	AU	AL	AA	AD	AM	AK
	HP	15	15	8	8	6	5	3	-1	-1	-1	-1	-2	-2	-2	-4	-4	-5	-6	-10	-10	-10
5	Workers	AV	AJ	AX	AT	AG	AR	AC	AH	AO	AS	AW	AF	AI	AE	AU	AQ	AA	AL	AD	AK	AM
	HP	15	14	10	10	9	3	-1	-1	-1	-1	-1	-2	-2	-2	-3	-3	-5	-6	-9	-9	-10

Fig. 11. Matching matrix

A grey-scale was set: black for bad matching (HP assessment index < -4), grey for acceptable matching (HP assessment index between from -4 to -1) and white for good matching. This method in reality is to be used as an optimization problem where the value to be optimized is the HP index. The index needs to be above 0 but as close to 0 as possible to ensure good matching of requirements and capabilities while at the same time avoiding waste. The matrix can be used as guidance tool to support manning activities.

5   Results

The project outlined a proof of concept for a model to evaluate workload requirement and matching operators skills as a predictor of human error in manufacturing tasks. The model was tested in a concrete case study involving an assembly line made of 21 individual workstations and 50 workers divided in two daily shifts named A and B. According to the data field collection scheme reported in Sect. 4, the application of the operational model entailed the WL assessment for the 21 work stations and HC assessment for all workers involved. Figure 12 summarizes the results obtained for the WL assessment.

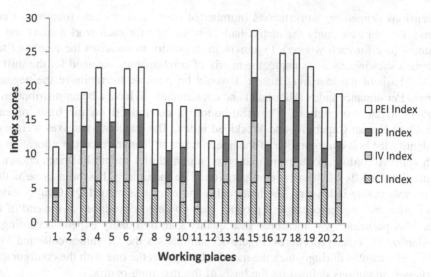

Fig. 12. Workload assessment of the assembly line

Figures 13 and 14 showed the HC values for the workers of the two shifts A and B.

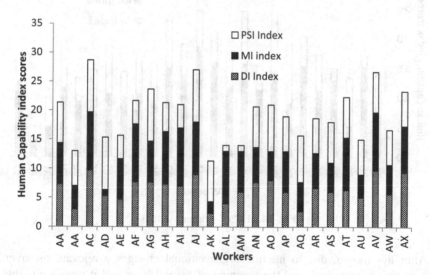

Fig. 13. HC of workers shift A

A Human Performance index was then defined to take into account the evaluation of all the possible matching combinations of workers and workstations. The final result of this activity was presented in two global matching matrixes, one for each shift, with dimensions defined by workstations (number of rows) and workers (number of columns). For our case study the matrix had 21 rows (one for each workstation) and 25 columns (one for each worker). Figure 16 in Appendix summarises the results of this approach showing, as an example, the matrix of combinations obtained for the shift B. On the basis of the matching matrix it would be possible to minimize the negative Human Performance index (HPminus) and consequently to have a better distribution of workers to the workstations. The distribution is determined on the basis of each individual Human Capability and Workload index. The matching-matrixes were used to identify the best configuration of the line in terms of human resources allocation for each shift. According to the plant managers, a period of 1 month has been chosen to monitor the results of the new configuration. The monitoring has been done with 2 observable quality indicators. The first quality indicator was named QI (Quality index) and it measured the percentage of product with no defects produced at the end of the line. This parameter was measured in a quality gate by quality experts according to standardized internal procedures. Figure 15 summarises the QI values collected for a period of 6 months during which the month of May was the one with the configuration workers-workstations defined on the basis of the matching matrix.

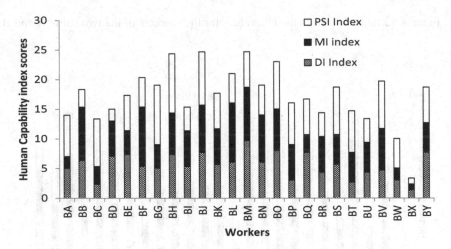

Fig. 14. HC of workers shift B

After this month, due to internal organisational changes a relevant turnover of workers significantly impacted the manning of several lines and it wasn't possible to maintain the observable optimized configuration any more.

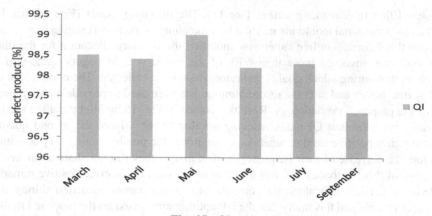

Fig. 15. QI values

The second quality indicator was based on the number of recovery activities performed to solve assembly errors before the quality gate. Supervisors observed a reduction of the recovery activities for both shifts.

6 Discussion

Currently the management of human resources on the production line is decided by the line supervisor, on the basis of his own judgement. The definition of a matching-matrix would means shifting from a total subjective assessment to one empirically and theoretically grounded on evaluation of required workload and available capabilities. The operational model application allowed an empirical quantification of WL and HC, but the model itself is generalizable to other context and configurations. Figure 12 highlights how the WL differs along the assembly line even if all workstations are part of system with a common tack time. In fact, WL varied from a value that goes from 11 (for workstation 1) to 28 (for workstation 15). Not only the total value of WL changes along the line but also the individual factors contributing towards it shows a significant degree of diversification. Some workstations were characterised by a small value of individual variability (IV) index and a relevant value of individual Parts (IP) index (e.g. workstation 16 and 17); while other workstations presented a small value of complexity Index (CI) and IV but a high value of Physical Effort Index (PEI) (e.g. workstation 11). This information shows how the skillset and capability required in term of human resources can significantly change across similar workstations. The assessment of Human Capability (HC) (summarized in Figs. 13 and 14), highlights how HC can significantly vary among workers too. As an example Fig. 13 reports the best HC score for an individual named "AC", who scored a total value of 28, while worker "AK" obtained the lowest HC score of 12; a significant gap is recorded between the two. Worker AK had very low score in the memory (MI) and dexterity (DI) indexes but an high score in Physical steadiness (PSI) and he can be allocated to those working-stations with lower requirement in Dexterity, Memory and higher requirement in

Physical Effort (e.g. working station 1 or 11). The matching matrix (Fig. 16) can be used as an operational tool to identify the best matching worker-workstation and on the basis of this information line supervisor modified the ordinary allocation for the line. This operation involved more than 60% of the workforce. Managers authorised 1 month of trial during which quality indicators have been collected. The comparison of quality data before and after the reconfiguration has been used to provide a preliminary test of the proposed methodology. Results reported in Fig. 15 highlight that the month of trial scored the best QI index reaching a value of 99%. Even the second quality indicator gave positive results; supervisors monitored the number of recovery activities and found a decrease of their frequency. Unfortunately they did not share a numerical reporting of these activities and this observation remains qualitative. Positive remarks in term of Quality indicators are correlated to human errors reduction during the assembly process and this imply that the HP optimization based on the proposed model can be improved. In addition the introduction of this reconfiguration on the daily working routine was positive perceived and workers generally contributed the rearrangements. On the basis of these preliminary results, plant managers approved an expansion of the project to demonstrate generalisation to more lines over a longer period of time.

7 Conclusion and Future Work

This project was developed to give an effective contribution towards addressing Human performance assessment for manufacturing tasks. The main scope of this work was to develop a model to estimate Human Performance for an assembly process and propose a model to leverage this information to optimize human resources allocation and workstation assessment. This work was carried out using a theoretical approach that was then operationalized to allow empirical data collection. This allowed the theoretical Workload and Human capability assessment to be customised for the real working condition under analysis. A preliminary test line, of 21 working station, was selected as case study and 50 workers have been involved into the testing phase. On the basis of the HP evaluation process a matrix workstations workers allocation was used. The quality indicators collected and the comparison of quality data pre and post reconfiguration has been used to assess the validity of the proposed methodology. On the basis of the preliminary results, plant Managers authorised an expansion of this action research to more production lines in collaboration with the Quality and Production Managers [34]. A set of 5 lines for 100 working stations has now been proposed considering different issues reported by the quality management for recorded human errors. The number of workers to be involved will rise to 340. On the basis of the model results a process of workstations assessment and manning allocation will be defined and a longer period of testing and monitoring will be allowed to discriminate improvements simply due to the so called Hawthorn effect [35]. The results are going to be monitored for a period longer than three months and they will be used to validate and or modify the model, assess its generalization and to verify the possibility to introduce individual motivation among the parameters being considered.

Appendix

Workingplaces		Matching shift B																							
1	Workers	BV	BJ	BC	BX	BT	BG	BA	BN	BO	BP	BR	BS	BW	BQ	BU	BB	BH	BK	BD	BE	BF	BI	BL	BM
	HP	26	25	23	20	20	20	17	16	15	15	14	12	11	10	8	6	-1	-1	-2	-2	-2	-2	-5	-6
2	Workers	BV	BC	BJ	BF	BX	BT	BI	BG	BH	BA	BN	BO	BP	BR	BS	BE	BW	BQ	BB	BU	BL	BK	BD	BM
	HP	20	19	19	15	14	14	14	14	13	11	10	9	9	8	6	6	4.666667	0	-2	-2	-3	-7	-8	-8
3	Workers	BV	BC	BJ	BX	BT	BG	BH	BA	BN	BP	BR	BE	BF	BI	BO	BS	BW	BQ	BB	BU	BL	BK	BD	BM
	HP	18	17	17	12	12	12	11	9	8	7	6	-1	-1	-1	-1	-1	-1	-1	-3	-3	-4	-8	-9	-10
4	Workers	BC	BV	BJ	BX	BT	BG	BA	BN	BP	Fi	BH	BO	BS	BW	BE	BF	BI	BQ	BU	BB	BL	BK	BD	BM
	HP	19	16	15	11	11	10	8	6	5	4	-1	-1	-1	-1	-2	-2	-2	-2	-3	-4	-5	-8	-9	-10
5	Workers	BV	BJ	BC	BX	BT	BG	BH	BA	BN	BP	BR	BE	BF	BI	BO	BS	BW	BQ	BU	BB	BL	BK	BD	BM
	HP	17	16	14	12	12	11	11	9	7	6	5	-1	-1	-1	-1	-1	-1	-2	-3	-4	-4	-8	-9	-9
6	Workers	BV	BJ	BX	BT	BG	BH	BA	BN	BP	BR	BC	BE	BF	BI	BO	BS	BW	BQ	BU	BL	BB	BD	BM	BK
	HP	15	15	10	10	9	9	7	5	5	3	-1	-1	-1	-1	-2	-2	-2	-4	-4	-5	-6	-10	-10	-10
7	Workers	BV	BJ	BX	BT	BG	BA	BN	BP	BR	BC	BH	BO	BS	BW	BF	BI	BE	BU	BQ	BB	BL	BD	BK	BM
	HP	15	14	10	10	9	7	5	4	3	-1	-1	-1	-1	-1	-2	-2	-2	-3	-3	-5	-6	-9	-9	-10
8	Workers	BC	BJ	BG	BO	BQ	BA	BN	BS	BT	BV	BP	BR	BU	BW	BX	BB	BD	BH	BE	BF	BI	BK	BL	BM
	HP	24	20	14	10	-1	-1	-1	-1	-1	-1	-2	-2	-2	-2	-2	-3	-3	-3	-4	-4	-4	-4	-7	-8
9	Workers	BV	BJ	BC	BT	BG	BA	BN	BO	BS	BP	BR	BW	BX	BQ	BH	BU	BE	BF	BI	BB	BD	BK	BL	BM
	HP	19	19	16	14	13	11	9	9	6	-1	-1	-1	-1	-2	-2	-2	-3	-3	-3	-4	-4	-5	-7	-7
10	Workers	BC	BV	BJ	BX	BT	BG	BA	BN	BO	BP	BR	BS	BW	BU	BH	BB	BF	BI	BE	BQ	BD	BK	BL	BM
	HP	21	20	19	14	14	14	11	10	9	9	8	6	5	2	-1	-2	-2	-2	-2	-2	-4	-5	-6	-8
11	Workers	BC	BJ	BG	BD	BO	BA	BN	BS	BT	BV	BQ	BP	BR	BU	BW	BX	BH	BK	BB	BE	BF	BI	BL	BM
	HP	20	20	14	-1	-1	-2	-2	-2	-2	-2	-3	-3	-3	-3	-3	-3	-4	-4	-5	-5	-5	-5	-9	-9
12	Workers	BV	BJ	BC	BF	BX	BT	BI	BG	BH	BA	BN	BO	BP	BR	BS	BE	BW	BU	BB	BQ	BK	BD	BL	BM
	HP	25	24	23	20	19	19	19	19	18	16	15	14	14	13	11	11	10	7	5	0	-3	-3	-3	-4
13	Workers	BV	BJ	BF	BX	BT	BI	BG	BH	BC	BA	BN	BP	BR	BE	BO	BS	BW	BL	BU	BQ	BB	BM	BK	BD
	HP	21	20	16	16	16	15	15	15	14	13	11	10	9	7	-1	-1	-1	-2	-2	-2	-3	-5	-6	-7
14	Workers	BV	BJ	BC	BF	BX	BT	BI	BG	BH	BA	BN	BO	BP	BR	BS	BE	BW	BU	BB	BQ	BL	BD	BM	BK
	HP	25	24	24	20	19	19	19	19	18	16	15	14	14	13	11	11	10	7	-1	-1	-2	-3	-3	-4
15	Workers	BC	BV	BJ	BT	BA	BG	BX	BH	EN	BP	BF	BI	BR	BO	BS	BE	BW	BQ	BL	BU	BB	BD	BK	BM
	HP	11	9	9	4	-1	-1	-1	-2	-2	-2	-3	-3	-3	-4	-4	-6	-6	-8	-8	-8	-10	-13	-14	-14
16	Workers	BC	BV	BJ	BT	BG	BA	BN	BO	BP	BR	BS	BX	BH	BW	BQ	BE	BF	BI	BU	BB	BD	BK	BL	BM
	HP	23	18	18	13	12	10	8	-1	-1	-1	-1	-1	-2	-2	-3	-3	-3	-3	-3	-5	-5	-6	-7	-7
17	Workers	BC	BV	BJ	BX	BG	BA	BT	BN	EH	BO	BF	BI	BP	BR	BS	BW	BE	BU	BQ	BD	BB	BL	BM	BK
	HP	16	12	11	-1	-2	-3	-3	-3	-4	-4	-4	-5	-5	-5	-6	-7	-8	-9	-9	-11	-11	-11	-11	-13
18	Workers	BC	BV	BJ	BX	BG	BA	BT	BN	BH	BO	BF	BI	BP	BR	BS	BW	BE	BU	BQ	BD	BB	BL	BM	BK
	HP	16	12	11	-1	-2	-3	-3	-3	-4	-4	-4	-5	-5	-5	-6	-7	-8	-9	-9	-11	-11	-11	-11	-13
19	Workers	BC	BV	BJ	BO	BG	BN	BA	BX	ET	BS	BR	BH	BP	BF	BW	BI	BU	BQ	BB	BE	BD	BK	BL	BM
	HP	22	14	13	3	0	0	-1	-1	-2	-2	-2	-3	-3	-3	-3	-4	-4	-5	-6	-6	-9	-10	-10	-12
20	Workers	BV	BJ	BC	BX	BT	BG	BA	BN	BO	BP	BR	BS	BW	BQ	BB	BH	BU	BE	BF	BI	BK	BL	BD	BM
	HP	20	19	17	14	14	14	11	10	9	9	7.666667	6	5	4	-1	-1	-1	-2	-2	-2	-5	-5	-7	-9
21	Workers	BC	BV	BJ	BT	BG	BA	BN	BO	BS	BP	BR	BW	BX	BQ	BH	BU	BB	BE	BF	BI	BK	BD	BL	BM
	HP	23	17.66667	17	12	12	9	8	7	4	-1	-1	-1	-1	-1	-2	-2	-3	-3	-3	-3	-6	-6	-6	-11

Fig. 16. Matching matrix for shift B

References

1. Hong, K., Nagaraja, R., Iovenitti, P., Dunn, M.: A socio-technical approach to achieve zero defect manufacturing of complex manual assembly. Hum. Factor Ergon. Manuf. **17**(2), 137–148 (2007). https://doi.org/10.1002/hfm.20068
2. Baines, T.S., Asch, R., Hadfield, L., Mason, J.P., Fletcher, S., Kay, J.M.: Towards a theoretical framework for human performance modelling within manufacturing systems design. Simul. Model. Pract. Theory **13**(6), 451–524 (2005). https://doi.org/10.1016/j.simpat.2005.01.003
3. Miller, D.P., Swain, A.D.: Human error and human reliability. In: Handbook Human Factor, Wiley, New York (1987)
4. Bosca, S., Comberti, L., Baldissone, G., Demichela, M., Murè, S.: Occupational accident precursors management systems. In: Proceedings of the 49th ESReDA Seminar, Brussels (2015)
5. Baldissone, G., Comberti, L., Bosca, S., Murè, S.: The analysis and management of unsafe acts and unsafe conditions. Data collection and analysis. Saf. Sci. (in press). https://doi.org/10.1016/j.ssci.2018.10.006
6. Comberti, L., Baldissone, G., Demichela, M.: A combined approach for the analysis of large occupational accident databases to support accident-prevention decision making. Saf. Sci. **106**, 191–202 (2018). https://doi.org/10.1016/j.ssci.2018.03.014
7. Lin, L., Drury, C.G., Kim, S.W.: Ergonomics and quality in paced assembly lines. Hum. Factors Ergon. Manuf. **11**, 377–382 (2001). https://doi.org/10.1002/hfm.1020
8. Leva, M.C., Ciarrapica Alunni, C., Demichela M., Allemandi, G.: Addressing human performance in automotive industry: identifying main drivers of human reliability. In: Irish Ergonomics Review 2016 Proceedings of the Irish Ergonomics society Annual Conference (2016)
9. Groth, K.M., Mosleh, A.: A data-informed PIF hierarchy for model – based human reliability analysis. Reliab. Eng. Syst. Saf. **108**, 154–174 (2012). https://doi.org/10.1016/j.ress.2012.08.006
10. Comberti L., et al.: Comparison of two methodologies for occupational accidents pre-cursors data collection, In: 25th ESREL (2015), pp. 3237–3244. CRC Press, Zurich (2015)
11. Baine, T.S., Benedettini, O.: Modelling human performance within manufacturing systems design: from a theoretical towards a practical framework. J. Simul. **1**, 121–130 (2007)
12. Eklund, J.: Ergonomics, quality and continuous improvement conceptual and empirical relationships in an industrial context. Ergonomics **40**, 982–1001 (1997). https://doi.org/10.1080/001401397187559
13. Leva, M.C., Comberti, L., Demichela, M., Duane, R.: Human performance modelling in manufacturing: mental workload and task complexity. In: H-Workload 2017: The First International Symposium on Human Mental Workload, Dublin Institute of Technology, Dublin, Ireland, 28–30 June 2017
14. Longo, L., Leva, M.C. (eds.): Human Mental Workload: Models and Applications. First International Symposium, H-WORKLOAD 2017, Dublin Ireland, Revised Selected Papers, vol. 726. Springer, Heidelberg (2017). https://doi.org/10.1007/978-3-319-61061-0
15. Wickens, C.D.: Mental workload: assessment, prediction and consequences. In: Longo, L., Leva, M.C. (eds.) H-WORKLOAD 2017. CCIS, vol. 726, pp. 18–29. Springer, Cham (2017). https://doi.org/10.1007/978-3-319-61061-0_2
16. Mijović, P., Milovanović, M., Ković, V., Gligorijević, I., Mijović, B., Mačužić, I.: Neuroergonomics method for measuring the influence of mental workload modulation on cognitive state of manual assembly worker. In: Longo, L., Leva, M.C. (eds.) H-WORKLOAD 2017. CCIS, vol. 726, pp. 213–224. Springer, Cham (2017). https://doi.org/10.1007/978-3-319-61061-0_14

17. Leva, M.C., Builes, Y.: The benefits of task and cognitive workload support for operators in ground handling. In: Longo, L., Leva, M.C. (eds.) H-WORKLOAD 2017. CCIS, vol. 726, pp. 225–238. Springer, Cham (2017). https://doi.org/10.1007/978-3-319-61061-0_15

18. Stanton, N.A.: Hierarchical task analysis: developments, applications and extensions. Appl. Ergon. **37**, 55–79 (2004). https://doi.org/10.1016/j.apergo.2005.06.003

19. Rasch, G.: Probabilistic model for some intelligence and attainment tests. University of Chicago Press, Chicago (1980)

20. Mijović, P., et al.: Communicating the user state: introducing cognition-aware computing in industrial settings. Safety Science in press available on line 5th of Janaury (2018). https://doi.org/10.1016/j.ssci.2017.12.024

21. Erdinç, O., Yeow, P.H.: Proving external validity of ergonomics and quality relationship through review of real-world case studies. Int. J. Prod. Res. **49**, 949–962 (2011). https://doi.org/10.1080/00207540903555502

22. Punnett, L., Fine, L.J., Keyserling, W.M., Herrin, G.D., Chaffin, D.B.: Shoulder disorders and postural stress in automobile assembly work. Scand. J. Work Environ. Health **26**, 283–291 (2001)

23. Jung, H.S., Jung, H.-S.: Establishment of overall workload assessment technique for various tasks and workplaces. Int. J. Ind. Ergon. **28**, 341–353 (2001). https://doi.org/10.1016/S0169-8141(01)00040-3

24. Grandejan, E.: Fitting the Task to the Man – An Ergonomic Approach. Taylor and Francis, London (1985)

25. Wickens, C.: Multiple resources and mental workload. Hum. Factors **50**(3), 449–455 (2008)

26. Cain, B.: A review of mental workload literature. Report No. RTO-TR-HFM-121-Part-II, Defense Research and Development Canada Toronto Human System Integration Section (2007)

27. Kahneman, D., Tversky, A.: Prospect theory: an analysis of decision under risk. Econometrica **47**, 263–291 (1979). https://doi.org/10.1142/9789814417358_0006

28. Kramer, A.F.: Physiological metrics of mental workload: a review of recent progress. In: Damos, D.L. (ed.) Multiple Task Performance, pp. 279–328. Taylor & Francis, London (1991). ISBN 0-85066-757-7

29. Di Domenico, A., Nussbaum, M.A.: Interactive effects of physical and mental workload on subjective workload assessment. Int. J. Ind. Ergon. **28**, 977–983 (2008). https://doi.org/10.1016/j.ergon.2008.01.012

30. Miyake, S.: Multivariate workload evaluation combining physiological and subjective measures. Int. J. Psychophysiol. **40**, 233–238 (2001). https://doi.org/10.1016/S0167-8760(00)00191-4

31. Falck, A.C., Örtengren, R., Rosenqvist, M.: Assembly failures and action cost in relation to complexity level and assembly ergonomics in manual assembly (Part 2). Int. J. Ind. Ergon. **44**, 455–460 (2014). https://doi.org/10.1016/j.ergon.2014.02.001

32. Lelis-Torres, N., Ugrinowitsch, H., Apolinário-Souza, T., Benda, R., Lage, G.M.: Task engagement and mental workload involved in variation and repetition of a motor skill. Sci. Rep. **7**(1), 14764 (2017). https://doi.org/10.1038/s41598-017-15343-3

33. Colombini, D., Occhipinti, E., Alvarez-Casado, E: The revised OCRA checklist method. Humans factor editorial, Barcelona. (2013). ISBN 978-84-616-2965-7

34. Greenwood, D.J., Levin, M.: Introduction to Action Research: Social Research for Social Change, 2nd edn. Sage Publications, London (2007). ISBN 1-4129-2597-5

35. McCarney, R., Warner, J., Iliffe, S., Van Haselen, R., Griffin, M., Fisher, P.: The hawthorne effect: a randomised, controlled trial. BMC Med. Res. Methodol. **7**, 30 (2007). https://doi.org/10.1186/1471-2288-7-30

Mental Workload in the Explanation of Automation Effects on ATC Performance

José Juan Cañas[1]([⊠]), Pedro Ferreira[1], Patricia López de Frutos[2],
Eva Puntero[2], Elena López[2], Fernando Gómez-Comendador[3],
Francesca de Crescenzio[4], Francesca Lucchi[4], Fedja Netjasov[5],
and Bojana Mirkovic[5]

[1] Mind, Brain, and Behaviour Research Centre, University of Granada,
Granada, Spain
{delagado, pedroferreira}@ugr.es
[2] CRIDA A.I.E ATM R&D + Innovation Reference Centre, Madrid, Spain
{pmldefrutos, epuntero, elopezb}@e-crida.enaire.es
[3] Aerospace Systems, Air Transport and Airports Department,
Polytechnic University of Madrid, Madrid, Spain
fernando.gcomendador@upm.es
[4] Industrial Engineering Department, University of Bologna, Forlì, Italy
{francesca.decrescenzio, f.lucchi}@unibo.it
[5] Faculty of Transport and Traffic Engineering, University of Belgrade,
Belgrade, Serbia
{f.netjasov, b.mirkovic}@sf.bg.ac.rs

Abstract. Automation has been introduced more and more into the role of air traffic control (ATC). As with many other areas of human activity, automation has the objective of reducing the complexity of the task so that performance is optimised and safer. However, automation can also have negative effects on cognitive processing and the performance of the controllers. In this paper, we present the progress made at AUTOPACE, a European project in which research is carried out to discover what these negative effects are and to propose measures to mitigate them. The fundamental proposal of the project is to analyse, predict, and mitigate these negative effects by assessing the complexity of ATC in relation to the mental workload experienced by the controller. Hence, a highly complex situation will be one with a high mental workload and a low complex situation will be one in which the mental workload is low.

Keywords: Automation · Air-traffic controllers · Mental workload

1 Introduction

The control of complex and dynamic environments is a risky and uncertain task [1]. A complex and dynamic environment is one in which a person has to find a solution by performing a series of operations that can be characterised as follows: the number of elements relevant to the solution process is large and these are highly interconnected; the system changes dynamically over time; part of the structure and dynamics of the system are opaque (not transparent) for the operator; and the objectives can be multiple

L. Longo and M. C. Leva (Eds.): H-WORKLOAD 2018, CCIS 1012, pp. 202–221, 2019.
https://doi.org/10.1007/978-3-030-14273-5_12

and sometimes conflicting [2–4]. Complexity is one of the most important causes of mental workload in many areas of human performance [5–10].

Air traffic control (ATC) has all the characteristics of a complex and dynamic task: there are many elements (aircrafts and obstacles) that are interconnected; all these elements are changing constantly due to both the actions of the air traffic controller (ATCo) and their own dynamics; some of the variables are not transparent to the ATCo; and the objective is to direct all aircraft traffic safely and orderly at the same time. For this reason, it has been indicated that the mental workload of the ATCo is related to the complexity of the ATC system [11, 12]. A great deal of theoretical and applied research has been directed over the years to reducing the complexity of the ATCo task and, thus, to make it safer and less uncertain. In this research study, the focus has been mainly on the design of automation tools to which part of the control task can be allocated. The results of introducing new automatic tools in the control task have been mainly successful, but – similar to other areas of human work – automation also has some negative effects on system performance and safety [13, 14]. Those negative effects have motivated further research, with the aim of better understanding the impact of automation on the ATCo. The goal of this research is to improve the benefits and to reduce the negative effects of automation. With this goal, project AUTOPACE (Grant 699238), funded by the SESAR joint undertaking as part of SESAR 2020 Exploratory Research Programme within the framework of the EU's Horizon 2020, was intended to carry out scientific research to address the effects of high automation on ATCos' performances. At AUTOPACE, we assume that high automation will have effects on the level of mental workload experienced by the ATCo. Those effects could have positive as well as negative consequences on ATCo performance. To determine those consequences, in the project we propose research, using a psychological model based on established theories of attentional resources, to predict the effects of automation on ATCo mental workload. This model, which is designed to reduce complexity, could be used as the basis of investigation into the required new competences and training strategies which ensure that the ATCo's mental workload levels are compatible with the requirements of safe operation. A safe operation implies that the controller, in their new role which requires supervision and monitoring, remains 'in-the-loop' to initiate an efficient decision-making process, especially when dealing with possible unforeseen operational conditions and malfunctions of automation. A safe operation would also imply that the controller performance would not be affected by stressful situations when the system fails. Unforeseen operational conditions and malfunction of automation could lead to disorientation and panicked behaviour.

In the following sections, we will discuss the approach taken in the AUTOPACE project to the problems associated to reducing the mental workload by introducing automation in the ATCo task. The main assumption of the AUTOPACE project is that workload is related to the complexity of the system in which the ATCo performs their work. Therefore, we start by explaining in Sect. 2 our vision of what complexity means within the field of ATC and ATM in general. Next, in Sect. 3, we will expose the fundamental problem that the AUTOPACE project wants to address: the possible negative effects of automation on the performance of the ATCo. It is true that automation reduces the mental workload by reducing the demand for mental resources.

However, automation can also cause phenomena such as out-of-the-loop or erratic behaviour when the automatic system fails. In consequence, in the AUTOPACE project there is a proposal to reduce complexity and mental workload by considering the negative effects of automation. This proposal is explained in Sect. 4. First, in Sect. 4 we expose the psychological model that we are developing based on the concept of mental workload. Then, in Sect. 5 we address the negative effects that we hypothesize that will be found in the future scenarios in ATC in which more automation will be introduced. In Sect. 6 we describe the methodology we are using to test the hypotheses contemplated in AUTOPACE. This methodology is based on the development of a computational model in which the psychological model of ATCo is implemented. In Sect. 6 some results obtained in the execution of this computational model are also presented. Finally, in the conclusions of the paper we indicate some consequences that the results of this project will have on the training of the ATCo designed to face the new automation scenarios.

2   Approaches to Defining and Measuring Complexity in ATC

Complexity features as a topic of scientific research and theory in many academic and applied fields [15]. However, a review of this research shows that all approaches to the complexity issue start from an explicit or implicit definition of what is meant by complexity. In particular, in the field of ATM (air traffic management) we can find three approaches in which complexity is defined and measured differently.

2.1   The Algorithmic Approach

In the algorithmic approach (see Fig. 1a), it is assumed that the complexity of the task can be calculated directly from the parameters of the environment (i.e., [16]). Thus, over the years, some formulas have been proposed in which complexity is calculated from parameters such as occupancy (number of aircraft in the sector) or the meteorological conditions. In this approach, the controller is not taken into account in the definition of complexity. Complexity is defined only by the traffic and the environmental conditions in which the task is performed. Although, obviously, traffic and environmental parameters are considered to have an effect on the cognitive system of the controllers (for example, these parameters affect their mental load, stress, etc.), in this approach, the behaviour of the cognitive system of the controller does not form part of the calculation of complexity.

2.2   The Behavioural (Activity) Approach

One could call the behavioural approach an attempt to include the ATCo in the calculation of complexity (see Fig. 1b). In this approach, complexity is defined and measured from the observable behaviour of the controller without any reference to the cognitive processing of traffic and environmental parameters. While it is assumed that controller behaviour is the result of cognitive processing of traffic and environment parameters, no attempt is made to model this cognitive processing. For example, the authors of [17] propose a method of measuring complexity from the actions of the controllers, and the authors of [18] have proposed another method where complexity is calculated from the commands issued by the controller.

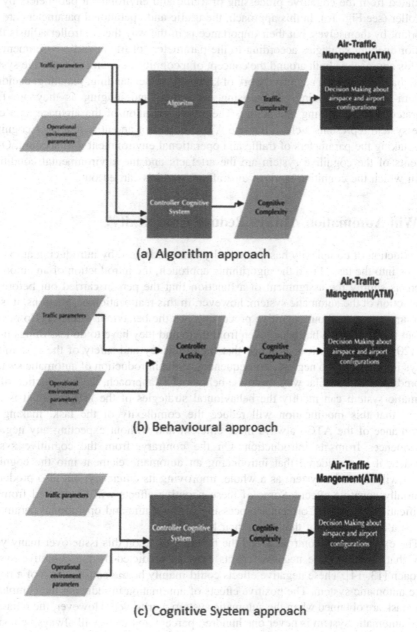

(a) Algorithm approach

(b) Behavioural approach

(c) Cognitive System approach

Fig. 1. The three approaches to the study of complexity in ATM

2.3   The Cognitive System Approach

Finally, in the approach known as the cognitive system approach [19], complexity is calculated from the cognitive processing of traffic and environment parameters by the controller (see Fig. 1c). In this approach, the traffic and operational parameters are not important by themselves, but their importance is in the way the controller adjusts their decision-making strategies according to the parameters of traffic and environment.

This approach is built around the concept of a cognitive system. A cognitive system is one that performs the cognitive work of knowing, understanding, planning, deciding, problem-solving, analysing, synthesising, assessing, and judging as they are fully integrated with perceiving and acting. The characterisation of the airspace as a cognitive system represents a claim that the ATCo is part of an entity that does cognitive work, taking the parameters of traffic and operational environment into account. Other elements of the cognitive system are the artefacts and the environmental conditions within which the cognitive work of air-traffic control is carried out.

3   Will Automation Always Reduce Complexity?

The reduction of complexity has traditionally been addressed by introducing automatic systems into the task. From the algorithmic approach, the introduction of an automatic system is simply the assignment of a function that the person carried out before the introduction of the automatic system; however, in this reallocation of functions, it is not necessary to worry about cognitive processing nor the behaviour of the ATCo beyond the fact that a function has been taken from them and they have to do less things in the task [20]. In this way, it is assumed that the efficiency and safety of the system will always improve and no negative consequences of the introduction of automatic systems are predicted. In a similar way, from the behaviourist approach, the introduction of the automatic system can modify the behavioural strategies of the ATCo, but it is considered that this modification will reduce the complexity of the task, making the performance of the ATCo always more efficient and without expecting any negative consequences from its introduction. On the contrary, from the cognitive system approach, it is considered that introducing an automatic element into the cognitive system will affect the system as a whole, improving its efficiency, but also producing potentially negative effects. Some of these negative effects will be derived from the modification of the ATCo mental processing of the traffic and operational parameters and, as a consequence of that, from their behaviour.

The experience of controllers and the research done on this issue over many years show that, in fact, these negative effects exist as predicted by the cognitive system approach [13, 14]. These negative effects could mainly be the consequence of a failure of the automatic system. The positive effects of automation in reducing the complexity of the task are obtained when the automatic system works well. However, the reliability of the automatic system is never one hundred percent and there will always be a small probability that the system will fail, affecting ATCo cognitive processing and behaviour. Neither the algorithmic nor the behaviouristic approaches would predict those negative consequences of automation failures.

For example, there is extensive literature on the well-known problem of being 'out of the loop' (OOTL). This problem occurs when the person, in our case the ATCo, is put out of the loop of the 'perceiving-acting-perceiving circle'. In a normal situation, a person is within a cycle of observation-action-feedback-action [21, 22]: the person observes the situation, acts on it, observes the results of their performance, and, if this is not correct or is insufficient, they act again to correct it. When the automatic system is introduced, the person is removed from that cycle by taking from them the functions of observing and receiving feedback on what the system is doing. If the system works well, removing the person from the loop will have no consequences; however, if the system fails, the person must note this failure and take control of the situation. The phenomenon of OOTL occurs when, after a change in the situation – in particular, high impact changes such as system failures – the person does not return to the loop either because they have not realised the failure or because they do not react in time to take control of the situation. This phenomenon is not taken into consideration by the algorithmic or behavioural approaches, but can be explained easily from the cognitive system approach.

It can also happen that a person experiences one or several failures of the automatic system and they enter a state of overexcitement that leads to panic and erratic behaviour. The authors of [23] have shown the importance of non-cognitive skills (for example, tolerance to stress) in the training of ATCos. If the automation fault experience affects the stress of the controllers, that stress will have a negative effect on their performance. As it has been demonstrated numerous times, over-activation affects cognitive processes, such as visual perception, that are essential in the task of air control [24].

Therefore, in line with the view of function allocation in the cognitive engineering perspective [19, 22], from the cognitive system approach it can be considered that automation will reduce the complexity of the task only if the negative effects are reduced. If, as hypothesised, automation produces negative effects in addition to positive ones, those negative effects will increase complexity by counteracting the reduction in complexity produced by the positive effects.

It is worth mentioning that the cognitive system approach can predict negative effects of both high complexity and low complexity. Neither of the other two approaches can predict these effects, since in both approaches it is assumed that automation always reduces the complexity and, therefore, the mental workload of the ATCo. However, much of the negative effects of automation are due to the reduction in mental workload after reducing the complexity of the system. As we will explain below, for the phenomenon known as OOTL, which occurs in situations of low mental workload, when we introduce automation to reduce complexity it is only possible to explain and predict it from the cognitive system approach.

4   AUTOPACE Proposal to Reduce Complexity
by Considering the Negative Effects of Automation

At AUTOPACE, the effects of automation are explained within the cognitive system approach by proposing hypotheses from a psychological model of the ATCo. In this psychological model there are two components: the functional structure of the ATCo's cognitive system and dynamic management of attentional resources.

4.1   The Psychological Model of the ATCo

At AUTOPACE, we propose a psychological model that has a structure which is the hypothesised cognitive system of the ATCo. In addition, the model includes a description of how the cognitive system functions by requiring attentional resources. It is very important to differentiate between these two aspects – the structure and the functioning of the system – in order to understand our hypotheses about the effects of automation on controller performance. Our hypotheses are developed in the context of the predicted future scenarios of automation.

The Functional Structure of the Cognitive System. All the cognitive models that have been proposed in the literature to explain the interaction between a person (i.e., the ATCo) and a system share the same scheme in which the human cognitive system is composed of sensory, perceptual, memory, and decision-making processes. We can take as a reference the model proposed in [25] (see Fig. 2). This model incorporates several interesting aspects of the recent theoretical developments in the science of human factors. In particular, we might highlight the incorporation in the model of the levels of processing that constitute what is called situation awareness (SA) [26]: perception, comprehension, projection, and decision.

Cognitive Functioning and Mental Resources. Human behaviour and mental activity require energy. In a sense, we could say that, in the life sciences, research has followed a mechanistic paradigm, according to which human machinery function depends on supplied energy [27]. Thus, for instance, it is assumed that performance of a task will improve or deteriorate depending, among other things, on the quantity and quality of the energy (resources) supplied [28]. In the tradition of attentional theories and human factors and ergonomics, this energy is called 'resources'.

Using a simple model of human functioning, we can say that when a person is confronted with the performance of a task, they do so with a certain amount of mental resources that we call available resources. The amount of resources that a person has depends on several factors, both individual and contextual. In addition to the available resources, we must talk about what we call demanded or required resources. Depending, essentially, on the complexity of the task, a person will need to apply more or less available resources to be able to perform it with a certain level of optimisation. Easy tasks will require fewer resources, while difficult tasks more resources.

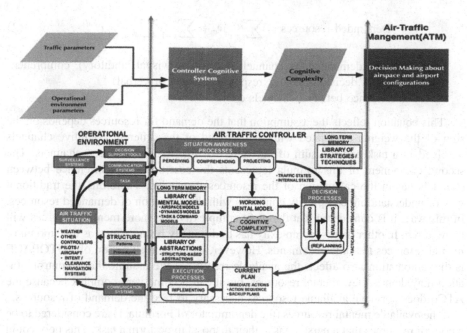

Fig. 2. The cognitive system approach and [25] model

Using these two concepts – demanded and available resources – psychological models have explained the functioning of the human cognitive system. The fundamental premise of all the models is that the functional structures, such as those described above, will work with an efficacy that will depend on the relationship between the demanded resources and the available resources. This relation is called the mental workload (MWL) [29–31] and is expressed according to formula 1:

$$MWL = \frac{Demanded\_resources}{Available\_resources} \tag{1}$$

The quantification of the cognitive demand resources can be made according to Wickens [32] and refined with reference to Wickens and McCarley [33]. When tasks overlap in time, the demanded resources depend on two factors: the resources demanded for processing for each cognitive channel (perception, comprehension, projection, decision-making, and manual or verbal actions) and the amount of interference between the two tasks. When two tasks are performed in parallel and use the same pool of resources, there would be interferences that increase the demanded resources. This increase could be reduced by the prioritisation of tasks. These two factors could be expressed as shown in Formula 2 [32]. In our model, this is the general formula used for calculating an ATCo's demanded resources.

$$\text{Demanded resources} = \sum_{c=1}^{u} w_c + \sum_{c=1}^{n} \sum_{d=c+1}^{N} i^{(c,d)} \tag{2}$$

w_c = resources demanded by channel: perception (visual, auditory), comprehension, projection, decision-making, response (manual or verbal)
$i^{(c,d)}$ = interference between channels c and d.

This equation reflects the assumption that the demand for resources depends on the sum of the weights associated with the demand of the different cognitive channels involved in a task and the sum of the values of interference between channels. The second component of this formula represents the cost that the interference between channels has in the calculation of the resources demanded. Therefore, the traditional way of understanding complexity coincides with the definition of demanded resources. In this way, it is considered that the more complexity, the more mental resources will be required. In other words, complexity has traditionally been defined as the amount of mental resources that a task demands. However, the basic assumption of AUTOPACE is that automation also affects the available resources. We assume that a control situation may demand few mental resources, but it can become very complex because the ATCo does not have available resources necessary to face the demand of resources.

The available mental resources (the denominator of Formula 1) are considered to be a pool of resources that a person has at their disposal to perform a task. This pool could be made up of different dimensions containing more or less available resources. In the traditional view of human factors research, it has always been considered that the person performing a given task uses the whole pool of available resources. In the case where the available pool is small, the denominator in the equation for calculating mental workload is small, contributing to a major probability of overload. On the contrary, when the pool is large, the person would use all the resources at his disposal, making the denominator large and the probability of underload higher. The dimension of the pool of available resources depends on a number of factors, such as stress, fatigue, emotions, etc., all of which are factors that affect the level of activation or arousal.

However, this traditional view of the pool of available resources has been reviewed in a sense that is very relevant for AUTOPACE. It is increasingly recognised that not all the available resources that a person possesses need to be allocated to perform the task. For many different reasons, the proportion of the available resources allocated to the performance of a task may vary considerably, both during task performance and from one iteration to another of that same task. This new understanding of the available resources is behind the recent interests of researchers of concepts such as engagement or effort. For example, a recent paper [34] has reviewed the literature on effort. For more than one hundred years, psychologists have been working on the concept of effort to understand why and how a person dedicates more or less available resources to a task. In educational psychology, there is a well-known theoretical model called Cognitive Load Theory [35] in which there are three components that are differentiated:

1. Intrinsic load which is directly related to the learning material and that is what we call demanded resources in our context of human factors;

2. Extraneous load which is the resources dedicated to other tasks, but not to the task of learning itself; and

3. Germane load, which refers to the mental resources devoted to acquiring and storing schemata in long-term memory (learning itself).

This third component refers to the mental resources that are in the pool of available resources at one point in time and actually allocated to the main task. This component of cognitive load is the issue of interest in [34]. The author realised that the available resources that are in the pool can be allocated to different tasks simultaneously and when we are calculating the total MWL of one task, we should enter in the denominator the real available resources that are dedicated to the task of our interest. For the same reason, researchers are talking more and more about engagement, another concept related to available resources and effort (i.e., [36]). It seems obvious that when performing a task, a person could be more or less engaged in it. Engagement affects the amount of resources that the person will make available to performing a task: the more engaged in the task, the more available resources are allocated to it. We can describe engagement as a continuum. At one end of the engagement scale, there is a 'passive cognitive engagement' that leads to allocating a small amount of resources. On the other end, there is an 'active cognitive engagement' that increases the amount of available resources allocated to the task. Therefore, engagement might affect the size of the pool of available resources, but more importantly, it would determine how much of those available resources are dedicated to the task. In that sense, engagement means something similar to germane load in educational psychology theories.

Our interest in these new interpretations of available resources for this project is clear: although we assume that automation reduces the demanded resources of the task, in our proposal, automation affects also the available resources in two ways:

1. The level of activation or arousal (psychophysiological activation), and, subsequently, the size of the pool of available resources; and

2. The amount of those available resources that are really dedicated to the task.

As we will explain in the following sections, the available resources that are allocated to the task will vary because ATCo responsibilities will change in the future automation scenarios. That means that there might be also a change in 'engagement' or 'effort' and, consequently, in the amount of available resources dedicated to the task.

In our proposal, these changes in responsibilities mean changes in available resources allocated to the task of control. Therefore, we will consider that automation will affect the available resources. An ATCo who is simply monitoring would be less engaged than another one who is approving or applying and, therefore the denominator of the MWL equation will be smaller (i.e., more risk of OOTL). Then, when the automatic system fails and the ATCo has to recover control, the probability of being out of the loop is higher when they are less engaged and dedicating less effort to the task. That explains why OOTL is more probable when monitoring than when approving or applying. Therefore, our hypotheses can be considered in relation to the attentional theories, as shown in Fig. 3. In the classical theories of attentional resources (i.e., [28]), automation affects only the demanded resources. These traditional theories are in line with the algorithmic and behavioural approaches to complexity; if automation affects only the demanded resources by reducing them, it is not necessary to take into account the human cognitive system because it directly benefits from changes made in the conditions of the traffic and the operational environment. The cognitive system benefits from automation, but it is not necessary to act on it. Although, it can be argued that knowing the functioning of the human cognitive system could be useful to better identify the aspects of traffic and the operational environment which would reduce the cognitive demands, the main assumption would be that any automatic system would have some positive benefit for the ATCo and no negative effects. However, when we consider the new attentional theories (i.e., [37]) which assume that automation also affects available resources, we must necessarily adopt the approximation of cognitive systems, since only from this approach is it considered that automation can modify the operation of the system as a whole (especially the interaction between the human cognitive system and the automatic system). For this reason, complexity cannot be calculated without considering the human cognitive system in its interaction with the automatic system.

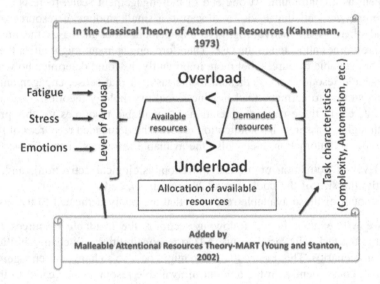

Fig. 3. Effects of automation according to the traditional and new attentional theories.

4.2   AUTOPACE Psychological Model in the Context of Related Research on Mental Workload

The psychological model proposed in AUTOPACE incorporates current theories and empirical results on mental workload [29–31]. The field of mental workload research has currently two major challenges. In the first place, the theoretical models proposed up to date should allow to make predictions in applied context where the mental workload of the operators is a fundamental factor to explain their performance. In this aspect, the research carried out in the AUTOPACE project demonstrates how the mental workload of the ATCo is fundamental to explain how she/he deals with the complexity of the control task. Secondly, although much progress has been made in these years, we are still in need of methodological development to validate the hypothesis derived from the theoretical models. In this second aspect, AUTOPACE contributes with a methodology based on the development of a computational model where the psychological model of the ATCo is implemented. We explain this methodology in the following section. But, first, we must describe in more detail the hypotheses that derive from the psychological model developed in AUTOPACE.

5 AUTOPACE Predictions for Future Automation Scenarios in ATC

In order to test our hypotheses, at AUTOPACE, we have defined the scenarios in which ATCos will work when automation is introduced in their work. We foresee two possible scenarios: one with medium automation and another with high automation. Those two scenarios will require different responsibilities and different levels of engagement with the task. We hope that by comparing these two scenarios, we can observe the behaviour of the ATC system when the psychological processes and the behaviour of the ATCos are affected by the different levels of automation. These two scenarios of future automation considered by AUTOPACE are described below.

The scenarios considered at AUTOPACE represent future traffic and mode of operations according to the SESAR Concept of Operations. The characteristics of this Concept of Operations are:

- It considers annual growth of 2.7% from 2015 to 2050 (an increase of 94.5%);
- It implements free route and 4D trajectory concepts;
- Trajectories are de-conflicted thanks to the implementation of de-complexing processes;
- Sectors are expected to be much bigger than current sectors; and
- Several ATCos will be operating in the same sector (flight centred ATS procedures).

AUTOPACE describes two different levels of automation that could be expected by 2050: high automation scenario (E1) and medium automation scenario (E2). These scenarios are defined by means of four scenario elements:

- **Actors:** the scenarios consider two actors as relevant for AUTOPACE purposes: the ATC System and the ATCo. Current executive and planner ATCo actors will not be needed thanks to automation. Therefore, AUTOPACE scenarios consider a unique human actor: the ATCo who will assume both executive and planner roles.
- **Responsibilities allocated to actors:** the responsibilities of each actor in each scenario is the most relevant factor for the cognitive modelling study. For this reason, we have defined three verbs to describe ATCo responsibilities with the following criteria:
  - Monitor: When the ATC System assumes the major ATC actions, the ATCo must monitor system behaviour to prevent deviations. Monitoring or vigilance is the activity that an operator performs to acquire situation awareness (SA). Due to the high level of automation, the ATCo must monitor in both high and

medium automation scenarios. It is important to note that the ATCo could not apply or approve actions without previously monitoring.

- Approve: Once the ATC System has proposed an ATC action, the ATCo must approve it before it is implemented. Approval requires previous monitoring, but also an evaluation of the correctness of the system decision. Approval does not imply the implementation of the action, but the ATCo must consider the consequences of the action carried out by the system. Therefore, we might say that approval requires a good SA (perception, comprehension, and projection, with projection being more relevant for approving than for monitoring).
- Apply. The ATCo analyses the situation, decides, and implements the most suitable solution from a set of provided ATC system solutions and with the support of the ATC tools. Application requires monitoring too, but, in contrast with approval, it is the ATCo who must elaborate the solution to the problem and then identify and implement the necessary actions to carry it out. Therefore, application should require not only SA (perception, comprehension, and projection), but also the use of decision-making and responding resources (verbal, manual).
- **Processes and services:** AUTOPACE ConOps identifies eight processes and describes the role that the ATCo plays in them for high automation and medium automation scenarios.
- **Human performance aspects:** a preliminary identification of the challenges that each scenario will have from the human factors perspective.

According to these criteria:

- In the high automation scenario, the ATCo is expected to have the responsibility of monitoring or monitoring and approving in the provision of the majority of the ATC services.
- In the medium automation scenario, the ATCo will be responsible not only for monitoring and approving, but also for applying many of the ATC services (after analysing the proposals made by the system).

Table 1 summarises the description of some of the ATC Controller responsibilities.

Table 1. Some responsibilities allocated to the ATC controller in the future automation scenarios

Responsibilities	Responsibilities allocation	
	High automation	Medium automation
Identify conflict risks between aircraft	Monitor	Monitor
Provide flight information to all known flights	Monitor	Monitor
Relay to pilots SIGMETS that may affect the route of a flight	Monitor	Monitor
Provide Alerting Service (ALRS) to all known flights according to the following three different phases (INCERFA, ALERFA, DETRESFA)	Monitor	Monitor

(*continued*)

Table 1. (*continued*)

Responsibilities	Responsibilities allocation	
	High automation	Medium automation
Check flightplans/RBT/RMTs for possible conflicts and complexity issues within area of responsibility	Monitor	Monitor
Plan conflict-free flight path through area of responsibility	Monitor	Monitor
Provide early conflict detection and resolution if the early resolution brings operational benefit (either on the ground side or the airborne side)	Monitor	Approve
Assign specified headings, speeds and levels	Monitor	Approve
Re-route flights to avoid non-nominal or hazardous weather areas	Monitor	Approve
Provide sequencing between controlled flights	Monitor	Approve
Resolve boundary problems by re-coordination	Monitor	Approve
Implement solution strategies by communicating trajectory changes to the aircraft through the concerned ATC Controller/System via Data Link	Monitor	Approve
Provide separation between controlled flights	Monitor	Apply
Apply appropriate separation to all controlled flights departing area of jurisdiction	Monitor	Apply
Monitor the air situation picture	Monitor	Apply
Monitor the weather conditions	Monitor	Apply
Monitor information on airspace status e.g. activation of segregated airspace Communicate with pilots by data link	Monitor	Apply
Monitor aircraft equipment status as provided by the system	Monitor	Apply
Co-ordinate with adjacent control areas/sectors for the delegation of airspace or aircraft	Monitor	Apply
In coordination with the ATC Supervisory or Local Traffic Management roles determine the need for Complexity Solution Measures in the case of overload situations forecast	Approve	Apply
Issue holding instructions	Approve	Apply

6 Methodology

When complexity is approached from a theoretical psychological model of the ATCo, it is possible to derive hypotheses from that model about how to reduce complexity with automation. These hypotheses refer to how the complexity varies depending on how the ATCo processes the traffic parameters and how the operational environment is designed and managed. These hypotheses can also be made about the measures that can be put in place to mitigate these effects. Then, these hypotheses must be tested using a scientifically valid method.

6.1 The ATCo Psychological Model Implemented in a Computational Model

There are several scientifically valid methods for testing hypotheses in a dynamic task. An alternative to the methods designed to obtain empirical data to test the hypotheses that are derived from a theoretical model, is the method that has been called the 'computational method' [38, 39], which consists of developing a computer model in which the psychological model is implemented. With this computer model, it is possible to run computer simulations where the hypothesis derived from the model can be tested. In order to do that, it is necessary that the computer model integrates the cognitive mechanisms responsible for the behaviour of the human actor, the task, and the environmental situation in which that task is performed. The hypotheses derived from the model are validated when the computer model responds in the way a human ATCo would respond when performing that task and in those traffic and environmental situations. For a recent review of this method and its applications for scientific discovery see [38].

At AUTOPACE, we have adopted this computational method. Subsequently, for the purpose of evaluating the effects of automation on the ATCo's cognitive system, we have employed a computational model prototype called COMETA (COgnitiveModEl for aTco workload Assessment), developed by CRIDA [40], that currently estimates the demanded resources required to perform the controller activity. The demanded resources are calculated based on the Wickens and McCarley algorithm [33]. Typically, COMETA inputs are the control events generated in real or simulation environments along with the ATCo task model expected in the scenario under study. For AUTOPACE, the control events have been generated by a fast-time simulation tool called RAMS. RAMS stands for 'reorganised ATC mathematical simulator'. This a FTS developed by ISA Software (http://ramsplus.com – taken on 06-03-2017)) where AUTOPACE Scenarios Environment (airspace and procedures) have been modelled. The ATCo task model (tasks associated with events, actions, behavioural primitives, and mental resources) has been adapted to the control activity expected in AUTOPACE

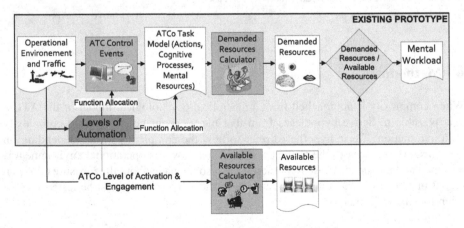

Fig. 4. COMETA functional architecture

scenarios (high and medium automation) in nominal (when the system works well) and non-nominal situations (after system failures). COMETA presents the results not only as a global figure for the demanded resources, but also as an apportionment for every dedicated cognitive process and dimension.

COMETA foundations share the functional structure and functioning of the ATCo cognitive system models of AUTOPACE. Figure 4 shows the complete functional structure.

6.2 Some Results to Validate the Predicted Effect of Automation on Mental Workload

Figure 5 shows some results obtained with COMETA related to the functional structure evolution and the expected cognitive process in future automation scenarios, all of which were compared with the current ATC paradigm. As observed, the distribution of the functional structure of the cognitive system changes drastically with automation. While current ATCos use the cognitive dimensions (visual, comprehension, projection, decision-making, and verbal resources) in a balanced way, future ATCos will focus their cognitive efforts mainly on comprehension and projection. The ATCo needs to project what is going to happen in order to understand the system performance without missing situational awareness. In a medium automation scenario where main actions are not only monitored and approved, but also applied, projection is more relevant than comprehension as the ATCo needs to invest more resources into the projection of future scenarios to correctly select among the options given by the system (approve) and their own instructions (apply). In the high automation scenario, the contrary occurs and what is important is to have a more robust mental picture of what is occurring, in order to monitor system performance (monitor) and to approve system proposals (approving); i.e., better comprehension than projection. These results are in line with the predictions of different levels of automation made by [41].

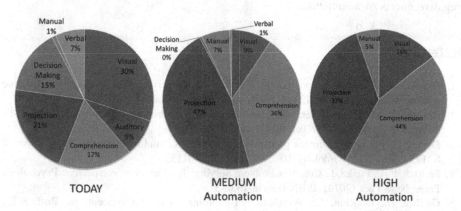

Fig. 5. Cognitive processes evolution in the current medium automation and high automation scenarios [42].

7 Summary and Conclusions

One of the main conclusions of Project AUTOPACE is that from a cognitive system approach to ATC complexity, it is possible to address the positive and negative effects of automation and propose measures to reduce its negative effects and improve system reliability and safety. Only from this approach is it possible to mitigate the negative effects of automation. The two other approaches do not predict negative effects since they consider that automation reduces the resources demanded (complexity is only dependent on the demanded resources). For this reason, in these approaches, many of the complex dimensions of human functioning are potentially ignored. An important consequence is that if the effects of automation are only considered with regard to traffic conditions and operational conditions, it is not possible to investigate the impacts of such profound transformations on human psychological processing and to adapt the way the human operator is prepared to manage such changes in their tasks. Therefore, only from the cognitive system approach is it possible to design training programs where cognitive and non-cognitive skills are taken into account in order to face the potentially negative effects of automation. It is very important to emphasise that when proposing a psychological model of the effects of automation, this model should be grounded in the consideration of mental workload because it is the psychological concept that defines the dynamic relation between the demanded and the available resources.

The ultimate goal of AUTOPACE is to indicate requirements for training competences resulting from the analysis carried out into the effect of automation on the ATCo psychological model. In future automation scenarios, some new training strategies and competences will be needed to cope with the effects of OOTL, stress, disorientation, panic, etc., to ensure that the ATCo performance is optimum. Therefore, the research carried out by AUTOPACE based on the ATCo psychological model will support future research on system design to balance the use of the different cognitive and non-cognitive processes and new training strategies to cope with the potentially negative effects of automation.

References

1. Osman, M.: Controlling uncertainty: a review of human behavior in complex dynamic environments. Psychol. Bull. **136**, 65–86 (2010). https://doi.org/10.1037/a0017815
2. Broadbent, D.E.: Levels, hierarchies, and the locus of control. Q. J. Exp. Psychol. **29**, 181–201 (1977). https://doi.org/10.1080/14640747708400596
3. Dörner, D., Funke, J.: Complex problem solving: what it is and what it is not. Front. Psychol. **8**, 1153 (2017). https://doi.org/10.3389/fpsyg.2017.01153
4. Frensch, P.A., Funke, J.: Complex Problem Solving: The European Perspective. Psychology Press, New York (2014). ISBN 0-8058-1336-5
5. Gopher, D., Donchin, E.: Workload: an examination of the concept. In: Boff, K.R., Kaufman, L., Thomas, J.P. (eds.) Hand-Book of Perception and Performance Cognitive Processes and Performance, vol. 2, pp. 41–49. Wiley, New York (1986). ISBN-13: 978-0471829577

6. Byrne, A.: Mental workload as an outcome in medical education. In: Longo, L., Leva, M.C. (eds.) H-WORKLOAD 2017. CCIS, vol. 726, pp. 187–197. Springer, Cham (2017). https://doi.org/10.1007/978-3-319-61061-0_12

7. Longo, L.: Designing medical interactive systems via assessment of human mental workload. In: 2015 IEEE 28th International Symposium Computer-Based Medical Systems (CBMS), pp. 364–365. IEEE Press (2015). https://doi.org/10.1109/CBMS.2015.67

8. Balfe, N., Crowley, K., Smith, B., Longo, L.: Estimation of train driver workload: extracting taskload measures from on-train-data-recorders. In: Longo, L., Leva, M. (eds.) H-WORKLOAD 2017. CCIS, vol. 726, pp. 106–119. Springer, Cham (2017). https://doi.org/10.1007/978-3-319-61061-0_7

9. Longo, L.: Mental workload in medicine: foundations, applications, open problems, challenges and future perspectives. In: 2016 IEEE 29th International Symposium Computer-Based Medical Systems (CBMS), pp. 106–111. IEEE Press (2016)

10. Tong, S., Helman, S., Balfe, N., Fowler, C., Delmonte, E., Hutchins, R.: Workload differences between on-road and off-road manoeuvres for motorcyclists. In: Longo, L., Leva, M. (eds.) International Symposium on Human Mental Workload: Models and Applications, pp. 239–250. Springer, Cham. (2017). https://doi.org/10.1007/978-3-319-61061-0_16

11. Edwards, T., Martin, L., Bienert, N., Mercer, J.: The relationship between workload and performance in air traffic control: exploring the influence of levels of automation and variation in task demand. In: Longo, L., Leva, M. (eds.) H-WORKLOAD 2017. CCIS, vol. 726, pp. 120–139. Springer, Cham (2017). https://doi.org/10.1007/978-3-319-61061-0_8

12. Loft, S., Sanderson, P., Neal, A., Mooij, M.: Modelling and predicting mental workload in en route air traffic control: critical review and broader implications. Hum. Factors 49, 376–399 (2007). https://doi.org/10.1518/001872007X197017

13. Parasuraman, R., Riley, V.: Humans and automation: use, misuse, disuse, abuse. Hum. Factors 39, 230–253 (1997). https://doi.org/10.1518/001872097778543886

14. Metzger, U., Parasuraman, R.: automation in future air traffic management: effects of decision aid reliability on controller performance and mental workload. Hum. Factors 47, 35–49 (2005). https://doi.org/10.1518/0018720053653802

15. Mitchell, M.: Complexity: A guided tour. Oxford University Press, Oxford (2009). ISBN-13: 978-0199798100

16. Netjasov, F., Janić, M., Tošić, V.: Developing a generic metric of terminal airspace traffic complexity. Transportmetrica 7(5), 369–394 (2011). https://doi.org/10.1080/18128602.2010.505590

17. Zhang, M., Shan, L., Zhang, M., Liu, K., Yu, H., Yu, J.: Terminal airspace sector capacity estimation method based on the ATC dynamical model. Kybernetes 45, 884–899 (2016). https://doi.org/10.1108/K-12-2014-0308

18. Tobaruela, G., Schuster, W., Majumdar, A., Ochieng, W.Y., Martinez, L., Hendrickx, P.: A method to estimate air traffic controller mental workload based on traffic clearances. J. Air Transp. Manag. 39, 59–71 (2014). https://doi.org/10.1016/j.jairtraman.2014.04.002

19. Kontogiannis, T., Malakis, S.: Cognitive Engineering and Safety Organization in Air Traffic Management. CRC Press, Boca Raton (2017). ISBN 9781138049727

20. Fitts, P.M.: Human Engineering for an Effective Air-navigation and Traffic-control System. National Research Council, Washington (1951)

21. Neisser, U.: Cognition and Reality: Principles and Implications of Cognitive Psychology. WH Freeman/Times Books/Henry Holt & Co (1976). ISBN-13: 978-0716704775

22. Hollnagel, E., Bye, A.: Principles for modelling function allocation. Int. J. Hum.-Comput. Stud. 52, 253–265 (2000). https://doi.org/10.1006/ijhc.1999.0288

23. Chappelle, W., Thompson, W., Goodman, T., Bryan, C.J., Reardon, L.: The utility of testing noncognitive aptitudes as additional predictors of graduation from US air force air traffic controller training. Aviat. Psychol. Appl. Hum. Factors 5, 93–103 (2015). https://doi.org/10.1027/2192-0923/a000082

24. Woods, A.J.: The consequences of hyper-arousal for human visual perception. Retrieved from Dissertations & Theses @ George Washington University (2010)

25. Histon, J.M., Hansman, R.J.: Mitigating complexity in air traffic control: the role of structure-based abstractions. Report no. ICAT-2008-05 (2008)

26. Endsley, M.R.: Toward a theory of situation awareness in dynamic systems. Hum. Factors: J. Hum. Factors Ergon. Soc. 37, 32–64 (1995). https://doi.org/10.1518/001872095779049543

27. Rabinbach, A.: The Human Motor: Energy, Fatigue, and the Origins of Modernity. University of California Press, Berkeley (1990). ISBN-13: 978-0520078277

28. Kahneman, D.: Attention and effort, Englewood Cliffs. Prentice-Hall, NJ (1973). ISBN-13: 978-0130505187

29. Longo, L., Leva, M.C. (eds.): Human Mental Workload: Models and Applications: First International Symposium, H-WORKLOAD 2017, Dublin, Ireland, June 28-30, 2017, Revised Selected Papers, vol. 726. Springer, Heidelberg (2017). https://doi.org/10.1007/978-3-319-61061-0. ISBN 978-3-319-61061-0

30. Hancock, P.A.: Whither workload? Mapping a path for its future development. In: Longo, L., Leva, M. (eds.) H-WORKLOAD 2017. CCIS, vol. 726, pp. 3–17. Springer, Cham (2017). https://doi.org/10.1007/978-3-319-61061-0_1. ISBN 978-3-319-61061-0

31. Wickens, C.D.: mental workload: assessment, prediction and consequences. In: Longo, L., Leva, M. (eds.) H-WORKLOAD 2017. CCIS, vol. 726, pp. 18–29. Springer, Cham (2017). https://doi.org/10.1007/978-3-319-61061-0_2. ISBN 978-3-319-61061-0

32. Wickens, C.D.: Multiple resources and performance prediction. Theor. Issues Ergon. Sci. 3, 159–177 (2002). https://doi.org/10.1080/14639220210123806

33. Wickens, C.D., McCarley, J.S.: Applied Attention Theory. CRC Press, Boca Raton (2007). ISBN 9780805859836

34. Wickens, C.D.: Effort in human factors performance and decision making. Hum. Factors 56 (8), 1329–1336 (2014). https://doi.org/10.1177/0018720814558419

35. Sweller, J.: Cognitive load during problem solving: effects on learning. Cogn. Sci. 12, 257–285 (1988). https://doi.org/10.1207/s15516709cog1202_4

36. Endsley, M.: From here to autonomy: lessons learned from human-automation research. Hum. Factors 59(1), 5–27 (2017). https://doi.org/10.1177/0018720816681350

37. Young, M.S., Stanton, N.A.: Malleable attentional resources theory: a new explanation for the effects of mental underload on performance. Hum. Factors 44, 365 (2002). https://doi.org/10.1518/0018720024497709

38. Sozou, P.D., Lane, P.C., Addis, M., Gobet, F.: Computational scientific discovery. In: Magnani, L., Bertolotti, T. (eds.) Springer Handbook of Model-Based Science. SH, pp. 719–734. Springer, Cham (2017). https://doi.org/10.1007/978-3-319-30526-4_33. ISBN 978-3-319-30526-4

39. Rizzo, L., Dondio, P., Delany, S.J., Longo, L.: Modeling mental workload via rule-based expert system: a comparison with NASA-TLX and workload profile. In: Iliadis, L., Maglogiannis, I. (eds.) Artificial Intelligence Applications and Innovations. AIAI 2016. IFIP Advances in Information and Communication Technology, vol. 475, pp. 215–229. Springer, Cham (2016). https://doi.org/10.1007/978-3-319-44944-9_19

40. Suárez, N., López, P., Puntero, E., Rodriguez, S.: Quantifying air traffic controller mental workload. Fourth SESAR Innovation Days (2014)

41. Endsley, M.R.: Level of automation effects on performance, situation awareness and workload in a dynamic control task. Ergonomics **42**, 462–492 (1999). https://doi.org/10.1080/001401399185595
42. Cañas, J.J., Ferreira, P.N.P., Puntero, E., López, P., López, E., Gomez-Comendador, V.F.: An air traffic controller psychological model with automation. In: 7th EASN International Conference: "Innovation in European Aeronautics Research", Warsaw, Poland (2017)

The Complementary Role of Activity Context in the Mental Workload Evaluation of Helicopter Pilots: A Multi-tasking Learning Approach

Ioannis Bargiotas[1,2](✉) , Alice Nicolaï[1,2] , Pierre-Paul Vidal[1,3] ,
Christophe Labourdette[2] , Nicolas Vayatis[2] ,
and Stéphane Buffat[1,4,5]

[1] Cognition and Action Group (COGNAG-G), UMR 8257,
CNRS, SSA, Université Paris Descartes, Paris, France
ioannisbargiotas@gmail.com
[2] Center for Mathematical Studies and their Applications,
CNRS, ENS Paris-Saclay, Université Paris-Saclay, 94235 Cachan Cedex, France
[3] School of Automation, Hangzhou Dianzi University, Zhejiang, China
[4] Institut de Recherche Biomédicale des Armées, Brétigny-sur-Orge, France
[5] Hôpital d'instruction des armées Percy, Clamart, France

Abstract. Manifestations of increasing mental demands may be related to the task's context. Additionally, to fundamental physiological changes, the workload may be also characterized sometimes by contextual task-related elements. We aimed to investigate the workload of helicopter pilots and develop predictive models related to the tasks' context. Eight pilots completed an unknown case-scenario (~ 1 h) in a helicopter simulator. The scenario included changing mission during flight and receiving/transferring an injured subject to the near hospital. We selected interesting scenario's periods/"tasks" (e.g., searching hospital, urgent landing) where pilots gave oral evaluations (0–100). Performed tasks had various contexts. We developed a multitasking learning approach to "pool together" all tasks because some of them, although different, may carry useful information about others, so they should neither be merged nor be processed totally independently. Interestingly, it seems that physiological and contextual parameters change order of descriptive power, depending on the task.

Keywords: Mental workload · Predictive model · Machine learning ·
Multitasking learning · Helicopter simulator

1 Introduction

The notion of mental charge is often described as fuzzy, ambiguous [1] or nebulous [2]. The vagueness often attributed to this concept results largely from its multidimensional character and the many definitions it is given. In the literature, we find many terms that are close to or overlap only partially: mental effort, cognitive cost, cognitive load, attentional load, mental strain or mental resources [1]. However, despite the absence of a clear and universally accepted definition by the scientific community [1, 3, 4], the

© Springer Nature Switzerland AG 2019
L. Longo and M. C. Leva (Eds.): H-WORKLOAD 2018, CCIS 1012, pp. 222–238, 2019.
https://doi.org/10.1007/978-3-030-14273-5_13

concept of mental load remains central for Human Factors, notably in aeronautics, because it is operational to gain assess the intricacy of human-machine interactions. The increasing complexity of information systems and automation has progressively transformed the operator's activity. The operator must now supervise these systems and develop effective mental models of their functioning that have an impact on his mental load and performance [5]. From the point of view of ergonomics [1, 2, 6], the mental load is conceived as a dynamic construction that emerges from the interaction between (i) the demands (or constraints) of the situation perceived and integrated by the operator, be they physical, cognitive, socio-cognitive, psychophysiological, or emotional, and (ii) the perception of the resources available to deal with these constraints. In this model, the workload evolves along a continuum, depending on the state of tension of this perceived resource-resource relationship. At the center of this continuum is a workload, viewed as a strain, considered optimal. It results from a subtle balance between constraints and perceived resources. At the ends of this continuum, two zones can be modeled: an underload zone, when the requirements of the situation are perceived as relatively low compared to the resources available to the operator, and an overload zone, when the requirements exceed the resources available to the operator. In each of these areas, the workload is said to be suboptimal and can lead to degraded performance, human errors or incidents. De Waard modeled these areas in his interpretation of the relationship between demand, workload, and performance [7].

The rest of the article is organized as follows: Related Work and practices are presented in Sect. 2, Scenarios, Acquisition Protocol, Calculated biomarkers and data mining strategy are presented in Sect. 3. Results and performance of the algorithm are presented in Sect. 4. Discussion of results and justification of technical choices are presented in Sect. 5. Finally, Conclusions and future perspectives are drawn in Sect. 6.

2 Related Work

The need to model the mental workload in complex situations comes from two directions. The first is the formalization of knowledge, to try to pinpoint definitions and rules. This entails developing knowledge-based models, such as the Adaptive Control of Thought-Rational (ACT-R) [8] or rule-based approaches [9]. The other one is the pragmatic one, and is more usually associated with measurement techniques, which are organized into three categories, [3, 10–12] (i) self-assessment measures: these include self-report measures and subjective rating scales; (ii) performance measures: these consider both primary and secondary task measures; and (iii) physiological measures.

In the last decades, researchers can quantify and evaluate mental workload through wearable sensors. Such sensors usually record basic physiological information (such as electrocardiogram - ECG, electroencephalogram - EEG, heart rate, breath rate, etc.) while the individual performs the given tasks and follows the clinician's instructions/protocol. Such measurements have been previously used in assessing mental workload in drivers [13, 14], pilots [15], etc. Since the above sensors became more portable and accessible, there has been an increasing interest in exploiting all available information of the given continuous signals. Many other parameters derived by this type of signals through signal processing methods, have been proposed previously (ex. heart rate variability - HRV, The 0.1 Hz HRV Components, etc. [7]), showing that physiological alterations can reflect individuals' mental workload.

The variety of methods indicates that researchers and industry increased their interest in the evaluation of mental workload [16–18]. Despite these efforts, there is no more consensus in the evaluation than in the definition of mental workload whether these physiological parameters alone can fully assess the individual's posture control. Many works questioned the ability of physiological measurements to measure accurately mental workload [19]. Others revealed that individuals generally overvalued their mental workload when the complexity of a task increases, although their internal state was not modified (HRV, heart rate-HR, etc. unchanged). Therefore they propose a distinction between subjective and objective mental workload [20, 21]. Therefore, recent works [22–24] proposed a combination of parameters derived from the physiological signals to evaluate workload. Data mining techniques gain reputability, and it seems that they can have an important additive effect on the workload research. Recently efforts have been done to understand better the advantages of basic data-driven approaches [24–26]. It has been shown that workload is better characterized by a combination of parameters [24, 25] (a "profile") rather than one dominant index. We are convinced that the latter multi-dimensional approaches open new perspectives in the analysis of complex phenomena such as workload. When there is only one task per individual, traditional modeling can provide useful information about the parameters that together are related to the workload. However, in the cases where consecutive tasks occur, traditional modeling might be not appropriate since it would either separate the tasks and create independent models or mix the tasks to create a global model. What naturally arises is that although each task is different and might be manifested differently, they might share some characteristics that might make simultaneous learning beneficial. Considering also the fact that investigated populations are often relatively few, recent multitasking learning approaches seem to provide an obvious advantage when is "pooling" together with data from different tasks [27]. The basic idea is that some tasks, although different, may carry useful information about others. So, to know which variables are more relevant to the corresponding workload of every task, tasks should not be processed entirely independently.

3   Design and Methodology

Our main hypothesis is that all tasks are not the same and so the corresponding workload would be manifested differently. Additionally to fundamental physiological changes, the workload may also be manifested by contextual task-related elements. In other words, depending on the task, contextual parameters might play an important (or even more important) role than physiology, in the overall evaluation of mental workload. Therefore, the primary objective of this research project is to investigate the workload of helicopter pilots. Through a realistic scenario, we aimed to select the important features depending on the task using multi-tasking learning techniques and develop predictive models related to the tasks' context monitoring and predicting subjective workload in the control of complex systems. Such models would enable to predict manifestations of increasing mental demands that may be related to the task's context.

The IKKY project (Integration of cockpit and its systems) is a major research and development project designed to define the cockpit of the future, organized around the consortium of the Council for Civil Aviation Research (CORAC). Within this large project, we worked in the part (work-package 1.6) called Cockpit centered on the method and tools for the evaluation of the cockpit of the future for helicopters. Airbus, Thales, and Physip were our industrial partners. One of the objectives of this work-package was to identify a set of measurements and methods for evaluating the psychophysiological state of the helicopter pilot in real time. In the end, these means of measurement will make it possible to evaluate the impact of new human-machine interfaces on the psychophysiological state of the pilot. Our protocol aimed to meet these limits as much as possible in the particular environment that a "full flight" simulator represents.

3.1 Participants and Procedure

Two expert pilots conducted calibration sessions prior to the experiment. Eight operational pilots from the gendarmerie air forces conducted the entire experiment. Pilot 1 was excluded from the analysis due to extensively noisy signals. The pilots are between 32 and 49 years old, and have between 300 and 2450 h of flight to their credit (aircraft combined).

3.2 Data Collection

3.2.1 Scenarios

Two scenarios were constructed to have two different records. We intended to use the first scenario as a baseline and therefore it was simple and had similarities with the second scenario. During the scenario, the pilot moves in the same region and the same zone as in the second scenario, in order to enhance the contextual coherence of the scenarios. This is a recognition mission for a ship that is suspected of oil spill off the coast. The second scenario begins in a similar way, but the pilot receives an emergency call to perform an aero-medical evacuation instead, a situation at the limits of the machine and his capabilities. The pilot would have to take several delicate decisions at the regulatory and operational level, in constrained conditions in terms of time and weather, to finally land safely at the end of the mission. Some of the tasks are missing to some pilots simply because they made different choices during the scenario (ex. Searching zone for urgent landing). Each scenario is described and analyzed in detail using a hierarchical task analysis method [28] (here expected tasks) carried out thanks to the support of pilot helicopter experts.

Expected mental load values are then predicted by the same experts for different phases of the scenario. The latter allowed the more precise identification of key moments of the scenario in terms of the expected workload variation. It also allows modifications and adaptations of the frame when the scenario presents risks in terms of operational realism. The veracity of the scenario 2 was demonstrated during the year 2017 by a real mission carried out in the Réunion (FR) Island according to an almost identical profile.

3.2.2 Simulator

We used a "Full Flight" Level D simulator, with a mobile base to simulate the movements of the cabin of the helicopter. The helicopter cockpit model selected is an EC135. There are currently four levels of full flight simulator for civilian pilots when converting from one type of aircraft to another (Levels A to D, with Level D being the highest level and qualifying for ZFT training), and the mobile base is likely to provide an additional degree of immersion (see Fig. 1). However, some equipment requires a time of handling by the pilots, including the navigation system specific to the version of the chosen helicopter.

Fig. 1. Full flight simulator with EC 135 helicopter cockpit (Thales ©).

3.2.3 Data Acquisition

We chose to take several reference measurements, which were used as ground truth for the modeling stage. Each scenario was divided into phases, thanks to an important work of hierarchical analysis of the tasks. During these phases, a subjective measure of the Instantaneous Self-Assessment (ISA) type was performed, orally and/ or using a tangible interface developed by the IRBA, according to the modality of preference chosen by the pilot at the moment. t of the scenario. A posteriori, measurements of NASA TLX [29], used in its simplified version [30], associated with explicit interviews [31] made it possible to specify the significant events encountered by the pilot during the scenarios. See Fig. 2 for an overview of an experimental session. The experiment was validated by the ethics committee of the University Paris Descartes, with the N ° CERES 201735.

Fig. 2. Above on the left, installation of the sensors. The electroencephalogram was not used for the model. It serves as measure control. Top right, an internal view of the simulator with the simulator operator. Below on the left, the Human Factor expert and the expert pilot. Bottom center, the simulator. Bottom right the data quality control station

3.2.4   Selected Sensors

The sensors selected were an Equival® type sensor, measuring heart rate, respiratory rate and cutaneous temperature, an eye tracker connected to a head movement capture device in the cabin reference (Thales Equipment). A Brain Products ® 32-channel electroencephalography helmet with amplified electrodes was also used, but the recordings were not intended to participate in the mental load modeling. In addition to the physiological measurements and contextual parameters, such as the simulated helicopter airspeed, height, roll, pitch, etc. All these measurements were collected synchronously by a device called CMS © for Cockpit Monitoring System.

3.3   Parameter Calculation

Most of the calculated parameters have been previously proposed as indicators of increased mental workload [13, 25]. However, the main idea of this feature engineering process is not only to use already proposed parameters but also to create new features form the available datasets, trying to describe the mental workload alterations with an exhaustive approach. Basic physiological characteristics (such as Heart Rate, Respiration rate etc.), as well as contextual characteristics based on the visual acquisitions, were included [7, 20]. The latter were used either in the absolute form or as a difference (incremental) by the mean value of a calibration period as proposed in [32]. The second part of the Scenario I served as the appropriate personalized calibration period. Moreover, in order to further exploit the richness of the eye movement coordinates changes, characteristics inspired by analytical studies with similar two-dimensional datasets (such as the center of mass coordinates changes in postural control research) were applied in the eye movement datasets [33, 34]. Table 1 provide the names and the description/values (where needed) of the biomarkers that were initially included in the model.

3.4 Multitasking Learning

The parts of the continuous signals that correspond to the investigated tasks (Fig. 3) were isolated and all the mentioned (31 overall) biomarkers (Table 1) were calculated and stored. So, every pilot's task (t_{ij}) has been represented by the above biomarkers. This representation is stored as a 1×31 dimension vector in the matrix that corresponds to the task's (T_i) corresponding matrix.

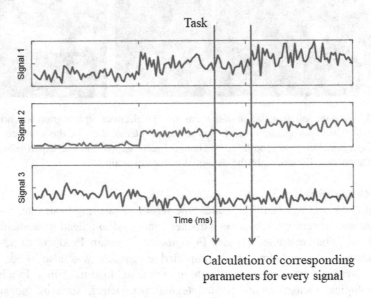

Fig. 3. Signals that corresponds to the period of a task are isolated and corresponding features are calculated for every signal.

Table 1. Names and descriptions of features that were included in the analysis. Features were separated in Physiological, Psychological and Contextual parameters. However, all features were equally included in the initial model.

Biomarkers	Description
Physiological	
HR (b/min)	Heart rate
HRV (ms)	The variation in the beat-to-beat interval
Energy01	The energy of HRV that lies at 0.1 Hz
BR (resp/min)	Average breath rate
ST (Co)	Skin temperature
IbiF95	(the F(Hz) were below that the 95% of ibi energy is)

(continued)

Table 1. (*continued*)

Biomarkers	Description
DHR (b/min)	Differential or incremental HR (DHR) (the difference between calibration/scenario I period and task period)
DHRV (ms)	Differential or incremental HRV (DHRV) (the difference between calibration/scenario I period and task period)
DEnergy01	Differential or incremental Energy01 (DEnergy01) (the difference between calibration/scenario I period & task period)
DBR (resp/min)	Differential or incremental BR (DBR) (the difference between calibration/scenario I period and task period)
DST (Co)	Differential or incremental ST (DST) (the difference between calibration/scenario I period and task period)
UpHR	HR > HR + 2 * SD of calibration/scenario I
UpHRV	HRV > HRV + 2 * SD of calibration/scenario I
Psychological + experience	
PSQI score	Overall of Pittsburgh sleep quality index (PSQI)
STAI - state	The state anxiety inventory
Hours	Total hours of flight
Vision parameters	
MaxFixation (ms)	The maximum duration of fixation during task
AverageFixation (ms)	The average duration of fixation during task
NFixation	Number of fixations per task
RateFixation	Rate between overall fixation period & task duration
MaxSaccade	The maximum duration of saccade during task
AverageSaccade	The average duration of saccades during task
NSaccade	Number of saccades per task
RateSaccade	Rate between overall saccadic period & task duration
Contextual parameters	
AOI	The areas of interest (AOI) where the pilot looks. Parts of Helicopter's cockpit (altitude, compass, radio etc.) & outside view where continuously registered during scenarios
Unique AOIs	How many unique areas of interest (AOI) the pilot fixed during the task
f95AOI	The frequency below that the 95% of AOI energy lays
GazeVelocityX (degrees/sec)	The average velocity of gaze position change in X-axis
GazeVelocityY (degrees/sec)	The average velocity of gaze position change in Y-axis
GazeAccelerationX (degrees/sec)	The average change rate of gaze velocity in the X-axis
GazeAccelerationY (degrees/sec)	The average change rate of gaze velocity in the Y-axis

Pilots were evaluated every task that they made. Therefore, having totally 10 different groups of tasks, we end up with 10 matrices ($T_{1:10}$) and 10 corresponding response vectors ($Y_{1:10}$) (see Fig. 4).

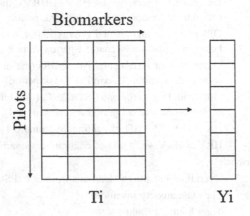

Fig. 4. Schematic representation of matrix Ti from the task i. Rows are the pilots that performed this task and columns are the 31 biomarkers that calculated by each task. Yi is the workload evaluation that pilots orally made after the scenario. For 10 groups of tasks, we have 10 matrices (Ti) and 10 response vectors (Yi)

We were interested in highlighting global commonalities (if any) between tasks and more importantly those elements that might play important role in the prediction of each task's workload evaluation. The Multi-Task Lasso with Least Squares Loss (MTLLeast) algorithm [35, 36] assumes that different tasks share the same sparsity parameter and so every task would be represented with different predictors but almost the same number per column. Briefly, the model solves multi-task least squares problem (1):

$$\min \sum_{i=1}^{t} \left\| W_i^T T_i - Y \right\|_F^2 + \rho_1 \|W\|_1 + \rho_{L2} \|W\|_F^2 \tag{1}$$

where T_i denotes the input matrix of the i-th task, Y_i denotes its corresponding response, W_i is the model for task i, the regularization parameter ρ_1 controls sparsity, and the optional ρ_{L2} regularization parameter controls the ℓ_2-norm penalty. In our study, we used only the Lasso $\ell1$-norm regularization (ρ_1).

The non-zero W elements show the particular representations for every task. Briefly, the proposed algorithm followed the following steps:

1. Already evaluated tasks were isolated by the datasets of every pilot.
2. Predictors from Table 1 were calculated for every task.

3. Similar tasks from every pilot were grouped and their parameters were standardized.
4. The MTLLeast regularization was applied,
5. For every task i, those predictors in W_i with non-zero coefficients were the variables that will contribute to the prediction of a relevant task by a future pilot. The most important predictors per task have been chosen and evaluated using the standardized coefficients of the Lasso regularization phase, as it has been already proposed in [36].
6. The model was cross-validated using the well-established and secure leave-one (pilot) - out method applying the well-known (and already used in such datasets) Random Forest regression algorithm [26, 37] as the prediction model.

Figure 5 below represents schematically the above cross-validated procedure.

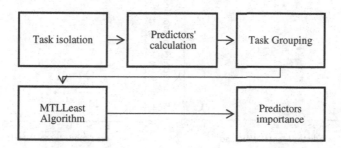

Fig. 5. Schematic representation of the design of the procedure.

4   Results

After the cross-validation procedure, the average root mean square error (RMSE) between true and predicted mental workload values was 15.3 ± 5.6. Interestingly, our strategy seems to have promising results, considering the limited number of pilots that are available. There are pilots whom their evaluation is predicted pretty accurately (Pilot 7, Pilot 5 etc.), others whom their predictions are generally either overestimated (pilot 8) or significantly underestimated (one case - pilot 4). All the predictions generally follow the "tendency" of the ground truth. Excessive RMSE values are always due to an important bias (such as in Fig. 6C) rather than an important variance. See Fig. 6 below.

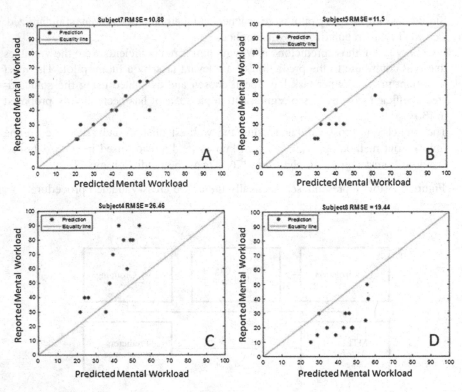

Fig. 6. Equality plots between reported mental workload (ground truth, y-axis) and the predicted values from the model (x-axis). Plots A and B show results for two pilots with an accurate prediction. C and D represent pilots where the RMSE was very high but due to an important bias in the prediction (either underestimation - C or over-estimation-D). All predictions follow the relative changes of corresponding mental workload.

We present also the predictive performance per pilot (Table 2). Interestingly, the model did predict accurately the evaluation of the less experienced pilots and the slight over/under-estimation were observed in pilots with higher experience.

Table 2. Prediction performance per pilot. The pilots that present very high RMSE have a large bias either due to general under- or overpredicted values.

Pilot	RMSE	Hours
2	14.2	2100
3	14.1	2450
4	26.5	1840
5	11.5	300
6	10.8	1200
7	10.9	965
8	19.5	1000

In terms of the descriptive power of predictors per task, there were 3 tasks where physiological elements where dominant, 2 tasks where contextual parameters where dominant and 5 where both categories were important. Table 3 summarizes the important elements of every task.

Table 3. Ten different tasks that pilots could perform during the Scenario 2. The median (whiskers) of reported mental workload is provided as well as the first two variables that were found to play a major role in the prediction process. The last column indicates the category of the chosen variables. P: Physiological, C: Contextual, PE: Psychological/Experience.

No of task	Scenario task	Reported evaluation median (whiskers)	Best predictors	Category
1	Take-off (calm)	25 (20, 40)	1. BreathRate 2. Hours	P - PE
2	Change mission	40 (25, 50)	1. DHR 2. RateSaccade	P - C
3	Flight towards a target	30 (20, 40)	1. UniqueAOI 2. RateFixation	C
4	Preparation for landing	40 (40, 65)	1. GazeVelocityX 2. PSQI score	C - PE
5	Take-off (urgent)	45 (40, 60)	1. UpHR 2. Hours	P - PE
6	Urgent trajectory towards the hospital	40 (30, 45)	1. f95AOI 2. HR	C - P
7	Searching zone for urgent landing	45 (30, 60)	1. UpHR 2. Hours	P - PE
8	Preparation for urgent landing	55 (45, 60)	3. GazeVelocityX 1. Average 1. Fixation	C
9	Urgent landing	40 (35, 45)	1. f95AOI 2. HR	C - P
10	Engine alert	55 (50, 70)	1. UpHR 2. f95AOI	P - C

5 Discussion

The objective of this study was to validate the hypothesis that the mental workload presented by the pilots is related not only to physiological but also to task-related contextual parameters. It was shown that although there are some important physiological characteristics (such as the incremental HR - UpHR), as one could expect from previous studies, there are tasks where mental workload is actually manifested mostly by the context (such as areas of interest - AOIs of looking, gaze movement and numbers of AOIs that the pilot needs to fix) rather than the physiology.

We introduced a multitasking method for highlighting the important features of every task. The proposed method offered the advantage of "pooling" the tasks the learning process and therefore taking into account the commonalities that may exist between several tasks before creating the predictive models per task. Moreover, the latter approach seems to handle more gently the problem of the low number of pilots. The cross-validation procedure showed that tasks are generally well predicted and pilots with high RMSE in prediction were mostly due to high bias rather than high variance. The latter drawback has also positive aspects. In cases either under or overestimated, the predictions are always relevant with the relative internal state of the pilot. The latter interpretation allows us to validate our feature selection methodology and conclude that physiological and contextual parameters (vision's areas of interest trajectories etc.) changed the order of descriptive power, depending on the task.

5.1 Data Acquisition and Scenarios

Emphasis is given on operational constraints and not on a difficulty related to an accumulation of system failures. The scenarios were designed according to an iterative process. A frame is designed to meet the specific needs of the workload variation project. This framework is elaborated by focusing on operational constraints and contextual elements, which constitute usual workload factors (weather conditions, time pressure, and deterioration of the injured person's state). It thus voluntarily moves away from the scenarios modeling an accumulation of breakdown, considered unrealistic by the pilots. Recent studies that used simulators showed encouraging results, but with a certain limit [24]. The models were found to be less effective than expected and not explicit enough (Bayesian Neural Networks). The latter is always an important issue, and the clarification is essential for the industrial processes. Interestingly, the authors reported a low confidence level in the baseline data from the subjective workload collection. Among the six participating pilots, two of them were test pilots. . They were "Super" expert of the machine and its technical limitations and trained for critical situations, thus introduced a degree of imbalance in the participants 'panel. Another difficulty was that the simulator was not dedicated to research, leaving only a two-hour window for equipment and mission. As a result, the environmental noise on the sensors was only partially controlled. The choice of an evolutionary scenario of failure accumulation was considered unrealistic by the pilots, who also emphasized a feeling of insufficient presence. Finally, there was a limited collection of complementary data (e.g., psychometric). Subjects also completed the PANAS questionnaire [38] after each session.

In our study, we tried to handle some of the above difficulties. On the one hand, to improve the operability of the interpretability and the performance of the model as well as provide a tool for continuous visualization of the mental workload. One of the major challenges that we met was the different choices that each pilot might make during the scenarios. As it was mentioned in the 3.4 and it is shown in Table 3, similar tasks were grouped intentionally in order to "catch" the fundamental aspects of each task helping the generalization of our conclusions (as possible as it can be with such small population). Giving an example will enlighten the above challenge. At the end of the scenario, the clinician demands an urgent landing before reaching the hospital due to the worsening of the patient's condition. The pilot, taking into account the bad weather conditions, took a decision either to proceed to urgent landing or to refuse and go directly to the hospital. So, at the end of the scenario, there are pilots that made two urgent landings (one somewhere before reaching the hospital and one at the hospital) and pilots that have only one. Even if these tasks are somehow slightly different both cases are close (in terms of the scenario's timeline) and both include strongly the notion of "emergency". So, it has been decided to be treated as one task. However, previous more easy landings were not included in this task since neither an emergency nor time&weather constraints were present. We are aware that these choices are conceptual choices around the "high-level" aspects of a task (landing, emergency, equal fatigue). Grouping the tasks is a trade-off between the beneficial effect of increasing the population of this task and the deleterious effect of grouping dissimilar elements. This is an open question and further research may be needed in order to clarify better the criteria that may lead to such decisions.

5.2   Parameters and Performance

Generally, we observed that the variable with the most descriptive power was the incremental HR (mostly as UpHR and sometimes as DHR). The latter results are in-line with previous reviews and studies that mentioned mean HR and the incremental HR seem to be the most correlated variables to mental workload [13, 39]. With a more careful observation we can notice that from the moment that the scenario increases complexity, multi-tasking and time pressure ($\geq$ Task 5 in Table 3), HR is present to 4/5 tasks. The reason why we see HR mostly in the high-demanding periods is probably due to the fact that the first tasks are not that complex and so pilots might activate compensatory mechanisms in order to lower the level of mental workload and to maintain a good performance [40]. For instance, pilots could reduce their speed to maximize the time to process the given information. Further research needed and the inclusion of helicopter's movements during the tasks might help in this direction. Surprisingly, HRV or incremental HRV has never shown significant importance. HRV and especially the Energy01 component have been reported as sensitive to mental workload [7]. Moreover, we expected that in tasks that the pressure of time would be extreme (ex. task 7 and 8 - Urgent landing) would have significant changes as proposed in [39]. Limited data, as well as the possible inter-correlation with other variables might explain the above finding. On the other hand, physiology is not dominant to all the tasks. In the same high demanding period ($\geq$ Task 5 in Table 3), the frequency that pilots change the fixation areas plays an important role. The index f95AOI was very important in the 3/5 tasks. Interestingly, the task with the highest median value of evaluation (task 8- Preparation for urgent landing) was the one where the contextual elements were the most important. In the last part of the scenario, the complexity is increased and so when pilots report their workload, they report also the subjective level of each task. Many studies revealed that the increase in complexity only increase the subjective level of mental workload, showing that drivers overvalued their objective mental workload [40]. It seems that this phenomenon is present to our findings but the general important role of HR indicates the objective workload increased (even overvalued). We would like to highlight also that a posture-inspired variable such as

GazeVelocity X and Fixations are important contextual factors. These findings are in-line with previous works, which showed that saccadic velocity can be seen as an indicator of a high level of mental workload in complex situations [41]. Even if eye activity is probably more dependent on visual demands than on cognitive demands [7], still the level of complexity, especially in extreme situations, could always indicate an increase in cognitive workload, and our findings support this conclusion.

6 Conclusions

We introduced a multitasking method for highlighting the fundamental features of every task when tasks are different and are not performed in the same way by the pilots. The proposed multi-task regression method searched for the high-level fundamental aspects that characterize a procedure. It seems that it performs very well even with a small available population, and showed that analyzing several tasks sharing mutual information before creating the predictive models is indeed beneficial. The conclusion of this study is dual. 1. In tasks with high complexity, context plays an important role in the workload evaluation. 2. The physiological and contextual parameters changed the order of descriptive power, depending on the task. Further research, larger population and the inclusion of helicopter's movement is needed to further establish the above findings.

Acknowledgments. The authors wish to thank the partners of work-package 1.6, Cockpit centered on the crew and Method and tools for the assessment of the future cockpit for heli-copters of the IKKY program, and in particular Serge Couvet, David Hartnagel, and Denis Demain for their very active participation. We also wish to express our gratitude to the French Gendarmerie air force and in particular the SAG Villacoublay.

References

1. Leplat, J.: Eléments pour une histoire de la notion de charge mentale. Charge mentale notion floue vrai problème. Octarès, Toulouse (2002, in French)
2. Young, M.S., Brookhuis, K.A., Wickens, C.D., Hancock, P.A.: State of science: mental workload in ergonomics. Ergonomics **58**, 1–17 (2015)
3. Cain, B.: A review of the mental workload literature. Defence Research and Development Toronto, Canada (2007)
4. Chanquoy, L., Tricot, A., Sweller, J.: Qu'est-ce que la charge cognitive?. In: La Charge Cognitive: Théorie et Applications, pp. 11–32. Armand Colin (2007, in French)
5. Burian, B.K., et al.: Single-pilot workload management in entry-level jets. National Aeronautics and Space Administraion, Moffeett Field, CA, Ames Research Center (2013)
6. Falzon, P., Sauvagnac, C.: Charge de travail et stress, chap. 11. In: Ergonomie, p. 175. Presses Universitaires de France (2004)
7. De Waard, D.: The measurement of drivers' mental workload. Groningen University, Traffic Research Center, Netherlands (1996)
8. Anderson, J.R., Bothell, D., Byrne, M.D., Douglass, S., Lebiere, C., Qin, Y.: An integrated theory of the mind. Psychol. Rev. **111**, 1036–1060 (2004)

9. Rizzo, L., Dondio, P., Delany, S.J., Longo, L.: Modeling mental workload via rule-based expert system: a comparison with NASA-TLX and workload profile. In: Iliadis, L., Maglogiannis, I. (eds.) AIAI 2016. IAICT, vol. 475, pp. 215–229. Springer, Cham (2016). https://doi.org/10.1007/978-3-319-44944-9_19

10. Tsang, P.S., Vidulich, M.A.: Mental workload and situation awareness. In: Handbook of Human Factors and Ergonomics, pp. 243–268. Wiley, Hoboken (2006)

11. Young, M.S., Stanton, N.A.: Taking the load off: investigations of how adaptive cruise control affects mental workload. Ergonomics 47, 1014–1035 (2004)

12. Wilson, G.F., Eggemeier, F.T.: Mental workload measurement. In: International Encyclopedia of Ergonomics and Human Factors, vol. 1 (2006)

13. Paxion, J., Galy, E., Berthelon, C.: Mental workload and driving. Front. Psychol. 5, 1344 (2014)

14. Yoshida, Y., Ohwada, H., Mizoguchi, F.: Extracting tendency and stability from time series and random forest for classifying a car driver's cognitive load. In: 2014 IEEE 13th International Conference on Cognitive Informatics and Cognitive Computing, pp. 258–265. IEEE (2014)

15. Lee, Y.-H., Liu, B.-S.: Inflight workload assessment: comparison of subjective and physiological measurements. Aviat. Space Environ. Med. 74, 1078–1084 (2003)

16. Longo, L., Leva, M.C.: Human Mental Workload: Models and Applications. Springer, Cham (2017). https://doi.org/10.1007/978-3-319-61061-0

17. Wickens, C.D.: Mental workload: assessment, prediction and consequences. In: Longo, L., Leva, M.C. (eds.) H-WORKLOAD 2017. CCIS, vol. 726, pp. 18–29. Springer, Cham (2017). https://doi.org/10.1007/978-3-319-61061-0_2

18. Cahill, J., et al.: Adaptive automation and the third pilot: managing teamwork and workload in an airline cockpit. In: Longo, L., Leva, M.C. (eds.) H-WORKLOAD 2017. CCIS, vol. 726, pp. 161–173. Springer, Cham (2017). https://doi.org/10.1007/978-3-319-61061-0_10

19. Kramer, A.F.: Physiological metrics of mental workload: a review of recent progress. In: Multiple-Task Performance, pp. 279–328 (1991)

20. Brookhuis, K.A., van Driel, C.J.G., Hof, T., van Arem, B., Hoedemaeker, M.: Driving with a congestion assistant; mental workload and acceptance. Appl. Ergon. 40, 1019–1025 (2009)

21. Dijksterhuis, C., Brookhuis, K.A., De Waard, D.: Effects of steering demand on lane keeping behaviour, self-reports, and physiology: a simulator study. Accid. Anal. Prev. 43, 1074–1081 (2011)

22. Lew, R.: Assessing cognitive workload from multiple physiological measures using wavelets and machine learning (2014)

23. Solovey, E.T., Zec, M., Garcia Perez, E.A., Reimer, B., Mehler, B.: Classifying driver workload using physiological and driving performance data. In: Proceedings of the 32nd Annual ACM Conference on Human Factors in Computing Systems - CHI 2014, pp. 4057–4066. ACM Press, New York (2014)

24. Besson, P., et al.: Effectiveness of physiological and psychological features to estimate helicopter pilots' workload: a Bayesian network approach. IEEE Trans. Intell. Transp. Syst. 14, 1872–1881 (2013)

25. Harrivel, A.R., et al.: Prediction of cognitive states during flight simulation using multimodal psychophysiological sensing. In: AIAA Information Systems-AIAA Infotech @ Aerospace, p. 1135. American Institute of Aeronautics and Astronautics, Reston (2017)

26. Moustafa, K., Luz, S., Longo, L.: Assessment of mental workload: a comparison of machine learning methods and subjective assessment techniques. In: Longo, L., Leva, M.C. (eds.) H-WORKLOAD 2017. CCIS, vol. 726, pp. 30–50. Springer, Cham (2017). https://doi.org/10.1007/978-3-319-61061-0_3

27. Argyriou, A., Evgeniou, T., Pontil, M.: Multi-task feature learning. Adv. Neural. Inf. Process. Syst. **19**, 41 (2007)
28. Stanton, N.A.: Hierarchical task analysis: developments, applications, and extensions. Appl. Ergon. **37**, 55–79 (2006)
29. Hart, S.G., Staveland, L.E.: Development of NASA-TLX (task load index): results of empirical and theoretical research. In: Advances in Psychology, pp. 139–183. Elsevier (1988)
30. Byers, J.C.: Traditional and raw task load index (TLX) correlations: are paired comparisons necessary? In: Advances in Industrial Ergonomics and Safety I, pp. 481–485. Taylor & Francis (1989)
31. Vermersch, P.: L'entretiens d'explicitation, 5th edn., ESF Éditeur, Issy-les-Moulineaux (2006, in French)
32. Brookhuis, K.A., de Waard, D.: Monitoring drivers' mental workload in driving simulators using physiological measures. Accid. Anal. Prev. **42**, 898–903 (2010)
33. Bargiotas, I., et al.: On the importance of local dynamics in statokinesigram: a multivariate approach for postural control evaluation in elderly. PLoS ONE **13**, e0192868 (2018)
34. Audiffren, J., Bargiotas, I., Vayatis, N., Vidal, P.-P., Ricard, D.: A non linear scoring approach for evaluating balance: classification of elderly as fallers and non-fallers. PLoS ONE **11**, e0167456 (2016)
35. Tibshirani, R.: Regression shrinkage and selection via the lasso. J. R. Stat. Soc. Ser. B. (Methodol.) **58**(1), 267–288 (1996)
36. Zhou, J., Chen, J., Ye, J.: Malsar: multi-task learning via structural regularization, vol. 21. Arizona State University (2011)
37. Breiman, L.: Random forests. Mach. Learn. **45**, 5–32 (2001)
38. Gaudreau, P., Sanchez, X., Blondin, J.-P.: Positive and negative affective states in a performance-related setting. Eur. J. Psychol. Assess. **22**, 240–249 (2006)
39. Nickel, P., Nachreiner, F.: Sensitivity and diagnosticity of the 0.1-Hz component of heart rate variability as an indicator of mental workload. Hum. Factors J. Hum. Factors Ergon. Soc. **45**, 575–590 (2003)
40. Gabaude, C., Baracat, B., Jallais, C., Bonniaud, M., Fort, A.: Cognitive load measurement while driving. In: Human Factors: A View from an Integrative Perspective (2012)
41. Di Stasi, L.L., et al.: Risk behaviour and mental workload: multimodal assessment techniques applied to motorbike riding simulation. Transp. Res. Part F Traffic Psychol. Behav. **12**, 361–370 (2009)

The Effect of an Exceptional Event on the Subjectively Experienced Workload of Air Traffic Controllers

Thea Radüntz[1(✉)], Norbert Fürstenau[2], André Tews[2], Lea Rabe[1], and Beate Meffert[3]

[1] Mental Health and Cognitive Capacity,
Federal Institute for Occupational Safety and Health, Berlin, Germany
raduentz.thea@baua.bund.de
[2] German Aerospace Center, Institute of Flight Guidance, Braunschweig, Germany
[3] Signal Processing and Pattern Recognition, Department of Computer Science,
Humboldt-Universität zu Berlin, Berlin, Germany

Abstract. There is a growing consensus concerning the negative consequences of inappropriate workload on employee's health and the safety of persons. In a simulator study, we focused on air traffic controllers during arrival management tasks. Our aim was to find out if the number of aircraft or the occurrence of an exceptional event added load to the subjectively experienced workload. The workload was assessed using the NASA-TLX, instantaneous self-assessment (ISA) questionnaire, and expert ratings. Our sample consisted of 21 subjects. According to standard ANOVA procedures, controllers' subjective ratings showed a high-significant discrimination between the different air traffic demands but only a weak-significant discrimination between sessions with and without event. In particular, we were not able to obtain a significant interaction effect between traffic volume and event. However, the examination of between-subject factors could reveal additional information about controller's rating behavior. We currently conclude that while the effect of the number of aircraft was evident, the impact of an exceptional event remained doubtful.

Keywords: Mental workload · Air traffic controllers ·
Subjective ratings · NASA-TLX · ISA

1 Introduction

There is a growing consensus concerning the negative consequences of inappropriate workload that can affect the individual itself but also other people that count on it. High mental workload is associated with increased anxiety, stress, and a lack of detachment from work during off-job time [8,9,24]. The missing recovery from work-related stress can then lead to weakness, tiredness, and exhaustion.

© Springer Nature Switzerland AG 2019
L. Longo and M. C. Leva (Eds.): H-WORKLOAD 2018, CCIS 1012, pp. 239–257, 2019.
https://doi.org/10.1007/978-3-030-14273-5_14

Thus, mental workload can influence the well being and health of a person. Furthermore, it can influence the individual performance because of forgetfulness, negligence, and a lack of concentration. The consequences are increased errors or inadequate decisions and might affect not only the own safety but also the safety of other persons. This is particularly true in safety-critical occupations such as air traffic control.

In order to understand workload changes in the air traffic sector, it is important to study the influence of different factors altering air traffic controllers' mental workload. In this article, we concentrated on two exposure parameters: air traffic volume and occurrence of an exceptional event. We were interested to find out if both of them have an effect on the experienced workload and if there was an interaction between both. In particular, we wanted to investigate if the occurrence of on exceptional event affected workload differently related to the current air traffic demands but also to individual characteristics. This understanding is relevant in order to improve working conditions by maintaining an appropriate level of workload that allows also the handling of unforeseen events.

In Sect. 2 we give a brief overview about the concept and current methods for registering mental workload. We introduce our hypotheses, the study design, and the way we proceeded for analyzing our data in Sect. 3. Finally, we outline and discuss our results in Sect. 4 as well as give prospects for future work related to our conclusions in Sect. 5.

2   Related Work

In general, mental workload was related to information processing theory [14]. High mental workload may arise from the inability to cope with increasing demands imposed on an individual's cognitive capacity [7,14,30] but also from a simultaneous interaction with emotional aspects [1], training and experience level [32]. Hence, increasing demands could originate among others from time pressure, task complexity, and individual's psycho-physiological state [11]. Methods for registering mental workload are categorized into subjective and objective methods. The subjective measurements use traditional questionnaires in order to assess subject's experienced workload. The objective methods are subdivided into performance measurement and biosignal registration. Recording and analysis of e.g. the brain activity [22,26], cardiovascular parameter [18,27] as well as ocular data [2] offered insight into subject's psycho-physiological state. The main idea underlying the assessment of workload using biosignals considered arousal and activation mechanisms of the organism reacting to the task load [21]. Measurement of individual's performance on a task was another way to determine workload. Hereby, identification of workload relied on the relationship concept between the two and implied that individual performance decreases under high mental workload [17,19,33]. However, studies also indicated that motivation, training, and experience could contribute to maintain performance at the same level by investing more effort and in this way mitigated the impact of workload [16,23]. Thus, the increased mental workload could not always be measured directly by means of performance break-down [12,20,29]. For a detailed overview of the mental workload literature including definitions and measuring methods of workload we advise the reader on the articles of Cain [5], Vidulich and Tsang [28] as well as Stanton et al. [25].

We conclude that identification of workload by means of performance measurements was problematic whereas physiological indicators and subjective ratings using questionnaires may better reflect workload changes. However, subjective measurements were problematic because of their susceptibility to subjective distortion, social desirability restrictions regarding the appropriateness of the answer, and subject's inability to introspect. Their main advantages were the simplicity of assessment and high user acceptance.

3 Design and Methodology

3.1 Research Questions

In our simulator study, we focused on air traffic controllers as an occupation with high cognitive demands and responsibility [6]. Air traffic controllers are dealing with safety-critical tasks and have to keep engaged and try to maintain their performance even under difficult situations. When task demands increase, they have to invest more effort. As a consequence, air traffic controllers work in a high pressure environment with high mental workload. This is mainly induced by the traffic load situation itself but might also arise by unexpected events [1]. Hence, the aim of our study was to find out if it is the number of aircraft or the occurrence of an exceptional event that stresses controllers the most. Furthermore, we were interested if there is an interaction effect between both and if between-subject factors, i.e. age or job demands, could reveal additional information about controller's experienced workload in both conditions. To this end, we formulated the following five research hypotheses:

1. The number of aircraft has a significant main effect on controllers' workload.
2. The occurrence of an exceptional event has a significant main effect on controllers' workload.
3. There is a significant interaction effect between number of aircraft and occurrence of an exceptional event regarding controllers' workload.
4. The experienced workload is related to controller's age.
5. The experienced workload is related to controller's current job demands.

3.2 Traffic Scenarios

Our research was performed in the Air Traffic Management and Operations simulator (ATMOS) of the German Aerospace Center (DLR) in Braunschweig. For our research design, we concentrated on arrival management tasks and manipulated the factors: exceptional event and traffic load. The traffic load was manipulated by the number of aircraft per hour (ac/h). We considered four levels of traffic flow that determined the more or less constant number of aircraft in the arrival sector (i.e., possible fluctuations according to controller's guiding behavior): 25 ac/h, 35 ac/h, 45 ac/h, and 55 ac/h. The second factor was by nature dichotomous: occurrence vs. absence of an exceptional event. The exceptional event was a flight that should be prioritized because of a sick passenger on board (in the following referred to as priority-flight event). The pseudo pilot was instructed to request priority for his flight but not to declare emergency by using the commands mayday or pan-pan. The rationale behind this was that in case of a mayday or pan-pan call there might be specific prescribed regulations that have to be implemented by the controller such as closing the sector, maintain a distance around the aircraft, or distribute the remaining aircraft on further controllers. These regulations would corrupt our experiment, in particular mitigate the air traffic demand factor. We decided to use the medical event communicated as priority request in order to get a workload increase in the sequence without activating additional measures which would be applicable in case of aircraft's engine failure or loss of controllability.

The combination of both factors, number of aircraft and priority-flight event, resulted in eight scenarios (Table 1). Scenario duration was 20 min for a scenario with no priority-flight event and 25 min for a scenarios with a priority-flight event. The priority-flight event occurred after the 10th min. The time parameters were chosen because of previous experiences related to simulator experiments with air traffic controllers. We gave controllers 10 min to get started and accustomed to their sector in order to control for any additional intrinsic, workload-relevant factors that could interfere with our exposure parameters. We assumed that in case of a priority-flight event the controllers would need maximally 10 min to solve it. We also knew that controllers' experience in the simulator used to be real and pervasive. By giving them 5 additional minutes in scenarios with priority-flight event, we aimed to allow them to leave the experiment with a positive impression and not with a bad feeling.

Table 1. Experimental design with two factors: number of aircraft and priority-flight event.

Simulation scenario	Traffic load (ac/h)	Priority-flight event
1	25	No
2	25	Yes
3	35	No
4	35	Yes
5	45	No
6	45	Yes
7	55	No
8	55	Yes

3.3   Procedure and Subjects

Our sample consisted of 21 subjects between the ages of 22 and 64 years (2 female, 19 male, mean age 38 ± 11). We had 13 approach controllers, 3 tower controllers, and 5 employees of the DLR, in the following referred to as novices. In real work life, subjects were working at different airports and different work positions. Thus, they had experienced different job demands. All of them had adequate expertise to handle the arrival management simulation and interact with the pseudo pilots who simulated the cockpit crews during the trials. Within two consecutive days, the subjects completed the above-mentioned eight traffic scenarios in randomized order. The first day started at noon with an introductory session where participants completed demographic questionnaires. They were briefed regarding the research goals, experimental procedure of the following two days, and workload scales used. Next, subjects completed a training session in order to get familiarized with the simulator and the questionnaires. Once they had a clear understanding of how everything worked and what was being measured, the experiment started. Four of the simulation scenarios were presented on the first day, the remaining four were conducted on the second day until noon. The Federal Institute of Occupational Safety and Health (BAuA) in Berlin was in charge of the project. All of the investigations acquired were approved by the local review board of the BAuA and the experiments were conducted in accordance with the Declaration of Helsinki. All procedures were carried out with the adequate understanding and written consent of the subjects.

3.4   Assessment of Workload

As dependent variable we assessed the experienced workload by means of the NASA-TLX, instantaneous self-assessment (ISA) questionnaire, and expert ratings. For the sake of completeness, we include the German versions used in the Appendix A.

NASA-TLX. Subjective workload was captured with a computerized version of the NASA-TLX [10]. After the training scenario, subjects were asked to rate the workload sources in 15 pairwise comparisons of NASA-TLX's six workload dimensions: mental demand, physical demand, temporal demand, performance, effort, frustration. Thereby, subjects chose the more relevant dimension of their workload. Thus, we got an individual weighting of the NASA-TLX subscales. After each simulation scenario subjects were asked to rate the scenario itself within a 100-point range regarding each of the six subscales. They indicated their rating by clicking on a 5-point step box of the scale. Finally, individual weightings S_d of the NASA-TLX dimensions d were combined with dimensions' ratings R_d according to Eq. 1 and yielded the overall workload index W_{idx} of the NASA-TLX [10].

$$W_{\mathrm{idx}} = \frac{1}{15} \cdot \sum_{d=1}^{6} S_d \cdot R_d \tag{1}$$

ISA. During all eight scenarios controllers performed the ISA questionnaire that was developed for the assessment of air traffic controller's mental workload [4,13, 15]. The ISA questionnaire consisted of a one-dimensional scale and was quick and easy to asses. It was presented in an interval of 5 min and subjects indicated their workload using a touch screen. Thereby, they had to select one of the following five values according to their feeling during the previous minutes: (1) under-utilized, (2) relaxed, (3) comfortable, (4) high, and (5) excessive. For our analysis, we only considered controller's rating after the possible occurrence of the priority-flight event, i.e., the rating of the 15th min.

Expert Ratings. At the end of each scenario, we asked the involved pseudo pilots from the simulated cockpit crews to rate the workload level of the air traffic controller during the scenario. The rating was conducted using the ISA scale. In order to have the same understanding of scale's levels as the air traffic controllers, pseudo pilots were previously briefed regarding the meaning of each level. Finally, ratings of the pseudo pilots were averaged for each scenario and participant.

3.5 Statistical Analysis

In order to answer our first three research questions regarding the effect of traffic flow, occurrence of an exceptional event, and interaction effect between both, we carried out three analysis of variance (ANOVA). The dependent variable of each was the workload index measured either with NASA-TLX, ISA, or expert ratings. For each ANOVA we utilized a repeated-measures design with two within-subject factors (two levels for the priority-flight event factor and four levels for the traffic-load factor). General differences between the levels were examined and tested with a post-hoc test (Bonferroni corrected). For testing the differences between priority-flight and no priority-flight event on each traffic-load level, we used four t-tests for each workload index and adjusted the values accordingly.

The research questions concerning group differences were examined using six mixed-factorial ANOVAs. Three of them were carried out with air traffic controller's age as between-subject factor and three with air traffic controller's current job demands. The dependent variable, within-subject factors, and levels were identical with those mentioned above. Similarly, we utilized a repeated-measures design and examined the differences with post-hoc tests (Bonferroni). In order to cluster the subjects in two groups by age, we took the median age of our sample. This yielded 11 subjects under 40 years (referred to as young) and 10 subjects over or equal 40 years (referred to as old). Work demand clustering in two groups was done by consideration of the airport traffic volume where the controller was working. Thereby, we took into account the annual report on the air transport by the DLR [3] and set a threshold in order to get two equally sized subject groups (Fig. 1). This resulted in 11 subjects working in busy airports (approach controllers or tower controllers) and 10 subjects working in smaller, less-busy airports (approach controllers, tower controllers, or novices). Finally, we have to note that 5 subjects had to be discarded from expert rating analysis because of missing values. Hence, expert rating ANOVAs were carried out with 9 subjects in the busy-airport group and 7 subjects in the less-busy airport group and respectively, 7 young and 9 older subjects.

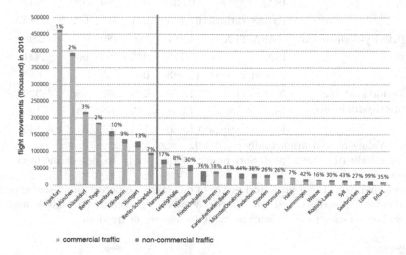

Fig. 1. Number of flight movements and share of non-commercial traffic per airport in Germany indicating our two-group split as green vertical line (figure from [3], p. 55). (Color figure online)

4 Results and Discussion

4.1 Effect of Traffic Load and Priority-Flight Event

Results of the ANOVAs for NASA-TLX, ISA, and expert ratings, each with the two within-subject factors traffic-load and priority-flight event, are summarized in Table 2.

Regarding traffic load, Bonferroni corrected post-hoc tests showed significant differences between all levels for all three measuring methods. Figure 2 shows the results. Our first hypothesis related to the effect of number of aircraft on controllers' workload proved to be true.

The impact of a priority-flight event varied across the questionnaire methods. Controllers' ISA and NASA-TLX ratings showed only week significant differences between sessions with and without priority flight. Expert ratings yielded a highly significant difference for the priority-flight event factor. In order to evaluate the effect of the priority flight for each traffic-load level, we computed t-tests and adjusted the values by means of Bonferroni correction. For expert and ISA ratings, we identified a significant difference between scenarios with and without priority-flight event for the 45 ac/h condition (experts: $t(15) = -4.28$, $p = 0.003$; ISA: $t(20) = -3.21$, $p = 0.018$). None of the other t-tests could reach significance. Our second hypothesis about the effect of an exceptional event on controllers'

Table 2. Analysis of workload scores across simulation conditions.

		F	p	η^2	Power[a]	Power[b]
Traffic load	NASA-TLX	68.224	.001	.773	.997	.414
	ISA	70.630	.001	.779	.920	.237
	Expert ratings	67.145	.001	.817	.672	.145
Priority-flight event	NASA-TLX	4.381	.049	.180	1	.998
	ISA	4.773	.041	.193	.994	.431
	Expert ratings	17.143	.001	.533	1	.684
Traffic load and priority-flight event	NASA-TLX	1.477	.230	.069	.986	.329
	ISA	1.031	.385	.049	.841	.195
	Expert ratings	1.800[c]	.183	.107	.612	.135

Note. Values of .001 are actually $p \le 0.001$.
[a]Power indicates the a posteriori power of our study to detect medium-size effects.
[b]Power indicates the a posteriori power of our study to detect small-size effects.
[c]Indicates Mauchly's test of sphericity was significant ($p < 0.05$) and a Greenhouse-Geisser correction was made to degrees of freedom.

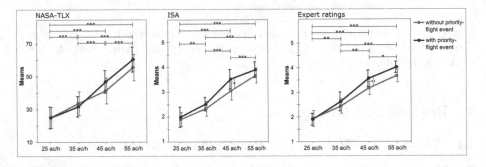

Fig. 2. Average workload over 21 participants measured using NASA-TLX (left), ISA (center), and expert ratings (right) across simulation conditions (Bonferroni corrected post-hoc tests: ∗∗∗: $p \le 0.001$; ∗∗: $0.001 < p \le 0.01$; ∗: $0.01 < p \le 0.05$; error bars indicate 95% confidence interval).

workload remained unclear, in particular regarding the 25, 35, and 55 ac/h scenarios and the ratings from the NASA-TLX questionnaire. Finally, no interaction effect could be obtained between both factors with any of the questionnaires used and our third hypothesis must be refused.

4.2 Effect of Age and Job Demands

No significant effect of age could be obtained with any of the questionnaire methods (NASA-TLX: $p = 0.627$, $\eta^2 = 0.013$; ISA: $p = 0.134$, $\eta^2 = 0.114$; expert ratings: $p = 0.398$, $\eta^2 = 0.051$;). The experienced workload was not related to controller's age and thus, our fourth hypothesis has to be rejected. However, by comparing the results descriptively (Fig. 3) we could assume that older subjects rated their workload slightly higher than younger ones during simulation scenarios with priority-flight event and higher traffic load. This held true for all three subjective measurement methods.

Regarding the between-subject factor of job demands, no significant main effect could be found using expert-rating values (F(1, 19) = 3.188, p = 0.096, $\eta^2 = 0.185$). Figure 4 (right column of top and bottom rows) shows the results scenarios with and without priority-flight event separately on two rows and indicates that it is hard to recognize a general tendency between the groups using experts' ratings.

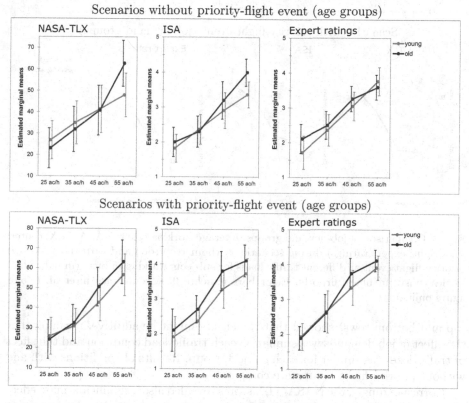

Fig. 3. Comparison of age groups. Average workload (left: NASA-TLX, center: ISA, right: expert ratings) during scenarios without (top row) and with (bottom row) priority-flight event at different traffic loads for young (in light blue) and older (in blue) subjects. Error bars indicate 95% confidence interval. (Color figure online)

Workload ratings of the subjects themselves seemed more indicative. The ISA ratings showed a significant main effect of the job demand factor (F(1, 19) = 12.221, p = 0.002, $\eta^2 = 0.391$). Although there was a significant difference in the workload means of the two groups averaged across all simulation conditions, we did not obtain a significant interaction effect of job demands with any within-subject factor. Descriptive evaluation of the results in Fig. 4 (middle column of

Scenarios without priority-flight event (job-demand groups)

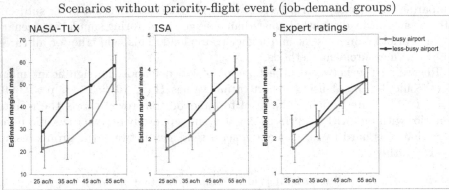

Scenarios with priority-flight event (job-demand groups)

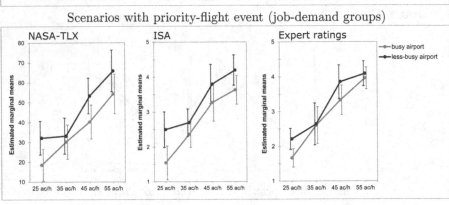

Fig. 4. Comparison of job-demand groups. Average workload (left: NASA-TLX, center: ISA, right: expert ratings) during scenarios without (top row) and with (bottom row) priority-flight event at different traffic loads for subjects working in busy (in light blue) vs. less-busy (in blue) airports. Error bars indicate 95% confidence interval. (Color figure online)

top and bottom rows) showed that the effects might be additive, meaning that the effect of job demands was similar on each traffic-load condition and the effect of traffic load was similar for each subject group. Results of conditions with and without priority-flight event were comparable.

Correspondingly, the NASA-TLX scores revealed also a significant main effect of current job demands ($F(1, 19) = 5.314$, $p = 0.033$, $\eta^2 = 0.219$). Furthermore, we were able to obtain a significant interaction between priority-flight event, traffic flow, and whether the controller was used to high job demands or not ($F(1, 57) = 3.319$, $p = 0.026$, $\eta^2 = 0.246$). The nature of this interaction is shown in Fig. 4 (left column of top and bottom rows).

In general, the subjective workload of the group working in busy airports increased gradually but to a lesser extent than the workload of the subjects working in less-busy airports. Furthermore, while workload of the subjects that work in busy airports increased almost exponentially over the traffic load of conditions without priority-flight event (i.e., between 45 ac/h to 55 ac/ah), subjective workload of subjects from less-busy airports seemed to increase somehow logarithmically (i.e., more pronounced slope between 25 ac/h and 35 ac/h and to a lesser extent between the following traffic-load scenarios). This tendency was not prominent during the priority-flight event conditions. Hereby, subjects from less-busy airports reported the same amount of workload between 25 ac/h and 35 ac/h whereas subjects from busy airports reported a gradual increase. The experienced workload as reported by the controllers was related to controllers' current job demands and our fifth hypothesis proved to be true.

5   Conclusion and Future Work

The aim of our study was to find out if it was the number of aircraft or the occurrence of an exceptional event that stressed controllers the most and if there was an interaction effect between both. Furthermore, we were interested if the factors age and experienced job demands during real-work life could reveal additional information about controllers workload. The subjective workload was measured using NASA-TLX, ISA, and expert ratings. The simulator experiment was expected to be representative for real operations because of its similarity to controllers' working environment and controllers' communication with pseudo pilots. While the effect of the number of aircraft was evident by all three questionnaire methods, the impact of the priority-flight event remained doubtful. Controllers' ISA and NASA-TLX ratings showed only a weekly significant discrimination between sessions with and without priority flight using standard ANOVA tests. Expert ratings yielded a highly significant difference for the priority-flight event factor, in particular during the 45 ac/h scenario. An additional model based in-depth analysis of controllers' ratings using a priori assumptions on non-linear dependencies considering resource limitations might modify this conclusion.

The examination of between-subject factors could reveal additional information about controller's rating behavior. Thereby, we observed the tendency that older subjects seemed to experience more workload than younger ones, in particular during the high-traffic conditions with priority-flight event. However, the differences did not reach significance. One reason for this could be the small number of participants. In order to have two equally-sized subject groups, we took the median age of our sample as threshold. For revealing differences between age groups the threshold age should be over 40 years. Regarding the factor of job demands, assumed by the number of flight movements of the airport where subjects were working for, we obtained significant differences by means of subjects' workload ratings but not using experts' ratings. Subjects working in busy airports seemed to experience lower workload compared to the group from less-busy airports. The effect of job demands was similar on each traffic-load level and the effect of traffic load was similar for each subject group. In the main, this held true for conditions with and without priority-flight event conducted using the ISA questionnaire. Thus, we assumed that the effect of job demands may be additive. Interestingly, only the NASA-TLX scores revealed an interaction between all three factors. During scenarios without priority-flight event, we observed that workload of subjects from busy airports increased slower among low traffic-load conditions and jumped to a higher value at the highest traffic-load condition. We suggested that experienced subjects realized their high-workload state suddenly when the traffic-load got the maximum value. In contrary, subjective workload of subjects working in less-busy airports increased most abruptly between the lowest and next-higher traffic-load condition and slower among higher traffic-load scenarios. It seemed that as subjective-workload ceiling approached the subjects of the less-busy airport group rated more cautiously. However, we have to note that this subject group included 5 (out of 10) subjects with no work experience in real airport environment. Thus, this difference between the groups could reflect the difference between novice and experienced subjects. Interestingly, subjects rated their workload more consciously during scenarios with priority-flight event.

To sum up, the number of aircraft contributed most to subjects' experienced workload while the priority-flight event became workload relevant only under high-traffic load. This observation fits well to controllers' reports. Most of them mentioned that during the scenarios with low and medium traffic volumes they had no difficulties to deal with the priority request. During the scenarios with higher traffic demands the situation changed and the priority-flight event became more demanding. Only few controllers were able to easily handle the situation. Regarding the effect of age, we conclude that more research with older controllers is necessary in order to gain more insight. Finally, the current job demands and thus, controllers habituation on higher workload states deserves more attention. The abrupt increase of perceived workload in controllers working in busy airports appears critical, in particular observed using the NASA-TLX during the high-load scenarios without priority-flight event. Objective registration of workload using bio signals may reveal if it is the workload itself that increases suddenly or if it is a lack of self-awareness that leads to these self-ratings. In this context, we want also to emphasize the importance of critical validation of metrics of mental workload as stated by [31].

Acknowledgments. We would like to thank Kerstin Ruta for her daily operational support, Emilia Cheladze for conducting the experiments, the numerous pseudo pilots for their contribution during the experiments, and Thorsten Mühlhausen for his conceptual, technical, and overall support. We would also like to thank Martin Schütte for his general project support.

More information about the project that acquired our data can be found at http://www.baua.de/DE/Aufgaben/Forschung/Forschungsprojekte/f2402.html.

Author Contributions. T.R. initiated the project and was responsible for the overall conception of the investigation. T.R., A.T., and N.F. developed the research design of the study. A.T. was responsible for the implementation of the simulation scenarios and the overall technical support. L.R. conducted the experiments and acquired the data. L.R. provided computational support for the data analysis with SPSS and graphic editing. The study was supervised by T.R. Data interpretation was performed by T.R. and B.M. The manuscript was written by T.R. Final critical editing was performed by A.T., N.F., and B.M.

Conflict of Interest Statement. The authors declare that the research was conducted in the absence of any commercial or financial relationships that could be construed as a potential conflict of interest.

A NASA-TLX Questionnaire

Bundesanstalt für Arbeitsschutz und Arbeitsmedizin   FB 3, Gruppe 3.4

ID:_____

NASA-TLX zur Erfassung der Arbeitsbeanspruchung

Geben Sie bitte an, welche relative Bedeutung für die empfundene Gesamtbeanspruchung bei der eben durchgeführten Aufgabe die sechs folgenden Beanspruchungsdimensionen

> Geistige Anforderung
> Körperliche Anforderung
> Zeitliche Anforderung
> Ausführung der Aufgaben
> Anstrengung
> Frustration

für Sie hatten. Lesen Sie sich bitte zuvor bezüglich der Bedeutung der Beanspruchungsdimensionen die unten stehende Beschreibung durch und wenden Sie sich bitte bei Unklarheiten an den Versuchsleiter.

Geistige Anforderungen	Wie viel geistige Anstrengung war bei der Informationsaufnahme und bei der Informationsverarbeitung erforderlich (z.B. Denken, Entscheiden, Rechnen, Erinnern, Hinsehen, Suchen)? War die Aufgabe leicht oder anspruchsvoll, einfach oder komplex, erfordert sie hohe Genauigkeit oder ist sie fehlertolerant?
Körperliche Anforderungen	Wie viel körperliche Aktivität war erforderlich (z.B. ziehen, drücken, drehen, steuern, aktivieren …)? War die Aufgabe leicht oder schwer, einfach oder anstrengend, erholsam oder mühselig?
Zeitliche Anforderungen	Wie viel Zeitdruck empfanden Sie hinsichtlich der Häufigkeit oder dem Takt mit dem Aufgaben oder Aufgabenelemente auftraten? War die Abfolge langsam und geruhsam oder schnell und hektisch?
Ausführung der Aufgaben	Wie erfolgreich haben Sie Ihrer Meinung nach die vom Versuchsleiter (oder Ihnen selbst) gesetzten Ziele erreicht? Wie zufrieden waren Sie mit Ihrer Leistung bei der Verfolgung dieser Ziele?
Anstrengung	Wie hart mussten Sie arbeiten, um Ihren Grad an Aufgabenerfüllung zu erreichen?
Frustration	Wie unsicher, entmutigt, irritiert, gestresst und verärgert (versus sicher, bestätigt, zufrieden, entspannt und zufrieden mit sich selbst) fühlten Sie sich während der Aufgabe?

ID:........................ | Datum: .... | VL: ....   Seite 1 von 4

Teil 1 - Beanspruchungsstruktur

Im Folgenden werden jeweils zwei der sechs Beanspruchungsdimensionen in verschiedenen Kombinationen gegenübergestellt. Geben Sie jeweils an, welche Beanspruchungsdimension für die Gesamtbeanspruchung, die Sie empfunden haben, bedeutsamer war. Es geht also zunächst nicht darum, wie hoch Sie die Beanspruchung in der einzelnen Dimension empfanden, sondern wie wichtig die jeweilige Dimension für das Gesamtempfinden war.

Beispiel:

Wenn für Sie die geistigen Anforderungen, die die Aufgabe gestellt hat, bedeutsamer für das Beanspruchungserleben waren, als die zeitlichen Anforderungen, die Sie empfanden, kreuzen Sie bitte so an:

Geistige Anforderungen   ☒   ☐   Zeitliche Anforderungen

Körperliche Anforderungen	☐	☐	Zeitliche Anforderungen
Anstrengung	☐	☐	Geistige Anforderungen
Frustration	☐	☐	Körperliche Anforderungen
Anstrengung	☐	☐	Frustration
Geistige Anforderungen	☐	☐	Zeitliche Anforderungen
Körperliche Anforderungen	☐	☐	Anstrengung
Zeitliche Anforderungen	☐	☐	Ausführung der Ausgaben
Frustration	☐	☐	Geistige Anforderungen
Zeitliche Anforderungen	☐	☐	Frustration
Ausführung der Aufgaben	☐	☐	Anstrengung
Anstrengung	☐	☐	Zeitliche Anforderungen
Frustration	☐	☐	Ausführung der Aufgaben
Ausführung der Aufgaben	☐	☐	Körperliche Anforderungen
Geistige Anforderungen	☐	☐	Ausführung der Aufgaben
Geistige Anforderungen	☐	☐	Körperliche Anforderungen

Kontrollieren Sie bitte, ob Sie kein Vergleichspaar vergessen haben.

ID:........................ | Datum: .... | VL: ....   Seite **3** von **4**

Teil 2 - Beanspruchungshöhe

Geben Sie jetzt bitte an, wie hoch die Beanspruchung in den einzelnen Dimensionen bezogen auf die gerade gelöste Aufgabe ausgeprägt war. Markieren Sie dazu auf den folgenden Skalen bitte, in welchem Maße Sie sich in den sechs genannten Dimensionen von der Aufgabe beansprucht oder gefordert gesehen haben. Machen Sie dafür, wie im Beispiel dargestellt, Ihre Einschätzung mit einem Kreuz kenntlich. Bei Unklarheiten wenden Sie sich bitte an den anwesenden Versuchsleiter.

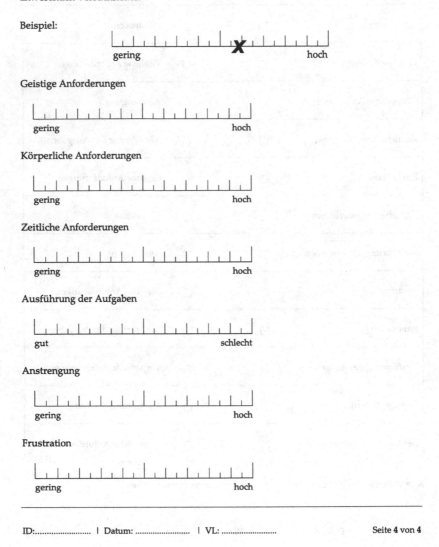

Beispiel:

    gering   hoch

Geistige Anforderungen

    gering   hoch

Körperliche Anforderungen

    gering   hoch

Zeitliche Anforderungen

    gering   hoch

Ausführung der Aufgaben

    gut   schlecht

Anstrengung

    gering   hoch

Frustration

    gering   hoch

B ISA Questionnaire

Bundesanstalt für Arbeitsschutz und Arbeitsmedizin   FB 3, Gruppe 3.4

ID:_____

ISA zur Erfassung der Arbeitsbeanspruchung

Geben Sie jetzt bitte an, wie hoch Ihre Beanspruchung in den letzten 5 Minuten war. Machen Sie dafür Ihre Einschätzung mit einem Kreuz kenntlich. Bei Unklarheiten wenden Sie sich bitte an den anwesenden Versuchsleiter.

Der Lotse hat sehr wenig bis gar nichts zu tun.	Der Lotse hat mehr als erforderlich, um die Aufgaben zu erfüllen. Die Zeit vergeht langsam.	Der Lotse hat ausreichend Arbeit. Alle Aufgaben sind unter Kontrolle.	Der Lotse ist „am Limit". Bestimmte nicht-zwingend notwendige Aufgaben werden verschoben. Die Zeit vergeht schnell	Der Lotse ist überlastet. Einige Aufgaben können nicht erledigt werden. Der Lotse spürt, dass er nicht die Kontrolle hat

ID:..................... | Datum: .... | VL: ....   Seite 1 von 2

References

1. Averty, P., Collet, C., Dittmar, A., Athènes, S., Vernet-Maury, E.: Mental workload in air traffic control: an index constructed from field tests. Aviat. Space Environ. Med. **75**(4), 333–341 (2004)
2. Beatty, J.: Task-evoked pupillary responses, processing load, and the structure of processing resources. Psychol. Bull. **91**(2), 276–292 (1982)
3. Berster, P., et al.: Luftverkehrsbericht 2016 - Daten und Kommentierungen des deutschen und weltweiten Luftverkehrs (2017). http://www.dlr.de/fw/Portaldata/42/Resources/dokumente/pdf/_Luftverkehrsbericht_2016_final_141217.pdf
4. Brennan, S.: An experimental report on rating scale descriptior sets for the instantaneous self assessment (ISA) recorder. Technical report. DRA Technical Memorandum (CAD5) 92017, DRA Maritime Command and Control Division (1992)
5. Cain, B.: A review of the mental workload literature. Technical report, Defence Research and Development Canada, Human System Integration Section, Toronto (2007). http://ftp.rta.nato.int/public/pubfulltext/rto/tr/rto-tr-hfm-121-part-ii/tr-hfm-121-part-ii-04.pdf. Accessed 11 Dec 2013
6. Edwards, T., Martin, L., Bienert, N., Mercer, J.: The relationship between workload and performance in air traffic control: exploring the influence of levels of automation and variation in task demand. In: Longo, L., Leva, M.C. (eds.) H-WORKLOAD 2017. CCIS, vol. 726, pp. 120–139. Springer, Cham (2017). https://doi.org/10.1007/978-3-319-61061-0_8
7. Eggemeier, F., Wilson, G.F., Kramer, A.F., Damos, D.L.: Workload assessment in multi-task environments. In: Multiple-task Performance, pp. 207–216. Taylor & Francis (1991)

8. Hancock, P.A.: Whither workload? Mapping a path for its future development. In: Longo, L., Leva, M.C. (eds.) H-WORKLOAD 2017. CCIS, vol. 726, pp. 3–17. Springer, Cham (2017). https://doi.org/10.1007/978-3-319-61061-0_1

9. Hancock, P.A., Desmond, P.A.: Stress, Workload, and Fatigue. Lawrence Erlbaum Associates Publishers, Hillsdale (2001)

10. Hart, S.G., Staveland, L.E.: Development of the NASA TLX: results of empirical and theoretical research. In: Hancock, P., Meshkati, N. (eds.) Human Mental Workload, pp. 139–183, North Holland, Amsterdam (1988)

11. Hendy, K.C., Hamilton, K.M., Landry, L.N.: Measuring subjective workload: when is one scale better than many? Hum. Factors 35, 579–601 (1993)

12. Hilburn, B., Jorna, P.G.A.M.: Workload and air traffic control. In: Hancock, A., Desmond, P. (eds.) Stress, Workload, and Fatigue, pp. 384–394. Erlbaum, Mahwah (2001)

13. Jordan, C.: Experimental study of the effect of an instantaneous self assessment workload recorder on task performance. Technical report. DRA Technical Memorandum (CAD5) 92011, DRA Maritime Command Control Division (1992)

14. Kahneman, D.: Attention and Effort. Prentice-Hall, Englewood Cliffs (1973)

15. Kirwan, B., et al.: Human factors in the ATM system design life cycle. In: FAA/Eurocontrol ATM R&D Seminar (1997)

16. Matthews, G.: Levels of transaction: a cognitive sciences framework for operator stress, pp. 5–33. Lawrence Erlbaum Associates Publishers Mahwah (2001)

17. Meister, D.: Behavioral Foundations of System Development. Wiley, New York (1976)

18. Mulder, L.J.M., van Roon, A.M., Althaus, M., Laumann, K., Dicke, M.: Determining dynamic cardiovascular state changes using a baro-reflex simulation model. In: Human factors in transportation, communication, health and the workplace, pp. 297–315. Shaker Publishing, Maastricht (2002)

19. O'Donnell, C.R.D., Eggemeier, F.T.: Workload assessment methodology. In: Boff, K., Kaufmann, L., Thomas, J. (eds.) Handbook of Perception and Human Performance, pp. 42–49. Wiley (1989). http://apps.usd.edu/coglab/schieber/docs/odonnell.pdf, Accessed 19 June 2015

20. Parasuraman, R., Hancock, P.: Adaptive control of workload. In: Hancock, A., Desmond, P. (eds.) Stress, Workload, and Fatigue, pp. 305–320. Erlbaum, Mahwah (2001)

21. Pribram, K.H., McGuinness, D.: Arousal, activation, and effort in the control of attention. Psychol. Rev. 82, 116–149 (1975). http://www.karlpribram.com/wp-content/uploads/pdf/theory/T-068.pdf. Accessed on 15 May 2015

22. Radüntz, T.: Dual frequency head maps: a new method for indexing mental workload continuously during execution of cognitive tasks. Front. Physiol. 8, 1019 (2017). https://www.frontiersin.org/article/10.3389/fphys.2017.01019

23. Saxby, D.J., Matthews, G., Warm, J.S., Hitchcock, E.M., Neubauer, C.: Active and passive fatigue in simulated driving: discriminating styles of workload regulation and their safety impacts. J. Exp. Psychol.: Appl. 19(4), 287–300 (2013)

24. Sonnentag, S., Kruel, U.: Psychological detachment from work during off-job time: the role of job stressors, job involvement, and recovery-related self-efficacy. Eur. J. Work. Organ. Psychol. 15(2), 197–217 (2006). https://doi.org/10.1080/13594320500513939

25. Stanton, N., Salmon, P., Walker, G., Baber, C., Jenkins, D.: Human Factors Methods: A Practical Guide for Engineering and Design, December 2005

26. Ullsperger, P., Metz, A.M., Gille, H.G.: The P300 component of the event-related brain potential and mental effort. Ergonomics **31**(8), 1127–1137 (1988). https://doi.org/10.1080/00140138808966752. pMID: 3191898
27. Veltman, J.A., Gaillard, A.W.K.: Physiological indices of workload in a simulated flight task. Biol. Psychol. **42**(3), 323–342 (1996). http://www.sciencedirect.com/science/article/pii/0301051195051651
28. Vidulich, A.M., Tsang, P.: Mental workload and situation awareness, pp. 243–273, 4th edn. Wiley, Hoboken (2012)
29. de Waard, D.: The measurement of drivers' mental workload. Ph.D. thesis, University of Groningen, Traffic Research Centre, Haren, Netherlands (1996)
30. Wickens, C.D.: Multiple resources and performance prediction. Theor. Issues Ergon. Sci. **3**(2), 159–177 (2002). http://www.tandfonline.com/doi/abs/10.1080/14639220210123806
31. Wickens, C.D.: Mental workload: assessment, prediction and consequences. In: Longo, L., Leva, M.C. (eds.) H-WORKLOAD 2017. CCIS, vol. 726, pp. 18–29. Springer, Cham (2017). https://doi.org/10.1007/978-3-319-61061-0_2
32. Xie, B., Salvendy, G.: Review and reappraisal of modelling and predicting mental workload in single- and multi-task environments. Work Stress **14**(1), 74–99 (2000)
33. Yerkes, R.M., Dodson, J.D.: The relation of strength of stimulus to rapidity of habit-formation. J. Comp. Neurol. Psychol. **18**, 459–482 (1908). http://psychclassics.yorku.ca/Yerkes/Law. Accessed 03 Nov 2011

The Effect of Education and Training on Mental Workload in Medical Education

Aidan Byrne[1,2,3](✉) (iD)

[1] ABM Local Health Board, Swansea, UK
aidanbyrne27@swansea.ac.uk
[2] School of Medicine, Swansea University, Swansea, UK
[3] Department of Anaesthesia, Morriston Hospital, Swansea SA4 4NL, UK

Abstract. Mental workload is now accepted as a significant factor in the performance of individuals conducting complex tasks in high risk environments such as healthcare and research shows that experience reduces the levels of mental workload. In order to determine the effect of training on mental workload, a systematic search of studies of the effect of education and/or training was conducted using standard research databases. Only 6 studies were identified and these showed either limited or no improvement after training/education, suggesting that educational interventions have limited utility in reducing mental workload. The apparent failure of education may suggest that the current, digital view of cognition is not adequate and an alternative concept of analogue cognition is proposed as a possible explanation.

Keywords: Mental workload · Education · Training · Human performance

1 Introduction

Mental workload is an abstract concept which reflects the demands of a particular task/environment on the cognitive resources of individuals [1, 2]. One of the main beliefs underpinning the study of mental workload as a concept is that high levels of mental workload lead to poor performance [3] and that interventions such as training/education can reduce mental workload and therefore improve performance [4]. In addition, measurement of mental workload could be used to develop improved educational techniques [5, 6]. Although education can be seen as peripheral to the more scientific process of characterising and measuring mental workload, the concept of mental workload would remain an abstract if it cannot be applied to real world applications [7, 8]. Although this form or research can be used to modify any specific task or the environment in which it is performed, it is a change in human behaviour that provides the greatest challenge to promoting safety [9, 10].

Within medicine, the concept of mental workload is not yet widely used to aid the design of either instructional materials or assessment tools, [6] although it is now being used to aid the design of systems and equipment [11, 12]. In addition, the concept of cognitive load theory has been introduced which, as the theories share so much, can lead to confusion [13, 14]. While Cognitive Load theory has mainly analysed classroom based teaching and is based on the premise that a reduction in the cognitive load

L. Longo and M. C. Leva (Eds.): H-WORKLOAD 2018, CCIS 1012, pp. 258–266, 2019.
https://doi.org/10.1007/978-3-030-14273-5_15

while learning provides learners with an increased cognitive capacity to learn. In contrast, mental workload theory has mainly analysed operators working in real or realistic environments and is based on the premise that either reducing the workload associated with the task or increased training will allow subjects to improve their performance. In addition, while mental workload theory posits mental workload to be a rather complex, multidimensional concept, cognitive load theory has the additional complication of splitting cognitive load into three separate components, making measurement difficult. This paper deals with mental workload theory rather than cognitive load theory.

Studies which measured the difference between novices and experts, completing tasks in simulated or real medical environments have shown that experience does reduce cognitive load [15–18]. However, studies within medical education which have measured the workload of subjects before and after a specific episode of training are problematic in that it appears to suggest that training does not reliably reduce workload [19–21].

If we accept the current definition of mental workload as the balance between the cognitive demands of the task compared to the ability of the subject [1] and that the purpose of training is to improve ability [6], then it follows that training should reduce mental workload. However, if training medical staff does not reduce their mental workload then either the training is ineffective or the tasks undertaken by medical practitioners have not been adequately characterised. This question is important as while mental workload is now accepted as a valid outcome in the assessment of both individual performance and that of systems in healthcare, [3, 22, 23] workers are currently in short supply and in many cases highly paid, so the allocation of staff to training rather than patient care provides a significant increase in cost or a reduction in patient care. In such circumstances, it is essential that any educational interventions are demonstrably effective. An initial search of the medical educational literature did not provide adequate evidence to address the question of whether training affects the mental workload of operators, so a wider search of the literature was undertaken. The aim was to identify all published papers which measured the effect of education/training on mental workload to determine which forms of training are most effective in reducing mental workload.

2 Methods

A systematic search of online research databases was performed by a single author, using the terms "mental workload" and "training" or "education". Inclusion criteria were any study which included an objective measure of mental workload before and after a period of training or education. Any form of educational intervention was included. Studies were excluded if only subjective measures of mental workload were used. The number of studies identified by each search engine are shown in Table 1. The abstract for each study identified was read to determine whether it was suitable for inclusion within this paper, with total numbers included also shown in Table 1. On full review of all the papers, none needed to be excluded. After the initial search, any authors identified were then used as search items to determine if they has authored similar papers, but this did not identify any additional studies. A search using Google Scholar using the terms "mental workload" and "training" produced 23,800 results. An informal search of the first 500 results did not reveal any further studies which met the criteria. Papers were then analysed to determine the task studied, the type and duration of educational intervention and the effect of mental workload.

3   Results

The search process identified six studies which met the inclusion criteria (Tables 1 and 2). A large number of papers were common to many of the database results, supporting the conclusion that the search identified all studies with the specified items in the title or abstract. However, it is likely that there are other studies which measure mental workload before and after some educational intervention, but which have not been identified by this process. The following six studies were identified:

1 - Lelis-Torres et al. [24] studied mental workload using a processed EEG signal before and after subjects practiced a task which involved repetitive key pressing and showed that the subject's workload decreased. The task or training were not well described but appear to be highly constrained with simple practice rather than a designed educational intervention. They found that repetitive practice resulted both in lower initial workload and a greater fall in workload with practice. However, they conclude that the increased cognitive effort involved in random practice showed more potential as an educational intervention.

2 - Boet et al. [21] performed a randomised trial of training in 20 junior surgical residents being trained on a full scale simulator to deal with medical crises. Mental workload was measured using a vibrotactile secondary task method. In the control group (n = 10) practicing crisis management without debriefing appeared to increase workload. In the intervention group (n = 10) targeted feedback over 15 min which included teaching on generic crisis management skills reduced workload.

3 - Byrne et al. [19] studied the performance of doctors being trained to act as examiners in a checklist based practical skills examination. Mental workload was measured by a vibrotactile secondary task method. Subjects completed four sequential video based training sessions with feedback. Overall, training appeared to have no effect on mental workload or the accuracy of their marking.

4 - Byrne et al. [25] studied anaesthetic trainees being trained on a full scale training simulator. Workload was measured with a vibrotactile secondary task method. After a single simulation with debriefing and targeted advice, each subject then completed a further simulation. There was no effect on mental workload or performance.

5 - Saus et al. [26] studied police cadets being trained to use firearms in a simulated environment. The training focussed on developing situational awareness on the

use of firearms in a variety of simulated situations. Mental workload was measured by a reduction in heart rate variability with the signal generated by a surface ECG. A single training session reduced mental workload and improved performance measured by the number of shots fired and the number of hits.

6 - Kang et al. [27] studied college students to complete simple mathematical calculations similar to "If A = 3, 7 + A = ?". Mental workload was measured by thermography of the nose. Although the measure appeared to correlate with perceived workload, there was no improvement during the short practice phase.

4 Discussion

Despite the large volume of literature on mental workload, there are few studies which have measured the effect of training or education on mental workload measured by an objective methodology. Including subjective measures [28] would have considerably increased the number of studies included in this paper, but as training/education would be expected to affect subjective measures of workload they were not included. The methodologies used to measure workload were diverse and although each methodology was supported by appropriate references to validate its use, the evidence for each appeared to be limited. In addition, it is recognised that to be effective, educational interventions need to use appropriate instructional design techniques, [29] usually incorporating repeated practice and feedback [30]. In contrast, the studies identified here used single educational interventions which were both short and appeared to lack any educational theory or design. They also appeared to focus on unaided practice or the provision of simple instruction.

Overall, the effect of training/education on mental workload appears to be variable, so that a logical conclusion from this review might be that there was insufficient evidence to recommend training/education as a valid intervention. However, two of the tasks studied were very limited, repetitive tasks, one of which showed improvement. This suggests that for such simple tasks, repetition may be effective. The other four studies looked at complex, rapidly evolving environments with the training either targeted at dealing with the specific scenario, or with training targeting generic crisis management or situational awareness. In these more complex situations, training staff to deal with specific problems had no effect, but where generic skills were emphasised, workload decreased.

Where the mental workload of medical staff, who work in complex environments, at different stages of their careers have been measured, it appears to show a gradual decrease in workload over many years of training [15, 17]. This gradual decrease in mental workload over many years of practice is not compatible with many existing models of learning, such as competency based training, where students acquire specific knowledge and skills during defined learning periods, with mastery of each component tested at the end of each section with a summative assessment. It also raises questions as to how this learning should be represented in models of neural processing.

Most educational theory posits cognition, at least implicitly, as a digital process using discreet items of knowledge acquired from sensory input which is then processed via a logical, Boolean or Bayesian logic process. The inferences from this conceptualisation of learning is that if a subject has acquired adequate knowledge relating to a specific situation, then they will be likely to select the correct solution to any given problem. Correspondingly, if the subject makes an incorrect choice, then they must have inadequate knowledge which needs to be addressed through an educational process.

An alternative view is to consider human cognition to be based on massive numbers of analogue circuits which integrate sensory inputs and develop responses in the same way as the electronic analogue computers used in the 1950/60s [31]. Although the term 'analogue' when applied to a computer describes the relationship between input and output of the computation, it does not specify the internal construction of the device, which can use, for example, physical connections or electrical circuits. Clearly, the human brain does not contain either physical linkages or continuous electrical currents. However, while neurones cannot conduct continuous currents which are turned up or down, they can form circuits which increase their firing rate or 'resonate' in response to specific conditions. The description of perception in terms of circuits which 'resonate' or 'vibrate' in response to incoming sensory information has already been described in Cognitive Resonance Theory [32]. This analogue view of learning would explain the learning process as one of gradual 'tuning' of circuits to improve their 'signal to noise ratio' and 'quality of reception' more in keeping with gradual improvements to an AM radio or the gradual redesign of a violin so that each becomes more responsive to any input and produces a progressively higher quality output [33].

Such a view of cognition would explain the lack of evidence to demonstrate that education is effective in reducing workload, as it might be expected that performance of simple, highly constrained tasks could be improved after short practice, extensive experience/practice would be required to 'retune' or develop the required analogue circuits where a more complex task required active selection and processing of information from a wide range of incoming sensory input [34]. It would also explain why short training interventions to deal with specific problems might fail, interventions which assisted subjects in making sense of the complexity around them might provide immediate reductions in mental workload, as rather than trying to analyse complexity, subjects could more easily select from a limited number of options. Further, new concepts of education may support the development of new and more effective teaching methods [35, 36].

5   Conclusion

The published literature on the effect of education on the mental workload of operators using objective methodology is extremely limited, with published studies limited to single educational interventions of uncertain utility. In addition, while the performance of highly constrained, simple tasks may be improved by short term practice or debriefing, they appear ineffective when applied to more complex tasks. In addition, while training subjects how to deal with specific complex tasks appears to be ineffective, teaching subjects a generic approach to a range of problems appears more effective.

These results may be better explained by an analogue theory of cognition rather than a digital one. Further research looking at the effects of education on mental workload will be required to determine whether this is true. In particular, studies which involve the measurement of mental workload in realistic environments before, during and after prolonged periods of training/education will be required to determine which forms of education are most effective in reducing mental workload.

Appendix

Table 1. Summary of databases searched and suitable studies identified. Terms used were "mental workload" and "training" or "education"

	Database	Match	Matches	Additional papers included	Total included in analysis
1	Pubmed	Training	153	5	5
2	Pubmed	Education	109	0	5
3	Science direct	Training	64	0	5
4	Science direct	Education	16	0	5
5	CINALH	Training	3	0	5
6	CINALH	Education	1	0	5
7	ERIC	Training	1	0	5
8	ERIC	Education	10	0	5
9	PsychInfo	Training	13	0	5
10	PsychInfo	Education	2	0	5
11	Scopus	Training	192	1	6
12	Scopus	Education	39	0	6
13	Web of science	Training	16	0	6
14	Web of science	Education	2	0	6
15	Wiley interscience	Training	9	0	6
16	Wiley interscience	Education	16	0	6

Table 2. Details of studies included in analysis.

	Study	Primary task	Outcome	Intervention	Duration	Retest	Outcome
1	Lelis-Torres et al. [24]	Sequential key pressing	Processed EEG	Repetitive practice	Post practice	Immediate	Improved
2	Boet et al. [21]	Managing simulated medical crisis	Secondary task	Debriefing training on crisis management	One training session	Immediate	Improved
3	Byrne et al. [19]	Marking skills assessment (OSCE)	Secondary task	Video based practice	One training session	Immediate	No effect
4	Byrne et al. [25, 37]	Simulated anaesthetic crisis	Secondary tasks	Video based debriefing on specific crisis	One training session	Immediate	No effect
5	Kang et al. [27]	Shooting simulator	Heart rate variability	Situational awareness training	One training session	Immediate	Improved
6	Kang et al.	Alphanumeric processing	Thermography	Practice	One session	Immediate	No effect

References

1. Wickens, C.D.: Multiple resources and mental workload. Hum. Factors **50**, 449–455 (2008). https://doi.org/10.1518/001872008X288394
2. Longo, L., Leva, M.C.: Human Mental Workload: Models and Applications: First International Symposium, H-WORKLOAD 2017, Dublin, Ireland, June 28-30, 2017, Revised Selected Papers. Springer, Heidelberg (2017). https://doi.org/10.1007/978-3-319-61061-0
3. Yurko, Y.Y., Scerbo, M.W., Prabhu, A.S., Acker, C.E., Stefanidis, D.: Higher mental workload is associated with poorer laparoscopic performance as measured by the NASA-TLX Tool. Simul. Healthc. J. Soc. Simul. Healthc. **5**, 267–271 (2010). https://doi.org/10.1097/SIH.0b013e3181e3f329
4. Carswell, C.M., Clarke, D., Seales, W.B.: Assessing mental workload during laparoscopic surgery. Surg. Innov. **12**, 80–90 (2005). https://doi.org/10.1177/155335060501200112
5. Menekse Dalveren, G.G., Cagiltay, N.E., Ozcelik, E., Maras, H.: Insights from pupil size to mental workload of surgical residents: feasibility of an educational computer-based surgical simulation environment (ECE) considering the hand condition. Surg. Innov. (2018). https://doi.org/10.1177/1553350618800078
6. Byrne, A.: Mental workload as an outcome in medical education. In: Longo, L., Leva, M.C. (eds.) H-WORKLOAD 2017. CCIS, vol. 726, pp. 187–197. Springer, Cham (2017). https://doi.org/10.1007/978-3-319-61061-0_12
7. Parasuraman, R., Sheridan, T.B., Wickens, C.D.: Situation awareness, mental workload, and trust in automation: viable, empirically supported cognitive engineering constructs. J. Cogn. Eng. Decis. Mak. **2**, 140–160 (2008). https://doi.org/10.1518/155534308X284417

8. Ayaz, H., Shewokis, P.A., Bunce, S., Izzetoglu, K., Willems, B., Onaral, B.: Optical brain monitoring for operator training and mental workload assessment. Neuroimage **59**, 36–47 (2012). https://doi.org/10.1016/J.NEUROIMAGE.2011.06.023

9. Young, M.S., Brookhuis, K.A., Wickens, C.D., Hancock, P.A.: State of science: mental workload in ergonomics. Ergonomics **58**(1), 1–17 (2015)

10. Wickens, C.D.: Mental workload: assessment, prediction and consequences. In: Longo, L., Leva, M.C. (eds.) H-WORKLOAD 2017. CCIS, vol. 726, pp. 18–29. Springer, Cham (2017). https://doi.org/10.1007/978-3-319-61061-0_2

11. Longo, L.: Mental workload in medicine: foundations, applications, open problems, challenges and future perspectives. In: 2016 IEEE 29th International Symposium on Computer-Based Medical Systems (CBMS), pp. 106–111. IEEE (2016)

12. Longo, L.: Designing medical interactive systems via assessment of human mental workload. In: 2015 IEEE 28th International Symposium on Computer-Based Medical Systems, pp. 364–365. IEEE (2015)

13. Sweller, J.: Cognitive load theory. Psychol. Learn. Motiv. **55**, 37–76 (2011). https://doi.org/10.1016/B978-0-12-387691-1.00002-8

14. van Merriënboer, J.J.G., Sweller, J.: Cognitive load theory and complex learning: recent developments and future directions. Educ. Psychol. Rev. **17**, 147–177 (2005). https://doi.org/10.1007/s10648-005-3951-0

15. Zheng, B., Cassera, M.A., Martinec, D.V., Spaun, G.O., Swanstrom, L.L.: Measuring mental workload during the performance of advanced laparoscopic tasks. Surg. Endosc. **24**, 45–50 (2010). https://doi.org/10.1007/s00464-009-0522-3

16. Guru, K.A., et al.: Cognitive skills assessment during robot-assisted surgery: separating the wheat from the chaff. BJU Int. **115**, 166–174 (2015). https://doi.org/10.1111/bju.12657

17. Byrne, A.J.J., Murphy, A., McIntyre, O., Tweed, N.: The relationship between experience and mental workload in anaesthetic practice: an observational study. Anaesthesia **68**, 1266–1272 (2013). https://doi.org/10.1111/anae.12455

18. Byrne, A.J., et al.: Novel method of measuring the mental workload of anaesthetists during clinical practice. Br. J. Anaesth. **105**, 767–771 (2010). https://doi.org/10.1093/bja/aeq240

19. Byrne, A., Soskova, T., Dawkins, J., Coombes, L.: A pilot study of marking accuracy and mental workload as measures of OSCE examiner performance. BMC Med. Educ. **16**, 191 (2016). https://doi.org/10.1186/s12909-016-0708-z

20. Muresan 3rd, C., Lee, T.H., Seagull, J., Park, A.E.: Transfer of training in the development of intracorporeal suturing skill in medical student novices: a prospective randomized trial. Am. J. Surg. **200**, 537–541 (2010). https://doi.org/10.1016/j.amjsurg.2009.12.018

21. Boet, S., Sharma, B., Pigford, A.-A., Hladkowicz, E., Rittenhouse, N., Grantcharov, T.: Debriefing decreases mental workload in surgical crisis: a randomized controlled trial. Surgery **161**, 1215–1220 (2017). https://doi.org/10.1016/j.surg.2016.11.031

22. Sato, H., Miyashita, T., Kawakami, H., Nagamine, Y., Takaki, S., Goto, T.: Influence of mental workload on the performance of anesthesiologists during induction of general anesthesia: a patient simulator study. Biomed. Res. Int. **2016**, 1058750 (2016). https://doi.org/10.1155/2016/1058750

23. Carayon, P., Gürses, A.P.: A human factors engineering conceptual framework of nursing workload and patient safety in intensive care units. Intensive Crit. Care Nurs. **21**, 284–301 (2005). https://doi.org/10.1016/J.ICCN.2004.12.003

24. Lelis-Torres, N., Ugrinowitsch, H., Apolinário-Souza, T., Benda, R.N., Lage, G.M.: Task engagement and mental workload involved in variation and repetition of a motor skill. Sci. Rep. **7**, 14764 (2017). https://doi.org/10.1038/s41598-017-15343-3

25. Byrne, A.J., et al.: Effect of videotape feedback on anaesthetists' performance while managing simulated anaesthetic crises: a multicentre study. Anaesthesia **57**, 176–179 (2002)

26. Saus, E.-R., Johnsen, B.H., Eid, J., Riisem, P.K., Andersen, R., Thayer, J.F.: The effect of brief situational awareness training in a police shooting simulator: an experimental study (2009). https://doi.org/10.1207/s15327876mp1803s_2

27. Kang, J., Babski-Reeves, K.: Detecting mental workload fluctuation during learning of a novel task using thermography. In: Proceedings of the Human Factors and Ergonomics Society Annual Meeting, vol. 52, pp. 1527–1531 (2008). https://doi.org/10.1177/1541931 20805201947

28. Rubio, S., Diaz, E., Martin, J., Puente, J.M.: Evaluation of subjective mental workload: A comparison of SWAT, NASA-TLX, and workload profile methods. Appl. Psychol. **53**, 61–86 (2004). https://doi.org/10.1111/j.1464-0597.2004.00161.x

29. Sweller, J., Sweller, J.: Instructional design. Aust. Educ. Rev. (1999)

30. Scerbo, M.W., Britt, R.C., Montano, M., Kennedy, R.A., Prytz, E., Stefanidis, D.: Effects of a retention interval and refresher session on intracorporeal suturing and knot tying skill and mental workload. Surgery **161**, 1209–1214 (2017). https://doi.org/10.1016/j.surg.2016.11. 011

31. Small, J.S.: The Analogue Alternative: The Electronic Analogue Computer in Britain and the USA, 1930–1975. Routledge, Abingdon (2001)

32. Grossberg, S.: Adaptive Resonance Theory: how a brain learns to consciously attend, learn, and recognize a changing world. Neural Netw. **37**, 1–47 (2013). https://doi.org/10.1016/J. NEUNET.2012.09.017

33. Ogiela, Lidia: Cognitive systems for medical pattern understanding and diagnosis. In: Lovrek, Ignac, Howlett, R.J., Jain, L.C. (eds.) KES 2008. LNCS (LNAI), vol. 5177, pp. 394–400. Springer, Heidelberg (2008). https://doi.org/10.1007/978-3-540-85563-7_51

34. Abela, J.: Adult learning theories and medical education: a review. Malta Med. J. **21**(1), 11–18 (2009)

35. Gobbo, F., Longo, L., Orru, G., O'sullivan, D.: An investigation of the impact of a social constructivist teaching approach, based on trigger questions, through measures of mental workload and efficiency. In: Proceedings of the 10th International Conference on Computer Supported Education, CSEDU 2018, Funchal, Madeira, Portugal, 15–17 March 2018, vol. 2 (2018)

36. Hancock, P.A.: Whither workload? Mapping a path for its future development. In: Longo, Luca, Leva, M.C. (eds.) H-WORKLOAD 2017. CCIS, vol. 726, pp. 3–17. Springer, Cham (2017). https://doi.org/10.1007/978-3-319-61061-0_1

37. Smith, M.A., Byrne, A.J.: 'Help! I need somebody': getting timely assistance in clinical practice. Anaesthesia **71**, 755–759 (2016). https://doi.org/10.1111/anae.13497

Author Index

Printed in the United States
By Bookmasters